Praise for *Winning at New Products*

"This book is an invaluable guide. . . . It's full of best practices, practical methods and real-world illustrations that demonstrate how to succeed at product and service innovation."
—DICK ARRA, chief technology officer, ITT Corporation

"This book provides insights into new approaches and offers very useful guidelines for creating a powerful innovation setting in your organization."
—HANNES ERLER, vice president of innovation, Swarovski K.G.

"[*Winning at New Products*] has been a mainstay of product-development literature for fifteen years."
—*Journal of Product Innovation Management*

"*Winning at New Products* by Robert G. Cooper has a clear place on your book shelf and will be most helpful in your innovation battles to explain the many in-built limitations to others less informed yet involved in the decision process."
—InnovationManagement.se

WINNING

AT

NEW PRODUCTS

OTHER PERSEUS BOOKS BY ROBERT COOPER

Product Leadership: Pathways to Profitable Innovation,
2nd edition, 2005

Portfolio Management for New Products, 2nd edition,
2001 (co-author with S. J. Edgett and E. J. Kleinschmidt)

Product Development for the Service Sector,
1999 (co-author with S. J. Edgett)

FIFTH EDITION

WINNING
AT
NEW PRODUCTS

Creating *Value* Through *Innovation*

Revised and Updated

Robert G. Cooper

BASIC BOOKS
NEW YORK

Basic Books
Hachette Book Group
1290 Avenue of the Americas, New York, NY 10104
www.basicbooks.com

Printed in the United States of America
First Edition: September 2017

Published by Basic Books, an imprint of Perseus Books, LLC, a subsidiary of Hachette Book Group, Inc.

The Hachette Speakers Bureau provides a wide range of authors for speaking events. To find out more, go to www.hachettespeakersbureau.com or call (866) 376-6591. The publisher is not responsible for websites (or their content) that are not owned by the publisher.

Library of Congress Control number: 2017949583.
ISBNs: 978-0-465-09332-8 (2017 paperback), 978-0-465-09333-5 (ebook)

LSC-C

10   9   8   7   6   5   4

To the three ladies in my life:
My wife, Linda, and my two daughters, Barbara and Heather

In memoriam

Jens Arleth,
managing director of U3-Innovation Management, Copenhagen
A leading innovator and a good friend

CONTENTS

PREFACE

Stage-Gate® has become the most widely used method for conceiving, developing, and launching new products in industry today. *Stage-Gate* is much more than a business process, however. The model was originally conceived by observing successful product developers as they drove major innovations to market. Those early observations led to the conclusion that there was a "better way"— that some innovation teams and project leaders had intuitively figured it out. I tried to capture their *secrets to success* on paper, and so was born the *Stage-Gate* system. Thus *Stage-Gate* is an idea-to-launch process, but one that encompasses a body of knowledge and set of best practices—best practices based on studies of thousands of successful new-product developments and hundreds of companies that *probed what the winners do differently from the rest.*

The emphasis in this 5th edition of *Winning at New Products* is on *bold innovation* and *in record time*. I've watched as companies, a few industries excepted, have shifted their innovation efforts from true innovations and major projects to much smaller and less ambitious ones over the last few decades. It's somewhat disheartening to see what these companies are calling "innovation" versus what it should be. In some firms, product development has been totally trivialized. I hope this 5th edition sounds a wake-up call that *true innovation* and *bold product development* are within your grasp.

I also emphasize speed—more specifically, *agility, flexibility, and acceleration and adaptability*, which are all linked. It seems that too many firms' innovation processes have become rigid and bureaucratic over the years—slow and cumbersome, unable to deal with today's pace of change. It's as though they're designed to impede bold innovation and to stand in the way of doing anything worthwhile fast. And so I build in some new techniques—some from the IT world—to get the innovation engine up to speed to where it should be: agile, accelerated, adaptive, and flexible.

The 1st edition of this book was published in 1986, before I had even begun to use the term "stage-gate." That first book reported the results of a number of research studies that colleagues and I had undertaken into new product success and failure. And it proposed the use of a *systematic and gated idea-to-launch business process* for the first time. To my surprise, the book had a profound impact on the way many companies approached product development, and firms such as P&G, DuPont, and Exxon Chemicals immediately embraced the concept of my stage-and-gate system.

But those were the early days of management of the innovation process. More research was undertaken, including some that focused on these early adopters of *Stage-Gate*. More success factors were uncovered in our *NewProd˜* research series and in our major benchmarking studies that followed; and more experiences were gained with the use of *Stage-Gate* methods (I first used the term "*Stage-Gate*" in an article that appeared in the *Journal of Marketing Management* in 1988). And so the 2nd edition was published in 1993. It went on to become the bible for those businesses trying to overhaul their new product process and implement *Stage-Gate*. The 3rd edition in 2000 continued the tradition, but with an emphasis on accelerating idea-to-launch. And the 4th edition in 2011 built in many of the new approaches, such as spiral or iterative development, lean processes, and "open innovation," that are widely embraced today.

This current 5th edition is more than a simple updating of the 4th edition, however—much in it is new too. Six years have passed since I wrote the last edition, and much more has been learned: For example, Agile development methods have gained a solid foothold in the IT or software-development world, and in the last few years have been employed within *Stage-Gate* and for *physical or manufactured new products*, achieving dramatic results. Indeed, incorporation of Agile methods as a project-management tool within the stages of *Stage-Gate* may be the *most significant change* to my durable gating system since it was first developed thirty years ago!

Stage-Gate has evolved and morphed in other ways too—it continues to be an evergreen process because of its many users globally! With these thousands of users, it's inevitable that new twists, approaches, and methods are uncovered, tested, proven, and incorporated into their idea-to-launch systems. Many of these novel approaches find their way into this book too. *Stage-Gate* is now faster and more streamlined—user firms have borrowed the concepts of lean manufacturing and Six Sigma and built these into *Stage-Gate*. Portfolio management has been integrated with gating methods, and the concept of "lean gates" and "gates with teeth" have been fashioned into the system in order to make sharper and more effective investment decisions. *Stage-Gate* has been made more adaptive and flexible in some firms, and it's now context based and risk dependent. It's also been automated with robust software. And there are new tools, such as "Design Thinking" and the "Innovation Project Canvas," that have been built in as well. Further, *Stage-Gate* approaches have even been extended to other types of projects, including technology developments (fundamental science) and process developments. So much that's new makes today's *Stage-Gate* hardly recognizable by early adopters of the original process! All of these new concepts and methods are in this latest edition.

Finally, this 5th edition takes a more *holistic approach* to succeeding at product innovation. There is more to winning than simply having a solid or agile idea-to-launch process! This holistic or "systems approach" is introduced in the *Innovation Diamond*, which includes strategy, resource and portfolio management, climate and culture, and process. Thus a new chapter on innovation strategy is built into this edition; and portfolio management—making the right investment decisions—is heavily emphasized too. And achieving the right climate and culture is a theme woven throughout.

A number of people have provided insights, guidance, content, and encouragement in the writing of this new edition. Several merit special attention. First, Mr. Jens Arleth, a long-time associate and business partner, former managing director of U3-Innovation Management in Copenhagen, who passed away in 2013, was leader in this field of management of innovation. He was a constant source of inspiration and ideas for improving the way we do new-product development; his Danish consulting firm specialized in *Stage-Gate* and portfolio management, and he was the first to introduce these concepts into Europe (specifically to Scandinavia) where they are now employed at leading firms throughout the region. With me, he co-owned the trademark for *Stage-Gate* in Europe. Indeed, it was a conversation with Jens in Copenhagen many years ago that convinced me of the potential for firms to adopt *Stage-Gate*, and motivated me to push on with *Stage-Gate* in those early days. His enthusiasm, good cheer, considerable knowledge and experience in this field, and especially his friendship, are sadly missed.

I also thank the following people for their contributions which made this edition so "new" and cutting edge:

- Dr. Angelika Dreher and Mr. Peter Fürst, managing partners at Five I's Innovation Management in Austria, who have taken up the challenge of implementing *Stage-Gate* in German-speaking countries for the last twenty-five years. They have pioneered in Europe some of the newer facets built into today's *Stage-Gate*, such as *Agile-Stage-Gate* methods, "Design Thinking," and the Innovation Project Canvas. Peter and Angelika, both business partners and good friends of mine, have provided many insights, exciting new methods, and examples that are found in this edition.

- Dr. Anita Sommer, who is a champion of *Agile-Stage-Gate* within the LEGO Group. She is a coauthor on recent articles into this new approach, and undertook the first basic research on the topic of Agile married to *Stage-Gate* for manufactured products. Her PhD research and the coauthored articles are heavily drawn on for this edition.

- Mr. Richard Peterson, formerly VP of New-Product Development at The Chamberlain Group, who provided insights based on his experiences (and also a case example) with the Agile and *Stage-Gate* approach. He and his firm were one of the first in the United States to experiment with this new approach.

- Mr. Tomas Vedsmand and Mr. Søren Kielgast, managing partners of the GEMBA Group, a consulting firm in Denmark, are both business partners of mine and pioneers in the application of Agile within *Stage-Gate*. They too provided valuable concepts for the current book, notably from an experimental program in their country by Dansk Indusri (Danish Industry Association) to introduce these concepts to medium-sized businesses.

- Mr. Lars Cederblad, a business partner and director of Level 21 (a strategy and innovation consulting firm in Sweden), who contributed ideas, experiences, and an application example for the current edition.

- Mr. Gerard Ryan, managing director of Prodex Systems in Australia, who implements *Stage-Gate* and automation software in Australia, New Zealand, and parts of Asia, and provided useful insights from his many experiences.

- And closer to home, the good folks at Stage-Gate International in North America, a company I cofounded (although I no longer have an ownership position in the firm), who continue to promote good management practices in product innovation and *Stage-Gate*.

Direct assistance was provided by several people: I would also like to thank my publisher, Ms. Lara Heimert, publisher at Basic Books (Perseus Books), who provided encouragement, and adeptly steered the progress of this book from inception to launch. Thanks is also due to Ms. Alia Massoud who works with Lara; and Michelle Welsh-Horst, manager, managing editor. And finally I thank Rachel King at Perpetua Editing, who did a superb job of copyediting the book, without whose perseverance and skill this book would not have been possible.

Robert G. Cooper
2017

1

THE INNOVATION CHALLENGE

Innovation is the specific instrument of entrepreneurship . . .
the act that endows resources with a new capacity to create wealth.

—PETER DRUCKER, *Innovation and Entrepreneurship,* 1985

HOW TO REALLY INNOVATE . . . AND DO IT IN RECORD TIME

Most companies have ambitious growth goals. The problem is that there are only so many sources of growth. Four of these—market growth, market-share increases, new markets, and acquisitions—are proving difficult or expensive. Markets in many industrialized countries and industries are mature and increasingly commoditized; gains in market shares are expensive; and acquisitions often don't work . . . witness share-price declines after major acquisitions are announced. New markets—India and China, for example—pose special problems; moreover, those firms that have entered Asia have already realized many of the benefits. Even traditional product development—for most companies, this means line extensions, improvements, and product modifications—seems depleted, and only serves to maintain market share.[1]

The dilemma is this: Shareholders and executives want a steady stream of profitable and high-profile new products—bold innovations that have a huge impact on the company's sales and profits and really *move the needle*. But management practices and today's competitive and financial environments are steering companies in a different direction . . . toward smaller, less risky, and less ambitious

1

initiatives. Indeed, recent pronouncements in authoritative publications have declared, perhaps prematurely, that *innovation is dead*![2] Part of the cause for the trend to less ambitious innovation is a preoccupation with short-term profitability, driven in part by the financial community. A second cause is that, even with a longer-term focus, it's really difficult to create that game-changing innovation these days—many markets and sectors simply appear barren!

Coupled with this goal of bolder innovations is the *goal of speed*. The implicit objective in new-product development (NPD) is "faster, better, cheaper." But is this goal realistic or is it simply a paradox—a contradiction in terms? It's difficult to create highly profitable new products, yet maximize short-term results. Bold innovations often take years to develop and cost millions to commercialize.

There is hope, and that's what this book is about! We see exceptional innovations and exceptional companies everywhere today. The trouble is, they are *the exception*—a minority of new products and companies. Odds are, you're not one of them. But these companies and big new products do provide a model, and by studying them, we learn *their secrets to success*.

Today, we see a handful of leading firms adopting new methods that achieve both bold innovation and in an accelerated fashion: They prove that *bold* and *fast* are both possible. These leading firms have adopted new methods and practices, some quite radical—in effect, they have reinvented their idea-to-launch methods, approaches, and processes—to make it more *agile, flexible, adaptive, and accelerated*. Indeed, some of the changes these firms have implemented represent the *most significant change to our approaches* in new-product development since the inception of gating processes three decades ago.[3]

In the next pages, you'll see a remarkable example of a big winner that was undertaken with record speed. We'll also probe into the reasons why and how, seeking lessons from this innovation. In so doing, you'll gain insights into the approaches, behaviors, and practices that made this new product so successful, so fast—lessons and insights that you can apply to your own business. The rest of the book then drills down into the details of these best practices—how to come up with big ideas, pick the winners, and drive them to market in record time, so that you and your company, too, can be a best-in-class innovator.

The Most Successful New Product ... Ever

Apple's iPod was the most successful new product ever launched, according to most metrics.[4] The speed of iPod's sales growth after launch in 2001 was staggering, with Apple reaching 50 million iPods sold globally in only 4.5 years after introduction. By contrast, it took Sony 10 years to sell 50 million Walkman units. And compare iPod's fast market growth to wireless phones, which took 12 years to reach sales of 50 million units, or digital cameras or cell phones, which had much slower starts. Apple also drove the MP3 market, whose cumulative sales reached 200 million units by the end of 2006, of which Apple was responsible for one quarter (and hit a 70 percent market share in the United States). Sales of the iPod peaked in 2008 with annual sales globally of an amazing 54.8 million units that year. By 2016, with sales slowing down as the iPod moved into the later stages of its product-life-cycle, Apple had sold *half-a-billion iPods!*[5]

Not only was the Apple iPod the most successful new product ever launched, it also reinvigorated the company, propelling Apple from a struggling, marginalized computer company in the late 1990s to the *most valuable publicly traded company today* (as of 2017). Some of you might remember Apple's challenges through the 1990s—how the firm's computer business faced tough competitors, such as IBM and HP, and suffered a number of product failures and disappointments. Its future back then was very much in doubt. So, by 1997, Steve Jobs was invited back as de facto head of the business after an absence of more than a decade.

Only a month after 9/11, and in the midst of an anthrax terrorist scare, Jobs went on stage to announce the first iPod.[6] And the rest is history: The iPod was the first of a series of inspirational i-products from Apple, including the iPhone and the iPad, which changed the way we communicate—some even say "changed the world"—and certainly skyrocketed the company to greatness.

How Did Apple Pull Off This Amazing Coup?

Contrary to popular belief, Apple *was not the innovator* in this industry—it did not invent the portable MP3 player. Indeed, when the iPod was introduced in November of 2001, almost fifty companies were selling portable MP3 players in the United States; many were Asian companies relying on the Internet to market their products.

The iPod grew out of Steve Jobs's digital-hub strategy. People were plugging all kinds of devices into their computers: digital cameras, camcorders, MP3 players. The home computer was becoming the central device, the "digital hub."[7] While Apple's programmers were busy creating software for editing photos and movies and managing digital music, they, like so many users, discovered that the early MP3 players were very much lacking.

Jobs thus asked his top hardware man, Jon Rubinstein, to see if Apple could develop a better music-playing device that would link into Apple's computers. But the challenge was a formidable one technologically: He was just about to give up when Toshiba, one of Apple's hard-drive suppliers, showed him a new 1.8-inch hard drive they had just prototyped. Rubinstein immediately recognized it as the key technology for the first iPod. And *in less than nine months*, the iPod team had a product ready to go: The iPod was assembled from off-the-shelf parts—a Toshiba hard drive, a Sony battery, and chips from Texas Instruments.[8]

Apple's success, where others failed, was due to a brilliantly conceived innovation strategy that was superbly executed. In broadest term's, Apple *saw the growing market need*, and then identified and *solved the major problems* with existing MP3 players—size, storage capacity, user interface, and the shortage of legally downloadable music. In solving the problems, Apple leveraged its unique strengths perfectly: its ability to vertically integrate and deliver an "amalgam of hardware, software, and content that made buying, storing, and playing music virtually effortless."[9] Apple achieved this success by relying on its legendary expertise in hardware and software but without going into the music business."[10] Apple also positioned the iPod cleverly, targeting its loyal customer base of young, media- and tech-savvy people (Apple's original target market) with a "cool and hip" product, almost a fashion statement. And the firm used its effective distribution-channel system, and maintained its high-quality image and avoided price discounting.

Sony, which had dominated the portable music market since the introduction of the Walkman in 1979, possessed many strengths and competencies as well: size, brand name and image, distribution and market presence, technology, and manufacturing capabilities. But it elected *a strategy that missed the boat*. As if Sony did not learn anything from its failed Betamax strategy years before, instead of attacking the embryonic but growing MP3 market, it rejected the opportunity, and instead tried to defend its languishing digital mini-disc player and establish it as the next device to supplant the declining CD player, the Discman. And so Sony and the Discman faded from the growing music marketplace.

> **Four lessons from the iPod case:**
>
> 1. Bold innovation is always possible—the right innovation strategy is critical, namely, focusing on the right strategic arenas.
> 2. Disruptive technology and "new science" is not necessary.
> 3. The odds of winning are about one in seven. But there are ways to beat these odds! One way to win is: Find big problems, then create big, bold solutions.
> 4. Accelerating major projects to market in record time is feasible. Just because they are "big" does not mean they need to take years.

Apple's successful iPod "imitation strategy" had a huge impact on the company's fortunes. Its revenue more than tripled from 2001 to 2006, while profits went from a $20 million loss to plus $2 billion in five years; and the iPod was the first of a series of breakthroughs that created the Apple we know today . . . another case of brilliant innovation strategy, flawlessly executed (and to Sony's chagrin, a case of a poorly conceived strategy doomed to failure). Strategy rules again!

Lessons Learned

Examples, such as Apple's iPod, are often cited but seem out of reach for most corporations. But a more careful examination of the iPod's success reveals *no magic here*, but simply *bold innovation* at work. And there are some lessons for us all here:

- *Bold innovation is indeed possible*; it's not just wishful thinking! One key is to have a clear *innovation strategy* that focuses the business's R&D effort on the right strategic arenas—on markets and sectors that are relatively new but still established, which are growing and have the potential for more growth, and where customers or users are largely dissatisfied with current solutions. Apple first identified this attractive *strategic arena* (MP3s), where it could leverage its strengths to advantage, and then developed a solution that solved users' problems: an easy-to-use, easy-to-download MP3 system, which also happened to be "cool."
- A *disruptive technology* or radical technological innovation *is not necessary* in order to achieve stellar new-product sales. Note that Apple did not invent the MP3 player, nor did it create this new-product category, nor was this opportunity in a blue ocean.* The MP3 category was an already existing market and product category: There were forty-three competitors selling MP3 players when Apple launched! And the components for the iPod were largely off-the-shelf—they already existed. True, Apple integrated several components—the iPod, iTunes (based on a firm, Jukebox, they had just purchased), and the home computer—in order to create a "new system." This "systems solution" was the innovation.
- One proven route to success is to *find big problems, then create big, bold solutions*. That's exactly what Apple did. Perhaps by chance, the development team discovered the many user dissatisfactions with existing MP3 players: Current products were cumbersome to use; downloading music legally was a challenge (remember Napster!); they had limited storage capacity; and so on. In spite of all the negatives, however, MP3s were still selling. By identifying these *points of pain*, and then by applying Apple's technical skills and using existing technology and components, they created and launched the winning solution.

---

* Blue ocean: an area in the ocean devoid of shipping traffic, where your "ship" is the one and only—as opposed to red ocean, which is a crowded area. In business, blue ocean refers to a totally new, open, and uncrowded market where you are the first business in; red ocean means a crowded, usually highly competitive market.

- *Accelerating to market*, even major new products, is most definitely feasible. It's quite incredible that this most successful new product in history *was developed in under a year*! Compare that to the time it takes to develop new products in your business . . . products probably nowhere as impactful as the iPod. How did they create a multibillion-dollar product so quickly? There's no question that the project leader and team were very talented people. They also were clever enough to use off-the-shelf components, so that invention and new science were not required. Leveraging the firm's core competencies and strengths was another key to speed. And the team was focused, *dedicated to this one project*. Finally, having executive sponsorship from the big boss no doubt helped too! There are other proven ways to speed new products to market that we'll see later in this book.

But Is Bold Innovation Dead?

Innovation in America is "somewhere between dire straits and dead," according to Peter Thiel, a founder of PayPal and the first outside investor in Facebook.[11] He goes on dismissively to say of this generation's inventors: "We wanted flying cars, instead we got 140 characters."* A world where all can use Twitter but hardly anyone can commute by air is less impressive than the futures dreamed of in the past.

The anecdotal evidence is damning: The recent rate of progress all around us seems slow compared with that of the early and mid-twentieth century. Take kitchens.[12] In 1900, kitchens were primitive things: no refrigerators, only ice boxes cooled by blocks of ice delivered on horse-drawn wagons, and stoves powered by wood or coal. Most households lacked electric lighting and running water. By 1970, middle-class kitchens in North America and Europe featured gas and electric stoves and ovens, fridges, food processors, microwaves, and dishwashers. But today, fifty years later, things have scarcely changed: Digital displays are on every kitchen appliance, but the appliances are basically the same as in the seventies. The breakthroughs happened in the first part of the century. The same is true of many industries—from automobiles to aircraft, from polymers and chemistry to construction materials and methods, from agriculture to food processing. It seems that only the IT industry—the software and hardware industries we associate with Silicon Valley—are truly innovating.

United States spending on R&D—both by companies and by the federal government—saw regular growth between 1950 and 1980, growing with the econ-

---

* The length limit for a Twitter message is 140 characters.

omy, according to professor of innovation and strategy at Babson College, Jay Rao.[13] But starting around 1980, this spending decreased and has remained flat ever since. "Unfortunately, there are fewer and fewer executives who are willing to spend more on R&D and long-term return," says Rao. "High-frequency trading and short-term incentives are killing innovation on all fronts. But for the venture capitalists, there are very few executives who are investing for the long term."

There are also challenges in conceiving, developing, and launching bold innovations. Whether you are a CEO, a marketing director, or a design engineer, you know that developing a truly differentiated new product is rare these days for most firms. Research shows that one of the foremost keys to profitability in new-product development is developing and launching *a unique superior product with a compelling value proposition.*[14] However, this creation is easier said than done: Markets are mature and increasingly commoditized, and hence it's difficult to create that breakthrough or game-changing new product—there seems to be "little headroom left." In many huge industries, such as food, consumer packaged goods, chemicals and plastics, or engineered products and heavy equipment, it is difficult to find opportunities for bold innovations. And disruptive technologies, a potential source of product innovation, are also scarce in most industries— those radical technologies that characterized so many industries, from plastics to automotive to home appliances, throughout much of the twentieth century.

Even today's high-tech industries struggle for the "next great innovation." New technologies, such as cell phones, digital cameras, software, or laptop computers, do emerge and dramatically generate new sales and profits. However, as these markets mature, users' needs change quickly and competitors launch new product after new product; thus it's difficult to sustain product competitive advantage in this leapfrog world.

Simply stated, managements in most companies, facing mature markets, tough competition, commoditization, and shareholder demands for short-term profits, not surprisingly has opted to focus on fast, low-risk, simple development projects—"low-hanging fruit" initiatives. Consider the development-pipeline breakdowns in Figure 1.1—a comparison of this century's development portfolio with the breakdown in the mid-1990s:[15]

- New-to-the-world products (true innovations) are down by almost half, to 11 percent of the typical development portfolio.
- By contrast, improvements and modifications to existing company-products—the least innovative category of developments—have almost doubled and now represent almost 40 percent of the typical development portfolio.

Figure 1.1: Breakdown of Development Portfolios by Project Type—Then and Now—Showing a Dramatic Shift to Less Innovative Products

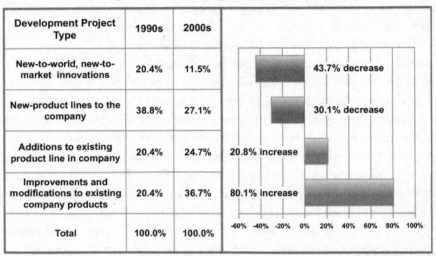

% of Projects in the Average Development Portfolio

Development Project Type	1990s	2000s
New-to-world, new-to-market innovations	20.4%	11.5%
New-product lines to the company	38.8%	27.1%
Additions to existing product line in company	20.4%	24.7%
Improvements and modifications to existing company products	20.4%	36.7%
Total	100.0%	100.0%

Artwork courtesy of Dave Caissy

WHAT'S THE SOLUTION?

The answer is a strong quest for *bold innovations*—breakthrough products, services, and solutions that create growth engines for the future. That is, instead of being content developing the "same old new-products"—extensions, modifications, upgrades, and tweaks that swamp the majority of companies' development portfolios—senior management should push for more breakthrough, game-changing, bolder product-innovation initiatives in their development pipelines.

The answer also *lies in speed.* Most product development initiatives seem to take far too long to undertake. Thus, firms must redouble their efforts to make their idea-to-launch engines faster, more adaptive, and more agile than ever before. The realities of today's competitive, fast-changing markets coupled with the demand for shorter financial paybacks mean that traditionally long cycle times—taking four or five years to develop that new product—are no longer acceptable. The goal must be to develop *breakthrough new products* but *in record time.*

The iPod case study provides a good model—a game-changing new product executed in months rather than years. There are dozens of similar examples of bold innovations—not as well-known as the iPod—in which a company created a "big concept" and bold innovation, and won, and in many cases, in far less time than traditional initiatives take. Gorilla Glass, developed by Corning for the iPad, is another example.[16] So is the Keurig coffee system, which propelled a small Vermont company to greatness. In reviewing these and other examples, a pattern emerges: In most cases, the developing company uncovered a *major customer problem*, and focused their resources and talents on developing a *bold solution*. Next, the project was properly resourced, usually with a dedicated team; used more agile, adaptive, and accelerated development methods and processes;[17] and had strong executive sponsorship and engagement. Industry needs this type of *bold innovation* to generate the growth desired by so many firms.

THE RESEARCH UNDERLYING THE BOOK

This book and its prescriptions are very much fact based. Since the 1980s, my colleagues and I have investigated over two thousand new-product launches and hundreds of companies. The goal: to uncover what winners do differently from losers, what the common denominators of successful new products and businesses are, and what distinguishes the best-performing innovators. The results have been published *in over one hundred journal articles* over the years.

NewProd Studies: Some of our studies have focused on *individual new-product projects*—over two thousand projects, both successes and failures. Multiple gauges of product performance—profitability, market share, meeting objectives, and so on—were measured. Similarly, many characteristics of the project—from the nature of the market through how well the project team executed key activities—were captured. These features characteristics were then correlated with success in order to identify those factors that distinguish the big new-product winners.

Benchmarking Studies: Other studies looked at the business unit or company rather than individual projects and asked the broader question: Why are some businesses so much better at product innovation than others? In such studies, the top-performing businesses in terms of product innovation were identified, and their practices were compared to the rest of firms. The drivers of new-product performance and their impacts were then identified.

Regardless of the study, the fundamental question was always the same: What makes for a winner? Note that the success drivers from our own and others' studies and reported in this book are *fact based, valid, and reliable*—they are based on solid research, usually published in peer-reviewed journals (they are not hearsay or merely opinion of some author). Chapter 1 in the *PDMA Handbook* summarizes these success drivers and the studies underlying them (see endnote 13).

A SYSTEMS APPROACH TO SUCCEEDING—THE INNOVATION DIAMOND

Winning at new products does not boil down to doing one or a few things well—it's not quite so simple! For example, there is more to winning than simply having a solid or agile idea-to-launch process. One must take a more *holistic approach* to succeeding at product innovation. This holistic or "systems approach" is illustrated in the *Innovation Diamond*, which includes strategy, resource and portfolio management, climate and culture, and process. That is, *four vectors* or *thrusts* must be in place to undertake innovation that yields bolder and imaginative projects yet undertaken in record time, according to our benchmarking studies (see sidebar for the research basis).[18] The Innovation Diamond in Figure 1.2 portrays these four vectors or drivers of innovation success:

Vector I: A Bold Product-Innovation Strategy to Focus R&D and NPD on the Right Strategic Arenas That Will Be Your Engines of Growth

Most businesses focus their new-product development efforts in the wrong areas—on flat markets, mature technologies, and tired product categories. To succeed in bigger, bolder innovation, it's necessary to break out of this box and to redirect R&D efforts on more fertile strategic arenas with extreme opportunities. If bolder innovation is your goal, your business needs a *product-innovation and technology strategy*—a strategy that focuses your business's R&D efforts on the most attractive arenas. Corning's decision to focus an existing capability on an embryonic market, namely, flat-panel screens, is an excellent example. The result was a huge business in a rapidly growing sector, flat-panel TV and monitor screens, which now dominate displays.[19] Sadly, the great majority of firms lack a clearly defined, robust, and well-communicated innovation strategy—there is no focus, or you're focused on arenas that won't yield the growth engines of tomorrow. Once decided, your strategic arenas become your "hunting grounds" in the search for breakthrough ideas, big concepts, and imaginative solutions.

Vector II: Making the Right Investment Decisions and Focusing Resources, Via Effective Portfolio Management

Many businesses have lots of good new-product ideas. But they *lack the appetite to invest* in these larger-scope and more risky projects, in spite of the fact that they promise to be tomorrow's winners. Part of the problem is climate and a risk-averse culture (Vector IV below). But our research shows that a major challenge in many firms is that senior management *lacks the right tools and methods* to

Figure 1.2: A "Systems Approach" to Winning—The Innovation Diamond, Showing Four Vectors that Drive Successful Innovation

A Bold Product Innovation-Strategy to Focus on the Right Strategic Arenas—Your Engines of Growth

An Innovative Climate and Culture, Right Organization, Leadership from the Top

Successful Innovation

Making the Right Investment Decisions and Focusing Resources via Effective Portfolio Management

Creating Big Ideas and Executing Developments with an Adaptive, Agile and Accelerated Idea-to-Launch Engine

Artwork courtesy of Dave Caissy

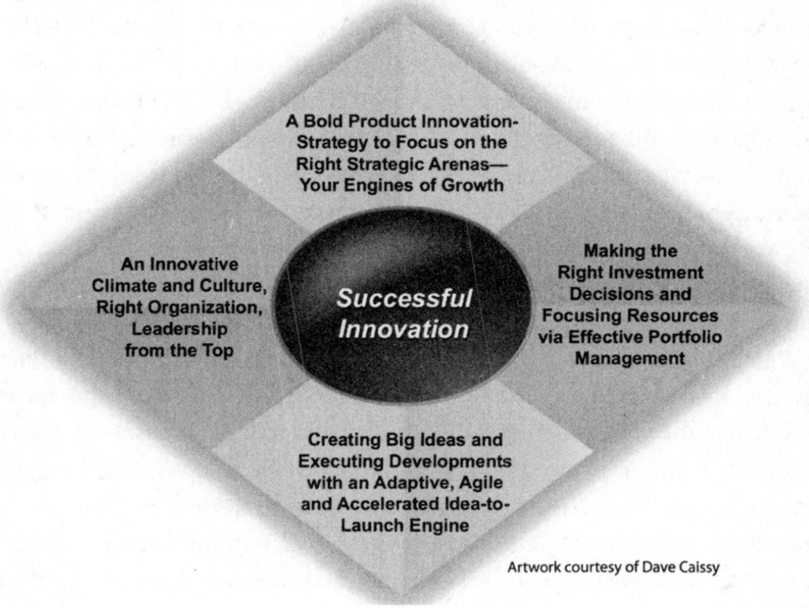

make these riskier decisions on "big concept" innovations. For example, they rely too much on financial tools, net present value (NPV), and return-on-investment methods to make the Go/Kill decisions, methods that work great for smaller, less innovative projects, but invariably lead to the wrong decisions when it comes to larger-scope, riskier innovation projects. And so the company retreats from these potential game-changing projects, and ends up doing the same old product improvements and modifications, with little real prospect for growth.

A second investment issue is that firms naturally gravitate toward a conservative, low-risk portfolio, ending up with the *wrong mix and balance of projects* in their development pipeline needed to deliver a steady stream of big winners. When management makes a series of Go/Kill decisions over many project on an ad hoc, one-at-a-time basis, usually the result is far too many little projects: The resources flow downhill to the lower risk, low-hanging fruit initiatives, almost by default. And the default option is usually wrong! Management must practice *strategic portfolio management*—much like you and I would for our personal investment portfolios—and deliberately strategically allocate resources into *strategic buckets*, one bucket reserved for more venturesome and higher-risk projects and investments. But what's the optimal allocation?

Vector III: Creating Big Ideas and Then Executing Developments With an Adaptive, Agile, and Accelerated Idea-to-Launch Engine

Big ideas lead to big concepts and big solutions—the growth engines of the future. Larger-scope and more imaginative development projects—bold innovations—begin with creating game-changing and blockbuster ideas. Our benchmarking studies have identified over twenty-five proven ways to create big, bold innovation ideas. But many firms rely on few of these methods, and instead look to traditional, somewhat depleted sources for their next breakthroughs—and of course there are no breakthroughs as a result. *Creating game-changing new-product ideas* provides the necessary feedstock for an innovative and bold product development effort; but how well does your business do here?

Generating great ideas is half the battle. The other half is *getting from the idea stage through to development and into the marketplace*—through the corporate equivalent of the "valley of death." (The "valley of death" describes the gap between conception or invention versus moving that concept or invention through to a commercialized product—the gap where so many projects die.) That's where an effective yet *rapid idea-to-launch engine* is needed. Without such a system, your "great ideas" and "big concepts" are like unpicked grapes on a vine—they'll wither and die. Driving bold innovations to market means installing a robust and efficient idea-to-launch engine or system that is designed to handle these major, "big concept" ideas and projects. Just because these projects are imaginative and bold is no reason to throw discipline out the window: The goal is "entrepreneurship but with discipline and due diligence," which is quite different than "shooting from the hip."

A second issue is that most businesses' current stage-and-gate systems are designed for "known projects" with few uncertainties and little ambiguity—modifications and product improvements—and are not well suited to big, innovative projects and technology-platform developments. Systems designed to handle bolder innovations must be more *adaptive and flexible* than in the past.

A final issue here is speed—more specifically, the need for your innovation process or idea-to-launch engine to be *agile and accelerated.* Many of the gating systems that companies use today have their roots in the 1980s and 1990s, and frankly are *too cumbersome, too linear, and too rigid* to deal with the realities of today's fast-paced world. A handful of leading firms have reinvented their innovation processes with the goal of improving productivity and driving cycle time down dramatically. By building in Agile[*] methods from the IT

---

[*] Agile: A set of methods and principles for developing software products, as outlined in the 2001 Agile Manifesto.

world, and making the process more *iterative and adaptive*, these firms get the product right early in the game, and move quickly to market.[20]

Vector IV: An Innovative Climate and Culture, the Right Organization, and Leadership from the Top

People working in the right climate is vital to success. Having the right climate and culture for innovation, an appetite to invest in innovative and more risky projects, and the right leadership from the top *distinguishes top innovation companies*, according to our extensive studies of innovation results. Those businesses that create a positive climate for innovation, support innovation at every opportunity, reward and recognize innovators and successful development teams, and welcome ideas from all employees do much better at product innovation.

Similarly, having the right senior leadership—men and women who drive and support the innovation effort with words as well as through actions, and foster an innovative climate—is vital to success. Not every senior executive can be a Steve Jobs, Elon Musk, Richard Branson, or Thomas Edison; but there are actions that any senior executive can take to make him or her a *leader of innovation* in their business. Sadly, research shows that most businesses lack the needed climate, culture, and leadership for innovation.

The next chapters delve into the details of the Innovation Diamond in Figure 1.2—the keys to being successful at bold product innovation—and how to implement them in your business. But first, let's step back and look at the vital role that innovation should play in your business and its impact on corporate prosperity and growth, and let's examine why executives need to spend more time thinking about how to become more proficient at leading the innovation effort.

NEW PRODUCTS: THE KEY TO BUSINESS PROSPERITY

New-product development is one of the riskiest, yet most important, endeavors of the modern corporation. Certainly the risks are high: You and your colleagues have all seen large amounts of money spent on new-product disasters in your own firm or industry. But then, the rewards are high too! A 2011 Deutsche Bank study of more than a thousand companies found that those that spent significantly more on R&D than their competitors were *more highly valued by investors*. And a 2014 study of companies that cut R&D spending in order to meet short-term earnings goals found that their stocks underperformed after earnings had been announced.[21]

Today, new products account for *a staggering 27.3 percent of company sales*, on average.[22] That is, more than one-quarter of the revenues of corporations come from products they did not sell three short years ago. In some dynamic industries, the figure is 100 percent! (Here a "new product" is defined as "new" if it has been on the market by that firm for three years or less, and includes extensions and significant improvements as well.) As might be expected, profits follow closely, with 25.2 percent of company profits derived from new products three years old or newer. The message is simple: Either innovate or die!

> The *best innovators* have four times the sales from new products and more than double the success rate as the worst performers. But why the huge differences?

Major Performance Differences Between the Best- and Worst-Performing Innovators

The percentages cited above—more than one dollar in four comes from new products—are only averages, and thus understate the true impact and potential of product innovation. What CEO wants to be *average*? A handful of companies do far better than average, according to our extensive benchmarking studies, and thus become the benchmark firms—see Figure 1.3.[23] The top 20 percent of businesses—the *best-performing innovators*—are compared to the worst performers (the bottom 20 percent). The best . . .

- have 36.3 percent of sales derived from new products launched in the previous three years, versus only 10.0 percent for the worst performers, a four-times difference in performance!
- have a commercial success rate of 79.5 percent of initiated development projects (double the success rate of the worst businesses at 37.6 percent).
- and see the great majority—70.1 percent—of new products they launch meet or exceed their target profit levels (targets set in the Business Case on which the project was approved). Only 30.0 percent of new products hit profit targets—less than one in three—in the worst performers.

Huge differences exist in product-innovation performance between the best and worst firms. But why? What distinguishes the best innovators? The point is that stellar performance is attainable in product innovation: These best innovators show the way. And the differences don't stop here. Most performance metrics in product innovation boil down to time and money, so besides the profit and sales data, also consider the time-to-market results in Figure 1.3:

Figure 1.3: Best Businesses Perform Very Much Better in Product Innovation versus the Rest—By Orders of Magnitude on Five Key Metrics—But Why?

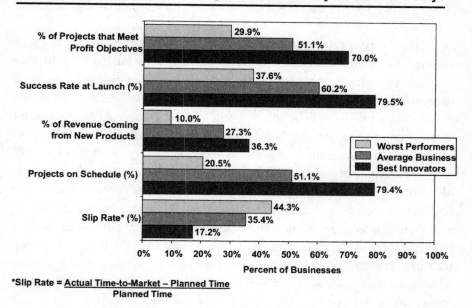

*Slip Rate = <u>Actual Time-to-Market – Planned Time</u>
Planned Time

- On average, about half of new-product development projects are launched on schedule. But the best innovators again really shine, with almost 80 percent of their new products launched on schedule. By contrast, the worst performers see only one in five products getting to market on time.
- The "slip rate" is a useful time metric, capturing the slippage between planned time-to-market (usually projected in the project's Business Case) and the actual time. High slip rates are bad. Note that the best firms in Figure 1.3 have a slip rate of only 17.2 percent, meaning that if the project was forecast to take twelve months, it actually took fourteen months; that is, two months late—not bad. By comparison, the worst businesses have a slip rate of 44.3 percent, meaning that a twelve-month time-to-market forecast in reality became 17.3 months!

Suggestion: Time to take stock and conduct a *current state assessment* of your performance in new products:

1. Look at your performance results in comparison to those in Figure 1.3. Are your results close to the best businesses? If so, well done! But if they're only "average" or worse, the time is ripe to determine why and what can be done.

2. Be sure to look not only at the popular "percentage of revenue from new products," but at other metrics such as "percentage of products hitting profit targets," "success rates," and the two time metrics in Figure 1.3.

I make three important points based on these best-versus-worst data in Figure 1.3. First, *huge differences exist* between the best and worst businesses—these are not a few percentage points difference in performance, but order-of-magnitude differences. These huge performance differences beg the question: Why? Why is it that some firms seem to be so successful at product innovation, whereas the majority pale by comparison? What are the secrets to such high productivity or superb new-product results? Our research shows that it is not just "a few good years" or a couple of lucky new-product winners; rather there are *clear, measurable, sustainable, and consistent behaviors, approaches, and methods* that the best companies embrace, and that the rest do not: the "best practices in innovation."

Second, the average business does fairly poorly in comparison to the best. Odds are that your business is closer to the average than the best, so your performance probably resembles the rather mediocre results achieved by average firms. Most businesses do have much room for improvement, so likely you have missed many of the pivotal best practices in innovation.

The final point is that the best firms do model the way: They prove that these results are not some mythical or theoretical result, but are achievable and realistic. That is, the common denominators or best practices that separate the best firms from the rest are both tangible and actionable, and within your grasp.

Suggestion: When you look at innovation performance in your own industry, do you see big differences? Why is it that some businesses are so successful? And when you analyze successes and failures in your own company, are there some patterns? What can you learn here about what it takes to be a best performer in product innovation? As this book unfolds, we lower the microscope on these and other results, and probe the factors that separate the winners from the losers—their best practices and their secrets of success.

HUGE AMOUNTS AT STAKE

Industry spends enormous resources in the quest for new products. Thus, not only are the potential upside rewards substantial, but there is much downside risk too. R&D expenditures are one metric that captures the magnitude of investments in product innovation. The figures are impressive: Globally, R&D expenditures from all sources (companies, government labs, institutes, and universities) were a staggering 1.1 trillion US dollars in 2104, or about 2.4 percent of global GDP.[24] Of that, the United States accounted for $430 billion. Domestic spending on R&D in the United States, but only by companies, amounted to $323 billion in 2013—that's 3.3 percent of these firms' annual sales![25] Table 1.1 provides breakdown of R&D spending by industry so that you can compare your firm with others in your industry.

Note that R&D spending is not the entire picture. It's estimated that for every one dollar spent on new-product R&D, another two dollars are spent on "other things" associated with the development and launch of the product—on marketing, capital equipment, and management costs.*

Why Product Innovation Is More Vital Than Ever

New products are clearly the key to corporate prosperity. They drive corporate revenues, market shares, bottom lines, and even share prices. But why is new-product development speeding up so much globally, and why is so much more emphasis being placed on product-innovation results? Here are *five external trends* that help to explain why innovation is picking up speed, and why your business cannot afford to wait on the sidelines:

> Technology advances, markets in turmoil, shorter product life cycles, globalization, and the Internet are all driving innovation—and they're not going away! Given these pervasive trends, product innovation is vital for your business's prosperity, and even survival, like never before.

1. *Technology advances:* The world's base of technology[†] and know-how increases at an exponential rate, making possible solutions and products not even dreamed of a decade or so ago. What was science fiction in *Star Trek* in the 1960s—for example, handheld computers, curing disease through DNA modification, driverless cars, magnetic induction cooktops, or portable video-communication devices—is suddenly a technological reality today. And here are some frightening statistics:[26] Until 1900, human knowledge doubled approximately every century. Today, on average, human knowledge doubles every thirteen months, and according to IBM, the "internet of things" will lead to a doubling every twelve hours.

2. *Changing customer needs:* Marketplaces are also in turmoil, with market needs and wants and customer preferences changing regularly. And

---

* However, not all R&D spending goes to new products; an estimated half—or more in some process industries—goes to process development (as opposed to product development).

† The term "technology" is used throughout this book to mean "the application of scientific knowledge for practical purposes" (not simply "a new product," as the word is often used in the IT industry).

TABLE 1.1: R&D SPENDING BY COMPANIES IN
THE UNITED STATES AS A PERCENT OF SALES

INDUSTRY	DOMESTIC R&D ($ MILIIONS)	R&D AS PERCENT OF SALES
ALL INDUSTRIES	322,528	3.3
Manufacturing industries	221,476	3.8
Food	5,028	0.7
Beverage and tobacco products	827	0.6
Textile, apparel, and leather products	662	1.2
Wood products	220	0.7
Paper	920	1.0
Printing and related support activities	252	1.1
Petroleum and coal products	242	0.1
Chemicals	61,664	4.5
Basic chemicals	2,658	0.6
Resin, synthetic rubber, and artificial synthetic fibers and filaments	1,065	0.7
Pesticide, fertilizer, and other agricultural chemicals	1,691	3.5
Pharmaceuticals and medicines	52,426	10.3
Soap, cleaning compound, and toilet preparation	2,469	2.4
Paint, coating, adhesive, and other chemicals	1,355	1.9
Plastics and rubber products	3,650	2.2
Nonmetallic mineral products	1,329	2.4
Primary metals	624	0.5
Fabricated metal products	2,212	1.6
Machinery	12,650	3.4
Agricultural implement	1,597	2.8
Semiconductor machinery	3,194	28.4
Engine, turbine, and power-transmission equipment	1,448	2.9
Other machinery	6,411	2.5
Computer and electronic products	67,205	10.6
Communications equipment	15,658	9.0
Semiconductor and other electronic components	30,800	18.5
Navigational, measuring, electromedical, and control instruments	14,478	8.3
Electromedical, electrotherapeutic, and irradiation apparatus	2,634	9.5
Search, detection, navigation, guidance, aeronautical, and nautical system and instrument	8,106	9.4
Other measuring and controlling device	3,738	6.2
Other computer and electronic products	6,269	5.2
Electrical equipment, appliances, and components	4,136	2.9
Transportation equipment	45,972	4.1
Automobiles, bodies, trailers, and parts	16,729	2.4
Aerospace products and parts	27,114	7.6
Aircraft, aircraft engine, and aircraft parts	D	D
Guided missile, space vehicle, and related parts	D	D
Military armored vehicle, tank, and tank components	9	2.7
Other transportation	2,121	3.4
Furniture and related products	374	1.1
Miscellaneous manufacturing	13,509	4.0
Medical equipment and supplies	10,954	4.4
Other miscellaneous manufacturing	2,555	2.7

INDUSTRY	DOMESTIC R&D ($ MILIIONS)	R&D AS PERCENT OF SALES
Nonmanufacturing industries	101,052	2.7
Mining, extraction, and support activities	3,997	0.9
Utilities	294	0.1
Wholesale trade	529	0.2
Electronic shopping and electronic auctions	1,357	2.1
Transportation and warehousing	D	D
Information	57,207	5.5
Publishing	35,675	8.6
Newspaper, periodical, book, and directory publishers	342	1.5
Software publishers	35,333	9.0
Telecommunications	3,041	0.7
Data processing, hosting, and related services	6,446	8.1
Other information	12,046	9.0
Finance and insurance	4,308	0.7
Real estate and rental and leasing	150	1.5
Lessors of nonfinancial intangible assets (except copyrighted works)	58	15.4
Other real estate and rental and leasing	92	0.9
Professional, scientific, and technical services	31,017	8.4
Architectural, engineering, and related services	3,133	3.4
Computer-systems design and related services	9,268	8.4
Scientific research and development services	14,201	20.1
Biotechnology research and development	4,499	19.3
Physical, engineering, and life sciences (except biotechnology) research and development	8,910	19.4
Social sciences and humanities research and development	792	61.1
Other professional, scientific, and technical services	4,415	4.5
Health-care services	526	1.0

in some fast-paced markets, customers aren't even certain what they want—there's much ambiguity regarding needs. The company that seemed omnipotent only a few years ago—for example, Nokia in cell phones, or Yahoo in search engines—suddenly falls from favor in the marketplace. And witness the number of mergers and acquisitions, as major corporations scramble to keep pace with fluid marketplaces. In other markets, customers have come to expect new products with significant improvements: Consumers wait with anticipation for the next release of that "neat product," and B2B customers constantly expect performance improvement from your offerings.

3. *Shortening product life cycles:* One result of the increasing pace of technological change coupled with changing market demands has been shorter

product life cycles. Product life cycles have been cut by a factor of about four over the last fifty years:[27] That new appliance that might have been sold for twelve years without major change in the 1960s now is replaced by a new model every four years! And your new product no longer has a life of five to ten years, but within a few years, sometimes even months, it is superseded by a competitive entry, rendering yours obsolete and necessitating a new product. These shortening life cycles have placed much pressure on businesses and their management teams.

4. *Increased globalization:* We have access to new and foreign markets like never before, but at the same time, our domestic market has become someone else's international one. This globalization of markets has created significant opportunities for the product innovator: The world product, locally tailored, targeted at global markets, makes possible a huge potential market size for the right innovation. As of 2015, Apple sold more iPhones in China than in the United States![28] Globalization has also intensified competition in every domestic market. These global factors have sped up the pace of product innovation.

5. *The Internet:* The Internet and related forms of communication have impacted just about every facet of modern product innovation. For example, the Internet and social media have revolutionized marketing, making global-market access available to almost everyone, even smaller firms and entrepreneurs, and making micromarketing—marketing strategies tailored to individual people or firms, the ultimate in segmentation—possible. Start-up firms raise venture capital on the Internet; markets and the competitive landscapes can be analyzed by online searches in record time; project team members can be in different locations yet be in constant contact; and new products (or *virtual* products) can even be tested with customers online. The Internet has also made possible outsourcing of many of the traditional labor-intensive tasks in product development, such as writing software code, undertaking engineering design work, and even patent searches, to lower labor-cost countries such as India and China.

A quick review of all five drivers of product innovation reveals that none is likely to disappear in the next decade or two. Technology advances and changes in market needs and demands will continue to occur; globalization of markets will march on; competition will drive life cycles to become even shorter; and the Internet and improved communication will keep advancing. In order to keep pace with these changes and trends, product innovation will be even more critical to corporate prosperity in the years ahead than it has been in the recent past. **Suggestion:** If you haven't already done so, conduct a review of the strategic role—past, present, and future—of new products in your company. Key questions include:

1. Where will your sales growth come from? What proportion from new products? From new markets? From growth in existing markets? Or from increased market share?
2. What proportion of your current sales comes from new products introduced by you in the last three years? How does this compare to the best innovators in Figure 1.3? What is your projection or objective for the future?
3. What will your portfolio of product offerings look like in five years?
4. What is your historical level of R&D spending as a percentage of sales? Has it been going up or down? How does it compare to your competitors' or your industry? Why is it higher or lower?
5. Are the answers to the questions above consistent with each other? Are you investing enough in R&D and new products to yield the results that you want?

HIGH ODDS OF FAILURE

Innovative products are critical to your long-term success. They keep your business's product portfolio competitive and healthy, and in many firms, provide you with long-term and sustainable competitive advantage. The dilemma is that product innovation is a crapshoot: Creating a steady stream of successful and high-impact new products is no small feat.

The hard reality is that the great majority of new products never make it to market. And those that do face a failure rate somewhere in the order of 25 to 45 percent. For example, our studies indicate that new products currently have a success rate of 60.2 percent at launch (Figure 1.3), and the PDMA[*] data show a 59 percent success rate at launch. These success-rate figures do vary from study to study, however, depending on what the industry is and how one defines a "new product" and a "failure." Note also that averages often don't tell the whole

---

[*] PDMA: Product Development and Management Association in Chicago, Illinois, is the major global association of product developers.

story: The success rate varies from a low of 37.6 percent for the worst firms to a high of 79.5 percent for the best!

Regardless of whether the success rate is 55 or 65 percent, the odds of a misfire are still substantial. Worse, the figures cited above *don't include the majority of new-product projects* that are killed along the way and long before launch, yet involved considerable expenditures of time and money. An estimated 46 percent of what industry spends on new-product development goes to initiatives that either fail in the marketplace or are cancelled prior to launch—that is, almost half of investment resources go to duds!

The *attrition curve* of new products as they move from idea to commercializing and beyond provides a more complete picture. A number of studies have revealed more or less the same-shaped curved in Figure 1.4: *For every 7 new-product ideas, about 4 enter development, 1.5 are launched, and only 1 succeeds.*[29] That's a seven-to-one ratio for success when starting at the idea stage— not good odds! The bad news continues: 40 percent of new-product projects fail to hit their profit targets and almost half are launched behind schedule; 32 percent of businesses rate their new-product development speed and efficiency as "very poor," while 80 percent rate their product development productivity (profits versus R&D spending) as "fair" or "poor." Finally, 28 percent of businesses don't even measure their new-product performance results![30] These are astounding statistics when one considers the magnitude of human and financial resources devoted to product innovation.

But all is not bad. Recall from Figure 1.3 earlier that a minority of firms—the 20 percent best innovators—do achieve an enviable 80 percent success rate at launch, 70 percent of their new products hit profit targets, and 79 percent are launched on schedule. These few firms show that it is possible to outperform the average, and by a considerable margin.

> The odds of winning are about one in seven. But there are ways to beat these odds!

Suggestion: How well is your company faring at product innovation? Do you know—do you keep score? (Many companies cannot provide reliable statistics on success, fail, and kill rates; on resources spent on winners versus losers; or on numbers of projects hitting time and profit targets.)

Keep score in product innovation. The adage "You cannot manage what you do not measure" certainly applies in new products. Key statistics to track include:

- Success versus failure rates at launch.
- Attrition rates: What percent of projects continue at each stage of the innovation process?

Figure 1.4: The Attrition Rate of New-Product Projects—Begin with Seven Serious Concepts, End Up with Only One Winner

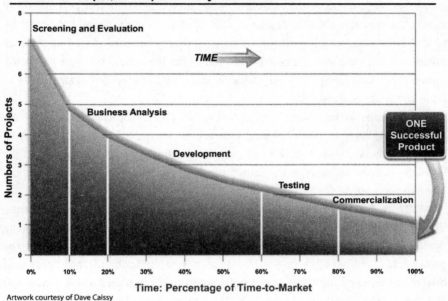

Artwork courtesy of Dave Caissy

- Proportion of resources devoted to winners versus losers versus killed projects, overall and per stage.
- Proportion of projects hitting time, profit, and sales targets.

Beating the Odds

New products are kind of like a steeplechase horse race: Relatively few new-product projects succeed. About seven horses leave the starting gate and must clear various hurdles, hedges, or gates along the way. And only one horse in seven crosses the finish line as the winner. Racetrack gamblers try to pick the one winning horse, but more often than not, they place their bets on the wrong one.

New-product management is even riskier than a horse race. True, the odds of picking a winner at the outset are somewhere on the order of seven to one. But the size of the bets is considerably greater—often in the millions of dollars. And unlike the gambler, new-product managers cannot leave the game—they must go on placing the bets, year after year, if the company is to succeed. The new-products game is very much addictive: Once in, it is difficult to quit!

Faced with these kinds of odds and risks, why would anyone want to play at product innovation? Maybe because there are some important differences between a horse race and creating new products. First, the payoff from one winning new product, like Apple's iPod or Corning's Gorilla Glass, can be enormous—enough to more than cover all your losses. Second, and perhaps more subtle, the way the bets are placed is different. At a racetrack, all bets must be placed *before the race begins*. But in new products, bets are placed *as the race proceeds*. Imagine a steeplechase horse race where bets could be placed after the horses clear each hedge or gate! Suddenly the odds are changed dramatically in favor of the shrewd gambler.

Product innovation, then, is much more like a game of five-card stud poker than a horse race. In five-card stud poker, after each card is dealt, the players place their bets. Toward the end of each hand, the outcome—who will be the winner—becomes clearer; at the same time, the betting and the amounts at stake rise exponentially.

Many an amateur poker player has sat down with a professional, assuming that he had equal odds of winning. True, each player has the same odds of being dealt a winning hand: The cards are dealt randomly. But over the long term, the professionals will always win—not because they get better hands, but because of how they bet, knowing when to bet high, when to bet low, and when to fold and walk away. The trick is in the betting! The professional player counts cards and has tangible criteria for betting.

Unfortunately, too many companies play at product innovation like the amateur poker player. They start with an equal chance of winning. But because they don't count cards (that is, they don't do their homework but operate on hunch and speculation instead) and lack solid betting criteria (that is, they have poor or nonexistent decision rules for making Go/Kill decisions), they lose to the professional. And so the odds of losing—especially for the amateur player—are exceptionally high.

The point of these analogies is to show that the new-products field is much more complex than a mere horse race: Product innovation features high risks, low odds of picking a winner, large amounts at stake, and an incremental betting process, with additional and increasing bets placed as the race proceeds. The second point is that effective betting is one key to winning. We all have the same odds of being dealt a good hand, but it's how we bet—the information we gather and the betting rules or criteria we use—that makes the difference between winning and losing. Finally, there is one important difference between product innovation, on the one hand, and poker or a horse race, on the other: *We can affect the outcome.* That is, through the actions that product developers take, they can change the outcome of the race or the poker hand. And thus much of what is to follow in this book is about gaining insights into the practices and methods that best innovators use to *change the outcome* and to *shift the odds in their favor*.

DEFINING NEWNESS AND A "NEW PRODUCT"

Serious players keep score in product innovation. But in order to keep score, one must have a definition of what counts as *a new product*. One of the problems with some of the scores cited above is that they include *different types* of new products: For example, the attrition rates for truly innovative new products are much higher than for extensions and modifications of existing company products.

Product: First, a "product" is anything referred to an *external marketplace* for sale, use, or consumption. This includes *physical products* as well as *software*, and *services* as well as *combinations of services, hardware, and/or software*. But the definition excludes "freebies" such as might be provided by a tech service-and-support group (for example, free user-training or free maintenance). Products are usually associated with businesses or corporations, and my many illustrations and examples are from companies. But "products" can also be from nonprofit organizations, industry associations, health-care and other societal organizations, or governments, although the term "program" might also be used there.

> Keep score in new-product development: How well is your business doing? But first, agree on a solid definition of what counts as a "new product."

New product: Next, how does one define a "new product," "innovativeness," or "newness"? Here are some definitions to help you when crafting your performance metrics:

- One major US B2B conglomerate defines a new product as "anything—service or physical product—that provides new functionality, features, or benefits that are clearly visible to the customer or user, and which involved at least fifty person-days in development time." The notion here is that the product should be perceived as "new" by the marketplace (and not just by the firm's engineering department), and that the firm should have made some minimum investment (there is something at stake).
- Some consumer-goods firms define a new product as a new stock-keeping unit (SKU) or new bar code. Such a loose definition, although very pragmatic, allows far too many launches to count as "new products" and thus inflates the numbers. To compensate for this overstatement, some of the same firms only count *incremental sales* from these same items—that is,

the *increase in sales*. So if a new version of a product is launched (a new SKU or new bar code), but it creates no new sales (that is, sales are low, or the product simply cannibalizes an existing company product), it may be a "new product" but its sales would not be counted in the tally.

- Another convenient definition is that a new product is "the result of any project or initiative that went through our idea-to-launch or gating system."

Yet another useful scheme recognizes that there are many different types of *new products*. "Newness" can be defined in two ways:[31]

1. New to the company, in the sense that the firm has never made or sold this type of product before, but other firms might have.
2. New to the market or "innovative": The product is the first of its kind on the market (or in *your market*).

Viewed on a two-dimensional map as shown in Figure 1.5, six different types of new products are identified:

1. *New-to-the-world products:* These new products are the first of their kind and create an entirely new market. This type represents only 10 percent of all new products, and is shrinking as a percentage.
2. *New-product lines:* These products, although not new to the marketplace, nonetheless are quite new to the developing firm. They allow a company to enter an established product category or market for the first time. About 20 percent of all new products are this type.
3. *Additions to existing product lines:* These are new items to the firm, but they fit within an existing product line the firm makes or sells. They may also represent a fairly new product to the marketplace. Such new items are one of the largest types of new products—about 26 percent of all new-product launches.
4. *Improvements and revisions to existing products:* These "not-so-new" products are essentially replacements of existing products in a firm's product line. They offer improved performance or greater perceived value over the "old" product. These "new and improved" products also make up 26 percent of new-product launches.
5. *Repositionings:* These are essentially new applications for existing products and often involve retargeting an old product to a new market segment or for a different application. Repositionings account for about 7 percent of all new products.

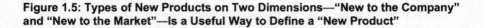

**Figure 1.5: Types of New Products on Two Dimensions—"New to the Company"
and "New to the Market"—Is a Useful Way to Define a "New Product"**

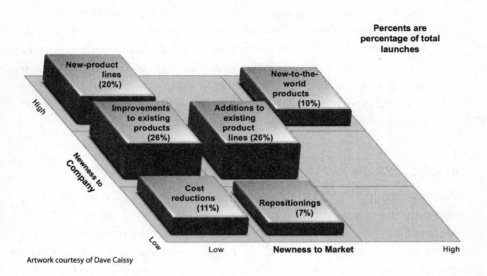

Artwork courtesy of Dave Caissy

6.   *Cost reductions:* These are the "least new" of all new-product types. They
     are new products designed to replace existing company products, but
     they yield similar benefits and performance at lower delivered cost. From
     a marketing standpoint, they are not new products; but from a design
     and production viewpoint, they could represent significant change. They
     make up 11 percent of all new-product launches.

Most firms count the first four types above—those in the upper part of Figure
1.5—as "new products" when measuring new-product performance and impact.
Suggestion:

1.   Develop a robust definition of what a "new product" is in your business.
     Ensure that the definition is both rigorous and operational, that is, one
     that is feasible (easy to use and measure, and gives reliable metrics), yet is
     tough (does not include every minor development project and thus over-
     state the numbers). Use this definition when determining your product-
     innovation results to compare with industry results in Figure 1.3.
2.   Next, review the new products that your business has introduced in
     the last three years. Then categorize them according to the six types in
     Figure 1.5. What is the split of projects by type (use a pie chart)? Does

the split differ much from the all-industry averages shown in Figure 1.5? Why?

3. What is the breakdown by project type in terms of total resources spent—that is, to which types of projects has your money and effort been devoted? What is the breakdown by sales and profits—that is, which types of products or projects are generating the revenues and profits? What is the success rate by type? Finally, what's the ratio of sales (or profits) to spending per project type (that is, the *productivity* of each type)?

4. Is your current breakdown or split the desirable one? What should be the split of new products by type in Figure 1.5?

THE PATH FORWARD

In this chapter, you have seen that *winning at new products* plays a critical role in determining company fortunes. The need is for bold and breakthrough new products that really move the needle . . . yet are executed in record time via a more agile, accelerated, and adaptive innovation engine. You have also seen some of the performance results, which show that this quest for *bold and fast* is not so easy! Then the huge differences between successful innovators and the typical company were highlighted, and provoke the question: *Why?* Four vectors that drive bold and successful innovation were laid out in the Innovation Diamond.

You have also read about some of the risks in product innovation: the huge expenditures that companies make on R&D, and the comparison of product innovation to a horse race with high odds of failure and significant rates of attrition. One key is in how you place your bets! But you can also affect the outcome—it's how you play the game that counts, not just how you bet. Finally, keeping score is an important facet of product innovation, so I provided definitions of "new products" and also laid out a scheme to help define and categorize new products in order for the scores to be more comparable.

In the next two chapters, we take a close look at the hard evidence. Our research into new-product practices and reasons for innovation success (and failure!) over the last thirty years has been noted by the Product Development and Management Association as the *most widely published research in the field* and has yielded perhaps the most comprehensive database on new-product winners and losers—over two thousand launches in over five hundred companies in both Europe and North America.[32] And from observing these many successes and failures, we learn the *keys to winning at new products*. Additionally, our benchmarking studies—in which we looked at the best-performing innovators versus the rest—yield many insights into best practices and *key success drivers*. These investigations, both at the project level and also at the business level, provide the basis for the book.

We begin our voyage in Chapter 2 with a look at the reasons new products fail, and what goes wrong. Focusing on failure is perhaps a negative way to start, but it's the right place too: Here, the hope is that we can learn from our past mistakes. We then look to *new-product successes* and pinpoint the *eight most important factors* that separate winning new products from the losers, and which ones most companies miss! Chapter 3 broadens the scope and looks at *successful companies*, and the *nine most important factors that make some businesses much more successful* at product innovation. We conclude that there are clear patterns to success, and indeed, that new-product success is both predictable and controllable. These "success drivers" are integrated into the key lessons for new-product success—the *critical success factors* that we then build into our *playbook for winning*.

Following that, Chapters 4 through 9 deal with crafting our playbook for winning. Here the focus is on the development and implementation of a stage-and-gate *new-product system* for driving new products to market successfully and efficiently. The majority of firms doing product development today already use some form of *Stage-Gate*, but in Chapter 4, we introduce the *newest version* of this popular *Stage-Gate* methodology—a best-in-class idea-to-launch product-innovation system.[*] Here, the critical success factors and best practices identified in Chapters 2 and 3 are integrated and translated into an operational blueprint for action, with a particular emphasis on bold innovation projects.

Chapter 5 moves *beyond traditional Stage-Gate*, and provides a look into some of the novel and more successful practices that companies have introduced into their idea-to-launch innovation engine, making it more *flexible, agile, faster, and adaptive*. Newer concepts such as context-based approaches, risk-based contingency models, and Agile methods are explored. Chapter 6 delves into the new *Agile-Stage-Gate hybrid mode* that a handful of leading hardware or physical-product firms have adopted in the last few years. Agile methods, borrowed from the IT world, are modified and adjusted to suit the manufacturing sector, and when combined with *Stage-Gate* principles, recently have proven to yield dramatic performance results.

But there is more to winning than merely having a robust idea-to-launch process. Consistent with the holistic and "systems approach" outlined in

---

[*] *Stage-Gate®* is a trademark of Stage-Gate International Inc. in the United States and Australia, and of R. G. Cooper & Associates Inc. in Canada. In the European Union, the *Stage-Gate®* trademark is held by R. G. Cooper.

the Innovation Diamond, Chapter 7 moves to another vital facet, namely, Discovery—coming up with *breakthrough new-product ideas*. This chapter highlights more than twenty-five proven methods for generating great ideas, along with results on which ones work best.

Chapter 8 moves to picking the winners: It is about *portfolio management* and focuses on ways to improve your "betting practices"—increasing your odds of *making the right R&D investment decisions*, and also on ways to achieve the *right balance and mix* of development projects. Focus is key here—focusing resources on the big winners! Picking winners is so vital that I devote another chapter (Chapter 9) to the same topic, but with emphasis on new approaches to make Go/Kill gates more effective, including the concept of "lean gates with teeth."

Developing a *product-innovation and technology strategy* for your business is the topic of the final chapter, 10. Strategy is one of the key facets or vectors of the systems approach shown in the Innovation Diamond. This final chapter helps provide direction to your business's total new-product effort: It gets into topics such as defining *innovation objectives* for your business, and identifying and selecting the *best strategic arenas* to focus your R&D resources—arenas that will become *your next engines of growth*. Developing *attack plans*—how to win in each strategic arena—is also a topic.

So read on! First, witness the critical success factors in the next two chapters, and then discover how they can and should be built into your *innovation system and playbook* in your business so that you, too, can be a *big winner* at new products.

2

WHY NEW PRODUCTS WIN

I am the master of my fate: I am the captain of my soul.
—W. E. Henley, "Invictus"

THE SECRETS TO SUCCESS

What are the factors that underlie new-product success? And why are some new-product projects and products so successful? Do you know? Most people don't or choose to ignore them—witness the high failure rates and the large number of businesses and new products with very poor performance (recall the poor performance results in Chapter 1, and also Figures 1.3 and 1.4). Because these *success drivers* are not well-known, I refer to them as "secrets to success."

There is help, however! Numerous studies have probed the question of why new products win (or fail)—they looked at large samples of successful versus unsuccessful new products and found what separates the two. Some studies have also lowered the microscope on businesses and their innovation performance and sought reasons for their results (see box in Chapter 1 for a quick description of these studies).[1]

An understanding of these "success drivers" is vital to designing systems and approaches for conceiving, developing, and launching new products—systems designed to deliver big winners and in record time. It's much like a coach and the football team watching video replays of football games: Patterns emerge and insights are gained into what to avoid in future games and what new plays or

TABLE 2.1: SEVEN REASONS WHY NEW PRODUCTS FAIL

1. *Me-too or tired new products*—the product is wrong! It *fails to excite the customer*—there is no "wow factor" and *no compelling value proposition* for the customer.

2. *Weak front-end homework*—the necessary due diligence (the market study, the technical assessment, the financial analysis) is superficially done or not done at all.

3. *A lack of customer or user input and market insights*—what the product should be and do is defined with little input from the marketplace. When the product goes to field trials or launch, it's not quite right or dead wrong!

4. *Unstable product specs and project scope creep*—the product and project definition keep changing as the project moves along, *the number one cause of delays later in the project.*

5. *Dysfunctional project teams, too many functional silos*—members from all the key functions are missing; the team leader is the wrong person; the team does not share a common vision; team members lack commitment; and team accountability is missing.

6. *Far too many projects in the pipeline (no focus)*—too many projects are approved, resulting in underresourced projects and people spread far too thin. Projects take too long, corners are cut, and project quality declines.

7. *A lack of competencies, skills, and knowledge*—people with the right skills, competencies, and knowledge to undertake the project are not available. The project, as defined, *never should have been approved in the first place.*

actions should be built into the new playbook. That is, when we identify a major and consistent reason for product failure, we build into our playbook or system steps to avert such failures in the future; and when we pinpoint success drivers—factors that distinguish winning new products—again we build in steps and actions to replicate those in our own idea-to-launch system. This chapter looks at the "tactical" success and failure drivers, specifically, factors that apply *at the project and product level* and that are immediately actionable; the next chapter focuses more on strategic and broader success drivers, which apply at the business-unit level.

WHY NEW PRODUCTS FAIL TO YIELD THE PROFITS THEY SHOULD

Perhaps the best place to begin the quest to improve innovation results is to understand *why new products fail*. Often, an understanding of past failures, problems, and pitfalls leads to insights that ultimately result in corrective action. This recognition is one premise of the process of continuous improvement and the learning organization. Why do so many new products fail to live up to their financial and sales expectations? In the last chapter, we saw that almost half of development projects fail to meet their profit objectives and that more than one-third of new products fail at launch! The following set of reasons and root causes for failure is compiled from an integration of research results from countless studies into new-product outcomes and from many problem-detection sessions held in companies (Table 2.1):[2]

1. Me-Too or Tired New Products

The first reason is that the product is wrong! It *fails to excite the customer*—there is no "wow factor" in the product, nor does it *satisfy an unmet need* or *solve a major problem* better than the competition. In short, it looks a lot like the competitor's product. What's missing is the *quest for competitive advantage*: The new-product idea is proposed, but the bar is never set high enough, and so the project team develops yet one more me-too, ho-hum, tired, and vanilla product, much the same as competitors'. There is *no compelling value proposition* for users or customers, and given no reason to switch, they don't! And sales fail to materialize.

One *root cause* is that management does not demand that project teams rise above competitors' offerings. By contrast, in one major consumer-goods firm, the expectation is that the new product will be "differentiated, unique, and deliver superior-to-competition performance"; otherwise, the project is simply rejected!

A second root cause is that businesses are *missing key elements* in their idea-to-launch systems: There is no emphasis on differentiated products and compelling value propositions. Indeed, if one were to slavishly execute according to the typical firm's new-product idea-to-launch guidebook, the result probably would be yet another vanilla product. Some firms' processes seem to be *designed to deliver mediocrity*.

Finally, for a variety of reasons ranging from pressure from the sales force to a pervasive risk averseness, the portfolio and development budget is consumed by an *overabundance of extensions, modifications, and tweaks*—renovations not innovations—so there's no room and no resources left for bold, innovative products with a "wow" factor.

2. Weak Front-End Homework

Some businesses simply fail to do the needed upfront or front-end work on projects. The necessary due diligence—the market study, the technical assessment, the financial analysis—is superficially done or not done at all. Figure 2.1 reveals the facts: Witness the high percentages of firms that do a poor job on key front-end tasks (note that results for average firms are shown, as well as results for the 20 percent worst-performing businesses). Among worst performers:

- 96 percent do a poor job on assessing the value of the product to the customer;
- 93 percent do the market research and voice-of-customer (VoC) work poorly or not at all;
- 77 percent carry out the technical assessment deficiently; and
- 77 percent don't do the business and financial analysis on the project well.

These are the 20 percent worst firms, so what about the typical firm? The data for average firms in Figure 2.1 are almost as damning, with more than half executing poorly across all six front-end tasks. These are frightening results, and they reveal a *quality crisis in the innovation process*—no, not product quality—but a crisis in "quality of execution." Simply stated, key tasks are not done, or not done well, which leads to too many underperforming new products.

The result of poor front-end homework is that when it comes time to make key decisions—product design or Go/Kill investment decisions—there are many assumptions, but *few hard facts*. Frequently this lack of front-end work is due to no time and no money to do the work, and very often because people are too busy on other tasks. Both are lame excuses. Another cause is the desire to reduce time to market. Cutting out the homework stage in order to save a few months sounds like a compelling argument, if it weren't for the huge body of evidence that proves otherwise—that poor or no homework actually lengthens, not shortens, cycle time, as well as damages new-product success rates.

> When it comes to doing the front-end or due diligence work on new-product projects—market research, product-value assessment, technical assessment, and building the Business Case—75 to 90 percent of worst performing firms are deficient (see Figure 2.1).

3. A Lack of Customer or User Input and Market Insights

Another reason so many new products fail to reach their sales and profit targets is the *lack of understanding of the marketplace and customer or user*. In

Figure 2.1: Serious Deficiencies Exist in the Early Stages of New-Product Projects, Especially for Poor-Performing Businesses

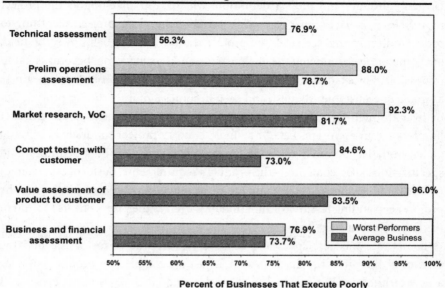

Percent of Businesses That Execute Poorly

many studies, this ignorance is the *number one reason for new-product failure!* Too often, the project team (or an executive) develops the concept of what the product should be and do, often with very little real input from the marketplace. For example, there is no voice-of-customer work done, and no visits to users by the project team to uncover insights into real needs and customer problems. Figure 2.1 again reveals the facts: The overwhelming majority of firms simply do a poor job on the market research, concept testing with the customer, and determining the value of the product to the customer. Note that the "voice of the salesperson" or "voice of the product manager" are not substitutes for the voice of the customer!

Also, if customer input is sought, it is often limited to one or only a few customers, and to immediate customers only—there is no attempt to broaden the customer base, or to move down the value chain to listen to the voices of the customers' clients, too. Further, as the product itself takes shape, and as various iterations of the product are crafted, there is little effort to validate the product with the customer until too late in the process. In short, *the customer or user is not an integral part of the development process.* And so, when the product goes to field trials, to customer tests, or even to launch, it's often not quite right or even dead wrong!

4. Unstable Product Specs and Project Scope Creep

Unstable product and project definition, which keep changing as the project moves along, is *the number one cause of delays later in the project*, according to some studies. In this scenario, the project team drives the ball down the field, but someone keeps moving the goalposts . . . and scoring a goal becomes next to impossible. For example, the project's scope changes: The project may begin as a simple one-customer request, and then becomes a multicustomer project. But halfway through Development, it's redefined again, this time as a new-product line serving an entire market. Or a single-country project suddenly becomes a global initiative. Another common scenario is that the product definition and specifications keep changing—the product's requirements, performance characteristics, and specifications are quite fluid, as different people who influence the project keep adding features or functionality, even as the project nears the end of the Development stage.

Sometimes unstable specs and scope creep are due to factors beyond the control of the project team, for example, a new competitive product entry or a new technology. But most often these definitional changes occur because of *new last-minute information:* A salesperson indicates that the product needs an additional feature, or an executive sees a competitor at a trade show and wants that function added, and so on. This "new information" is not really new at all. It could have, and should have, been available to the project team near the beginning of the project. The root cause is often traced back to point #2 above, a lack of front-end homework.

5. Dysfunctional Project Teams, Too Many Functional Silos

The lack of true cross-functional project teams is *a major fail point* in many new-product projects. Indeed, there is strong indication that *an effective crossfunctional team is the number one key to driving cycle time down.* But many companies get it wrong. In some companies, the project resembles a relay race: The marketing department "owns" the project for the first lap, and then hands it off to R&D for development; after R&D completes its phase or lap, it gets handed off to manufacturing, which throws it over the wall to the sales force for launch—the opposite of a cross-functional team. In other businesses that have attempted to field cross-functional teams, often the experience is marred: The team lacks members from all the key functions (for example, often the Operations person does not join the team until well into Development—too late!); the team leader is the wrong person and not really much of a leader at all; the team lacks cohesiveness and does not share a common vision of the project; some team members lack a strong stake in and commitment to the project; and team accountability is missing. What we witness are "dysfunctional teams" rather than cross-functional teams!

6. Far Too Many Projects in the Pipeline—No Focus

One of the greatest sins in product development is a senior-management issue, namely, *overloading the development pipeline.* Far too many projects are approved at the early Go/Kill gates for the resources available. And there's no real attempt to deal with the resource issue later on: Projects keep getting added to the active list. The result is that *projects are underresourced and people are spread far too thin.* And with so much multitasking (people working on far too many projects), many inefficiencies creep into the system, as much time is wasted switching from project to project. One result is that projects take far longer than they should, as the development pipeline begins to resemble a logjam in a river. Another is that project quality starts to decline: Corners are cut, a needed market study gets skipped, or the field trials are abbreviated, often with disastrous results.

7. A Lack of Competencies, Skills, and Knowledge

In some businesses and projects, not only are project team members spread too thin, there aren't even the people available with the right skills, competencies, and knowledge to undertake the project. Or the business is missing a key success driver, such as access to a marketplace or to a needed technology. Sometimes the cause is that management approves the project, yet fails to understand that key resources and competencies are indeed missing: The project, as defined, *never should have been approved in the first place.* Other times, this skills lack comes about because certain businesses have downsized so much that they've lost key technical and marketing talent: The people who are good at doing major and longer-term projects (but are not needed for day-to-day marketing and technical work) are gone. Finally, the necessary partnerships and alliances are not in place: Management does not insist that outside business partners be found to bring the missing and needed skills to the table, or the wrong partners are enlisted.

If you are typical, you've probably witnessed some or all of these seven reasons that new products fail to achieve their financial goals. No doubt, it is comforting to hear that other businesses suffer from the same maladies that you do. It's also motivating to hear that many companies have identified these and similar causes, and are taking steps to overcome them. For example, a quick review of these seven causes above reveals potential solutions—a stronger customer focus, better front-end work, fewer but better projects in the pipeline—that are built into prescriptions for improving results. So read on to see what the success drivers are and what actions can be taken.

TABLE 2.2: WHY NEW PRODUCTS SUCCEED— EIGHT CRITICAL SUCCESS DRIVERS

1. A unique superior product—a differentiated product that delivers unique benefits and a compelling value proposition to the customer or user—is the number one driver of new-product profitability.
2. Building in the voice-of-the-customer—a market-driven and customer-focused new-product process—is critical to success.
3. Doing the homework and front-end loading the project makes the difference between winning and losing: Due diligence done before product development gets underway pays off!
4. Getting sharp and early product and project definition—and avoiding scope creep and unstable specs—means higher success rates and faster to market.
5. Spiral development—build, test, get customer feedback, and revise—putting something in front of the customer early and cheaply, and often gets the product right.
6. The world product—a global product or "glocal" product (global concept, locally tailored) targeted at international markets—is far more profitable.
7. A well-conceived, properly executed launch is central to new-product success. And a solid marketing plan is at the heart of the launch.
8. Speed counts! There are many good ways to accelerate development projects, but not at the expense of quality of execution.

Source: R. G. Cooper, *PDMA Handbook,* endnote 1.

EIGHT COMMON DENOMINATORS OF WINNING NEW PRODUCTS

The challenge is to design a playbook, blueprint, or process for successful product innovation—a process by which new-product projects can move from the idea stage through to a successful launch and beyond, quickly and effectively. Before charging into the design of this playbook, let's first understand the secrets to success—what separates successful innovation projects from the failures, the *critical success factors* that make the difference between winning and losing.

Some are fairly obvious, but before you dismiss them as "too obvious," recognize that most firms still miss them, either due to neglect or simply lack of knowledge. We begin this insightful journey next, and as we probe each success driver, reflect on how you can translate each into an operational facet of your new-product playbook (see Table 2.2 for a summary).[3]

1. A unique superior product—a differentiated product that delivers unique benefits and a compelling value proposition to the customer or user—is the number one driver of new-product profitability.

Delivering products with *unique benefits and real value to users* separates winners from losers more often than any other single factor! Such superior products have five times the success rate, over four times the market share, and four times the profitability of products lacking this ingredient, according to our research.[4] Product advantage, superiority, or differentiation as the key determinant of success is a recurring theme in many new-product studies. That differentiated, superior products are key to success should come as no surprise to product innovators. Apparently, it isn't obvious to everyone: Study after study shows that "reactive products" and "me-too" offerings are the rule rather than the exception in many businesses' new-product efforts, and the majority fail to produce large profits![5] A second very popular scenario, which also yields poor results, is *the "techie" building a monument to himself*—the technical solution in search of a market.

What do these superior products with unique customer or user benefits have in common? These winning products:

> A superior and differentiated product— one that delivers unique benefits and superior value to the customer—is the *number one driver of success* and new-product profitability.

- are superior to competing products in terms of *meeting users' needs*, offering *unique features and benefits* not available in competitive products, or *solving a problem* the customer has with a competitive product;
- offer product benefits that are *highly visible*, and benefits or attributes easily perceived as useful by the customer;
- feature good *value for money* for the customer, reduce the customer's total costs (high value-in-use), and boast excellent price/performance characteristics; and
- provide excellent *product quality* relative to competitors' products, and in terms of how the user measures quality.

Note that there are at least two types of product advantage: As one study notes, *product meaningfulness* concerns the benefits that users receive from buying and using a new product, whereas *product superiority* captures the extent to which a new product outperforms competing products.[6] Note also that the term "product" includes not only the evident or physical product but the "extended product"—the entire bundle of benefits associated with the product, including the system supporting the product, product service and support, as well as the product's branding or image.

The "best-performing innovators" were introduced in Chapter 1—businesses that model the way.[7] A closer look at these exceptional businesses shows that the best innovators emphasize certain factors in their new-product efforts—see Figure 2.2. Best innovators are much stronger in terms of offering important and unique product benefits, a superior value proposition, and better value for the customer in their new products, by more than two-to-one versus the worst performers.

The evidence in Figure 2.2 is strong, and provides a vital message here:

1. First, these ingredients of a superior product (Figure 2.2) provide a useful checklist of questions to assess the odds of success of a proposed new-product project: They logically become *top priority questions* in a project screening checklist or scorecard.
2. Second, these ingredients become *challenges to the project team* to build into their new-product design. In short, the list of these five ingredients of product advantage above become personal objectives for the project leader and team, and must be molded into the playbook.

But how does one create or build in product superiority? Note that superiority is derived from design, features, attributes, performance, quality, and specifications, and even branding, image, and positioning. The important point here is that *superiority* is defined from the *customer's or user's standpoint*, not in the eyes of the R&D, technology, or design departments. Sometimes product superiority is the result of new technology or a technological breakthrough. But more than technology and unique features are required to make a product superior. Note that *product features and functionality* are things that cost the developer money. By contrast, *benefits* are what customers pay money for! Often the two—features and benefits—are not the same. So, in defining *unique benefits*, think of the product as *a bundle of benefits for the user* and a benefit as *something that users or customers view as having value to them*.

An example: Green Mountain Coffee Roasters began humbly as a small café in rural Vermont in 1981; it was soon doing its own coffee roasting, selling to local hotels and restaurants. Management saw a huge consumer need, a problem

Figure 2.2: A Unique Superior Product Is the Number One Driver of New-Product Success—Best- versus Worst-Performing Innovators

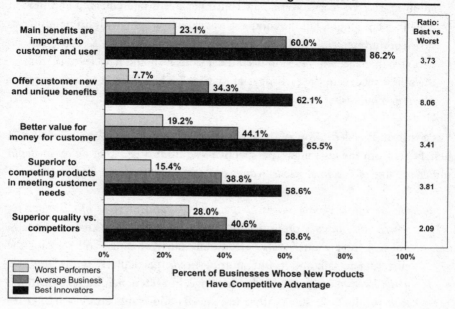

Worst Performers
Average Business
Best Innovators

Percent of Businesses Whose New Products Have Competitive Advantage

waiting to be solved: the need for an inexpensive and convenient single-serving coffee making machine for home use. Note that coffee makers, even single-cup, were not new; many of the better coffee makers were imported from Europe, but were quite expensive and did not suit American coffee drinkers.

Green Mountain created the K-Cup and Keurig system, a unique and inexpensive product that met the unmet consumer need in the United States. Keurig relied on easy-to-use prepackaged coffee pods (K-Cups), brewed a single cup of coffee quickly and with no fuss and no waste, and offered a variety of coffee types and brands. So the company also signed up other well-known coffee companies: Tully's in Seattle, Newman's Own, Timothy's in Canada, and others.

The business model was similar to Gillette's razor-and-blade model: namely, sell the machine inexpensively and make money on the K-Cups. Since Keurig was introduced in 1998, the company has been enormously successful, hitting sales of $4.7 billion in 2014—taking over the US at-home coffee market and one of the biggest American successes of modern times, with a "sales explosion" between 2000 and 2014.[8]

An important lesson is that a *unique superior product* that offers *unique customer benefits* and meets *customer needs* better than competitive products was really the *key to success* for this illustration! But even here, there is bad news and new lessons. By the end of 2015, the product and company were in trouble. Keurig's possible demise might be a story as incredible as its stunning rise. In recent years, new consumer needs had emerged and new benefits were sought, but the company was slow to act—namely, its painfully slow commitment to eco-friendly recyclable pods or "green K-Cups." Apparently, management failed to heed the lessons it should have learned from the initial success in the early days of Keurig. By the end of 2015, sales were down precipitously.[9]

Suggestion: The definition of "what is unique and superior" and "what is a benefit" is from the customer's perspective—so it *must be based on an in-depth understanding of customer needs, wants, problems, likes, and dislikes.*

1. *Determine customer needs at the outset—build in voice-of-customer research early in your projects.* The goal here is to identify customer needs, not just their wants. *Wants* are usually fairly obvious, and easy for the customer to talk about. But spotting *needs*, particularly *unmet and unarticulated needs*, is more of a challenge, but often yields a breakthrough new product. So start with a user needs-and-wants study—market research and seeking customer insights—to probe customer needs, wants, problems, preferences, likes, and dislikes. Determine the customer's "hot buttons"—the order-winning criteria, the customer's problems, and what the customer is *really seeking* in a much-improved or superior product.

2. *Do a competitive product analysis.* There is no such thing as a perfect competitive product. If you can spot the competitors' products' weaknesses, then you're halfway to beating them. Remember: The goal is product superiority, and that means superiority over current or future competitive offerings. Take the competitor's product apart in your lab or design department, and when you do the VoC research, be sure to ask your customers for their opinions about the strengths and weaknesses of competitors' products. One more point: Anticipate what the competitor's product will likely be in the foreseeable future; never assume the competitor's current product will be the competitive benchmark by the time you hit the market! Once these two investigations are complete, the project team can translate the information into a product definition, paying special attention to *the benefits* and the *value proposition* that the product will offer to the customer.

3. *Build in multiple test iterations to test and verify your assumptions about your winning-product design.* Once the product concept and specs are de-

fined (based on user inputs above), *test the product concept with users*—and make sure they indicate a favorable response. That is, even before serious development work begins, start testing the product—even though you don't yet have a product!—via iterations using concepts, virtual prototypes, or "protocepts" (something between a concept and a prototype) tests. This disciplined approach to discovering product superiority is decidedly customer focused, which leads to success factor number two, the need for a strong customer input.

2. Building in the voice of the customer—a market-driven and customer-focused new-product process—is critical to success.

A thorough understanding of customers' or users' needs and wants, the competitive situation, and the nature of the market is an essential component of new-product success. This finding is *supported in virtually every study of product success factors.* Recurring themes include:

- need recognition,
- understanding user needs,
- market need satisfaction,
- constant customer contact,
- strong market knowledge and market research,
- quality of execution of marketing activities, and
- more spending on the front-end market-related activities.

Conversely, a failure to adopt a strong market focus in product innovation, an unwillingness to undertake the needed market assessments and to build in the voice of the customer, and leaving the customer out of product development spells disaster. Poor market research; inadequate market analysis; weak market studies, test markets, and market launch; and inadequate resources devoted to marketing activities are common weaknesses found in almost every study of why new products fail.

Sadly, *a strong market focus is missing in the majority of firms' new-product projects.* Detailed market studies are frequently omitted (in more than 75 percent of projects, according to one investigation). Further, market-facing activities are the weakest-rated activities of the entire new-product process, rated much lower than corresponding technical actions. Moreover, relatively few resources and little money are spent on the marketing actions (except for the launch), accounting for less than 20 percent of the total project cost.

Figure 2.3: Voice-of-Customer and Market Insight Strongly Impact on Innovation Performance Results—Best- versus Worst-Performing Innovators

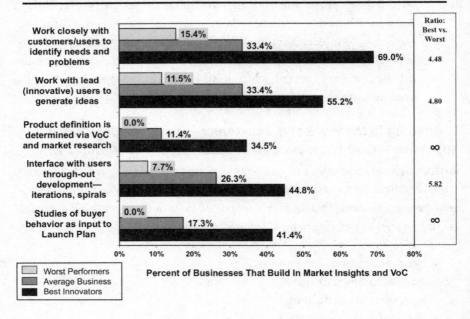

The best innovators are leaders when it comes to a strong market focus—see Figure 2.3. Best-innovating businesses:

- work closely with customers and users to identify needs, problems, and customer "points of pain"—4.5 times more so than do worst performers;
- work with lead or innovative users—users that are "ahead of the wave"—to generate new-product ideas (by a 5:1 ratio versus worst performers);
- determine their product definitions via market research—that is, VoC insights are a major input to the product definition (remarkably, *none* of the worst-performing businesses do this, and such input is a practice of only 11 percent of average businesses);
- interface with customers throughout the entire development process, not just at the beginning and end—by a 6:1 ratio versus worst performers; and
- seek market input to help design the launch plan.

An example: Drägerwerk is an international leader in the field of medical and safety technology, and its Dräger Safety subsidiary provides products, services, and solutions for risk management for personal and facility protection.[10] One of the company's product lines, breathalyzer testing devices, is used by police forces to test alcohol levels in suspected drunk drivers. The goal was to develop a new European breathalyzer product line, but the project *lacked blockbuster ideas for features*. Two VoC study teams were formed, and after some training on how to do *ethnographic research*, they began their camping-out exercises in the United Kingdom, the Netherlands, and Germany.

In all countries, the teams spent time at police stations, conducting traditional interviews with police officers and their supervisors. But the real learning and insights came from their nighttime vigils—the camping-out exercise—in which the VoC teams worked beside the police officers as they ran their nighttime roadside spot checks on drivers. These insights provided the *key to a new product with significant competitive advantage*. For example, by watching the police at work, the British VoC team soon realized how difficult a job the police officers have trying to maintain order and control. One officer had pulled over a car full of exuberant young drinkers fresh from the nearby pub and issued the standard command: "Remain in the car!" The officer, wearing latex gloves for fear of HIV, then passed the breathalyzer device through the driver's window, instructing the driver to blow into the mouthpiece. It takes two minutes to get a full reading!

Meanwhile, the other officer had pulled over another car, so now the officers had to manage two cars full of intoxicated young men. Quite clearly, the police officers were somewhat intimidated by the task of crowd control, as they were outnumbered and the lads in the cars were twice the size and half the age of the officers (who do not carry guns). Note that the officers never admitted to intimidation during the formal daytime interviews!

To overcome the problem of crowd control and intimidation, the VoC team came up with one solution: Speed up the process. The aim was to substantially reduce the two-minute waiting time that was creating the queue. The goal became to develop a ten-second test device. A second observation was that because of the location of dials, the British version of the instrument could only be used on right-hand-side drivers. Thus, when a left-hand-side driver from France or Germany was pulled over in the United Kingdom, the police could not conduct the test quite as easily. And because of time pressures, they really had no option but to simply "wave the car through." This behavior was never reported to their supervisors nor revealed in the formal interviews. The solution here was to

> Building in the voice of the customer is one of the strongest drivers of new-product profitability, and also of time efficiency. But the great majority of companies miss the mark here—with insufficient VoC and no fact-based customer insights.

Figure 2.4: A Strong Customer Focus Means Key Actions from Beginning to End in the Innovation Process

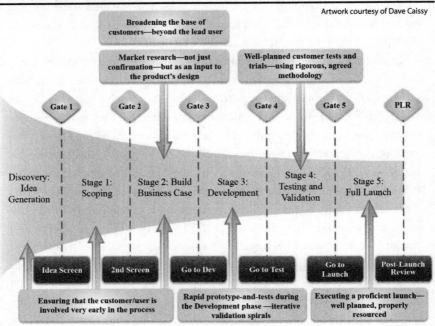

Artwork courtesy of Dave Caissy

design an ambidextrous testing instrument—an arm with the mouthpiece that could be swung over to accommodate either a right- or left-side driver.

These novel feature-ideas are just two of the ten that made the new Dräger product line a huge success. Each feature was not, in itself, a breakthrough, but when the ten such new features and benefits were added together, the new product was indeed a blockbuster and absolutely delighted police forces.

Suggestion: Huge differences in practices exist between best innovators and worst performers, according to the results in Figure 2.3, and these actions in Figure 2.3 are clearly "best practices." Thus, a strong market focus must prevail throughout the entire new-product project, as shown in Figure 2.4, starting with idea generation:

1. *Idea generation:* The *best ideas* come from customers! Devote more resources to market-oriented idea-generation activities, such as focus groups and VoC research with customers to determine customers' needs and their problems. Use the sales force to actively solicit ideas from customers and develop relationships with innovative or lead users. Robust ideas also come from online and social-media sources. There is more to come on effective ideation in Chapter 7.

2. *The design of the product*: User and customer inputs have a vital role in the *design of the product*—when the product's requirements and specs are being defined. Often, market research, when done at all, is done too late—after the product design has already been decided and simply as an after-the-fact check. Note that market research must be used as an *input to the design decisions*! Best innovators determine customer and user needs at the outset, starting with a user needs-and-wants study (VoC research) in tandem with a competitive product analysis (competitive benchmarking). Best practices here include in-depth personal interviews with customers and users, customer site visits (done by the entire project team), "camping out" with the customer (extended site visits or ethnography), customer panels, and large-sample quantitative market research. Even in the case of a technology-driven new product (where the idea comes from a technology, perhaps a technological breakthrough), the chances of success are much greater if customer and marketplace inputs are built into the project soon after its inception.

3. *Before pushing ahead into Development*: Be sure to *test the product concept with the customer* by presenting a representation of the product—via models, mock-ups, protocepts, CAD drawings, and even virtual products—and gauging the customer's interest, liking, and purchase intent. It's much cheaper to test and learn before Development begins than to fully develop the product, and then begin customer testing!

4. *Throughout the entire development project*: Customer inputs shouldn't cease at the completion of the predevelopment market studies. Seeking customer inputs and testing concepts or designs with the user is very much an *iterative process*—"spiral development" as outlined in success driver #5 below. By bringing the customer into the process to view facets of the product via a series of concept tests, rapid prototyping and tests, and customer trials, the developer verifies all assumptions about the winning design.

An example: ComCo (disguised name) is a smaller Canadian firm which produces communication devices for use in heavy-duty transport trucks operating in remote locations. The system is built into the truck, and operates via satellite rather than cell towers. The devices are sold for use in remote areas where trucks operate outside of cell-tower range, for example, in northern Canada, Alaska, or Brazil. To date, *only voice communication* was provided, so that drivers could stay in touch with their dispatcher.

The new-product project, which had already passed the first few gates and was almost into development, was to provide *additional information to the fleet manager* and maintenance department, namely, information about the engine, transmission, and truck performance (such as engine temperature, oil pressure, etc.). Using on-board sensors, the new product would convey this information to the truck fleet home-base, again via satellite, so that maintenance could be appropriately scheduled.

It was only when the project leader with some team members undertook their VoC study—in essence, a *concept test* as in item three above—that *new and provocative insights* were gained. In-depth on-site personal interviews were used. When the team tried to probe exactly what engine and operating information might be desired, to their great surprise, users were rather dismissive of the proposed features of the new product; the VoC study revealed that, instead, the *real need* was for iPad-to-head-office communication . . . the truck driver with an iPad in a remote location communicating directly to the dispatch, for example, and downloading forms, data, information about load drop-off, who signed for the delivery, etc.

The project team quickly regrouped and redefined the project and product based on the new information. Thus a *"very significant change in direction* to this major project took place as a result of our VoC, and [it was] a big win for the company!"* declared a buoyant project leader. Once again the value of seeking customer inputs was proven, and the danger in using untested assumptions about customer needs was revealed.

3. Doing the homework and front-end loading the project makes the difference between winning and losing: Due diligence done before product development gets underway pays off!

We all learned in eighth grade how distasteful homework was. Many of us haven't forgotten: We hate homework! But then, as now, homework or due diligence is critical to winning. Countless studies reveal that the steps that precede the actual design and development of the product make the difference between winning and losing. The best innovators are much better when it comes to these activities in *the "fuzzy front end" of projects—they do their homework* and make the front end a *lot less fuzzy* (see Figure 2.5):

- Initial screening: the first decision to get into the project (the idea screen).
- Preliminary market assessment—the first and quick market study to assess market size and likely product acceptance and sales.

Figure 2.5: Quality of Execution in the Fuzzy Front End Impacts Strongly on New-Product Success—Best- versus Worst-Performing Innovators

Percent of Businesses That Execute Well

- Preliminary technical assessment—a technical appraisal of the project, looking at technology risks and the likely technical route.
- Preliminary operations assessment—looking at source-of-supply, manufacturing, and operations issues.
- The detailed market study, market research, and VoC research (described above).
- Concept testing—testing the product concept with the customer or user to ensure customer liking and purchase intent (also described above).
- Value assessment—determining the value or economic worth of the product to the customer.
- The business and financial analysis just before the decision to "Go to Development" (building the Business Case).

Where do the best innovators excel in the early days of a new-product project? Compared to worst performers, the stand-out practices for the best innovators include: undertaking voice-of-customer research as input to the product's design, determining the economic value of the product to the customer, and the executing business and financial analysis as part of building the Business Case. But these are not easy tasks, and even the best firms struggle here. Another issue is *balance* within the homework stage. Best innovators strike an *appropriate balance between market/business-oriented tasks and technology activities*, whereas worst performers tend to push ahead on the technical side and pay lip service to marketing and business issues in the early stages of the project. Figure 2.5 shows how much better the best innovators execute the homework activities, but especially the early stage marketing/business tasks. Surprisingly, most firms confess to serious weaknesses in the front-end or predevelopment steps of their new-product process. Pitifully small amounts of time and money are devoted to these critical steps: only about 7 percent of the dollars and 16 percent of the effort.

> Sold front-end homework pays for itself: much higher likelihood of product success if the homework is done well; better project definition which *speeds up* the development process; and fewer surprises and fewer last-minute changes needed as the project nears launch.

The front-end tasks are important because they *qualify and define the project*, answering vital questions, such as:

- Is the project economically attractive? Will the product sell at sufficient volumes and margins to justify investment in development and commercialization?
- Who exactly is the target customer? And how should the product be positioned?
- What exactly should the product be to make it a winner? What features, attributes, and performance characteristics should be built into it to yield a unique superior product?
- Can the product be developed and at the right cost? What is the likely technical solution?
- What about source of supply? By us or by others? And at what cost and investment?

"More homework means longer development times" is a frequently voiced complaint. This is a valid concern, but experience has shown that homework pays for itself in reduced development times as well as improved success rates, for three reasons:

1. First, all the evidence points to a much *higher likelihood of product failure* if the homework is omitted. So the choice is between more work early on, or much increased odds of failure: no pain, no gain!

2. Second, better project definition, the result of solid homework, *actually speeds up* the development process. One of the major causes of time slippages is poorly defined projects as they enter the Development stage—that is, vague targets and moving goalposts.

3. Third, given the inevitable product-design evolution that occurs during the life of a project, the time to make the majority of these design changes is not as the product is moving out of Development and into the market. More homework up front *anticipates these changes* and encourages them to occur earlier in the process rather than later, when they are more costly.

Suggestion: The message is clear: Don't skimp on the homework! First, cutting out homework drives success rates down; second, eliminating homework to save time today will lead to wasted time tomorrow. It's a "penny wise, pound foolish" way to save time. As Toyota's new-products handbook recommends: *Front-end load the project.*[11] That is, undertake a higher proportion of the project's work in the early stages and ensure that no significant project moves into the Development stage without the actions listed in Figure 2.5—early stage activities that should be built into your idea-to-launch system.

4. Getting sharp and early product and project definition—and avoiding scope creep and unstable specs—means higher success rates and faster to market.

How well the project and product are defined prior to entering the Development stage is a major success factor, impacting positively on both profitability and reduced time-to-market. Look at the facts in Figure 2.6, and notice how much better the best innovators *get the product defined before embarking on the Development stage*. This definition includes five main elements:

1. the project's scope (for example, domestic versus international, line extension versus new-product item versus platform development, etc.);
2. the target market: exactly who the intended customers or users are;
3. the product concept and the benefits to be delivered to the user (including the value proposition);
4. the positioning strategy, including the target price; and
5. the product's features, attributes, requirements, and high-level specifications (prioritized: "must have" and "would like to have").

Note the major differences on each of these five items when best innovators are compared to the worst performers in Figure 2.6. These elements of

Figure 2.6: Having Sharp, Stable, and Fact-Based Product Definition Before Development Begins Drives Innovation Success—Best vs. Worst Innovators

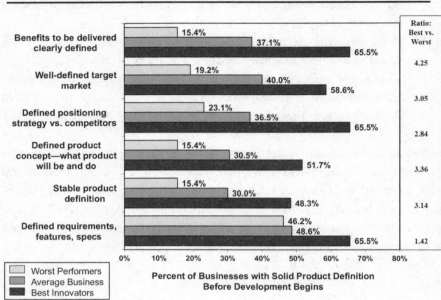

Percent of Businesses with Solid Product Definition
Before Development Begins

Worst Performers
Average Business
Best Innovators

product definition are vital to success and distinguish the best innovators. By contrast, a failure to *define the product and project scope* before Development begins is a major cause of both new-product failure and serious delays in time-to-market. In spite of the fact that *early and stable product definition is consistently cited as a key to success*, businesses continue to perform poorly here, as shown in Figure 2.6. Terms such as "unstable products specs" and "project scope creep" plague too many new-product projects.

> Securing sharp, early, stable, and fact-based project and product definition during the homework phase is one of the strongest drivers of cycle-time reduction and new-product success.

Suggestion: Build a *mandatory product definition step* into your idea-to-launch system. Unless the five items cited above are clearly defined, written down, fact based, and agreed to by all parties prior to entering the Development stage, the odds of failure skyrocket. Here's why:

- Building in a product definition step forces *more attention to the front-end* or homework activities, a key success driver.

- This definition serves as a *communication tool* and guide. All-party agreement or buy-in means that all functional areas involved in the project have a clear and consistent definition of what the product and project are and are committed to them.
- The product definition also provides a *clear set of objectives* for the development stage of the project and for development team members: The goalposts are defined and clearly visible, and the development team can speed towards them—no moving goalposts and no fuzzy targets!

Achieving a stable product definition is a challenge—even the best innovators struggle, as shown in Figure 2.6. Recognize that many markets are quite fluid and dynamic, there is much ambiguity, and "things change." So the notion of the traditional "100 percent design freeze" before Development is obsolete in some markets, certainly in the IT and software sectors, and increasingly in other industries. But *dynamic markets and ambiguity are poor reasons* for throwing one's hands in the air and declaring that "product definition is impossible—we'll decide it as we go along." With solid front-end homework and due diligence (success driver #3 above), some elements can indeed be nailed down before Development begins even in fluid markets, while some elements of the product's design will remain "variable" and "to be decided" as the project proceeds.

Suggestion: The recommendation is this: For those of you who face *ambiguity* and *fluid and dynamic markets*, where product definitions are difficult to nail down before Development commences:

- Build in the *necessary front-end homework*, as in success driver #3. Facing fast-paced markets is no excuse for taking lazy shortcuts. So take your choice: fast failures or thoughtful successes!
- Develop your "product definition" as best you can *before Development begins*—use the list of five elements above.
- Specify in advance which part of the product requirements and specs are "known and fixed" versus which are "fluid, uncertain, and variable" before Development begins (one hopes that more than 40 to 50 percent is fixed or "known" on entering Development). Use two columns in your product definition template: "fixed" and "variable."
- Build *iterative validations* with users, or *"spirals,"* into your development process to gather data so that the "variable elements" of your product definition can be confirmed as development proceeds . . . which brings us to success driver #5.

5. Spiral development—build, test, get customer feedback, and revise—putting something in front of the customer early and often gets the product right.

Spiral or iterative development is the way fast-paced teams handle the dynamic information process with fluid, changing information. Spiral development *helps the project team get the product and product definition right*, in spite of the fact that some information is fluid and some may even be unreliable or uncertain when the team moves into the Development stage.

Many businesses use *too rigid and linear a process* for product development. The project team diligently visits customers in the front-end stages and determines customer needs and requirements as best they can. Front-end work or homework is properly done, and the product specs are determined and the product definition is fixed. So far, so good.

The Development stage gets underway but proceeds in *a linear and rigid fashion*. The project team moves the project forward following a "heads-down" rather than a "heads-up" approach. Some ten or fifteen months pass, and at the end of this linear development stage, the product is ready for field trials or full customer tests. Then everything goes wrong: When presented with the prototype or beta product for testing, the original intended customers now indicate that "this is not quite what we had in mind" or that "things have changed." Or perhaps a new competitive product has been launched that alters the competitive landscape.

> People don't know what they're looking for until they see it or experience it. So get something in front of the customer or user fast—and keep repeating these tests all the way through to formal product testing or field trials. Multiple iterations and product validations—spiral development—are essential when facing fluid markets with customers that are uncertain about their needs.

By proceeding in a linear and rigid process, the project team and business has set themselves up for failure. Maybe the initial product requirements were not quite right: Key points were missed when the initial VoC work was done; or due to ambiguity, no amount of VoC work could have nailed down all the product requirements; or perhaps things really did change. And now the project team must backtrack to the Development stage for another attempt at the product . . . back to the drawing board! And we witness another victim of a rigid, linear process that did not encourage the team to adapt to changing circumstances.

Smart project teams and businesses practice *spiral development* (based somewhat on Agile development, as used in the software industry). For example, a study of two leading B2B European manufacturers revealed that, on

Figure 2.7: Spiral Development—A Series of "Build-Test-Feedback-Revise" Iterations—Gets the Product Right with No Time Wasted

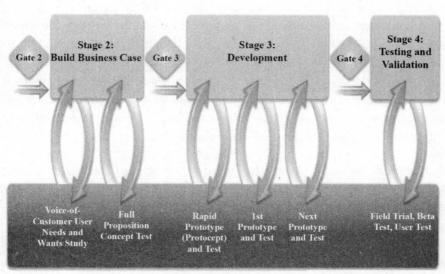

The Customer or User

Artwork courtesy of Dave Caissy

average, between 3 and 4.5 versions of the product—from early model through to prototype—were presented to validate the design with customers through the Development and Testing stages (while product ideation-and-design contractors, such as IDEO, iterated on average *15 times with the customer* per project!).[12] And best-innovator businesses are six times more likely to interface with customers and users throughout the entire Development stage, as indicated in Figure 2.3. They build in a series of *iterative steps* or *"loops,"* whereby successive versions of the product are shown to the customer to seek feedback and verification, as shown in Figure 2.7. These loops are a series of "build-test-feedback-and-revise" iterations (their iterative nature leads to the term "spiral development").

Note that "spiral development" is not quite the same as Agile development. Spiral loops are measured in months, whereas Agile sprints and validations are measured *in weeks*. And Agile, when built into *Stage-Gate*, has many more facets than simply frequent-and-rapid customer validations, as we'll see in Chapter 6.

Suggestion: *Use spirals—a series of "build-test-feedback-and-revise" iterations.* This spiral approach is based on the fact that customers don't really know what they are looking for until they see it or experience it—so get something in front of the customer, anything, even if it's still a long way from the final product; and start early. Then seek fast and confirmatory feedback, making the necessary changes to the product, getting an even more complete version in front of the customer for the next iteration. But some words of warning: Don't fully develop the product and start presenting real prototypes early in the process: The notion here is to get something in front of the customer initially that you can put together quickly and inexpensively.

How does spiral development work in practice? A sample set of spirals is shown in Figure 2.7. Note that these loops or spirals are built in from the front-end stages through the Development stage and into the Testing stage, beginning with a VoC study and culminating in full product tests.

6. The world product—a global product or "glocal" product (global concept, locally tailored) targeted at international markets—is far more profitable.

The world is the business arena today! Thus, corporate growth and profitability depend on a *globalization strategy married to product innovation*. In global markets, product development plays a primary role in achieving a sustainable competitive advantage.[13] And multinational firms that take a *global approach* to new-product development outperform those that concentrate their R&D spending in their home market.[14] International products designed for and targeted at world and nearest neighbor export markets are the best-performing new products (see Figure 2.8).[15] By contrast, products designed for only the domestic or home market, and later adjusted and sold to nearest neighbor and international target markets, fare worse. The magnitude of the differences between international new products and domestic products is striking: two- or three-to-one on various performance gauges.

The management implication of these and other studies is that *globalization of markets demands global new products*. To define the new product's market as domestic, and perhaps a few other nearby convenient countries, severely limits market opportunities. For maximum success in product innovation, the objective must be to *design for the world* and *market to the world*. Sadly, this international dimension is often overlooked or, if included, is *handled late in the development process* or as a side issue.

A global orientation means defining the market as an international one and designing products to meet international requirements, not just domestic ones. The result is either a *global* product (one version for the entire world) or a *glocal* product (one development effort, one product concept or platform, but perhaps *several product variants* to satisfy different international markets). Another op-

Figure 2.8: Impact of Various International Strategies on Performance

New-Product Target-Market Strategy

	Domestic Target Market	Regional (Nearby) Foreign Target Markets	Global Target Market
Domestic Product Strategy	Develop products for home market. Sell only to home (domestic) market **Adequate Results**	Develop products for home market & adjust domestic product for nearby foreign markets **Poor Results**	Develop products for home market & adjust domestic product for global markets **Poor Results**
Global Product Strategy	✗	Develop single product with multiple inputs from regional markets. Sell product to regional target markets	Develop single product with multiple inputs from global markets. Sell product to global target markets
'Glocal' Product Strategy	✗	Develop regional product with multiple versions tailored to regional target markets (often based on one platform)	Develop global product with multiple versions tailored to international target markets (often based on one platform)
		Best results	

(left axis label: NPD Product Strategy)

tion is *two glocal* products—as an example, one product or platform designed for developed countries, but with different product-versions to suit different developed countries or regions, and a more basic product or platform to sell to developing countries, but, again, which can be tailored to suit different needs in each of these countries.

A global orientation also means undertaking VoC research, concept testing, and product testing in multiple countries rather than just the home country; and also launching in multiple countries concurrently or in rapid succession. It also means relying on *a global project team* with team members in multiple countries (only one new-product project team in five is reported to be a global development team!).

7. A well-conceived, properly executed launch is central to new-product success. And a solid marketing plan is at the heart of the launch.

Emerson once said, "Build a better mousetrap and the world will beat a path to your door." The problem is that Emerson was a poet, not a businessman. This old adage may never have been true, and it certainly hasn't been true for years.

Not only must the product be superior, but its benefits must be communicated and marketed aggressively. A quality launch is strongly linked to new-product profitability. Look at how the best innovators fare in Figure 2.9:

- They do the necessary market research—understanding buyer or customer behavior—in order to better craft the launch plan (interestingly, less than half the best innovators undertake such a study, but then not one worst performer does so—thus I include this action as a key difference between best and worst firms).
- Best innovators conduct a test market or a trial sell to validate the marketability of the new product and also to test elements of the market launch plan.
- They undertake a solid prelaunch business analysis.
- But most important, best innovators execute the launch more proficiently—by a three-to-one ratio when compared to worst performers.

The message is this: Don't assume that good products sell themselves, and don't treat the launch as an afterthought. Just because the launch is the last

Figure 2.9: Market Launch and Related Actions Strongly Impact on Innovation Results—Best- versus Worst-Performing Innovators

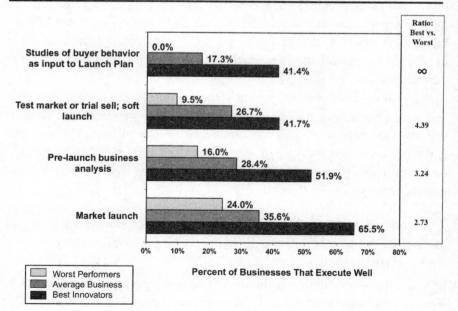

step in the process, never underestimate its importance. A well-integrated and properly targeted launch does not occur by accident, however; it is the result of a *fine-tuned marketing plan*, properly backed and resourced, and proficiently executed.

Marketing planning—moving from marketing objectives to strategy and marketing programs—is a complex process. Entire books have been devoted to the subject. But this complex marketing planning process must be woven into your new-product system. For example, defining the target market and the development of a positioning strategy, one of the core steps in developing a marketing plan, is part of the product-definition step just before Development begins (success factor #4 above). And answers to many key questions—How do customers buy? Via what channels of distribution? What are their sources of information? What servicing do they require?—are central to developing the nuts and bolts of the marketing programs. Answers to these questions must come from market-research investigations that are built into your new-product process or playbook.

Suggestion: I make five important points regarding new-product launch and the marketing plan:

1. The development of the market launch plan is an *integral part of the idea-to-launch process*. It is as central to this process as the development of the product itself.

2. The development of the market launch plan *must begin early* in the new-product project. It should not be left as an afterthought to be undertaken as the project nears commercialization.

3. A market launch plan is only as good as the *market intelligence* upon which it is based. Market studies designed to yield information crucial to marketing planning should be built into the new-product project.

4. The launch must be *properly resourced* in terms of both people and dollars. Too often, an otherwise great new product fails to achieve its sales goals simply because of a underresourced launch.

5. Those who will execute the launch—the sales force, technical support people, other front-line personnel—should be engaged in the development of the market launch plan and therefore should be *members of the project team*. This ensures valuable input and insight into the design of the launch effort, availability of resources when needed, and buy-in by those who must execute the launch—elements critical to a successful launch.

8. Speed counts! There are many good ways to accelerate development projects, but not at the expense of quality of execution.

The challenge highlighted in Chapter 1 is *bold innovations developed in record time*. Speed to market is indeed an admirable goal—there are a number of valid reasons that cycle-time reduction should be a priority:[16]

1. *Speed yields competitive advantage: First in will win!* There is conflicting evidence on this caveat, however; often the *number-two product entrant learns from the mistakes* of the pioneer and ends up making more money. Nonetheless, on average, the first entrant usually does better, as shown in Figure 2.10, which reveals the impact of order-of-entry.
2. *Speed yields higher profitability.* Again there is mixed evidence. Nonetheless, first-in products certainly have the advantage of realizing revenues sooner (money does have a time value!) and may also see more revenues and profits over the product's life.
3. *Speed means fewer surprises and lower risk.* There is much less likelihood that the market has changed if one gets to market quickly. Surprises from market fluidity are less likely.
4. *Speed is an unwritten goal of innovators—both senior management and project team members.* Most people involved in product development by nature are impatient. They have seen too many projects take far too long. Long cycle times often destroy project-team morale and also cause senior management to lose interest in or patience with the project.

The point is: Speed is important, but it is only a means to an end, the ultimate goal being profitability. Further, some of the practices naively employed in order to reduce time-to-market ultimately cost the company money: They are at odds with sound management practice. Thus, there is also a "dark side" to accelerated product development:

- Shortcuts are taken with the best intentions, but far too frequently result in disaster: serious errors of omission and too many ill-conceived shortcuts, which not only add delays to the project but often lead to higher incurred costs and even product failure.
- Reducing cycle time often results in focusing on easy and quick hits—the "low hanging fruit" projects such as line extensions and minor modifications—but that means paying the price later via a lack of significant new

Figure 2.10: First Entrant ("1st In") Products Tend to Do Better—Higher Success Rates and Profitability

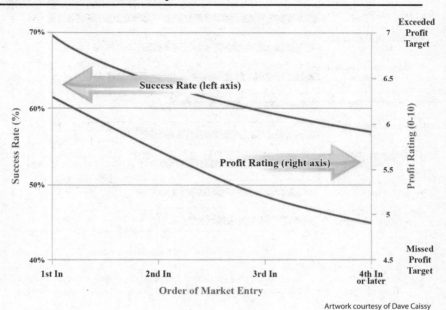

Artwork courtesy of Dave Caissy

products and loss of longer-term competitive advantage (recall the negative shift in development portfolios Figure 1.1 in Chapter 1).

- Setting unrealistic timelines to achieve launch deadlines creates frustration, tension, and morale problems among project team members when milestones are invariably missed.

Suggestion: Be careful in the overzealous pursuit of speed and cycle-time reduction. There are ways to reduce cycle time, however, that are consistent with sound management practice and are also derived from the critical success drivers outlined above. Figure 2.11 shows how some of the success drivers not only impact positively on new-product profitability, but also on time reduction or efficiency. In Chapters 6 and 7, we'll see some of the better and more radical approaches that leading firms are

There is also a "dark side" to accelerated product development. Shortcuts frequently result in errors, add delays, and lead to higher incurred costs and even product failure. Reducing cycle time can result in focusing on quick hits—"low hanging fruit" projects, and a lack of bold new products. And setting unrealistic timelines creates morale problems on project teams when milestones are invariably missed.

Figure 2.11: What Drives New-Product Profitability and Time-to-Market?

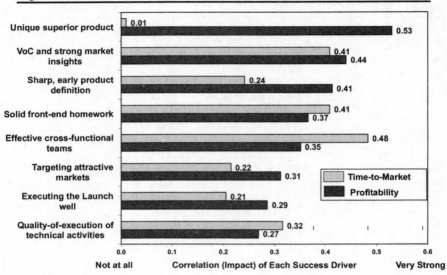

Profitability: profits relative to target (%); return-on-investment (%); payback period (years).
Time-to-market: time relative to scheduled; time efficiency (time relative to fastest possible).

using to make their idea-to-launch systems more agile, accelerated, and adaptive. Table 2.3 lists six basic, low risk, and sensible ways, perhaps less radical, to *increase the odds of winning* but also to *reduce time-to-market*!

BUILDING THE SUCCESS DRIVERS INTO YOUR PLAYBOOK

Many businesses have "operating procedures" or guides on how to do things right. Imagine you are crafting a new-product guidebook or set of operating principles for how to do a new-product project right—for example, an "idea-to-launch playbook" or a stage-and-gate system to drive new products to market. What would be the first eight principles that might underpin your system? The eight success drivers outlined above in this chapter, and in Table 2.2 of course. Here's how:

1. Make sure your idea-to-launch system includes actions as well as decision criteria that yield bold, differentiated products with a compelling value proposition for the customer. Most systems do not, and so they miss the number-one profit driver!

TABLE 2.3: SIX BASIC, LOW RISK WAYS TO REDUCE TIME-TO-MARKET

1. Do the *front-end homework* and develop early and stable *product and project definitions* based on facts rather than hearsay and speculation (success drivers #3 and #4 above); this saves time downstream.

2. Build in *quality of execution* at every stage of the project. The best way to save time is by avoiding having to cycle back and do it a second time.

3. Employ effective *cross-functional teams*: "Rip apart a badly developed project and you will unfailingly find 75 percent of slippage attributable to: 'siloing,' or sending memos up and down vertical organizational 'silos' or 'stovepipes' for decisions; and sequential problem solving" (T. J. Peters, *Thriving on Chaos* [New York: Harper & Row, 1988]).

4. Use *parallel processing*: The relay race, sequential, or series approach to product development is antiquated and inappropriate for today's fast-paced projects. Overlap tasks to accelerate the process (more in Chapter 5).

5. Use *spiral development*, success factor #5 and in Figure 2.7. These build-test-feedback-revise iterations begin early with a concept test and end with the full field trials or user tests before launch. This gets the product right, thus avoiding costly recycles later in the project.

6. Prioritize and focus—do fewer projects but higher-value ones. Use dedicated project teams, and concentrate resources on the truly deserving projects. Not only will the work be done better, it will be done faster.

2. Build a hefty dose of VoC and market information work into your system—make VoC a mandatory action. VoC tends to be a weak area generally, so it needs bolstering.

3. Ensure that projects are front-end loaded; thus, build a robust "homework stage" or two (perhaps a "light homework" stage followed by a "heavy homework" stage) before Development gets underway.

4. Build in a step to secure fact-based product and project definitions—to plant the goalposts firmly in the field. And get sign-off by all members of the project team and senior management.

5. Incorporate validation iterations or spirals into your system—a series of build-test-feedback-and-revise iterations to get the product definition right in the face of fluid information and changing requirements.

6. Ensure your system is a global one, integrating global inputs into your project and product design, and perhaps conceiving a global platform with glocal products.

7. Make the development of a launch plan a key ingredient in your system, along with the input and agreement of the functional areas that will execute the plan. Get sales people on the project team!

8. Speed is vital and accelerated development has many potential benefits, but many downsides, too. Six basic and sensible ways to accelerate developments were highlighted above—build these into your idea-to-launch system.

The next chapter continues with the theme of success drivers, but those that are broader and more related to the business rather than to the project. So read on and see *how some businesses distinguish themselves* in product innovation.

3

DRIVERS OF SUCCESS—WHY THE BEST INNOVATORS EXCEL

The secret of success is constancy to purpose.

—BENJAMIN DISRAELI, British prime minister (1804–1881)

WHAT THE WINNERS DO DIFFERENTLY

Why are some businesses so much more successful at product innovation than others? We saw in Chapter 1 the huge differences in performance between best-performing innovators and the rest. What are their secrets to success? The last chapter revealed some of these "secrets," notably, those most closely connected to how some new-product projects yield big winners. Seeking unique, superior products; building in solid front-end homework and VoC input; spiral iterations with users; planning and executing an effective launch; and accelerating the process (with some provisos) were but some of the drivers of success revealed in Chapter 2. In this current chapter, we continue with the theme "drivers of success," but *this time focused on the business unit* and not so much on the project as the unit of analysis: In short, *what distinguishes the most successful businesses* when it comes to innovation performance?

Consider now the big lessons—the critical success drivers that *make the difference* between winning and losing businesses; and reflect on how you can benefit from each, and how you can translate each into action in your business (see Table 3.1 for a summary).[1]

TABLE 3.1: WHY BUSINESSES EXCEL— NINE CRITICAL SUCCESS DRIVERS

1. Businesses with superlative performance in new-product development have a *product-innovation and technology strategy* to focus the business on the best strategic arenas, and to provide direction for ideation, roadmapping, and resource allocation.
2. *Successful businesses focus:* They do fewer development projects, better projects, and the right mix of projects. They achieve this by adopting a *systematic portfolio-management* system and by building tough Go/Kill decision points into their new-product idea-to-launch system.
3. *Leveraging core competencies* is vital to success; "step-out" development projects, which take the business into new areas (new markets or new technologies), tend to fail. However, collaborative development and open innovation can mitigate some risks here.
4. *Target attractive markets:* Projects aimed at attractive markets do much better, and thus certain key elements of market attractiveness are important project-selection criteria.
5. The *resources must be in place!*
6. The right *organizational structure* and *design* for project teams is a major driver of product-innovation success.
7. Businesses that excel at new-product development have the *right climate and culture* that supports and fosters innovation.
8. *Top management support* doesn't guarantee success, but it certainly helps. However, many executives get it wrong.
9. Companies that follow a *multistage, disciplined stage-and-gate idea-to-launch system* fare much better than an ad hoc approach or no system at all.

SOME SUCCESS DRIVERS ARE STRATEGIC

1. Businesses with superlative performance in new-product development have a product-innovation and technology strategy to focus the business on the best strategic arenas, and to provide direction for ideation, roadmapping, and resource allocation.

We live in turbulent times. Technology advances at an ever-increasing pace; customer and market needs are constantly changing; competition moves at lightning speed; and globalization brings new players and opportunities into the game. More than ever, businesses need *a product-innovation and technology strategy* to help chart the way.[2] Having a new-product strategy for the business is clearly linked to positive performance. The ingredients of such a strategy with the strongest positive impact on performance include the following (Figure 3.1):[3]

1. *Clearly defined product-innovation goals and objectives:* Best practice suggests that a business should clearly define its *long-term goals for product innovation*—for example, deciding what percentage of the business's sales, profits, or growth will come from new products over the next three or five years. Surprisingly, this is a weak area for most firms, with less than 40 percent having such defined and communicated goals and objectives for their total new-product effort.

2. *The role of product innovation in achieving the overall business's goals:* Strategists recommend that the product-innovation goals of the business be *linked to the overall business goals* so that the role of product innovation in achieving business goals is clearly articulated. For example, what percent of your business's growth will come from new products? Defining such "role goals" clearly links your innovation strategy to your overall business strategy.

3. *Strategic arenas defined—areas of strategic focus on which to concentrate one's new-product efforts:* Focus is the key to an effective innovation strategy. The goal is to select strategic arenas that are rich with opportunities for innovation—those that will generate the *business's future engines of growth.*[4] The great majority of businesses do designate strategic arenas— markets, product areas, industry sectors, or technologies—in order to help focus their product-development efforts, although evidence suggests that many business are focused on *the wrong arenas*—on traditional and sterile areas that fail to yield the opportunities and development portfolios needed. In Chapter 10, where we delve into developing your business's innovation strategy, this topic of *picking the best strategic arenas* is probed in considerable depth as a vital facet of strategy. Without such clearly defined strategic arenas, the business often ends up with a scattergun approach to product development, or worse, in markets, sectors, and product categories that offer little headroom for real growth.

4. *Strategic Buckets employed:* Studies reveal that earmarking buckets of resources—funds or person-days—targeted at different project types or different strategic arenas helps to ensure strategic alignment and the right

mix and balance of development projects. Best-performing innovators utilize Strategic Buckets two-and-a-half times more often than worst performers, according to results in Figure 3.1.

5. *Product roadmap in place:* A product roadmap is an effective way to map out a series of development initiatives over time in an attack plan, often three to five years into the future. A *roadmap* is simply a management group's view of *how to get to where they want to be* or achieve their desired objective, and provides *placemarks* for specific future development projects. Roadmaps are used by best innovators twice as often as by worst performers.

6. *Long-term commitment:* Does the business have a long-term view of its new-product efforts? Or is product development largely a short-term effort—essentially a list of development projects for this year and next, with an absence of longer-term projects? Many businesses are deficient here: Only 38.1 percent have a long-term product-innovation strategy. By contrast, the majority of best innovators have such a strategy.

More on the topic of developing an innovation strategy for the firm in Chapter 10.

2. Successful businesses focus: They do fewer development projects, better projects, and the right mix of projects. They achieve this by adopting a systematic portfolio-management system and by building tough Go/Kill decision points into their new-product idea-to-launch system.

Most companies suffer from too many projects and not enough resources to mount an effective or timely effort on each. And there are too few of the right kinds of projects—the bolder innovations. This lack stems from a lack of adequate project evaluation and prioritization—poor portfolio management—with negative results:

- Scarce and valuable resources are wasted on mediocre or low-value projects.
- The truly deserving projects—the bolder, higher value initiatives—don't receive the resources they should.

The desire to weed out bad projects, coupled with the need to focus limited resources on the best projects, means making tough Go/Kill and prior-

Figure 3.1: Best Innovators Develop a Product Innovation and Technology Strategy to Guide the Business's New-Product Efforts

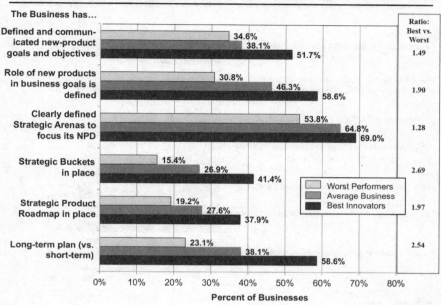

itization decisions. That is, *effective portfolio management—making the right development investment decisions—*must be an integral part of your idea-to-launch system. This results in sharper focus, higher success rates, and shorter times-to-market.

Project evaluations, however, are consistently cited as weakly handled or nonexistent: Decisions involve the wrong people from the wrong functions (no functional alignment); no consistent criteria are used to screen or rank projects; or there is simply no will to kill projects at all—projects are allowed to get a life of their own. For example, only 31.1 percent of businesses properly screen new-product ideas, and only 26.3 percent undertake a proficient business and financial analysis as part of the Business Case (see Figure 2.5 in Chapter 2). And the great majority of businesses lack a *formal portfolio-management system*, as shown in Figure 3.2:[5] Three-quarters have *too many projects* for their limited resources; most don't prioritize projects well; and four-out-of-five businesses have a poor mix and balance of projects in their pipelines, with too many small, insignificant developments. By comparison, the best innovators do a much better job on project selection and portfolio management—good portfolio management practices really do make a difference!

Figure 3.2: To Achieve Optimum Portfolios—the Best Projects and the Right Mix—an Effective Portfolio-Management System Is Essential

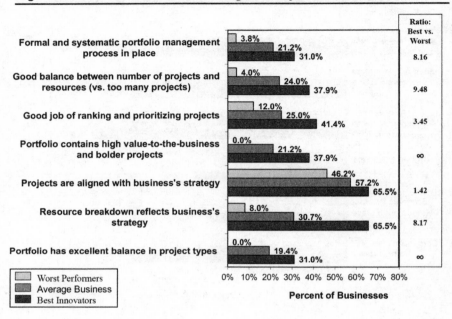

A critical problem is having too many projects for the limited resources available, as seen in Figure 3.2. This problem stems from the reluctance to kill projects: There are no project priorities! As one frustrated executive put it, "We never kill projects, we just wound them." He was referring to the fact that resources are removed from projects a little at a time (rather than making a tough kill decision), and end up being spread so thinly that all projects are set up for failure. In many cases, managers confessed that projects simply aren't killed once they're into development: "Projects get a life of their own!"

What senior management must learn to do is to *walk away from some weaker projects*, much like an astute poker player walks away from a weak poker hand. Killing weak projects is not easy, especially after some time and effort has been invested, but no one does anyone any favors by saying "yes" to all projects. For one thing, not all projects are equally "good"—there is a bell-shaped curve, and in terms of value-to-the-business, some projects are excellent and some are mediocre. Lopping off the bottom third increases the "average project value" in the portfolio and thus improves R&D productivity overall. Further, by saying "yes to all," resources get thinly spread, quality of execution suffers, and cycle time and time-to-market increase.

Often the problem of poor project prioritization boils down to *the lack of a mechanism or system* for ranking, rating, prioritizing, or even killing projects. There are no specified *decision points or gates*; it's not clear who the right decision-makers are—the locus of decision-making is ill-defined; and finally, there are no formal or agreed criteria against which to judge or evaluate projects. **Suggestion:** What some companies have done is to redesign their new-product process: They have created a *funneling process*, which successively weeds out the poor projects; and they have built in decision points in the form of *tough gates*.

At gate reviews, senior management rigorously scrutinizes projects, then makes Go or Kill and prioritization decisions. The use of visible Go/Kill criteria at gates improves decision effectiveness; moreover, certain project characteristics have been identified that consistently separate winners from losers, which can be used as criteria in *scorecard format* for project selection and prioritization. These criteria include some of the important success drivers cited in this and the last chapter:

> Introduce tough *gates with teeth* and kill the weak projects. The result is better focus—fewer but better development initiatives.

1. *Strategic:* how well the project aligns with the business's strategy, and how strategically important it is.
2. *Competitive and product advantage:* whether the product is differentiated, offers unique customer benefits, and represents a compelling value proposition to the user.
3. *Market attractiveness:* how large and growing the market is, and whether the competitive situation is positive (not intense, few and weak competitors).
4. *Leverage:* whether the project leverages the business's core competencies, such as marketing, technology, and manufacturing/operations.
5. *Technical feasibility:* the likelihood of being able to develop and manufacture the product—is this new science and a technically complex project? Or a technology repackage?
6. *Risk and return:* the financial prospects for the project—for example, NPV (net present value), IRR (internal rate of return), and Payback Period—versus the risk.

Project selection and picking winning new-product initiatives is only part of the task, however. Other goals are selecting the right *mix and balance* of projects for your development portfolio, seeking strategic alignment in the portfolio, and ensuring that the business's spending on development projects mirrors its

Figure 3.3: Portfolio Breakdown by Project Type Shows the Different Portfolios for Best versus Worst Performers in Product Innovation

Percent of Development Portfolio*

	Worst Performers	Average Business	Best Innovators
Promotional Developments and Package Changes	12%	10%	6%
Incremental Product Improvements and Changes	40%	33%	28%
Major Product Revisions	19%	22%	25%
New-to-the-Business Products	20%	24%	24%
New-to-the World Products	7%	10%	16%

* Adds to 100% down each column

~45%　　~55%　　~65%

|————— 10 Point Steps —————|

Best-Performing Innovators focus more on innovative and game-changing projects

strategic priorities. Figure 3.3 shows dramatically that portfolio management and project mix really do matter: The best innovators have more aggressive development portfolios and undertake a higher proportion of more innovative new-product projects, while the worst-performing businesses have a very timid new-product project portfolio.[6] We come back to this vital but challenging topic of project selection and portfolio management in Chapters 8 and 9.

3. Leveraging core competencies is vital to success; "step-out" development projects tend to fail.

"Attack from a position of strength" may be an old adage, but it certainly applies to the launch of new products. Where new-product synergy with the base business is lacking, new products fare poorly. *Synergy*, or *leverage*, is a familiar term, but exactly what does it translate into in the context of new products? Synergy (or leveraging core competencies) means having a strong fit between the needs of the new-product project and the resources, competencies, and experience of the firm in terms of:

- R&D resources (ideally the new product should leverage internal and existing technical competencies).

- Marketing, selling (sales force), and distribution (channel) resources.
- Brand, image, and marketing-communications and promotional assets.
- Manufacturing or operations capabilities and resources.
- Technical support and customer-service resources.
- Market-research and market-intelligence resources.
- Management capabilities.

Leverage and synergy are the common thread binding the new business to the old. When translated into product innovation, the ability to leverage existing and in-house strengths, competencies, resources, and capabilities increases the odds of success of the new-product project. By contrast, "step-out" projects take the firm into territory that lies beyond the experience, competencies, and resource base of the company and increase the odds of failure.

Familiarity is a parallel concept to synergy, and many companies use the "familiarity matrix" to categorize development projects: New markets and new technologies are the axes (Figure 8.7). Some new-product projects take the company into unfamiliar territory: a product category new to the firm; new customers and unfamiliar needs served; unfamiliar technology; new sales-force, channels, and servicing requirements; or an unfamiliar manufacturing process. Sadly, the firm often pays the price: Step-out projects have a higher failure rate due to lack of experience, knowledge, skills, and resources.

> The ability to leverage core competencies—both marketing and technical—are important project screening criteria. Attack from a position of strength!

If at all possible, always *attack from a position of strength* when it comes to new products. That is, *select projects that leverage your in-house resources and skills*, seeking synergies in your product-development projects. This message comes from a number of studies into new-product success and failure. The reasons for this impact of leverage are clear:

- *Knowledge*: Operating within one's field of expertise—either markets or technology—provides considerable "domain knowledge," which is available to the project team. By contrast, moving into new fields for the business often yields unpleasant surprises.
- *Experience*: The more often one does something, the better one becomes at doing it: One develops a track record, and moves "down the experience curve." The result: It takes less time and costs less to do each successive project.

Figure 3.4: Leveraging Technology Core Competencies Almost Triples the Success Rate and Impacts Strongly on New-Product Profitability

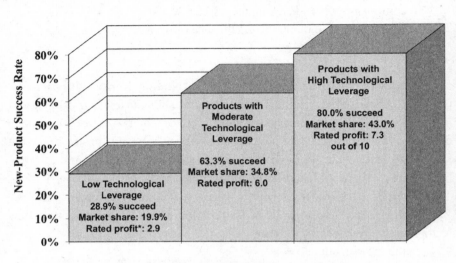

* Rated profit: 10 = far exceeded our expected profit;
0 = fell far short; 5 = just met expectations

Figure 3.5: Leveraging Marketing Core Competencies Almost Doubles the Success Rate, Doubles Market Share, and Impacts Strongly on Profitability

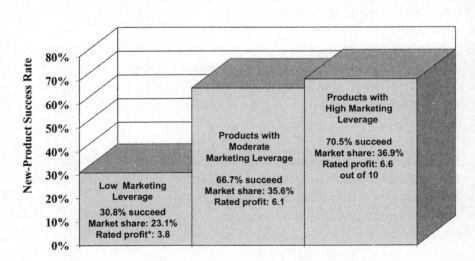

* Rated profit: 10 = far exceeded our expected profit;
0 = fell far short; 5 = just met expectations

- *Resources are available and at marginal cost*: Developing the new product using existing and in-house technical skills or selling it to existing customers through an already established sales force or distribution channel is usually less expensive and less risky than buying outside technology and skills, or building a new sales force and targeting unfamiliar customers.

Two types of leverage are important to product innovation:

1. *Technological leverage*: High technology-leverage or synergistic products are those that build on the firm's existing or in-house development technology and skills, utilize inside engineering or design skills, and use existing manufacturing or operations resources and competencies.
2. *Marketing leverage*: High marketing-leverage or synergistic new products are those that are sold through the firm's existing sales force or distribution system; make use of existing customer relationships; and leverage a brand name or image, or build off the firm's promotional and marketing communications skills and assets.

Look at the compelling results showing the impacts of both dimensions of leverage in Figures 3.4 and 3.5:

- New products with *high technology leverage achieve almost three times the success rate* as those with low technology leverage. Such "high leverage" new products also have a much higher rated profitability than do new products in which there is little or no technological leverage or synergy (Figure 3.4).
- Similarly, new products that *leverage the firm's existing marketing resources* and skills have more than double the success rate. Such high market-leverage products also achieve 1.6 times the market share and have a much higher rated profitability on average than low leverage products (Figure 3.5).

Suggestion: In designing new-product strategies and selecting which new products to develop, never underestimate the *role of leverage*. Arenas and projects that lack any leverage from the base business invariably cost the firm more to exploit. Further, projects without leverage usually take the firm into new and uncharted markets and technologies, often with unexpected pitfalls and barriers. There are simply too many unpleasant surprises in arenas that are new to the firm.

These two dimensions of leverage—technological and marketing, and their ingredients—become obvious checklist items in a scoring or rating model to help prioritize new-product projects. If your *leverage score* is low, then there *must be other compelling reasons to proceed* with the development project. Leverage and synergy are not essential—there are other ways to fill the void—but they certainly improve the odds of winning.

Sometimes it is necessary to venture into new and unfamiliar markets, technologies, or manufacturing processes. Note that the odds of disaster are not so high to deter making the move altogether. If leverage is low, yet the project is attractive for other reasons, then steps can be taken to bolster the internal resources and competencies. Low leverage scores signal the *need for outside resources*—partnering, outsourcing, or other "open innovation" approaches. For example, through *open innovation*, the developer obtains resources and knowledge from sources external to the company: ideas for new products, intellectual property and outsourced development work, marketing and launch resources, and even licensed products ready to launch.[7]

4. Target attractive markets. Projects aimed at attractive markets do better, and thus certain key elements of market attractiveness are important project-selection criteria.

Market attractiveness is an important strategic variable. Porter's "five forces" model considers various elements of market attractiveness as a determinant of industry profitability.[8] Similarly, various strategic planning models—for example, the two-dimensional GE-McKinsey map or business portfolio grid used to allocate resources among various existing business units (stars, cash cows, dogs, and wildcats)—employs market or industry attractiveness as a key dimension of the grid.[9]

In the case of new products, market attractiveness is vital: Products targeted at more attractive markets are far more successful. There are two dimensions of market attractiveness:

1. *Market potential:* positive market environments, namely, large and growing markets; and markets in which there is a strong customer need for such products, and in which the purchase is an important one for the customer. Products aimed at such attractive markets are far more successful.
2. *Competitive intensity:* negative markets characterized by intense and tough competition; competition on the basis of price; high-quality and strong competitive products; and competitors whose sales force, channel system, and support service are strongly rated. Poor competitor margins is also a negative. Products aimed at these competitive and unattractive markets fare more poorly.

Figure 3.6: Market Attractiveness Almost Doubles the New-Product Success Rate and Impacts Positively on Market Share and New-Product Profitability

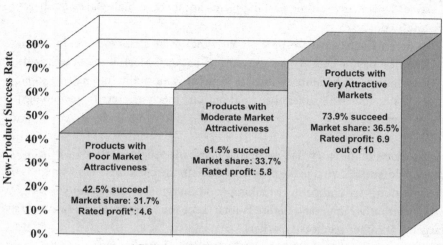

New-Product Success Rate

Products with Poor Market Attractiveness

42.5% succeed
Market share: 31.7%
Rated profit*: 4.6

Products with Moderate Market Attractiveness

61.5% succeed
Market share: 33.7%
Rated profit: 5.8

Products with Very Attractive Markets

73.9% succeed
Market share: 36.5%
Rated profit: 6.9 out of 10

* Rated profit: 10 = far exceeded our expected profit;
0 = fell far short; 5 = just met expectations

The significant impact of market attractiveness, measured by these two dimensions, is shown in Figure 3.6. New products aimed at attractive markets have almost double the success rate and achieve higher market shares and much better profits. Consistently picking the right development projects to invest in is one way to win at innovation, and market attractiveness is an important criterion for making these correct investment decisions.

These dimensions of market potential and competitive intensity are obvious, of course, but are often overlooked or rationalized away when evaluating the odds of success for a new product, especially in the emotion of the moment:

An example: One of the speakers at a small-business conference was presenting a new product his business was launching. The product was very high tech and used a complex mathematical algorithm on data from a digitized picture to move a robotic arm on a production line. The demo unit on stage had a fascinating application: packing sardines into a sardine can. We all watched the stage with anticipation as the first sardine moved up the conveyer belt; then we heard the picture being taken and watched with amazement as the small robotic arm seized the sardine and packed it just perfectly—head and tail in the right places—in the small sardine can. We all clapped.

The business owner (and his highly competent technical staff) were jus-
tifiably proud of their technical achievement and took a bow on stage. Then
the tough questions started: What is the value of the product to the user?
How many sardine packers on a production line will it replace? At what wage
scale? How many sardine packing plants are there in high-wage countries?
And so on.

It turns out that there were (at the time) three sardine plants in North
America, paying decent wages to sardine packers. Most of the other plants
were in low-wage countries, thus limiting the value of the automated packer.
At last count, the business had sold but one machine. Terrific technology,
lousy market!

The point of the story is to remind us to ask the tough questions—What is the
market potential? What is the product's value to the customer? How tough is the
competition? Are competitors making good margins?—*before jumping into Development* rather than days before launch. I see too many "clever new products"
targeted at rather mediocre markets.
Suggestion: The message is this: Both elements of market attractiveness—market potential and competitive intensity—impact the new product's fortunes, and
both must be criteria in your *scoring or rating system* for project selection and
prioritization. That's why market attractiveness is part of the scorecard checklist
illustrated in success driver #2 above.

THE ORGANIZATION—PEOPLE, RESOURCES, CULTURE, AND SENIOR MANAGEMENT

5. The resources must be in place.

Having a sound game plan does not guarantee success. There must be players on
the field as well—not just part-time or Saturday afternoon players—but full-time
dedicated resources. But too many projects and businesses suffer from a lack of
time and money commitment to product innovation. The results are predictable:
much higher failure rates, longer times-to-market, and underperforming development projects.

The high failure rates and poor performance data in product innovation were
highlighted in Chapter 1. Many reasons for new-product failures have been uncovered over the years, including well-known and recurring themes such as a
lack of market information, a failure to listen to the voice of the customer, poor
front-end or predevelopment homework, unstable product definition, poor

Figure 3.7: Serious Resource Deficiencies Exist in Product Innovation Regardless of the Functional Area—Best Innovators Are Better Resourced

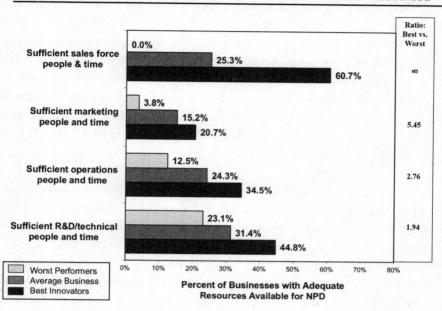

Worst Performers
Average Business
Best Innovators

Percent of Businesses with Adequate Resources Available for NPD

quality of execution of key tasks, and even poorly structured, ineffectual project teams.[10] We saw some of these direct causes in Chapter 2.[11]

An examination of the many failure reasons shows that many are themselves interlinked and are traceable to a much more fundamental or root cause, namely, *major resource deficiencies* in key areas.[12] For example, poor quality of execution and leaving out important tasks, such as VoC work or front-end due diligence, are often not so much due to ignorance or a lack of willingness; it's more often because of a lack of time and people. As one senior project leader declared: "We don't deliberately set out to do a bad job on projects. But with seven major projects underway, on top of an already busy 'day job,' I'm being *set up for failure*—there just isn't enough time to do what needs to be done— and so I cut corners."

This project leader is not alone in her concern. Surveys and benchmarking studies reveal that the new-product development resource deficiency is perverse and widespread. Consider the evidence:

- A lack of focus and inadequate resources are *the number-one weaknesses* in businesses' new-product development efforts in major benchmarking

studies: Project teams are working on too many projects or are not sufficiently focused on new-product development work.[13] Only a minority of
businesses indicates that sufficient resources are available to project teams
to do a quality job in new-product development—see Figures 3.7 and 3.8.[14]
The weakest areas are marketing resources followed by manufacturing/
operations resources available for product development—Figure 3.7.

- Even worse, what limited resources are available to product innovation are
  thinly spread. Figure 3.8 reveals this lack of focus. For example, 91 percent
  of businesses suffer from people being *spread over too many development
  projects*; and 79 percent have their people *doing too many other tasks,* and
  thus are not sufficiently focused on product-innovation work.

A lack of resources has many negative consequences. First, *quality of execution suffers:* Corners are cut, as project teams scramble to meet timelines but
lack the needed resources. A second result is that cycle time or *time-to-market
lengthens:* The "time to get things done" is not so much execution time, it's waiting time—waiting for people to get around to doing the work (or WIP, work in
process). And *morale suffers:* Lacking the necessary personnel and their time
commitments from functional bosses, the project team is stretched; deadlines
are missed and pressure mounts; people are blamed; and team morale starts to
deteriorate.

The most costly outcome of resource deficiencies, however, is the *lack of
game-changers and bold innovations.* New-product failures and being late or slow
to market are the *measurable costs* of poor or untimely execution, often brought
on by insufficient resources. A *far greater cost* cannot be measured because it's
an *opportunity cost.* How many *big projects are simply not done* due to a lack of
resources? With very limited time and resources, the "necessity projects" and
renovations get done—*the urgent always seems to take precedence over the important*—and the major or bold projects get put on hold . . . which may explain
why 79 percent of businesses lack high value or bold projects in their development portfolios (Figure 3.2)!

Adequate resources for projects—focused and dedicated people—are vital
to strong innovation performance. Properly executed initiatives take time and
money: "Faster, better, cheaper" is a myth! Look at the facts:

- Devoting sufficient resources to new-product development is strongly
  linked to new-product performance.[15] Indeed, the strongest single driver
  of *percentage of sales* from new products is how much the business spends

Figure 3.8: Project-Team Focus and Dedicated Resources (Dedicated Team Members) Have Strong Positive Impacts on Performance

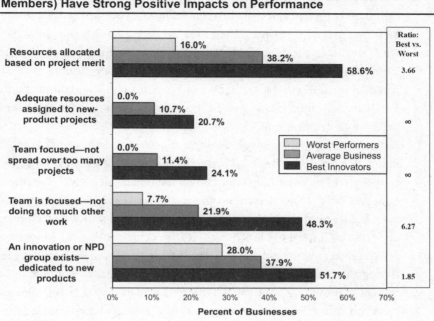

on R&D (as a percentage of sales). Further, note from Figure 3.8 that even though the best innovators are resource deficient, they suffer much less from resource gaps than do the worst performers.

- Best innovators are considerably more focused and boast dedicated resources for product innovation, as seen in Figure 3.8: Half of these better performers have dedicated resources to product development (project team members are not working on a lot of "other tasks"); and more than half of the best innovators have a focused and dedicated group—often cross-functional (R&D, marketing, operations, and so on)—working 100 percent on product innovation!

Suggestion: The challenge of too many projects and too few resources can be attacked by undertaking a current-state assessment that includes *resource capacity analysis*:

1. *Determine if you have enough of the right resources to handle the active projects currently in your development pipeline.* Begin with your current

list of active projects. Determine the resources required to complete them according to their timelines (get that data from project leaders—resources approved and realistic requirements, expressed as person-days by functional department). Then look at the availability of resources—who's available for new-product work, what percentage of their time, from what department? Develop one spreadsheet per month—projects listed and people (or departments) and person-days—and do the math! You'll usually find major gaps, especially in some departments, and hence potential bottlenecks.

2. *Determine if you have enough resources to achieve your business's product-innovation objectives.* Begin with your new-product objectives: What percent of your business's sales—and thus what dollar sales—will come from new products? Now, determine the resources required to achieve this goal: Figure out the number of major, medium, and minor development projects you'll need to launch each year to achieve this goal; how many active projects you need at each stage of the development process, idea through to launch; and how many resources per year it will take to do this set of projects. Again you'll likely find a major gap between demand based on your goals, and your capacity available. It's time to make some tough choices about the realism of your goals or whether more resources are required.

Other solutions include:

- Develop a *product-innovation and technology strategy* for your business (success driver #1 above, and in Chapter 10). The issue of resources invariably surfaces, and this is the time to debate whether you have sufficient resources in place to achieve your objectives, whether resources should be increased for strategic reasons, or whether your innovation objectives for the business are simply too ambitious and unrealistic.
- *Ring-fence the resources:* That is, make product-innovation people dedicated resources—dedicated full-time to product development—rather than dividing them among many duties.
- *Portfolio solutions:* Consider the Strategic Buckets method to set aside resources for different types of projects. More on this topic in Chapter 8 on portfolio management.
- *Focus:* Do fewer but better projects (success driver #2). A solid one-time pruning exercise to kick-start the process culls out the weak projects and refocuses the resources on the excellent projects.

Figure 3.9: The Way New-Product Development Project Teams Are Organized Strongly Impacts Innovation Performance

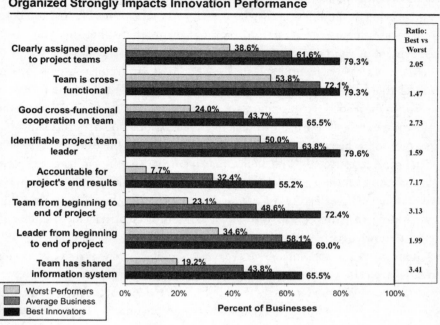

6. The right organizational structure and design for project teams is a major driver of product innovation success.

Product innovation is very much a team effort! Do a postmortem on any bungled new-product project and invariably you'll find each functional area doing its own piece of the project, with very little communication between players and functions—a fiefdom mentality—and no real commitment of individual players to the project. Many studies concur that how the project team is organized and functions strongly influences project outcomes.[16]

Suggestion: Design your organization for product innovation. Product innovation is not a one-department show! It is very much a multidisciplinary, cross-functional effort. Organizational design—how you organize for new products—is critical. Except for the simplest of projects—simple line extensions and product updates—product innovation must cut across traditional functional boundaries and barriers. The ingredients of good organizational design should be familiar ones, but surprisingly, many businesses have yet to get the message.

Best innovators organize their new-product project teams as shown in Figure 3.9. First, there is a *clearly assigned team* of players for each significant development project—people who are part of the project and *do work for it* (not just come to meetings). That is, coming out of every Go/Kill or gate decision meeting, it should be clear who is assigned to the project team (and their time commitments specified, too). What is surprising is that this practice is not evident in almost all businesses today.

There is a clearly *identified team leader* in best innovators—a person who is in charge and responsible for driving the project. The team leader's role is similar to the leader of a business start-up: an entrepreneurial role, in which the leader not only leads the team—much like a team captain on a sports team—but also promotes the project, seeks resources, and handles the external interfaces of the project, especially with senior management. The project leader is often likened to the entrepreneur in a start-up business, with the project being his or her start-up. Characteristics of effective project team leaders include: credibility, enthusiasm, entrepreneurship, people skills, project-management skills, and project knowledge.*

Some firms also appoint a *project manager*—quite a different role—especially in large projects. The project manager has an administrative and less entrepreneurial role; this person manages the day-to-day activities of the project, handles the nuts-and-bolts items, gets the team meetings organized, manages the timeline and the budget—all the tasks associated with good project management.

Project-team accountability is key to innovation success, as seen in Figure 3.9. That is, when a project leader and team present a Business Case to senior management—for example, projections of first-year sales, profit estimates, and expected launch date—and the project is approved, these projections now become *commitments*: They become the team's targets, and the project team is ultimately accountable for their achievement. Many firms now build in a "post-launch review" in which the team presents the *results of the project* a year or so after launch to the same group of senior management—a closed-loop feedback system. Although the concept of accountability makes sense, note that only one-third of businesses actually apply the principle, but that the *best innovators embrace team accountability for results by a seven-to-one ratio.*

In order to foster team accountability, it's essential that the project team remain "on the field for the entire game." In too many firms we have benchmarked, the prevailing philosophy was "launch and leave"—that is, launch the product and get onto some other assignment before the results are known. This

---

* Based on a content-analysis review of articles appearing over a twenty-year period in the *Journal of Product Innovation Management* that probed for the characteristics of effective project team leaders.

lack of accountability and team continuity led to many negative results: wildly overestimated initial projections (in order to get the project approved), and a failure to follow through and work to achieve the promised results. Thus, a best practice is that *the project team remain on the project from beginning to end*—not just on the project for a short while or a single phase: Almost half of businesses practice this end-to-end approach, and it is particularly evident among best innovators.

> A cross-functional team, with clearly assigned and accountable team members, on the team from beginning to end, and led by a highly visible team leader, is a common denominator in best-innovating businesses.

How does one design a *system that integrates* many activities and multifunctional inputs and fosters a cross-functional team approach? One answer is to develop a systematic approach to product innovation—a blueprint or roadmap from idea to launch—which *cuts across functional boundaries* and requires the active participation of people from different functions. Make every stage in the process a cross-functional one.

A second and equally important answer lies in *organizational design*. What type of organization structure will bring many players from different walks of life in the company together in an integrated effort? In short, how do you take a diverse group of players and turn them into a team? The three approaches that appear to work best are:

1. *Balanced matrix:* A project leader is assigned to oversee and lead the project; team members are assigned from functional areas. The team leader *shares the responsibility and authority* for completing the project with the functional managers: There is joint approval and direction.
2. *Project matrix:* A project leader is assigned to oversee and lead the project, and again team members are assigned from the functional areas. In this model, however, the team leader has *primary responsibility and authority* for the project. Functional managers assign personnel as needed and provide technical expertise and mentoring; the gate meetings are where resources are committed and personnel assignments are agreed on.
3. *Project team:* A project leader is put in charge of a project team composed of a core group of personnel from several functional areas. Once the team members are assigned (likely at a gate meeting and by the senior functional bosses), the functional managers have *no more formal involvement or authority over their people.* The project leader is now "their boss."

Figure 3.10: Climate and Culture for Product Innovation—Values, Attitudes, and Policies, Rank Ordered (Highest Impact to Lowest)—Has a Major Impact

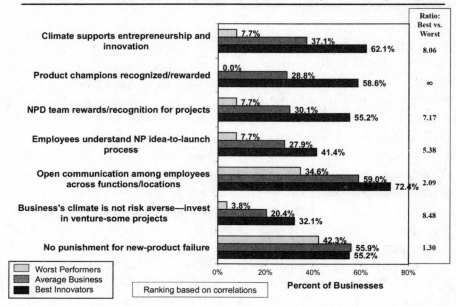

Of the three designs above, the last one appears to be best suited for large, complex projects, whereas a project-matrix approach works best for both complex and simpler projects.

Regardless of which of the three structures above you elect, strong project *leadership—a dedicated and empowered project leader—*appears essential for timely, successful projects. The leader must have formal authority (co-opting authority from functional heads); and the leader and team must be empowered to make project decisions and not be second-guessed, overruled, or "micromanaged" by the functional heads or senior management.*

To work well, team members should be located close to each other. Colocation is one solution—team members from different functions in the company are relocated in one area or department, and in the Agile model, in one room! Colocation is not possible in the case of global or outsourced projects; thus, excellent communications technology—electronic meeting rooms, with reliable and easy-to-use audio-visual links—combined with timely and periodic face-to-face

---

* "Micromanage" is a term used to describe the behavior of senior management, meaning day-to-day meddling in the affairs of the project team.

meetings, are vital to success. The final organizational ingredients essential to making this multifunctional team work is a *climate and culture* that fosters creativity, innovation, and a team approach, the next driver.

7. Business has the right climate and culture that supports and fosters innovation.

Climate and culture for innovation is a pervasive topic, with many elements and facets. And it's sometimes difficult to put one's arms around what is meant by "climate and culture," or worse yet, what to do about it. One thing is clear from all the research: One cannot ignore climate and culture if exceptional new-product results are the goal. Indeed, climate and culture proves to be among *the strongest discriminators* between best- and worst-performing innovators in the Innovation Diamond in Figure 1.2.

What are the elements of a positive climate; how many businesses really embrace these; and what impact on performance do they really have? A number of characteristics of a positive climate have been investigated, and Figures 3.10 and 3.11 reveal that there are some *major differences in the climate* for innovation between best and worst innovators. The twelve elements considered are split into two main factors or themes: The first is the general climate (Figure 3.10), and the second centers on specific actions to promote a positive climate (Figure 3.11).

1. *A supportive climate for entrepreneurship and product innovation:* A supportive climate is a major difference between the best and worst performers, with 62.1 percent of best innovators scoring very strongly here.

    An example: Grundfos, a major European pump manufacturer, openly promotes new-product development at every opportunity. NPD is evident everywhere—in the company's annual report, which devotes more pages to product innovation than to finances; its show-case of new products that occupies its entire headquarters front lobby; and its campaign of posters seen throughout company premises emphasizing innovation. And it works: The company boasts a very motivated staff—both junior and senior people—who are strongly committed to product innovation.

2. *Rewards and recognition for champions:* Best innovators typically recognize and/or reward their new-product project leaders and entrepreneurs (new-product champions or product innovators). But this again is a weak area, with a minority of businesses providing such rewards.

3. *Rewards and recognition for project teams:* This is also a weak area on average: When a new-product project team does a good job on their project (for example, gets to market on time, meets sales revenue targets, has a winner), less than one-third of firms reward or recognize them. Best innovators are much stronger here: 55.2 percent reward their teams.

     An example: Emerson electric has a "wall of fame" off the main lobby in their St. Louis headquarters building. Here, the pictures of project teams that delivered are featured for all to see and admire. Grundfos has a display of new products in its front lobby, complete with a description of the project and team that executed it.

4. *Understanding of the business's innovation process:* Employees should understand the firm's new-product idea-to-launch system, so they're able to participate in it. But, on average, ignorance is a major weakness: Employees do not understand nor support the business's innovation process in four out of five businesses, sometimes the result of lack of training, a lack of leadership, or simply a negative or skeptical attitude within the business.

5. *Open communication:* Best innovators provide for open communication among employees across functions, departments, and locations—this openness helps to stimulate creativity, and makes for more effective cross-functional communication on project teams.

6. *Risk averseness:* Best innovators appear far less risk averse—they are not afraid to invest in more venturesome projects—with almost one-third opting for riskier projects (although risk averseness is a weakness overall: On average, only one-fifth of businesses take on riskier projects). *Strategic Buckets*—which reserves designated resources for higher-risk projects—is one solution (more on this topic in Chapter 8).

7. *No punishment for failure: Fear of failure* and *creativity* cannot coexist! Thus, mitigating fear of failure is particularly evident in best innovators and indeed in most businesses in Figure 3.10. Removing this fear through a policy of "no punishment for failures—it's OK to fail" encourages more innovative and risk-taking behavior (although this encouragement should not be confused with lack of accountability).

Table 3.2 shows some of the values and attitudes evident in more progressive and innovative companies: the "new game" players versus the "old game"

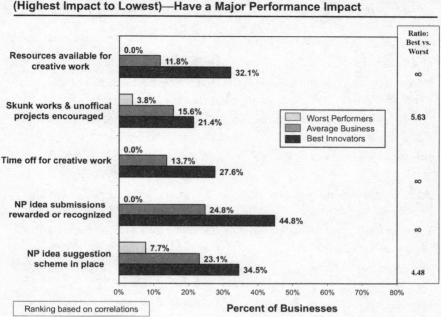

Figure 3.11: Climate and Culture for NPD—Specific Actions Rank Ordered (Highest Impact to Lowest)—Have a Major Performance Impact

adherents, and may serve as a *set of* values *for your business* as you move forward.

The second culture and climate factor contains more action-oriented items and specific efforts designed to promote a positive climate (Figure 3.11); in descending order of impact they are:

1. *Resources available for creative work:* A significant number of best innovators provide support and resources for creative employees to pursue their own projects—seed money, equipment, etc. But, overall, providing such resources is a very weak area.

2. *Skunk works projects encouraged:* In some best innovators, *skunk works* projects are encouraged. A skunk works is a team that works *outside the official bureaucracy and structure* of the business, often on very innovative, critical, and sometimes secret projects. In many cases, this team *reports directly to a senior executive*, and team members are seconded from their functional departments: They no longer work in a department, but instead are full-time members of the project team.

**TABLE 3.2: THE NEW GAME VERSUS THE OLD GAME—
VALUES, ATTITUDES, ACTIONS[17]**

Old Game	New Game
Renovations and modifications in traditional markets	Innovative bold new products in new markets
Stable, predicable markets, competitive and mature	Customer and competitor uncertainty, disruptive trends
Many incremental bets . . . few kills	Bold investments, but disciplined kills—a correct kill is a 'success'
Traditional stage-and-gate process—linear, rigid, not adaptive	New stage-and-gate system—adaptive, flexible, agile, and accelerated
Late stage-customer feedback—in Testing or Field Trials phase	Early and frequent customer feedback via iterations—spiral development
Do it right the first time—no mistakes!	Fail often, fail early, fail cheaply—learn from mistakes
Internal environment for control—avoid risk	Internal environment for big and bold—take and mitigate risks
Do the obvious and build on what already exists	Search for unconventional, radical ideas and solutions
Project teams focused on delivering documentation	Project teams focused on delivering something physical—on development results

3. *Time off or scouting time:* Many best-innovator businesses provide resources and time off to creative employees to work on their own projects—this time off is often the source of creative innovation. Overall, this scouting-time provision is a very weak area, with only 13.7 percent of businesses providing it.

> *An example:* 3M has a policy that anyone in the firm can get a project going, and spend 15 percent of their workweek on it—formal start and management approval or a gate is not required. Thus, not every project begins in the formal new product innovation (NPI) process (3M's *Stage-Gate* system). Most of the leaders of these 15 percent projects tend to be technical people, although the system is open to anyone in 3M.

These 15 percent projects enable the leader to acquire enough resources and time "to put together something to get feedback from a customer," allowing one to bridge from technology to the marketplace. Ultimately, these projects are brought into 3M's formal NPI once resource commitments are significant. Some at 3M avow that the firm's most significant innovations have come via this route.

4. *NP ideas rewarded*: The best innovators often provide rewards or recognition to employees who submit new-product ideas.

   An example: In one major materials company, idea submitters received "points," depending on how many gates their idea passes. Points can be accumulated, and ultimately cashed in for prizes, much like in an airline loyalty program.

5. *A new-product idea-suggestion scheme in place*: This scheme, a fairly common practice in best-performing innovators, actively solicits new-product ideas from employees. Although a weak area across all businesses, as we shall see in Chapter 7, idea suggestion schemes can be a major potential source of new-product ideas.

The climate and culture for product innovation is surprisingly and dangerously weak in many businesses, as noted in Figures 3.10 and 3.11. Particular weaknesses include anything to do with off-line or creative but unofficial work: free time or scouting time, resources to support creative projects, skunk works, and free-time projects or unapproved "underground" projects. Yet a significant proportion of top-performing businesses embrace this type of activity and support it. Another very weak area is idea submission from employees: many businesses have no idea scheme in place, and no rewards or recognition for ideas. And finally, the third major area of weakness is the unwillingness to invest in more venturesome projects—a general risk averseness.
Suggestion: If the goal is to improve the climate and culture for bold innovation in your business, then look at the list of items above and the illustrations of best practice. Some actionable items include:

- Provide scouting time and make resources available to creative, passionate employees to pursue their dream projects—free-time projects as at 3M (that is, allow some unofficial projects).

- Try a skunk works approach for critical projects—the project team working outside the official organization.
- Put a new-product idea submission scheme in place.
- Reward and/or recognize idea generators and also project team members for their efforts.
- Make it a rule: No punishment for hard and competent work that sadly resulted in a killed or failed project!
- Set aside a specific percentage of resources for bold innovation projects (a separate "bucket"). And do take on some venturesome projects—and make sure everyone is aware that you allow and encourage these.
- Make sure that employees really understand your idea-to-launch system; provide some training and leadership here, so they can be more engaged in product innovation.
- Encourage open communication between functions (no silos allowed!), locations, and countries.
- And most important—support and encourage product innovation openly and passionately.

8. Top management support doesn't guarantee success, but it sure helps. But many executives get it wrong. There are seven habits of successful executives in leading product innovation.

Top management support is a necessary ingredient for successful product innovation. Look at the strengths of the impacts of senior management's role in Figure 3.12:

- In 80 percent of best-innovator businesses, the executives are *strongly committed to product innovation*. Compare this to the 27 percent commitment in worst-performing businesses!
- New-product *metrics* are part of senior management's annual objectives in half of the best firms, but are noticeably absent in worst performers.
- Executives provide *strong support and empowerment* to teams and team members in two-thirds of the best innovators, but do so in only 8 percent of worst performers.
- Across the board, executives leave the day-to-day activities and decisions to the project team—they *do not micromanage*—but this freedom is especially true in best innovators.
- Senior management is very much engaged in the key Go/Kill decisions in 80 percent of the best innovators (versus in only 42 percent of worst performers).

Figure 3.12: Senior Management (Executive) Practices and Commitment Are Key to Driving Innovation Results

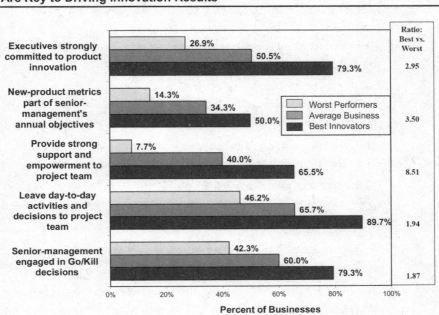

Leaders must lead by being passionately committed to product innovation. Although not always possible in today's financially driven firms, *putting products before profits* is the ultimate leadership commitment to innovation. Some great business leaders have managed to achieve this: "In the book [Jobs's biography], Jobs said that he had hoped he had infused Apple with a rare desire to keep putting products ahead of profit—the quality that he held responsible for the success that made it the world's most valuable technology company."[18] Indeed, Jobs is quoted as saying: "I learned that my perspective was right. Products are everything."[19] If you are committed to product innovation and to unequalled new products, then profits will ultimately follow. But a sole commitment to profits probably will yield a hollow result.

> Innovation is a prerequisite for sustained growth. No other path to profitable growth can be sustained over time.
>
> —A. G. Lafley, former CEO, Procter & Gamble

Suggestion: Senior management must make a long-term commitment to internal product development as a source of growth and embrace it passionately. They must develop a vision, objectives, and strategy for product innovation that is driven by corporate objectives and strategies. They must make avail-

SEVEN HABITS OF SUCCESSFUL LEADERS OF INNOVATION

1. They embrace and support product innovation at every opportunity—both in words and in actions:

   • They are passionate about innovation.
   • They put the resources in place.
   • They put products before profits! (Profits will ultimately follow.)

2. They lead the creation of an Innovation Strategy for their business.
3. They are actively involved in making Go/Kill decisions at gates:

   • They practice effective gatekeeping.
   • They develop "rules of engagement" and commit to these rules.

4. They are the innovation portfolio managers:

   • They understand the business's development portfolio.
   • They play an active role at portfolio reviews.

5. They understand and embrace their business's idea-to-launch stage-and-gate system.
6. They foster the right climate and culture for innovation.
7. They keep score:

   • They hold themselves, other executives, and project teams accountable for results.
   • When targets are missed, they find out why—they promote continuous improvement.

able the necessary resources and ensure that these resources aren't diverted to more immediate needs in times of shortage. They must commit to a disciplined process to drive products to market and be actively engaged in it as gatekeepers. And most important, senior management must empower project teams and support committed champions by acting as mentors, facilitators, "godfathers," or executive sponsors to project leaders and teams—acting as "executive champions."[20]

Senior management's role is *not to get involved* in development projects on a day-to-day basis, nor to be constantly meddling and interfering in the project, nor to "micromanage" projects. This meddling behavior is wrong for two reasons: It usurps the authority of the team (and hence defeats the "empowered team" concept); and frankly, the research evidence is that senior management doesn't do so well with "executive pet projects" or at managing such projects! The seven behaviors of effective senior management are outlined in the box.

HAVING A NEW-PRODUCT PLAYBOOK PAYS OFF

9. Companies that follow a multistage, disciplined new-product process—a Stage-Gate® system—fare much better.

The product-innovation or idea-to-launch process in many companies is broken. It is a process plagued by errors of omission and commission: Things don't happen when they should, or how they should, or as well as they should! The process lacks consistency and quality of execution, and it is very much in need of repair. Study after study reveals that many businesses' idea-to-launch systems are deficient or nonexistent and point to the need for a complete and a quality process.

A systematic new-product process—such as a *Stage-Gate®* system—is the solution that many companies have turned to in order to overcome the deficiencies that plague their new-product efforts. *Stage-Gate* systems are simply roadmaps, "cookbooks," or "playbooks" for driving new products from idea to launch, successfully and efficiently. About 68 percent of US product developers had adopted early versions of *Stage-Gate* processes by the year 2000, according to a PDMA best-practices study done then. More recent benchmarking studies reveal

> Leading companies have adopted a Stage-Gate® system, a method developed by the author, to accelerate new-product projects from idea to launch.

that 73 percent of businesses employ such a process, and a more current study reveals that "nearly all of our best performers (90 percent, compared to only 44.4 percent of worst performers) have a clear, defined new-product development process—a game plan, playbook, or *Stage-Gate* system that guides new-product development projects from idea to launch . . . suggesting that simply having a formal process is itself a best practice."[21]

Managing new products without a system in place is like putting a dozen players on a football field with no huddles, no playbook, and no preplanned plays, and expecting them to score. It works once in a while, but over the long run, the better disciplined competitor will win.

The goal of a robust idea-to-launch system is to build the best practices outlined in this and the previous chapter into a single process, so that these

Figure 3.13: A High-Quality *Stage-Gate*® System Yields Higher New-Product Success Rates, with More Projects Hitting Sales and Profit Targets

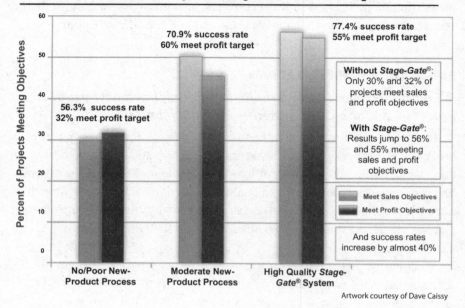

Artwork courtesy of Dave Caissy

success drivers or practices happen by design, not by accident. Operationally, an idea-to-launch system breaks the product-innovation process into a *series of cross-functional stages*—think of these as "plays" in a North American football game. Each stage is composed of a number of prescribed "best practice" activities or tasks, undertaken by a cross-functional team, with many tasks executed in parallel. Best practices, such as front-end homework, spirals with users, planning the launch, and VoC are built into the various stages. A set of visible and prescribed deliverables is the result of each stage.

Each stage is preceded by a gate or Go/Kill decision point—think of these as the huddles in a football game. Here the team meets with management to decide whether to move to the next play, and if so what the play (actions) will be; or to stop the game and walk away from a bad situation. This stage-and-gate format leads to terms such as "gating," "gateways," "stage-gate," "phase-gate," or "tollgate" systems. The term *Stage-Gate*, now widely in use, was originally coined by me in early articles on the topic.[22] A typical *Stage-Gate* system is shown in Figure 4.10 in the next chapter for major new-product projects (note that there are abbreviated versions for smaller, lower-risk developments).[23]

The evidence in support of a systematic idea-to-launch or stage-and-gate system is strong. Booz Allen Hamilton was first to find that companies that

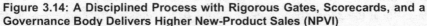

Figure 3.14: A Disciplined Process with Rigorous Gates, Scorecards, and a Governance Body Delivers Higher New-Product Sales (NPVI)

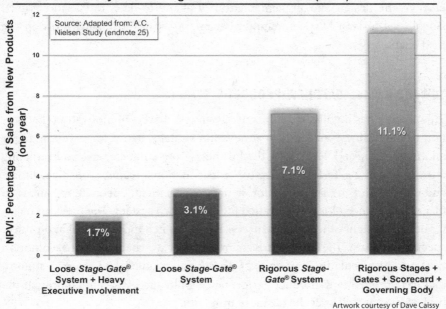

Artwork courtesy of Dave Caissy

had implemented new-product processes are more successful, and that those firms with the most experience with a new-product process were even more successful. As one vice president put it, "The multistep new-product process is an essential ingredient in successful new-product development."[24]

P&G's idea-to-launch SIMPL stage-and-gate system is considered vital to the company's product-innovation performance: "*Stage-Gate*® is not optional . . . [it is] essential to succeed in today's environment."[25] And the payoffs of such processes have been frequently reported: improved teamwork, less recycling and rework, improved success rates, earlier detection of failures, a better launch, and even shorter cycle times.[26] P&G notes that its SIMPL *Stage-Gate* system "improves functional interfaces (when and how to work together; defines responsibilities)" and "delivers individual initiatives [new products] to market effectively and efficiently. *Stage-Gate* works!"[27]

Note the measured impacts of a formal stage-and-gate process in Figure 3.13: much higher success rates and about double the proportion of projects hitting sales and profit targets.[28] A study by A. C. Nielsen in the consumer packaged goods industry reveals that best results come from an idea-to-launch system that features rigorous stages, with gates, scorecards used at gates, and an engaged governing body (often called gatekeepers)—see Figure 3.14.[29]

Suggestion: If your firm does not have an effective new-product process in place—or if it is more than three years old, or it seems a little cumbersome and creaky—the design and implementation of an up-to-date, rapid, and professional idea-to-launch system should become a top-priority task. More in the next chapter.

TOWARD A *STAGE-GATE* NEW-PRODUCT SYSTEM

This chapter has highlighted nine critical success drivers of innovation that pertain to the business unit: a clear innovation strategy, better focus (doing fewer and better projects), leveraging the business's core competencies and targeting attractive markets, fostering effective cross-functional teams, a positive climate and culture and the right role for senior management, adequate resources in place, and the need for a well-crafted idea-to-launch system. The previous chapter delivered eight other critical success drivers, much more tactical and project specific in nature. The success drivers from these two chapters are based not on hearsay and speculation, but on facts—on the many published research studies[*] that have probed new-product performance, both successes and failures, at the project level as well as at the business-unit level.

Now the challenge begins: to translate these success drivers into operational reality. That's the role of a new-product stage-and-gate system. In the next chapter, we'll fashion these success drivers into a roadmap, a blueprint, or a playbook that is designed to drive new-product projects from idea through to launch—successfully and in a time-efficient manner: *Stage-Gate*.

---

[*] By published, I mean "published in a legitimate refereed journal," not just self-published, as so many research or consulting firms do. Thus, the research and results presented here have stood the test of a rigorous and independent peer review by experts in the field. The results are therefore credible.

4

THE *STAGE-GATE®* IDEA-TO-LAUNCH SYSTEM*

A process is a methodology that is developed to replace the old ways and to guide corporate activity year after year. It is not a special guest. It is not temporary. It is not to be tolerated for a while and then abandoned.

—THOMAS H. BERRY, *Managing the Total Quality Transformation*[1]

WHATE IS *STAGE-GATE?*

Stage-Gate® is a *conceptual and operational map* for moving new-product projects from idea to launch and beyond—a blueprint for managing the new-product development process to improve effectiveness and efficiency. *Stage-Gate* is a system or process not unlike a playbook for a North American football team: It maps out what needs to be done, play by play, huddle by huddle—as well as how to do it—in order to win the game. *Stage-Gate* is based on the premise that some projects and project teams really understand how to win—they get it![2] Indeed, *Stage-Gate* was originally developed *from research that modeled what the winning teams that undertake bold innovation projects do.*[3] But too many projects and teams miss the mark—they simply

---

* *Stage-Gate*® is a trademark of the Stage-Gate International Inc. in the United States and Australia, and of R. G. Cooper & Associates in Canada. In the European Union, the trademark is held by R. G. Cooper.

fail to perform. A closer inspection often reveals that these failed projects are plagued by missing steps and activities, poor organizational design and leadership, inadequate quality of execution, unreliable data, and missed timelines. So these teams and projects need help—help in the form of a *playbook* based on what winning teams do. *Stage-Gate* is simply that playbook.

Stage-Gate Now Used in Most Leading Firms

A world-class process for product innovation, such as *Stage-Gate*, is one solution to what ails so many firms' new-product efforts.[4] Facing increased pressure to *reduce the cycle time yet improve their new-product success rates*, companies look to *Stage-Gate* systems to manage, direct, and accelerate their product-innovation efforts. That is, they have developed a systematic process—a blueprint or playbook—for moving a new-product project through the various stages and steps from idea to launch. But most important, they have built into their playbook the many *critical success drivers* and *best practices* in order to heighten the effectiveness of their programs. Consider these examples:

- 3M has traditionally had an enviable new-product track record. An innovative corporate culture and climate are often cited as 3M's secret to success. But for years 3M has also had in place various stage-and-gate systems for managing the innovation process: 3M's NPI (new product innovation), a five-stage system for new products; and their NTI (new technology innovation), a three-stage process that is more iterative, for technology projects (closer to fundamental science projects).[5]
- Corning Glass has always been a leading innovator, beginning generations ago with Pyrex glass, and in more recent years with fiber optics and glass for flat-panel displays. Corning's successes continue. What drives new products to market at Corning is the company's version of a *Stage-Gate* process, designed and originally installed in 1987. The process has been refined and streamlined over the years (see Figure 4.1) and has gone through many evolutions, with the latest version recently introduced and used for the Gorilla Glass project (more on that in Chapter 5).[6]
- Exxon Chemical began piloting a *Stage-Gate* process in its polymers business unit in the late 1980s. So successful was the process that Exxon Chemical then rolled the method out throughout its entire chemical business, and around the world. According to the father of Exxon's product-innovation process (PIP), "The implementation of the PIP has probably had more impact on the way we do business than any other initiative at Exxon Chemical undertaken in the last decade." Today, the process

Figure 4.1: Corning's *Stage-Gate* Process Has Gone Through a Number of Evolutions, Including Overlapping Stages (Concurrency) and Streamlining

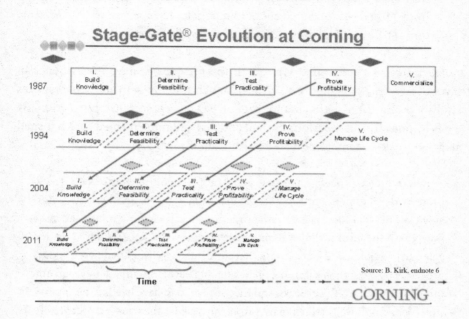

Source: B. Kirk, endnote 6

has been adopted by other parts of Exxon, and has become a pervasive decision process: It is used for virtually *every type of project* in the corporation—from process developments to major capital expenditures (plant expansions), and even for oil-well drilling!

- LEGO, the successful Danish toy manufacturer, replaces about one-third of its product line every year with new items. In order to accomplish this rapid introduction of new products consistently, successfully, and year after year, a process was needed. Today, LEGO relies on a *Stage-Gate* new-product process to ensure that everything comes together for these many and rapid launches each year. And in 2016, LEGO introduced its latest version of *Stage-Gate*—a hybrid model with Agile built in—in the LEGO Education business unit (more on this topic in Chapter 6).[7]

- ITT implemented a five-stage *Stage-Gate* system in the early 2000s, called Value-Based Product Development (VBPD). At that time, new product sales were far below other global manufacturers of engineered products, hovering around 15 percent of annual sales. ITT's new VBPD forced a number of best practices into the business units, such as voice-of-customer studies, solid front-end homework, rigorous gates complete with scorecards for gatekeepers, and effective cross-functional teams. The performance improvements were dramatic: With *Stage-Gate* in place, along with other elements of the Innovation Diamond, new-product sales had more than doubled—going from 15 percent to 35 percent of annual sales in nine years![8] (At the same time, ITT also adopted the "diamond" shown in Figure 1.2.)

Stage-Gate methods work! We saw in the previous chapter the evidence in favor of adopting stage-and-gate idea-to-launch systems. A major best-practices study of product innovation found that *having such a process was just a given.* By a ten-to-one ratio, best performers had adopted and implemented such a formal stage-and-gate system. Here is an excerpt from that study:[9]

A new-product process—a "game plan" or playbook to guide NPD [new-product development] projects from idea to launch—is another much heralded key to NPD success. By "new-product process," we mean more than just a flow-chart; the term includes all process elements—the stages, stage activities, gates, deliverables, and gate criteria that constitute a well-defined new-product process. For more than a decade, managements have been urged to design and implement such a NPD process, and they appeared to have heeded the experts. Indeed, having a well-defined new-product process is the *strongest practice* observed in the sample of businesses [in the study].

A more recent study reveals even stronger results: "Nearly all of our best performers (90 percent, compared to only 44.4 percent of worst performers) have a clear, defined new-product development process—a game plan, playbook, or *Stage-Gate* system that guides new-product development projects from idea to launch. In fact, best performers are between two and three times more likely to have implemented a successful new-product development process than worst performers, suggesting that simply having a formal process is itself a best practice."[10]

SEVEN GOALS OF A NEW-PRODUCT IDEA-TO-LAUNCH SYSTEM

The challenge in this chapter is this: Given the eight critical success drivers in Chapter 2 about how to manage new-product projects, and given the next nine success drivers in Chapter 3 that capture practices at the business-unit level—drivers all gleaned from new-product success-and-failure experiences and the various benchmarking studies—how can we translate these findings into an operational and effective new-product playbook? For example, how does one build in quality of execution, or a strong market focus, or better predevelopment homework? Let's begin with a quick look at what this new-product system must achieve.

Goal #1: Quality of Execution

The argument that the proponents of total quality management make goes something like this: "The definition of quality is precise: It means meeting all the requirements all the time. It is based on the principle that all work is a process. It focuses on improving business processes to eliminate errors." The concept is perfectly logical and essentially simple. Most smart things are. And the same logic can be applied to new-product development.

Product innovation is a process: It begins with an idea—in a best-practice system, even earlier—and culminates in a successful product launch or beyond. But processes aren't new to the business environment. There are many examples of well-run processes in business: for example, manufacturing processes, information processes, and so on.

A *quality-of-execution crisis* exists in the product innovation process, however. Simply stated, things don't happen as they should, when they should, and as well as they should. We saw in the last two chapters clear evidence that many key actions, from VoC work and front-end homework to planning and executing the launch, were deficient in too many firms and projects. Serious gaps, such as omissions of steps and poor quality of execution, are the rule rather than the exception. And these deficiencies are strongly tied to product failures. We also saw that these activities—their quality of execution and whether these activities are carried out at all—have a dramatic impact on success or failure, with best-performing innovators typically executing these tasks far more proficiently than the rest.

This quality-of-execution crisis in product innovation provides strong evidence in support of the need for a more *systematic and quality approach* to the way firms conceive, develop, and launch new products. The way to deal with the quality problem is to visualize product innovation as a process, and to apply *process management* and *quality management techniques* to this process. Note that any process in business can be managed with a view to quality. Get the details of your process right, and the result will be a high-quality output.

Quality of execution is the goal of the new-product process. More specifically, the ideal playbook should:

1. *Focus on completeness:* Ensure that activities that are central to the success of a new-product project are indeed carried out—no gaps, no omissions, a complete process.

2. *Focus on quality:* Ensure that the execution of these activities is first class; that is, treat innovation as a process, emphasize DIRTFT (do it right the first time), and build in quality controls and checks.

3. *Focus on the important:* Devote attention and resources to the pivotal and to particularly weak steps in the new-product process, notably the front-end and market-facing activities.

The new-product system is simply a *process-management tool.* We build into this process quality of execution, in much the same way that quality programs have been successfully implemented on the factory floor.

Goal #2: Sharper Focus, Better Prioritization

Most companies' new-product efforts suffer from a lack of focus: *too many projects and not enough resources.* Earlier, adequate resources were identified as a principal driver of companies' new-product performance; but a lack of resources plagues too many firms' development efforts. And quality of execution (Goal #1 above) certainly won't be achieved until the resource problem is solved.

Sometimes this lack of resources is simply that: Management hasn't devoted the needed people and money to the business's new-product effort. But often, this resource problem stems from a lack of focus, the result of inadequate project evaluations: the failure to set priorities and make tough Go/Kill decisions. In short, the gates are weak—they lack teeth! Indeed, most of the critical evaluation points—from initial screening through to prelaunch business analysis—are characterized by serious weaknesses: decisions not made, little or no real prioritization, poor information inputs, no criteria for decisions, and inconsistent or haphazard decision-making.

The need is for a *new-product funnel, rather than a tunnel.* A "new-product funnel" builds in tough Go/Kill decision points throughout the process; poor projects are weeded out; scarce resources are redirected toward the truly deserving projects (the high-value ones); and more focus is the result. One funneling method is to build the new-product process around *a set of gates* or Go/Kill decision points. These gates are the "get-out" points where we ask, "Are we still in the game?" Gates are analogous to the *quality-control checkpoints* on a manufacturing plant. They pose two fundamental questions:

1. Are we doing the project right?
2. Are we doing the right project?

Gates are preset at different points throughout the new-product system. Each gate has its *own set of metrics and criteria* for passing, much like a quality-control check in production. These criteria and questions deal with various facets of the project, including:

- Readiness check criteria: Is the project ready for the gate meeting? Are the deliverables in place? Do we have data integrity?
- Criteria that gauge the business rationale for investing in the project—Go/ Kill and prioritization criteria. For example, what's the NPV of the project?
- Criteria that focus on the forward plan (the *action plan* for the next stage), resources needed, resource availability, and the decision to commit resources to the project.

These gates serve to map and guide the new-product system. They signal a "Kill" decision in the event of a project whose economics and business rationale become negative, when barriers to completion become insurmountable, or when the project is far over budget or way behind schedule. Gates prevent projects from moving too far ahead into the next stage until the critical activities have been completed, and in a quality fashion. And gates chart the path forward: They determine what tasks and milestones lie ahead, and the resources, budgets, and time frames for these tasks.

Goal #3: Fast-Paced Parallel Processing with Spirals

New-product project leaders face a dilemma. On the one hand, they are urged by senior management to compress the cycle time—to shorten the elapsed time from idea to launch. On the other hand, they are asked to improve the effectiveness of product development: Cut down the failure rate—do it right! This desire to "do it right" suggests a more thorough, perhaps longer process.

Parallel processing is one solution to the need for a complete and quality process, yet one that meets the time pressures of today's fast-paced business world. Traditionally, new-product projects have been managed via a *series approach*—one task strung out after another, in series. The analogy is that of a relay race, with each department running with the project for its one hundred meters. Phrases such as "hand off," "passing the project on," "dropping the ball," and even "throwing it over the wall" are common in this relay-race approach to new products.

In marked contrast to the relay-race or sequential approach, with parallel processing many activities are undertaken *concurrently* rather than in series.

The appropriate analogy is that of a rugby football match rather than a relay race. In rugby, the entire team runs down the field in parallel, vigorously interacting with each other all the way; and a lot happens fast! With parallel processing, the effort is far more intense than a relay race and more work gets done in an elapsed time period: Three or four activities are done simultaneously and by different members on the project team. Second, there is less chance of an activity or task being dropped because of lack of time: The activity is done in parallel and hence does not extend the total elapsed project time. And finally, the entire new-product process becomes cross-functional and multidisciplinary: The whole team—marketing, R&D, engineering, operations—is on the field together, participates actively in each play, and takes part in each gate review or scrum.

A second key is *building validation spirals* into this rugby approach—a series of "build-test-feedback-and-revise" loops or iterations with customers, introduced in Chapter 2. Spirals validate the product design early and minimize wasted time; they prevent moving too far down the field with incorrect requirement assumptions. Spiral development is based on the premise that customers don't know what they want until they see it, so *get something in front of customers fast*. It's the approach that some people call "fail early, fail often," except here I'm not advocating deliberate failures but rather a series of *quick-easy-and-cheap tests*—relying on early and inexpensive versions of the product (a model, virtual prototype, or protocept) to seek fast feedback and confirm the design before sinking more money into the project. Spiral development fits well into parallel processing, and both approaches lead to accelerated development, but not at the expense of quality of execution.

Goal #4: A True Cross-Functional Team Approach

The new-product process is multifunctional: It requires the inputs and active participation of players from many different functions in the organization. The multifunctional nature of innovation coupled with the desire for parallel processing means that a *true cross-functional team approach is* mandatory in order to win at new products. I emphasize the word "true" in describing a cross-functional team, as opposed to the many "fake" or "pretend" teams one sees in business. You can tell a *fake team* when:

- So-called team members show up at meetings, but they aren't really committed to the team—they're there as *functional representatives* at the meeting.
- They aren't given release time from their "day job"—this team activity is just piled on top of an already hectic schedule.

- They promise to get things done by the next team meeting, but invariably their "real job" gets in the way and their functional boss gives them some other assignment.
- They are given lots of responsibility for the project and very little authority—the functional bosses still make the decisions about the project, often micromanaging from on high.
- Team members receive no recognition based on the results achieved by the team (for example, individuals' key performance indicators (KPIs) are not based on the team's performance).

Sound familiar? Time to have a hard look at the way you're organized for new products. The ideal new-product system demands that every significant new-product project have a true cross-functional project team. Essential characteristics of this team are (from Chapter 3 and Figures 3.8 and 3.9):

- The project team is *cross-functional*, with committed team players from the various functions and departments—marketing, engineering, R&D, and operations. *Release time from their normal jobs* to spend on the project is provided to team members (typically people and time commitments are decided at gate meetings).
- The project team has a *clearly defined team captain or leader*. This leader is dedicated to the project (not spread across numerous other duties or projects) and is accountable from beginning to end of the project—not just for one stage.
- The leader has *formal authority*: This means co-opting authority from the functional heads. When those in senior management approve the team's action plan at gate meetings, they also commit the resources—money, people, and release time—to the project leader and team. At the same time, senior management *transfers decision-making power* to the team. Expectations and the scope of this authority are made very clear to the team at each gate.
- The leader has an *entrepreneurial role*, as highlighted in Chapter 3, in which the leader not only *leads the team*, but also promotes the project, seeks resources, and handles the external interfaces of the project, especially with senior management.
- For larger projects, a *project manager* can also be on the team, but this is a different and more mechanical job than the project leader—a project manager is responsible for project management, namely, timelines, budgets, meetings, etc.

- Some of these resources are "ring fenced": That is, people working on the project *are 100 percent dedicated* to new-product efforts—to this one project and perhaps one other. New-product development *is* their full-time job!
- The team structure is fluid, with new members joining the team (or old ones leaving it) as work requirements demand. But *a small core group of responsible, committed, and accountable team players should be present from beginning to end of project.*
- Senior management holds the entire team accountable for results—all team members, not just the team leader. And rewards—such as merit increases, KPIs, bonuses, or variable salary—are tied to the team's performance and results.

Goal #5: A Strong Market Focus with Voice-of-the-Customer (VoC) Built In

A market focus is the *missing ingredient in too many new-product projects*. A lack of VoC inputs and inadequate market assessment are consistently cited as reasons for new-product failure. Moreover, the market-facing activities tend to be the weakest in the new-product process, yet are strongly linked to success. Although many managers profess a market focus, the evidence—where the time and money are spent—proves otherwise. If higher new-product success rates are the goal, then a market focus—executing the key marketing activities in a quality fashion—must be built into the new-product system as a matter of routine rather than by exception. Market inputs must play a decisive role from beginning to end of the project. *Ten market-facing actions are integral and recommended actions* in the new-product playbook (but they are often missing)—see Table 4.1.

Goal #6: Better Front-End Homework

New-product success or failure is largely *decided in the first few plays of the game*—in those crucial steps and tasks that precede the actual development of the product. Solid front-end homework and sharp early product definition are key ingredients in a successful new-product process, according to our benchmarking studies, and result in higher success rates and profitability in studies of project performance. The front-end homework helps to define the product and to build the Business Case for development. Ironically, most of the money and time spent on projects is devoted to the middle and back-end stages of the process, while the front-end actions suffer from errors of omission, poor quality of execution, and underresourcing. The ideal new-product system ensures that these early stages are carried out before the project is allowed to proceed—

TABLE 4.1: TEN VITAL MARKET-FACING ACTIONS TO BUILD INTO YOUR NEW-PRODUCT PLAYBOOK

1. *Customer-based idea generation:* working with lead users and key customers to identify problems, "points of pain," gaps, and emerging opportunities for new solutions.
2. *Preliminary market assessment:* an early, relatively inexpensive step designed to assess market attractiveness and to gauge possible market acceptance for the proposed new product.
3. *Market analysis:* a more detailed study to determine market size and potential, to define market segments and industry structure, and to identify success factors (what it takes to succeed in this market).
4. *VoC work to determine user and customer needs and wants:* in-depth, face-to-face and onsite interviews with customers or camping out with customers (ethnography) to determine customer problems, needs, wants, preferences, likes, dislikes, buying criteria, and so forth, as an input to the design of the new product.
5. *Competitive analysis:* an assessment of competitors—their products and product deficiencies, prices, costs, technologies, production capacities, and marketing strategies.
6. *Concept test:* a test of the proposed product—perhaps as a virtual product or protocept—to determine likely market acceptance. Note that the product development is not underway yet, but a model or representation of the product is displayed to prospective users to gauge reaction and purchase intent, the first of many spirals.
7. *Customer iterations during Development:* continuing concept, protocept and product testing throughout the Development stage—spirals—using rapid prototypes, models, and partially completed products to gauge customer reaction, validate the product, and seek feedback.
8. *User tests:* field trials, preference tests, in-use tests, or beta tests using the finished product (or commercial prototype) with users to verify the performance of the product under customer conditions, and to confirm intent to purchase and market acceptance.
9. *Test market or trial sell:* an optional mini-launch or "soft launch" of the product in a limited geographic area, single sales territory or to a handful of customers (or a simulated test market). This is a test of all elements of the marketing mix, including the product itself.
10. *Market launch:* a proficient launch, based on a solid market launch plan, and backed by sufficient resources.

before the project is allowed to become a full-fledged development. Activities essential to building the Business Case become mandatory plays before the project is given formal approval for Development. What are these essential front-end activities in a well-designed system? They are outlined in Table 4.2.

Goal #7: Products with Competitive Advantage— Bold Innovations

Don't forget to build in product superiority at every opportunity—differentiated products, unique benefits, and a *compelling value proposition* for the customer. This is perhaps the most important driver of new-product profitability, yet all too often, when redesigning their new-product processes, firms fall into the trap of repeating current, often faulty, practices: There's no attempt to seek *truly superior products*. And so the results are predictable—more ho-hum, tired products. Here's how to drive the quest for product advantage and bolder innovations:

- Ensure that at least *some of the criteria at every gate focus on product superiority*. Questions such as "Is there a 'wow' factor in the product—will it excite the customer or user?" "Is there a compelling value proposition here? Show me!" "Does the product solve a major customer problem?" "Does it have at least one element of competitive advantage?" and "Does it offer the user new or different benefits?" become vital to rate and rank would-be projects. These questions put some pressure on this team to dig harder to find real competitive advantage, and may also rightly kill some major projects where no competitive advantage exists.
- Require that certain *key actions designed to deliver product superiority be front and center* in each stage of the process. Some of these have been highlighted above (Goal #5 above and also in Table 4.1) and include: customer-focused ideation, VoC studies, competitive product analysis, concept and protocept tests, spirals and constant and iterative validations with customers during the Development stage via rapid-prototype-and-tests, and trial sells.
- Demand that project teams deliver evidence of product superiority to project Go/Kill reviews: Make product superiority an important deliverable and discussion issue at such meetings (rather than just dwelling on the financial projections).
- Ensure that the product definition, so critical to new-product success, not only includes performance requirements and specs but is also very clear about the *compelling value proposition* for the customer.

TABLE 4.2: DO THE FRONT-END HOMEWORK—
TEN KEY ACTIONS TO BUILD IN

1. *Initial screening:* the initial decision to spend time and money on the project.
2. *Preliminary technical assessment:* an initial attempt to assess technical feasibility, outline manufacturing/operations implications, and identify technical risks and issues.
3. *Preliminary market assessment:* highlighted in Table 4.1, this is the first-pass market study.
4. *Detailed technical assessment:* detailed technical work (not development!) to show technical proof of concept (a technical solution envisioned) and identify and address technical risks and roadblocks.
5. *Operations (source-of-supply) assessment:* technical work to determine manufacturing, operations or source-of-supply implications and options, capital expenditures, and probable manufacturing or delivered costs.
6. *Detailed market studies:* includes the VoC user needs-and-wants study, market analysis, competitive analysis, and concept tests outlined in Table 4.1.
7. *Financial and business analysis:* probes the expected financial consequences and risks of the project.
8. *Product definition and Business Case:* integrates the results of the technical, operations, market, and financial analyses into a product definition, project justification, and project plan.
9. *Development of forward plan:* an action plan that includes tasks, timeline, and resources required.
10. *Decision on the Business Case:* a thorough project evaluation and decision to go to full Development.

Suggestion: Take a close look at the idea-to-launch process within your firm. Does it ensure quality of execution? Is it built around a set of gates or decision points to dump bad projects and focus resources on the truly deserving ones? Does it emphasize parallel processing—a rugby match—or does it resemble a relay race; and does it incorporate customer spirals to confirm the product design early? Does it build in an empowered, cross-functional team headed by a leader with authority? Or are you still largely functionally based, with the project moving from department to department? Does it promote a market focus, and what proportion of project expenditures goes to market-facing actions? Do you devote enough resources to the front-end or homework stages? Do you build in the actions laid out in Tables 4.1 and 4.2? And do you emphasize activities and criteria designed to yield unique, bold, superior products with real competitive advantage (or does your system favor small, simple, me-too efforts)?

If some of the answers are no, then the *time is ripe to rethink your new-product playbook*. Maybe it's time to *overhaul your idea-to-launch system*—it's a bit dated, or too cumbersome, or misses many of the vital success drivers and goals outlined above. Perhaps the time is now to reinvent your innovation system with the objective of building in the best practices from Chapters 2 and 3, and the seven goals outlined above, to create your *Stage-Gate* system for the next decade.

HOW TO MANAGE RISK

The management of new products is the management of risk, so your playbook must also be designed to manage risk. Indeed, if you look closely, you'll see that most of the critical success drivers outlined in the previous two chapters investigate ways of dealing with risk. Total risk avoidance in new-product development is impossible, unless a company decides to avoid all innovation—and face a slow death.

Most of us know what is meant by the phrase "a risky situation." In product innovation, a high-risk situation is one in which much is at stake (for example, the project involves a lot of money or is strategically critical to the business) and the outcome is uncertain (for example, it is not certain that the product will be technically feasible or will do well in the marketplace). The components of risk are: *amounts at stake* and *uncertainties* (see Figure 4.2).

Russian Roulette: A Life-or-Death Gamble

Imagine for a moment that you are facing the gamble of your life. You've been invited to a millionaire's ranch for a weekend. Last night, you played poker and lost more money than you can afford—around $100,000. All of the other players are enormously wealthy cattle and oil barons. Tonight, they've given you the opportunity to get even. Each of the other ten players antes into the pot $1 million.

That's $10 million—more money than you are ever likely to see again. Here is the gamble. One of the players takes out a six-shooter pistol, removes all the bullets, and in full view of everyone, places one live bullet in the gun. He then spins the chamber. For $10 million, you are asked to point the gun at your head and pull the trigger. Will you take the gamble?

Figure 4.2: The Risk in a Development Project Has Two Components—Amounts at Stake and Level of Uncertainty—and *Stage-Gate* Manages Both

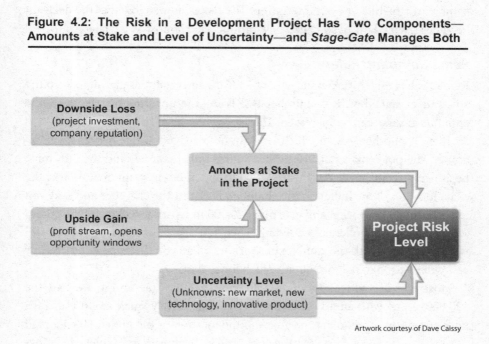

Artwork courtesy of Dave Caissy

Most people would say no! But the situation exhibits the key elements of risk: a great deal at stake (the $10 million or your life) and a high degree of uncertainty—the bullet could be in any location.

Reducing the Stakes

This hypothetical gamble represents an unacceptable risk level. Yet this is precisely the way some managers play at new products: huge amounts at stake, coupled with high levels of uncertainty. Others are simply fearful of any risk, and walk away, which may also be the wrong decision. How can the risk be reduced to an acceptable level—so that you can take the bold gamble? And how can risk be reduced in new-product management so that you can feel comfortable about taking those bold gambles too?

One route is to *lessen the amounts at stake*. For example, use blank bullets along with ear protectors to deaden the noise, and point the gun, not at your head, but at your foot. The potential downside loss, if the gun were to fire, is that now you would merely be laughed at by a group of poker players. But upside gains are inevitably tied to downside losses. So, instead of anteing up $1 million, every player now puts in only one dollar. Will you still take the gamble? Most would reply, "Who cares?" There is no longer enough at stake to make the gamble worthwhile or even interesting. The risk is now so low that the decision becomes trivial. Lots of so-called new products are almost as trivial.

Some Gambling Rules

Rule number one in risk management is: If the uncertainties are high, keep the amounts at stake low. Rule number two is: As the uncertainties decrease, the amounts at stake can be increased. These two rules keep risk under control.

There is another way in which risk can be managed in our hypothetical example. The pot remains at $10 million, a live bullet is used, and the gun must be aimed at your head. But this time, your opponent, in plain view, marks the exact location of the bullet on the chamber. He spins the chamber and asks you to reach into your pocket and give him $20,000 in return for a look at the gun to see where the live bullet has ended up. Then you decide whether or not you still wish to proceed with the gamble. In short, he offers you the opportunity to *buy an option*—to "have a look"—for a much lower cost.

Most of us would consider this a "good gamble" (assuming we had the $20,000)—one with an acceptable risk level. A relatively small amount of cash buys an option or a look at the gun and the location of the bullet. Having paid for the look and determined the bullet's location, you then make your second decision: Are you still in the game? It's much like buying options on a property you might wish to purchase. The risk has been reduced by converting an "all-or-nothing" decision into a two-stage decision: two steps and two decision points or gates. Your ability to purchase information was also instrumental in minimizing risk: Information has reduced the uncertainty of the situation. Finally, the ability to withdraw from the game—to get out—also reduced risk.

> Manage risk by breaking the process into increments. When the uncertainties and unknowns are high, keep the spending low.

Three more gambling rules designed to manage risk evolve from this second gambling situation. Rule number three is: Incrementalize the decision process— break the all-or-nothing decision into a series of stages and decisions—in effect, buying options and doing due diligence. Rule number four is: Be prepared to pay for relevant information to reduce risk. And rule number five: Provide for get-out points—decision points that provide the opportunity to fold your hand, walk away, or get out of the game.

Risks in New-Product Management

These five rules of risk management apply directly to new products. Near the beginning of a project, the amounts at stake are usually low, and the uncertainty

Figure 4.3: As Amounts at Stake (Investment) Increase Over the Life of the Project, Uncertainties Are Driven Down and Risk Is Managed

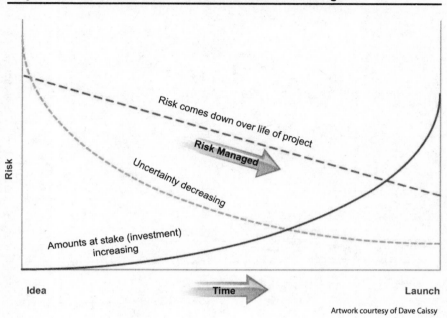

Artwork courtesy of Dave Caissy

of the outcome is very high. As the project progresses, the cost of the project and thus the amounts at stake begin to increase (see Figure 4.3). If risk is to be managed successfully, the uncertainties of outcomes must be deliberately driven down as the stakes increase. Further, the stakes must not be allowed to increase unless the uncertainties do come down.

Uncertainties and amounts at stake must be kept in balance. Unfortunately, in many new-product projects, the amounts at stake increase as the project progresses while the uncertainties remain fairly high (see Figure 4.4). Additional spending fails to reduce the uncertainties! The project moves ahead with decisions based on assumptions and hearsay—a lack of facts. By the end of the project, as launch nears, management is no more sure about the commercial outcome of the venture than at day one of the project. The amounts at stake have increased, uncertainty remains high, and the risk level is unacceptably high.

For every thousand-dollar increase in the amounts at stake, the uncertainty curve in Figure 4.3 must be reduced by an equivalent amount. To do otherwise is to let risk get out of hand. In short, every expenditure in the new-product process— every notch up on the amounts-at-stake curve in Figure 4.3—must bring a corresponding reduction in the uncertainty curve. The entire new-product process,

Figure 4.4: Amounts at Stake (Investment) Increase, but Uncertainties Don't Come Down Much and Risk Runs Out of Control

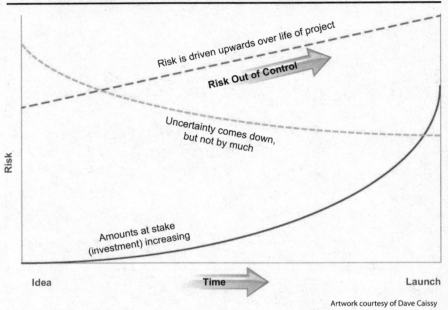

Artwork courtesy of Dave Caissy

from idea to launch, can be viewed as an *uncertainty reduction process* involving the *purchase of options*. Remember the five gambling rules:

1. When the uncertainties of the new-product project are high (that is, when the prospects of success are uncertain), keep the amounts at stake low. When you don't know where you're going, take small steps—buy a series of options rather than investing the entire amount.
2. As the uncertainties decrease, let the amounts at stake increase. As you learn more about where you're going, take bigger and bigger steps.
3. Incrementalize the new-product process into a series of steps or stages. Treat it as a series of *options purchases*. Each step should be more costly than the one before.
4. View each stage as a means of reducing uncertainty. Remember that information is the key to uncertainty reduction. Each step in the process that involves an expenditure must reduce uncertainty by an equivalent amount.
5. Provide for *timely evaluation, decision, and get-out points*. These decision points (or gates) pull together all the new information from the previous stage and pose the questions, "Are you still in the game? Should you proceed to the next stage, or kill the project now?"

Figure 4.5: *Stage-Gate* Is a Conceptual and Operational Roadmap from Idea Through to Launch and Beyond

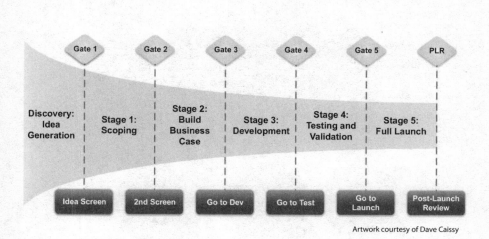

Artwork courtesy of Dave Caissy

Suggestion: The five decision rules outlined above apply to almost any high-risk situation. Does your company follow them in its day-to-day management practices? Review your firm's new-product practices, perhaps using an actual case, and assess whether your management group is handling risk appropriately.

> Seven best-practice goals together with the key success drivers from the last two chapters have been fashioned into the *Stage-Gate system—a conceptual and operational model* for moving a new-product project from idea to launch.

A BEST-PRACTICE NEW-PRODUCT SYSTEM
The Structure of the Stage-Gate System

The seven key goals and the five gambling rules, together with the success drivers from the last two chapters, have been fashioned into a best-practice *Stage-Gate* system—a *conceptual and operational* model for moving a new-product project from idea to launch.[11] This *Stage-Gate* system is a playbook or blueprint for managing product innovation to improve effectiveness and efficiency—see Figure 4.5.

Stage-Gate is elegantly simple, and makes a lot of sense: a series of information-gathering stages followed by decision-making gates. *Stage-Gate* treats product innovation as a process, and any process can be modeled and made better and more efficient. Instead of viewing product development as a black box—ideas go in and commercially ready products come out (or a black

Figure 4.6: The *Stage-Gate* System Breaks Product Development Into a Series of Manageable Stages with Increasing Resource Commitments

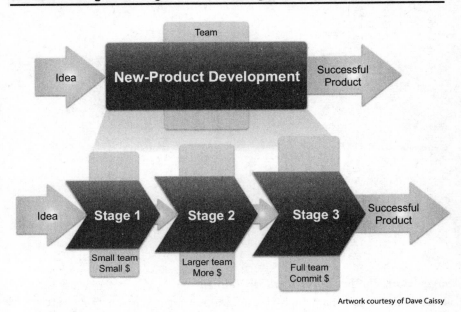

Artwork courtesy of Dave Caissy

hole—ideas go in and nothing comes out)—*Stage-Gate* breaks the innovation process into a predetermined set of manageable, discrete stages (see Figure 4.6). Each stage consists of a set of prescribed, cross-functional, and parallel activities:

- Teams of people undertaking some vital activities to gather some data,
- followed by data analysis and interpretation,
- to create the key deliverables (information),
- on the basis of which senior management—the resource owners—make the Go or Kill decision.

And the process repeats (see Figure 4.7). The entrance to (or exit from) each stage is a gate: The gates control the process and serve as the quality control and Go/Kill checkpoints. This stage-and-gate format leads to the name "*Stage-Gate* system."

The Stages

Each stage is designed to gather information needed to move the project to the next gate or decision point. Different types of information—market, technical, operations—is important, and so the work within each stage is cross-functional:

Figure 4.7: *Stage-Gate* Consists of a Set of Information-Gathering Stages Followed by Go/Kill Decision Gates

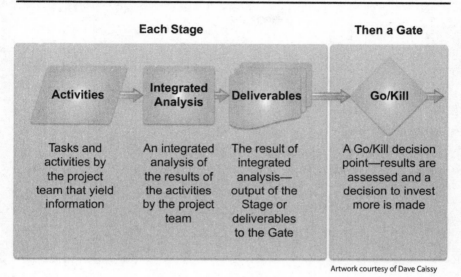

Artwork courtesy of Dave Caissy

There is no "R&D stage" or "marketing stage." And each stage is defined by the activities within it—a set of parallel and cross-functional tasks that incorporate best practices, for example:

- the ten vital market-related actions and the key homework activities listed above in Tables 4.1 and 4.2;
- some of the success drivers, for example, quality of execution and sharp, early product definition; and
- the seven goals, for example, the quest for a superior, differentiated product, that we saw earlier in this and the last two chapters.

Some of these activities are mandatory; others are merely prescribed and highly recommended—*Stage-Gate is a guide, not a rule book*. These stage-activities are designed to gather information and drive uncertainties down. And each stage typically costs more than the preceding one: The process is an incremental commitment one, like buying a series of options.

The general flow of the typical *Stage-Gate* system is shown pictorially in Figure 4.8. The stages are:

0. *Discovery*: prework designed to discover and uncover opportunities and generate ideas.

Figure 4.8: The Five Stages in the Typical Idea-to-Launch *Stage-Gate* System from Discovery (Ideation) Through to Launch

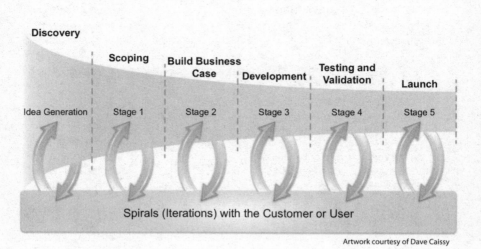

Artwork courtesy of Dave Caissy

Figure 4.9 Each Stage Is Preceded by a Gate—the Decision or Go/Kill Points in the System

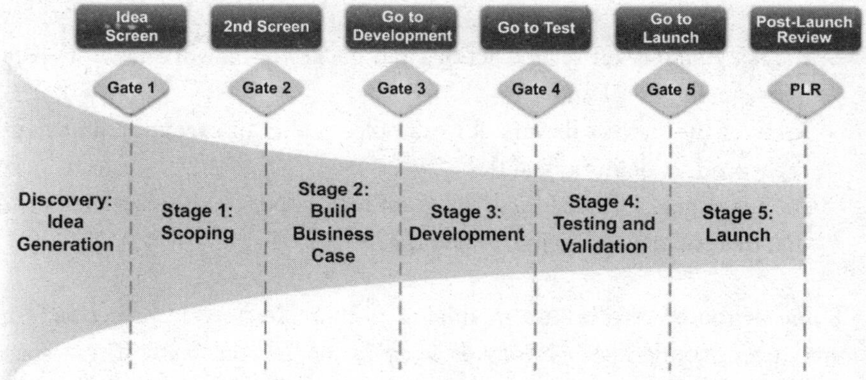

Gates are where projects get resources and are prioritized—
they get on management's radar screen

Gates are also the quality-control checkpoints in the system:
- Are you doing the project right?
- Are you doing the right project?

Artwork courtesy of Dave Caissy

1. *Scoping:* a quick, preliminary investigation and scoping of the project—largely desk research.
2. *Build the Business Case*: a much more detailed investigation involving primary research—both market and technical—leading to a Business Case, including product and project definition, project justification, and a forward plan (or action plan).
3. *Development:* the actual detailed design and development of the new product, and the design of the operations or production process.
4. *Testing and Validation:* market tests or trials, technical tests, and operations trials to verify and validate the proposed new product, and its marketing and production/operations.
5. *Launch:* commercialization—beginning of full operations or production, marketing, and selling.

The Gates

Preceding each stage is a gate or a *Go/Kill decision point*—see Figure 4.9.* The gates are the huddles on the football field: They are the points where the team converges and where all new information is reviewed. Gates serve as quality-control checkpoints, as Go/Kill and prioritization decision points, and as points where the path forward for the next play or stage of the process is agreed to.

The structure of each gate is similar (Figure 4.10). Gates consist of:

1. A set of required *gate deliverables*: what the project leader and team must bring to the decision point (e.g., the results of a set of completed tasks). These deliverables are visible, are based on a standard menu for each gate, and are decided at the output of the previous gate. Management's expectations for project teams are thus made very clear. Deliverables are usually defined in the format of *templates*.
2. *Gate criteria* against which the project is judged: These can include "must meet" or knock out questions (a checklist) designed to weed out misfit or "nonstarter" projects quickly, for example:

    • Is the proposed project within our business or strategic mandate?
    • Does it meet our EH&S policies (environmental, health, and safety)?

---

* Strictly speaking, the gates follow the stages—gather information, then make a Go/Kill decision. But it's more practical to treat them as entrance gates—opening the door to the next stage.

Figure 4.10: Gates Have a Common Format—Inputs, Criteria, and Outputs

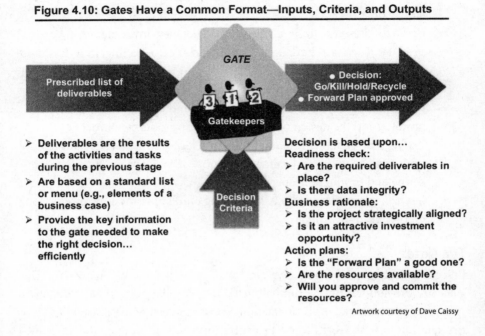

Artwork courtesy of Dave Caissy

There are also scorecard criteria ("should meet" criteria or desirable factors), which are scored and added (a point count system), which are also used to make Go/Kill decisions as well as to prioritize projects, for example:

- the strength of the value proposition or product's competitive advantage,
- ability to leverage core competencies in this project,
- relative market attractiveness, and
- size of the financial return versus the risk.

3. Defined *gate outputs*: for example, a decision, usually one of four possible outcomes: *Go, Kill, Hold, or Recycle;* and in the event of a Go decision, an approved action plan for the next stage complete with resource commitments (people required, money, and person-days), an agreed timeline, and a list of deliverables and date for the next gate.

Gates are usually staffed by senior managers from different functions, who own the resources required by the project leader and team for the next stage. They are called the *gatekeepers*, and are a predefined group for each of the five gates. For example, for larger projects, Gates 3, 4, and 5 are often staffed

Figure 4.11: This Five-Stage Idea-to-Launch *Stage-Gate®* System Is for Major and Higher Risk New-Product Projects

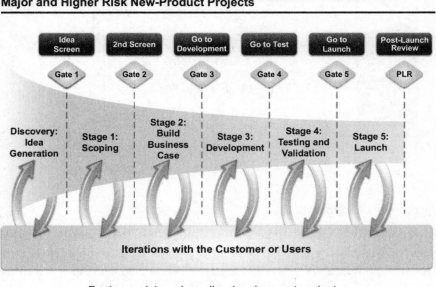

For lower-risk and smaller development projects,
use an abbreviated version: two to three Gates

Artwork courtesy of Dave Caissy

by the leadership team of the business—the head of the business and the heads of marketing/sales, technology, operations, and finance. Earlier gates are often staffed by middle management, as the resource commitments are less.

> Gates feature deliverables (what the project team delivers to the gate); criteria to make the Go/Kill and prioritization decisions (often in the form of a scorecard); and gate outputs (the Go/Kill/Hold/Recycle decision and what each decision translates into in practice).

AN OVERVIEW OF THE *STAGE-GATE* SYSTEM

Now for a bird's-eye look at the *Stage-Gate* system—an overview of what's involved at each stage and gate. In later chapters, we'll lower the microscope on the Discovery stage, or how to generate breakthrough ideas (Chapter 7). Chapters 8 and 9 take a close look at how to design and operate gates or decision points. And Chapters 5 and 6 look at next generation versions of the gating system. But for now, let's just have a *quick walk-through* of the *basic model* designed for larger new-product projects, which you can follow stage by stage in Figure 4.11.

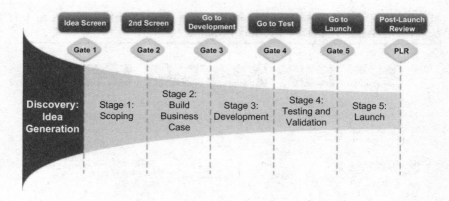

Discovery or Ideation

Ideas are the feedstock or trigger to the process, and they make or break the system. Don't expect a superb new-product process to overcome a deficiency in good new-product ideas. The need for great ideas coupled with the high attrition rate of ideas means that the idea-generation stage is pivotal: You need great ideas and lots of them.

Many companies consider ideation so important that they handle this as a formal stage in the process, the one we call Discovery—that is, they build in a *defined, proactive idea-generation and capture system.* Many activities can be part of the Discovery stage in order to stimulate the creation of great new-product ideas. Such activities include: undertaking fundamental but directed technical research; seeking new technological possibilities; working with lead or innovative users; utilizing VoC research to capture unarticulated needs and customer problems; competitive analysis and inverse brainstorming of competitive products; installing an idea-suggestion scheme to stimulate ideas from your own employees; scanning the outside world and employing "open innovation" to seek external ideas; and using your strategic planning exercise to uncover disruptions, gaps, and opportunities in the marketplace. More in Chapter 7.

> Ideation is a proactive and defined set of activities designed to generate breakthrough new product ideas—ideas with real competitive advantage. Many sources and methods exist for generating great ideas.

The deliverable to Gate 1 is the idea, usually captured on a one-page simple *idea template.*

Gate 1: Idea Screen

The Idea Screen is the first decision to commit resources to the project: The project is born at this point. If the decision is Go, the project moves into the Scoping or preliminary investigation stage. Thus, Gate 1 signals a preliminary but tentative commitment to the project: a flickering green light. Gate 1 is a "gentle screen" and amounts to subjecting the project to a handful of key must-meet and should-meet criteria. These criteria deal with strategic alignment, project feasibility, magnitude of opportunity and market attractiveness, product advantage, ability to leverage the firm's resources, and fit with company policies. Financial criteria are typically not part of this first screen, because so little is known, and besides, the resources to be committed are quite small at this point. A checklist for the must-meet criteria and a scorecard (point-count rating scales) for the should-meet criteria can be used to help focus the discussion and rank projects in this early screen:

An *example*: Exxon Chemical implemented its PIP (product-innovation process), whose initial gate has a handful of key yes/no criteria:

- Strategic fit: Does the proposal fit within a market or technology area defined by the business as an area of strategic focus?
- Market attractiveness: Are the market size, growth, and opportunity attractive?
- Technical feasibility: Is there a reasonable likelihood that the product can be developed and produced?
- Killer variables: Do any known killer variables exist (e.g., obsolescence, environmental issues, legislative actions)?

At this "Start Gate" meeting, project ideas are reviewed against these four criteria, using a paper-and-pencil approach: This list of must-meet criteria is scored (yes/no), and the answers to all questions must be "yes"; a single "no" kills the project. The gatekeepers include both technical and business (marketing) people.

Stage 1: Scoping

This first and inexpensive homework stage—"light homework"—has the objective of determining the project's technical and marketplace merits. Stage 1 is a quick scoping of the project, involving desk research or detective work—little

Figure 4.12: Stage 2 Scoping Actions and Deliverables

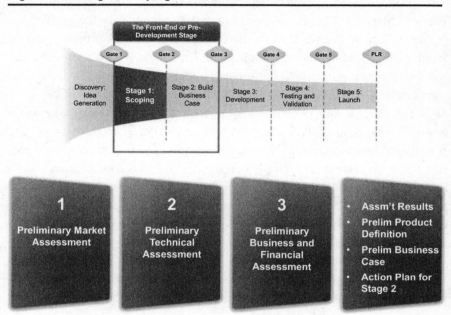

or no primary research is done here (see Figure 4.12). This stage is usually done in less than one calendar month's elapsed time, and ten to twenty person-days' work for a major project.

A preliminary market assessment is one facet of Stage 1 and involves a variety of relatively inexpensive activities: an Internet search, a library search, in-house information, a meeting with the salesforce, contacts with key users, focus groups, and even a quick concept test with a handful of potential users. The purpose is to determine market size, market potential, and likely market acceptance, and also to begin to shape the product concept.

Concurrently, a *preliminary technical assessment is* carried out, involving a quick and preliminary in-house appraisal of the proposed product. The purpose is to assess development and operations (or source-of-supply) routes; technical and operations feasibility; possible times and costs to execute; and technical, legal, and regulatory risks and roadblocks.

Stage 1 thus provides for the gathering of both market and technical information—at low cost and in a short time—to enable a cursory and first-pass financial and business analysis as input to Gate 2. A preliminary Business Case is delivered here, but based on fairly uncertain or "guesstimates" data.

Because of the limited effort, and depending on the size of the project, very often Stage 1 can be handled by a team of just several people—from marketing and technical.

The deliverables to Gate 2 are the results of the preliminary market and technical assessments, a preliminary product definition (first draft), and a preliminary Business Case, based on very rough financial estimates.

Gate 2: Second Screen

The new-product project is now subjected to a second and somewhat more rigorous screen at Gate 2. This gate is similar to Gate 1, but here the project is reevaluated in the light of the new information obtained in Stage 1. If the decision is Go at this point, the project moves into a heavier spending stage, Build Business Case.

At Gate 2, the project is subjected to a list of readiness-check questions, and also a set of must-meet and should-meet criteria similar to those used at Gate 1. Here, additional should-meet criteria may be considered, dealing with sales force and customer reaction to the proposed product, and potential legal, technical, and regulatory "killer variables," the result of new data gathered during Stage 1.

Again, a checklist and scorecard facilitate this gate decision. The financial return is determined at Gate 2, but only by a quick and simple financial calculation (for example, the Payback Period).

An example: At ITT's five-stage, five-gate *Stage-Gate* system, the second gate, called the "Value Screen," follows the preliminary investigation, namely, the "Scoping Stage," and opens the door to a more detailed investigation, "Build the Business Case," much like Figure 4.10.

The essence of this "Value Screen" gate is a reevaluation of the proposed project in light of the additional information gained from the Scoping Stage. The gate features a combination of must-meet and should-meet criteria.

The must-meet items must yield "yes" answers and deal with strategic alignment and meeting company safety, legal, and ethical standards. Most projects at Gate 2 pass these potential knock-out questions.

The tougher evaluation occurs with the "should-meet" criteria: Gatekeepers rate the project on ten-point scales on six criteria on a scorecard in this point-count system; ratings are added and scores displayed:

1. Strategic (importance and fit)
2. Product and competitive advantage (unique superior product?)

Figure 4.13: The Key Activities in Stage 2, Based on Best-Practice Firms and Teams, Required to Build a Robust Business Case

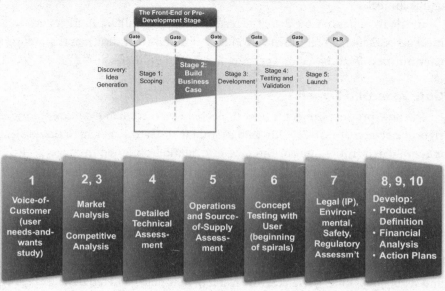

Artwork courtesy of Dave Caissy

3. Market attractiveness (size, growth, competiveness?)
4. Synergies (leverages our core competencies)
5. Technical feasibility
6. Financial reward versus risk

The total score as well the ensuing discussion are important inputs to the Go/Kill decision and project prioritization.

Stage 2: Build the Business Case

The Business Case opens the door to full product development (heavy technical work), and thus Stage 2 is where the Business Case is constructed. This stage is a detailed investigation stage, which clearly defines the product and verifies the attractiveness of the project prior to heavy spending. It is also the *critical home-work* stage—the one found to be so often weakly handled. (See Figure 4.13 for a list of suggested activities in Stage 2).

The definition of *the winning new product* is a major facet of Stage 2. The elements of this definition include target-market definition; delineation of the product concept; specification of a product-positioning strategy, the product benefits to be delivered, and the value proposition; and spelling out essential and desired product features, attributes, requirements, and high-level specifications.

Stage 2 sees *market analysis* undertaken to determine market attractiveness and market characteristics: This analysis is a more detailed study than in Stage 1, and is designed to determine market size and potential, to define market segments and industry structure, and to identify success factors (what it takes to succeed in this market).

VoC should also be undertaken to really understand the details of customers' needs, wants, and preferences—that is, to help define the "winning" new product prior to beginning development work in the next stage. While earlier VoC and customer insight work helps to create the idea, the details of the product's requirements, based on more in-depth VoC work, must be agreed on here.

Competitive analysis is also a part of this stage. Another market activity is concept testing: A representation of the proposed new product is presented to potential customers, their reactions are gauged, and the likely customer acceptance of the new product is determined—the first of the customer-validation spirals.

In Stage 2, a detailed *technical appraisal* focuses on the technical feasibility and risks of the project. That is, customer needs and "wish lists" are translated into a technically and economically feasible conceptual solution. This translation might even involve some preliminary design or laboratory work, but it should not be construed as a full-fledged development project. An operations (or manufacturing) appraisal is often a part of building the Business Case, where issues of manufacturability, source-of-supply, costs to manufacture, and investment required are investigated.

> Build the Business Case is the "make or break" phase of the project. It's here where so many project teams get into trouble and where the seeds of disaster are sown. A number of key tasks are recommended for this stage, highlighted in Tables 4.1 and 4.2 and Figure 4.13—all based on best practices and what winning teams do. So do have a close look at these tasks, and build them into your new-product system and into your projects.

If appropriate, detailed legal, patent, and regulatory assessment work is undertaken in order to remove risks and to map out the required actions.

Finally, a detailed *business and financial analysis is* conducted as part of the justification facet of the Business Case. The financial analysis typically involves a discounted cash flow approach (NPV and IRR), complete with sensitivity analysis to check the impact of major assumptions. A risk assessment is also part of this business analysis.

Figure 4.14: The Objective of Stage 2 Is a Business Case, Which Has Three Main Elements

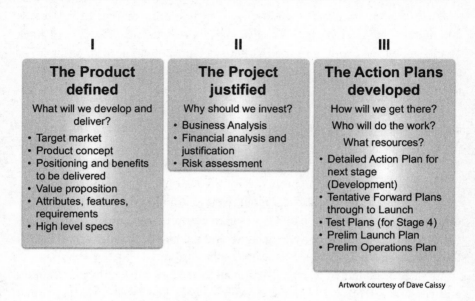

I	II	III
The Product defined	**The Project justified**	**The Action Plans developed**
What will we develop and deliver?	Why should we invest?	How will we get there?
• Target market	• Business Analysis	Who will do the work?
• Product concept	• Financial analysis and justification	What resources?
• Positioning and benefits to be delivered	• Risk assessment	• Detailed Action Plan for next stage (Development)
• Value proposition		• Tentative Forward Plans through to Launch
• Attributes, features, requirements		• Test Plans (for Stage 4)
• High level specs		• Prelim Launch Plan
		• Prelim Operations Plan

Artwork courtesy of Dave Caissy

The result of Stage 2 is a *Business Case* for the project, with three main elements (Figure 4.14):

1. the *product definition*—a key to success.
2. a thorough *project justification* (financial and business rationale, risk assessment).
3. the *detailed project plan* (the action plan or "go-forward" plan), spelling out the timeline and resources required, especially for the next stage, Development.

Stage 2 involves considerably more effort than Stage 1 and requires inputs from a variety of sources. Stage 2 is best handled by a team consisting of cross-functional members—the core group of the eventual project team.

Gate 3: Go to Development

Gate 3 is the *final gate prior to the full Development stage*, the last point at which the project can be killed before entering heavy spending. Some firms call it the "money gate": Once past Gate 3, financial commitments are substantial. In effect,

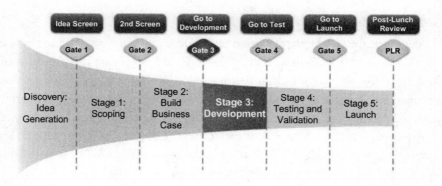

Gate 3 means "go to a heavy spend." And it's here that the shape of the funnel changes, as shown in Figure 4.10, taking on a gentler slope—that is, most of the Kill decisions are made in the early gates, at Gates 1, 2, and this Gate 3; relatively few projects are killed after Gate 3. Gate 3 also yields a sign off of the product and project definition.

The qualitative side of this gate evaluation involves a review of each of the tasks in Stage 2: checking that the tasks were undertaken, that quality of execution was sound, and that the results are positive. Next, Gate 3 subjects the project once again to the set of must-meet and should-meet criteria used at Gate 2, but this time with much more rigor and with benefit of more solid data. Finally, because a heavy spending commitment is usually the result of a Go decision at Gate 3, the results of the financial analysis are an important part of this screen.

If the decision is Go, Gate 3 sees commitment to the product definition and agreement on the project plan that charts the path forward: The Development Plan and the Preliminary Operations and Marketing Plans are reviewed and approved at this gate. The full project team—an empowered, cross-functional team headed by a project leader with authority—is assigned; and resources—person-days and funds—are formally committed.

> The Development stage is where technical people on the project team translate the Development Plan and project definition into reality—they *develop the product!* The details of this stage obviously vary by industry, thus I leave it to you to map this out for your firm. Don't forget the "other" or nontechnical tasks too: validations or spirals with the customer, updating the Business Case and financial analysis, and creating plans for following stages in the project.

Stage 3: Development

Stage 3 begins the implementation of the Development Plan and the physical development of the product. That is, the technical people on the project team undertake the necessary technical work to deliver the prototype and testable product. Source-of-supply and operations issues are resolved. For service products, the detailed service design is finalized and the operating procedure for service delivery with the client and/or the SOP (standard operating procedure) are mapped out in this stage. Alpha tests, in-house tests, or lab tests in Stage 3 ensure that the product meets requirements under controlled conditions.

For lengthy development projects, numerous milestones and periodic project reviews are built into the Development Plan. These *milestone reviews are not gates per se:* Go/Kill decisions are not made here; rather, these milestone checkpoints provide for project control and management, checking that the project is on time and moving forward as planned. However, missing a milestone or two usually signals that the project is off course, which calls for an immediate and emergency gate review. The emphasis in Stage 3 is clearly on technical work. But marketing and operations activities also proceed in parallel. For example, customer-feedback work continues concurrently with the technical development, with constant customer opinion sought on the product as it takes shape during Development. These are the "build-test-feedback-revise iterative spirals" in Figure 4.11—the back-and-forth *customer-validation loops*, with each development result—for example, protocept, rapid prototype, working model, first prototype, and so on—taken to the customer for assessment and feedback. Meanwhile, detailed test plans, market launch plans, and production or operations plans, including production facilities requirements, are developed. The financial and business analysis is also updated with new insights gleaned from the technical, operations, and customer-feedback work, while regulatory, legal, and patent issues are resolved.

A few leading firms are now combining *Agile project-management methods* from the IT world with *Stage-Gate*, initially for software products, but most recently *for physical (hardware) new products*, and in many different industries. These Agile methods emphasize short time-boxed sprints (typically two to four weeks); rapid delivery of product iterations that can be demonstrated to stakeholders (in weeks rather than months); dedicated, colocated teams; and rapid response to customers' needs and changes in needs. Initial integration of *Stage-Gate* and Agile often takes place first in the technical stages, namely, Development and Testing (Stages 3 and 4 in Figure 4.11), but more experienced

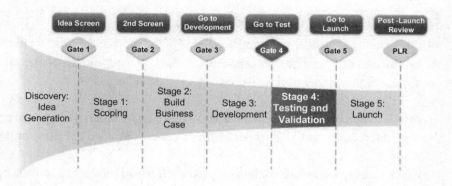

firms employ this Agile-Stage hybrid across the entire idea-to-launch process in Figure 4.11.[12] We get more into the *Agile-Stage-Gate* hybrid approach in Chapters 5 and 6.

The main deliverable at the end of Stage 3 is a partially tested prototype, one which the customer has vetted several times, but ready for full customer tests in the next stage. Other deliverables include a full Market Launch Plan; an Operations Plan to provide product or service delivery; the plans for the next stage, namely, Testing; and an updated financial and business analysis.

Gate 4: Go to Testing

This postdevelopment review is a check on the progress and the continued attractiveness of the product and project. Development work is reviewed and checked, ensuring that the technical work has been completed in a quality fashion, that the product "works" (that is, has technical integrity, based on the results of the in-house or alpha tests), and that it meets customer requirements and needs, receiving positive feedback . . . that it delights the customer!

This gate also revisits the economic questions via a revised financial analysis based on new and more accurate data. The Testing or Validation Plan for the next stage is approved for immediate implementation, and the detailed Marketing and Operations Plans are reviewed for probable future execution.

The Testing and Validation Stage is an important one: Often, glaring product errors, which were not caught by the quick validation iterations, are discovered in a more in-depth and lengthy field trial. But this stage is more than just customer validation—it also includes extended in-house tests and production or operations trials as well. Sometimes production equipment is purchased during this stage, and installed and commissioned.

Stage 4: Testing and Validation

This stage tests and validates the entire viability of the project: the product itself, the production or operations process, customer acceptance, and the economics of the project. A number of activities are undertaken at Stage 4:

- *In-house product tests:* extended technical lab tests or alpha tests to check on product quality and product performance under controlled operating or lab conditions.
- *User, preference, or field trials of the product:* the final product tests to verify that the product functions under actual use conditions and also to gauge potential customers' reactions to the product—to establish purchase intent.
- *Trial, limited, or pilot production/operations:* to test, debug, and prove the production or operations process and to determine more precise production costs and throughputs. (Production equipment may be required for these trials, so it is purchased and commissioned in this stage as well.)
- *Simulated test market, "soft launch," test market, or trial sell:* an attempt to *actually sell the product* to a limited set of customers, in order to gauge customer reaction, measure the effectiveness of the launch plan, and determine final estimates of market share and revenues.
- *Revised business and financial analysis:* to check on the continued business and economic viability of the project, based on new and more accurate revenue and cost data.
- Sometimes Stage 4 yields negative results, so it's back to Stage 3. Iterations back and forth, even between the stages, throughout the *Stage-Gate* system are quite possible, indeed likely.

Gate 5: Go to Launch

This final gate opens the door to full commercialization—market launch and full production or operations start up. It is the final point at which the project can still be killed. This gate focuses on the quality of the activities in the Testing and Validation stage and their results. Criteria for passing the gate focus largely on whether the Stage 4 test results are positive, the expected financial return, whether the launch and operations start-up plans remain solid, and the readiness check—that all is commercial-ready for the launch. The Operations and Market Launch Plans are reviewed and approved for implementation in Stage 5, and in some firms, so is the Product Life Cycle Plan (the plan that

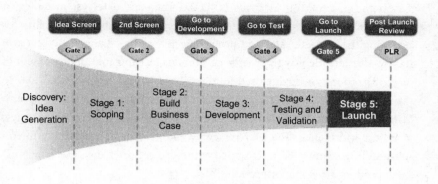

takes the product well beyond the Launch phase, into maturity and even to product exit).

Stage 5: Launch

This final stage involves implementation of both the Market Launch Plan and the Operations Plan. Production equipment is acquired, installed, and commissioned (although as mentioned above, sometimes this is done earlier in Stage 4, as part of the Stage 4 operations trials); the logistics pipeline is filled; and selling begins. And barring any unforeseen events, it should be clear sailing for the new product . . . another new-product winner!

Post-Launch Review

At some point following commercialization (often twelve to eighteen months later), the new-product project is terminated. The team is disbanded, and the product becomes a "regular product" in the firm's product line. This is also the point where the project and the product's performance are reviewed. The latest data on revenues, costs, expenditures, profits, and timing are compared to projections made at Gates 3 and 5 in order to gauge performance. Issues of team accountability are topics here. Finally, a post audit—a *retrospective analysis* of the project, mapping the steps from the project's beginning to end, what was done well and what was done badly, what can be learned, and how to do the next one better—is carried out. This retrospective analysis is vital to the process of continuous improvement or *kaizen*.

This final review marks the end of the project. Note that the project team and leader remain responsible for the success of the project through this post-launch period, right up to the point of the Post-Launch Review.

An example:[13] Emerson Electric's NPD 2.0 stage-and-gate system builds in a rigorous post-launch follow-up as a way to ensure team accountability for achieving the project's sales and profit objectives. "Post-Launch Review also sets up a systematic way to provide continuous learning and improvement of the NPD process through closed-loop feedback." These reviews occur *one to two months after launch*, and again *twelve to twenty-four months after launch*. "The initial follow-up would allow corrective action and a complete review of team performance. The later review would provide accountability for results, and determine the next steps for the project or change the new NPD [new-product development] process."[14]

Like Emerson Electric, many firms undertake *two Post-Launch Reviews*: one shortly after launch to make immediate course corrections and to undertake a retrospective analysis of the project—the continuous improvement exercise—while memories are still fresh and team members are still around; and the final review some twelve to twenty-four months after launch to review actual versus promised results and to terminate the project.

So there you have it—very simple in concept, yet remarkably robust as a way to drive new products to market. Before getting into the details of the added sophistication, flexibility, and new techniques that some companies are now building in (outlined in the next few chapters), let's first make sure we're all on the same page regarding what *Stage-Gate* is and is not!

THE FIVE MAIN ARTEFACTS OF *STAGE-GATE*

I'm often invited into a firm to work with a task force designing or overhauling their gating system. What I often see are well-intentioned efforts, but the result is a *system that lacks some vital components*—in short, the task force missed some key components of what should be in a well-crafted *Stage-Gate* system. The components found in *Stage-Gate* can be summed up in *five major artefacts*; leaving any one out means you really don't have a complete *Stage-Gate* system—like a car missing an engine or a wheel. Here's what to look for:

1. *The Stages: Stage-Gate* has well-defined Stages, each stage labelled and with a well-defined purpose. Stages also have *recommended activities based on best practices* within each stage—for example as shown in Figure 4.13 (every stage should have a sketch like Figure 4.13).

2. *Deliverables:* These are what the project team seeks to have at the end of each stage—the endpoint of the stage—and to deliver to the upcoming gate. Deliverables must be clearly defined in the system, as they *provide the objectives for the team* for that stage, and also the *vital information needed by management* to make an effective gate decision. Deliverables are often defined by way of short and clear templates—but keep them lean!

3. *Gates: Stage-Gate* also has Gates; each gate is clearly labelled (simple, understandable names) with a clear purpose. Gates also *must have criteria for Go*—that is, a set of Go/Kill and prioritization criteria for each gate. Often these are in the form of a scorecard, used to "score" or rate the project.

4. *Outputs:* Gates also have Outputs, namely, a decision: Go/Kill/Hold/Recycle. These decisions must also be defined, for example, what happens in the event of a "Go decision": as noted above, "in the event of a Go decision, the action plan for the next stage is approved complete with resource commitments (people required, money, and person-days); the timeline for the stage is agreed; and a list of deliverables and date for the next gate are decided."

5. *Roles:* A number of *Stage-Gate* roles are outlined in this and other chapters, and include:

   a. *Project team members:* a core group of project people—cross-functional, usually from technical, marketing, operations, and sales—who undertake the project and are *accountable for its commercial results*; team members have *designated time allocated* to the project (ideally are dedicated to the one project in the case of major projects).

   b. *Project leader:* the "captain" of the project team, an entrepreneurial and critical role. He or she is a *member of the project team* and has *significant authority* (obtained at gates); also promotes the project, seeks resources, and handles the external interfaces of the project, especially with senior management.

   c. *Project manager* (optional): uses *project-management tools* and methods (Gantt charts, budgeting, meeting facilitation) to ensure that the project functions well according to sound project-management practices. (For smaller projects, often the project leader handles these tasks.)

d. *Gatekeepers:* the senior people who "own" the resources required for the project to move to the next stage, and who make the Go/Kill and prioritization decision; are a cross-functional group.

e. *Process manager:* oversees the entire *Stage-Gate* process, and is responsible for seeing that project teams understand and adhere to the process and its practices; also facilitates gate meetings (more in Chapter 9 and Table 4.3).

f. *Executive sponsor:* for larger projects, a member of senior management (can be a gatekeeper) that *mentors and guides the project team*, and to whom the project leader can turn to for advice and help; is sometimes called "the godfather" of the project.

WHAT TYPES OF PROJECTS DOES *STAGE-GATE* HANDLE?

Stage-Gate is used by producers of physical products—both consumer goods and industrial or B2B goods; also by service providers, such as banks, insurance, consulting, and telecommunications companies. The specific model described above and in Figure 4.11 has been designed for *major and bolder new-product projects.* A *new product* can be a radical or bold innovation, but also a significant product improvement, or merely a line extension (as defined in Chapter 1, Figure 1.5)—all these types of new product projects are handled by *Stage-Gate.* There are *different versions* of *Stage-Gate* for these different types of new products, as we'll see in the next chapter.

> *Stage-Gate* can be used for other types of projects, such as process developments, mergers and acquisitions, and capital projects. The concepts are the same—stages (work with defined deliverables, followed by gates and a decision to move forward), but the details of the *Stage-Gate* models used for these other applications are quite unique to each application.

Some companies have extended the use of this *Stage-Gate* approach—the concept of stages with defined tasks and resulting deliverables, together with gates, defined gatekeepers, and visible Go/Kill criteria—to a wide variety of investment decisions. Besides new-product projects, these other applications of *Stage-Gate* include:

- internal projects (such as an IT project where the "customer" is inside the company),
- new-*process* developments—where the "deliverable" is a new or improved manufacturing process, again an "internal customer,"

- new business developments—outside the current market and technological boundaries of the firm,
- alliance and partnership projects,
- mergers and acquisitions,
- fundamental research or science projects,
- platform developments,
- exploration projects (one major petroleum firm uses *Stage-Gate* for oil well drilling exploration projects), and even
- capital projects (plant expansion or plant construction).

For these different types of projects, the principles of the system are much the same, but clearly the details—the specific stages and gates, the Go/Kill criteria, and the expected deliverables to gates—are customized to suit each type of project.

DEBUNKING THE MYTHS ABOUT *STAGE-GATE*—WHAT *STAGE-GATE* IS NOT!

The concept sounds simple, but it is surprising how some people get it so wrong. They read the book and claim to have implemented a stage-and-gate process "just like in the book"; but something gets *lost in the translation*. Here are some of the frequent ways people misread, misapply, and abuse an otherwise excellent system. What *Stage-Gate* should not be:

Not a Functional, Phased Review Process[15]

Don't confuse *Stage-Gate* of the twenty-first century with the traditional "phased review" process of the 1960s–1980s. Surprisingly, some companies still use this ponderous phased-review system. The phased-review process, endorsed by NASA and others, broke the innovation process into stages, each stage reporting to a function or a department. Implemented with the best of intentions, the process managed to almost double the length of developments. Why? The process was designed like a relay race—activities in sequence rather than in parallel; there were handoffs throughout the process, as one function passed the project on to the next department (and with handoffs, there arise the inevitable dropped balls or worse yet, just throwing it over the wall!); and there was no commitment to

> **What *Stage-Gate* is not:**
>
> - Not a functional, phased review process.
> - Not a rigid lock-step nor a linear system.
> - Not a project-management system nor a project-control system.

the project from beginning to end by any one group—accountability was missing. Moreover, the process was a technical one, not a business process; and gates were more like milestone review points or *technology readiness checks* (projects were rarely killed).

By contrast, today's *Stage-Gate* system is built for speed. The stages are cross-functional, and not dominated by a single functional area: This is a *business process*, not an R&D, engineering, or marketing process. The play is rapid, with activities occurring in parallel rather than in series. The governance model is clear, with defined gates and criteria for efficient, timely Go/Kill decision-making. And the project is executed by a dedicated and empowered team of cross-functional players, led by an entrepreneurial team leader or team captain.

Not a Rigid, Lockstep Process

Some companies' idea-to-launch systems resemble rule books—a lockstep process full of rules, regulations, mandatory procedures, and "thou shalts" that every project should follow, regardless of the circumstances. If this describes your process, no wonder people try to avoid it or circumvent it!

Stage-Gate is a map to get from Point A (idea) to Point B (successful new product). As in any map, when the situation merits, detours can be taken. For example, many companies tailor the model to their own circumstances and build lots of flexibility into their process:

- Not all projects pass through every stage or every gate of the model.
- In any project, activities and deliverables can be omitted or bypassed.
- Similarly, activities can be moved from one stage to another—for example, moving an activity ahead one stage in the event of long lead times.

More on these facets of flexibility in the next chapter.

Not a Linear System

Because of the visual graphics associated with *Stage-Gate*, some people see it as a linear model, with both the stages and the activities within each stage being linear. They miss the point that although the stages are laid out one after the other, within each stage, activities and tasks *are anything but linear*. Indeed, inside the stages there is much *looping, iterating, and back-and-forth play* as the project proceeds; some activities are undertaken sequentially, others in parallel, and others overlapping. And then there are the ever-present spirals outside the company to customers and users. Even the stages are allowed to overlap (beginning one stage before the previous one is completed, as in Corning's model in

Figure 4.1); and often the project must iterate back to a previous stage. So the process is anything but linear, even though the traditional graphics depict a neat, linear, and logical process.

Not the Same as Project Management

Stage-Gate is a *macro* process—an overarching process. By contrast, *project management* is a *micro* process. *Stage-Gate* is not a substitute for sound project-management methods. Rather, *Stage-Gate* and project management are used together. Specifically, project-management methods are applied *within the stages* of the *Stage-Gate* process. For example, during the larger, more complex stages (Stages 3, 4, and 5, Development, Testing, and Launch in Figure 4.11), *project-management methods* must be applied, such as:

- Timelines, Gantt charts, and critical path plans.
- Milestone review points (built into the action plans approved at each gate) to check on on-time performance
- A team-initiation task to define the project for this stage—its mission and goals.
- Regular project reviews.

Increasingly, *Agile project-management methods* are used within the stages of *Stage-Gate* instead of the traditional Gantt-chart style (or waterfall) project-management method.

Not a Project Control Mechanism

I visited an internationally renowned company near Frankfurt, Germany, and was introduced to its *Stage-Gate* process via a PowerPoint presentation. The title slide said it all: "Project Kontrolling System," and the presentation went downhill from there. *Stage-Gate* is not, and never was, intended to be a *control mechanism* so that executives, auditors, and financial people could control, or worse yet, micromanage projects from their lofty offices. Rather, *Stage-Gate* is a playbook designed to enable project teams and team leaders to get resources for their projects and then speed them to market using the best possible methods to ensure success.

Not a Dated, Stagnant System

Although *Stage-Gate* has endured many years, today's versions are almost un-recognizable from the original model. *Stage-Gate* has evolved a lot over time. The world has been the laboratory for *Stage-Gate*, and ingenious people from every continent have made many improvements and adaptations to the system. Many novel improvements have been built into the standard model outlined in this chapter; you'll see more in the next two chapters.

To put things in perspective, the *marketing concept* was first published in 1960, and its principles—putting the customer first—are still valid today;[16] but the way we practice marketing today is very different from the way it was in 1960. It's the same with *Stage-Gate*: The principles still hold, but today's modern *Stage-Gate* system bears little resemblance to the original model. It has evolved considerably to include new principles of lean and rapid product development; it has built in a number of new best practices that were not envisioned back in the early days; and now there are many different and tailored versions of *Stage-Gate*.

The point is that *Stage-Gate* is not a static tool; rather, it's a comprehensive, integrated, evolving, and evergreen system that builds in many best practices and methods. And it's always changing. Many pundits promote one favorite tool or a particular method as the "answer" or replacement to *Stage-Gate*. Although some of these new tools are no doubt useful and indeed many *Stage-Gate* users incorporate them into their *Stage-Gate* process, be careful—these tools are typically not a replacement for or alternative to *Stage-Gate*. For example, *lean product development* offers some very good techniques, principles, and methods for removing waste in the innovation process, which companies simply build into *Stage-Gate*. Six Sigma is another valuable tool, and a number of firms such as Ethicon (a division of J&J) have integrated DFSS (Design for Six Sigma) right into their *Stage-Gate* process.[17]

> *Stage-Gate* has evolved a lot over time, and today versions of *Stage-Gate* are almost unrecognizable from the original model. The world has been the laboratory for *Stage-Gate*, and ingenious people from every continent have made many improvements and adaptations to the system.

Not a Bureaucratic System

Sadly, some managers see *any system* as an opportunity to impose more paperwork, lots of forms, long PowerPoint presentations, unending meetings and committees, and needless red tape. Remember: The objective here is a systematic, streamlined process, not a bogged down bureaucratic one. Take a hard look at your idea-to-launch process. If any procedure, meetings, committee, mandatory activity, form, or presentation does not add value, then get rid of it!

An example: A major Swiss firm engaged in the power-transmission belt industry faced a time-to-market challenge. On first arriving at the firm (and coming from a company that used *Stage-Gate* effectively), the new CTO was alarmed at how slowly the company's gating process moved. "It was heavy with bureaucracy," he declared. Thus, at the CTO's insistence, a task force was set up; the process was reinvented and streamlined, and all unnecessary activities and procedures removed, so project leaders could get on with their job of driving their product to market. The process works now!

Not a Data-Entry Scheme

A notable producer of automotive tires in the United States installed its version of a *Stage-Gate* process, which I was asked to review. What surprised me was that the entire system design was led by the IT department (which knew little about product development), and that software constituted the dominant part of the process. When I logged on to the new system, the first screen asked me for information such as "customer requirements for the new tire" and "intended vehicles and their volumes."

What the system appeared to be was an *order entry system*, but it was not; it was their take on what a *Stage-Gate* process should be. There were no gates in the process; and the stages were just nominal ones, each stage asking for additional information. But nowhere were best practices, such as doing voice-of-customer work, undertaking a competitive analysis, or doing a technology assessment, ever mentioned. Indeed, as one astute employee pointed out: "If I were prepared to 'fake the numbers,' I could get through the entire idea-to-launch system without even leaving my keyboard." And this tire company is not alone. I have since seen similar IT-driven models in other well-known companies whose managements should know better.

Stage-Gate is *not* a data-entry system or an IT model. Although software, with its required data entry, can be a valuable facilitator to the process, don't let the tail wag the dog here. *Stage-Gate* comprises a set of information-gathering activities; the data that these activities yield can be conveniently handled by IT to facilitate document management and communication among project team members. But the software and data entry are a tool, not the process!

Not Just a "Back-End" or Product-Delivery Process

One executive in a large engineering and manufacturing firm boasted to me, "Once the product is defined and the business case accepted, then our stage-and-gate process kicks in and it's usually clear sailing from there. It's all that front-end stuff—before we get into our stage-and-gate process—that causes the problems." Shocked at his lack of understanding of *Stage-Gate*, I politely explained that "all

TABLE 4.3: A GOOD CHECKLIST— KEY FEATURES OF AN OPERATIONAL FIRST-CLASS *STAGE-GATE* SYSTEM[17]

A visible and fully-documented process: Some firms *claim* to have a new-product development process, but on closer inspection, it's more of a high-level, conceptual model—a few flow diagrams with boxes and diamonds and little more. To be operational, an effective new product process should be *well mapped and well documented*: stages defined, activities within stages spelled out, gates named, criteria and deliverables for gates delineated, and even the gatekeepers identified, the five main artefacts of *Stage-Gate* outlined previously. An estimated two-thirds of all businesses have a reasonably well-documented process, and three-quarters of best innovators do.

Really "living the process": The true test of a process is whether or not it is really used or is merely "window dressing." Having an idea-to-launch process mapped out and in place is one thing, but really *living the process* and diligently using it for most development projects is something else. Less than half of companies—44.9 percent—actually do live their development process; 60 percent of the best innovators do, whereas only 18.5 percent of worst performers do.

Helps project teams access the resources they need: Another test of a successful idea-to-launch process is whether or not it facilitates development, helping project teams secure needed resources and get products to market (or, in the converse, acts as a bureaucratic barrier). An estimated 70 percent of best innovators have a *facilitating process* compared to only 45.8 percent of average firms. Among worst performers, only 23.1 percent have a process that is a facilitator and enabler, marking this as another best practice.

Fosters compliance: Monitoring to see how well the process is followed is a good way to determine if the system is truly deployed. Metrics that gauge whether projects are really "in the process" or hitting gates and milestones on time, and the quality of gate meetings, attempt to capture compliance. Overall this is a fairly weak area, with only 39.1 percent of firms employing of such compliance checks and metrics and only half of best innovators doing so.

Adaptable and scalable: Is the process flexible, able to adapt to the needs, size, and risk of the project? Or is it a rigid, one-size-fits-all process that does not recognize differences between high- and low-risk projects, or between large and small projects? The process should be *flexible and scalable*, having different versions—for instance, a full five-stage, five-gate process for major projects and a shorter, three-stage process for lower risk projects, such as enhancements, modifications, and extensions. More on this topic in Chapter 5. Almost two-thirds of businesses (62.3 percent) boast a flexible, adaptable, and scalable process; 75 percent of the best innovators have flexible processes, twice the proportion of worst performers.

A process manager in place: Most firms (72.2 percent) have appointed a *Stage-Gate* process manager to guide and oversee their gating system. This person's role is to ensure that the process works, coach teams, facilitate gate meetings, maintain the project database, provide for training, and maintain the system and its documentation and IT support.

Continuous improvement built in: Internal learnings should be leveraged and the process should improve over time. Too many processes, implemented with the best of intentions, appear to create bureaucracy and include much non-value-added work. Thus, one must be constantly on the alert for non-valued work or outdated methods, eliminating bureaucracy or waste that may creep into the process. Periodically review the process to make needed improvements: most companies revamp their processes, 73.2 percent within the past three years and 83.8 percent within the past five years.

that front-end stuff" is very much part of *Stage-Gate*. Look at the flow chart in Figure 4.11: Three of the stages (or half the model) occur before Development begins. The fuzzy front end—ideation, scoping the project, defining the product, and building the business case—is perhaps the *most critical part* of *Stage-Gate*! Indeed, the game is won or lost in the first few plays, and so the front end of *Stage-Gate* is vital, and the part of the model that contributes the most to much higher success rates.

Suggestion: As soon as you finish this chapter, take a hard look at your own new-product idea-to-launch system. First, do you have such a process? If yes, lay it out in front of you. Go through the *seven goals* listed earlier in this chapter, and ask yourself: "Does my new-product process build in each of these items?

Where? Can I point to them? Are they clearly visible?" Next, check that your system includes the *five main artefacts* of a *Stage-Gate* system outlined above—many systems do not! Then review the "what *Stage-Gate* is not" list just above, and see if your process is guilty of any items.

Finally, answer the next question: "Is my system really operational, and is it first class?" The key features of *Stage-Gate* that translate the model from a handful of PowerPoint slides to a *fully operational and first class system* are in Table 4.3.[18] Review the list in Table 4.3, asking whether your system passes. If the answers are "no" to these questions, then it's time to reinvent your firm's idea-to-launch system and to get it operational and practiced.

5

BEYOND *STAGE-GATE*[1]

Learning and innovation go hand in hand.
The arrogance of success is to think that what
you did yesterday will be sufficient for tomorrow.

—WILLIAM POLLARD, English clergyman (1828–1893)

NEXT GENERATION *STAGE-GATE*®

As the creator of the *Stage-Gate* process, I am often asked, "What's next after stage-gate?" For years, I've not had an answer. The original *Stage-Gate* system was created in the 1980s, based on an in-depth study of successful "intrapreneurs" within major corporations as they drove successful new products to market. Their practices and the lessons they learned provided the foundation for that early stage-and-gate model, as seen in Chapter 4. Over the years, *Stage-Gate* has evolved and incorporated many new practices,[2] and some companies have also developed their own versions of *Stage-Gate*, building in some positive elements, but also some negative ones.

> Progressive companies are developing a new generation of idea-to-launch gated processes.

Today, we're seeing new approaches emerging from leading-edge companies that represent *a new generation of idea-to-launch processes*. In some cases, it's *an evolution* of *Stage-Gate* to a better, faster model; in other firms, it's closer to *a revolution*, moving to a very different system. But there is anything but unanimity as to what the next generation idea-to-launch system should be. This chapter looks at what leading firms are doing to move beyond their current idea-to-launch methodology and tries to integrate these practices into a next-generation system.

Some Criticisms

Stage-Gate has had a significantly positive impact on the conception, development, and launch of new products.[3] But there are also criticisms, some the result of the nature of the process and others of the way companies implemented the system. The world has changed a lot since the first *Stage-Gate* system was implemented—it is now faster paced, more competitive and global, and less predictable. And there's far more ambiguity—for example, more and more, customers don't seem to know what they need or want! In this context, *Stage-Gate* has attracted a number of criticisms: It is accused of being too linear, too rigid, and too planned to handle more innovative or dynamic projects. It's not adaptive enough and does not encourage experimentation. It's not context based—one size should not fit all. Its gates are too structured or are too financially based, and the system is too controlling and bureaucratic, loaded with paperwork, checklists, and too much non-value-added work.[4]

Some authors and experts have taken issue with these criticisms, arguing that most are due to faulty implementation,[5] while some deficiencies have been corrected in more recent evolutions of *Stage-Gate*.[6] Too often, I find a company is using a very old version of *Stage-Gate*, one that was obsolete years ago! But issues do remain, and thus a handful of leading firms are *rethinking and reinventing* their idea-to-launch gating system. Through my ongoing studies of benchmarking best practices, conferences where progressive firms engage in "what's next" discussion sessions, and personal interactions with leading firms, in this chapter I've constructed an overview of directions for the next generation of idea-to-launch systems.

THE TRIPLE A SYSTEM

At first glance, the practices and recommendations of firms creating new idea-to-launch systems look a lot like the traditional process; there are *still stages* where work gets done, and there are *still gates* where decisions are made. Look at Corning's *Stage-Gate* evolution over twenty-five years in Figure 4.1. But the details of the process and its function are quite different: What emerges is a more agile, vibrant, dynamic, flexible gating process that is leaner, faster, and more adaptive and risk based. This is what I call the Triple A or A-A-A system—it is adaptive and flexible, agile, and accelerated (Figure 5.1).

Figure 5.1: The Next-Generation System May Look Similar to Traditional *Stage-Gate*, but Functions Quite Differently

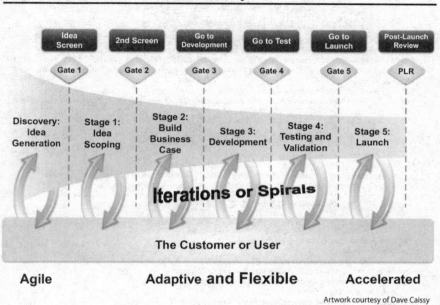

Artwork courtesy of Dave Caissy

A1—Adaptive and Flexible: The next-generation idea-to-launch system is adaptive . . . *adapting to changing circumstances* as the project moves forward. Innovations often unfold in unpredictable ways; thus, to boost the chances of success, the next generation system is based on the principle of "invest a little, learn a lot."[7] It incorporates *spiral or iterative development* to get something in front of customers early and often through a series of build-test-revise iterations. We had an introduction to spiral or iterative development in Chapters 2 and 4. Further, the product may be less than 50 percent defined when it enters Development, but via the spirals, the *product evolves, adapting to new information* as it moves through the Development and Testing stages.

The next-generation system is also *flexible* insofar as the actions for each stage and the deliverables to each gate are *unique to each development project*, based on the context of the market and the needs of the development process. This is the opposite of an SOP (standard operating procedure) approach to product development, which prescribes standardized actions and deliverables. There are also *fast-track versions* of the process for lower-risk projects. And in the next-generation system, a *risk-based contingency model* dictates that appropriate activities and deliverables be determined, based on an assessment of project assumptions and risks. Finally, Go/Kill criteria are flexible—there

Figure 5.2: The Elements of the Next-Generation *Stage-Gate* System

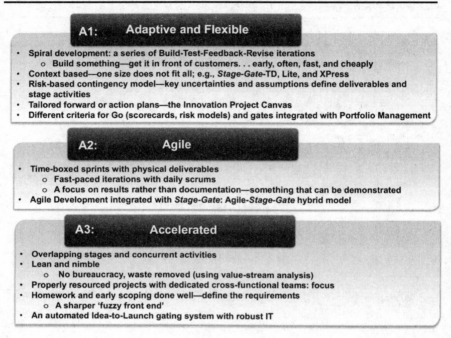

A1:   Adaptive and Flexible

- Spiral development: a series of Build-Test-Feedback-Revise iterations
  - Build something—get it in front of customers. . . early, often, fast, and cheaply
- Context based—one size does not fit all; e.g., *Stage-Gate*-TD, Lite, and XPress
- Risk-based contingency model—key uncertainties and assumptions define deliverables and stage activities
- Tailored forward or action plans—the Innovation Project Canvas
- Different criteria for Go (scorecards, risk models) and gates integrated with Portfolio Management

A2:   Agile

- Time-boxed sprints with physical deliverables
  - Fast-paced iterations with daily scrums
  - A focus on results rather than documentation—something that can be demonstrated
- Agile Development integrated with *Stage-Gate*: Agile-*Stage-Gate* hybrid model

A3:   Accelerated

- Overlapping stages and concurrent activities
- Lean and nimble
  - No bureaucracy, waste removed (using value-stream analysis)
- Properly resourced projects with dedicated cross-functional teams: focus
- Homework and early scoping done well—define the requirements
  - A sharper 'fuzzy front end'
- An automated Idea-to-Launch gating system with robust IT

are *no standard set or universal criteria* for each gate—and gates are integrated with portfolio management.

A2—Agile: The next-generation system also incorporates elements of Agile Development, the rapid development system developed by the software industry, but now starting to be used for *physical products and services*. For example, sprints with scrums—very short increments in which the deliverable is something that can be demonstrated to stakeholders (rather than documentation)—are part of the new system. This *new Agile-Stage-Gate hybrid model* emphasizes adaptive planning (responding quickly to new requirements), evolutionary development (minimal product definition at the beginning), and an iterative time-boxed approach undertaken by a dedicated development team.

A3—Accelerated: The next-generation idea-to-launch system is focused on accelerating the development process. Projects in the system are *properly resourced*, especially major projects, and fully staffed by a *dedicated cross-functional team* for maximum speed to market. Activities within stages overlap, and *even stages overlap*; the notion of a "stage" is less relevant. The new system is *much leaner* with all waste removed—no bureaucracy, no unnecessary activities. There is more emphasis on the *fuzzy front end*, making it sharper and less fuzzy, so that the project is clearly scoped and key unknowns, risks, and uncertainties identified as early as possible. Finally, *robust software support* is provided to reduce work, provide better communication, and accelerate the process.

The elements of these three As—accelerated, adaptive, and agile—are summarized in Figure 5.2. Let's now probe what each means in practice.

AN ADAPTIVE AND FLEXIBLE PROCESS

Spiral or Iterative Development

Emerging idea-to-launch systems take their power from being adaptive and flexible—able to *shape themselves to the context of particular projects*. These qualities arise from four practices: spiral development cycles, context-based stage definitions and activities, risk-based contingency models to drive decision-making, and flexible criteria for Go/Kill decisions.

The traditional *Stage-Gate* process requires that the *product and project be defined* before the project moves into Development. Indeed, "sharp, early, and fact-based product definition" is a fundamental principle of *Stage-Gate*.[8] But the world moves too fast today to make a stable and rigid product definition possible for some businesses, markets, and projects. Often customers are not clear on what they want (or need) in the first place, so it's impossible to get a 100 percent accurate product definition prior to Development. As Steve Jobs, never a proponent of traditional

> Smart firms have made the idea-to-launch system much *more adaptive:* They have built in multiple spirals or iterations that permit experimentation with users, with each spiral consisting of build-test-feedback-and-revise. Thus the *product definition evolves and solidifies over the course of Development.*

market research, famously said, "People don't know what they want until you show it to them."[9] And sometimes requirements simply change in the time that passes between the beginning and end of development—for example, a new customer need, a new competitive product, or a new technological possibility emerge—and the original product definition is no longer valid.

Thus smart firms, especially those doing riskier and bolder projects, have made the idea-to-launch system much *more adaptive*. The product may be less than 50 percent defined as development begins, but comes together during development; the product's design and definition adapts to new information, customer feedback, and changing conditions on its way to launch. That is, the *product definition evolves and solidifies over the course of Development*, not at the beginning of Development. Such firms have built in multiple spirals or iterations (what we saw in Chapter 2, but often faster and more frequent) that permit experimentation with users, with each spiral consisting of:

- *Build.* In each iteration, build something to show the customer, and be creative here: Build computer-generated graphics, a virtual prototype, a protocept*, a rapid prototype, a crude working model, an early beta version, or an MVP† (minimally viable product).[10]
- *Test.* Test each version of the product with users or customers—gauge interest, liking, preferences, and purchase intent, and let them tell you what they like and what value they see.
- *Feedback.* Find out the customer's reactions firsthand and, most important, what must be fixed or changed.
- *Revise.* Reset your thinking about the value proposition, benefits sought, and the product's design based on the feedback; and get ready for the next iteration of build-test-feedback-and-revise, but this time with a product version one step closer to the final product.

Figure 5.3 shows some example spirals.

Each spiral moves the project closer to the final product design. This spiral approach promotes experimentation, encouraging project teams to *fail often, fail early, fail fast, and fail cheaply,* a principle that Jobs applied throughout his development career at Apple.[11] This looping or spiral development is consistent with two core tenets of the Agile Manifesto for software development: a focus on quick response to change and continuous customer or stakeholder involvement in the development of the product:

> *An example:* Corning provides an example of spiral development. For special projects, namely large, higher-risk, bold projects such as Gorilla Glass,‡ Corning subdivides the development and testing phases into discrete increments defined in a sixty- to ninety-day plan. Each increment includes numerous iterations that yield testable versions of the product as a deliverable at key milestones (often weekly or biweekly). These increments are much like Agile

---

* Protocept: something between a concept (usually drawings and words) and a ready-to-trial prototype.

† MVP: a feature-limited product that can actually be sold and thus generate revenue; more common in start-up and high-tech businesses.

‡ Gorilla Glass®, a durable glass from Corning developed for the screen on Apple's iPad.

Figure 5.3: The Next-Gen System Is Adaptive—Spiral Development—with Build-Test-Feedback-Revise Iterations Built in (Sample Spirals Are Shown)

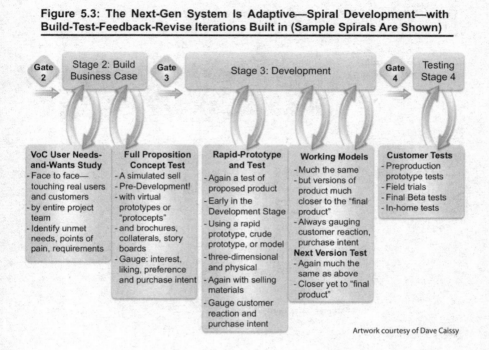

Artwork courtesy of Dave Caissy

sprints, but they sometimes last months rather than weeks. Within these increments, there are multiple one-day meetings with senior management—sometimes weekly—to review and move the project along. At the end of each increment, there is a major milestone review at which the project team must deliver something that can be demonstrated to stakeholders (customers and management).[12]

Suggestion: Build a series of "build-test-feedback-and-revise" spirals into your projects' development plans, much like Corning does for major projects. Allow the project to start out in the Development stage with the *product only partially defined*, knowing that multiple iterations with customers throughout the Development and Testing stages will evolve the product and get it right.

Context-Based Stages and Gates

In the first generation of *Stage-Gate*, companies typically developed a single gating model intended to handle the most difficult or complex new-product projects. The irony is that most projects were much simpler, and only a handful were the complex initiatives that the process had been designed for.

Figure 5.4: Stage-Gate Is Context Based and Scalable—One Size Does Not Fit All

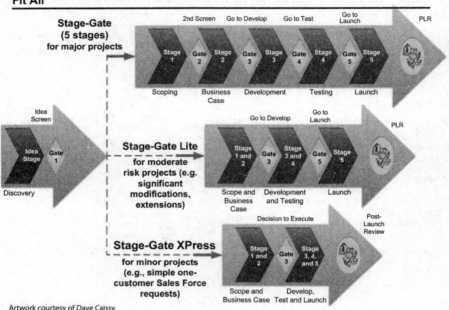

Artwork courtesy of Dave Caissy

Many firms have now developed faster-track or lighter versions of *Stage-Gate* to handle their many but less risky, better-defined, and less complex development projects; recent benchmarking studies show that 75 percent of best-performing innovators use a scalable idea-to-launch process.[13] For example, there are often three versions of *Stage-Gate* (Figure 5.4):

1. the full five-stage process to handle major, higher-risk developments;
2. a light version for moderate risk projects, such as significant modifications, improvements, and extensions—*Stage-Gate* Lite; and
3. an express version for very small developments, such as a sales-force request requiring a minor product change for one customer—*Stage-Gate* XPress.

In addition, many firms have introduced special versions of *Stage-Gate* to handle technology-development projects where the deliverable is not a new product, but rather a *technological capability*.[14] Such projects still require the discipline of a gating process, but the activities, deliverables, and criteria for Go are unique to these types of projects; hence, they merit their own system. Some examples of context-based approaches:

The Kellogg Company has three versions of its K-Way innovation process: the regular five-stage process to handle new products, a lighter three-stage process for smaller projects, and a three-stage process to handle technology developments such as new science or invention projects.[15]

3M has its regular new-product innovation (NPI) system, a standard five-stage model to handle typical new-product projects. There is also a shorter three-stage, three-gate version used by international subsidiaries, where the US-developed product is modified for sale locally. Finally, there is the *three-stage new technology innovation* (NTI) system for managing the design and development of a new technology.[16]

P&G, by contrast, has decided not to employ different processes for fast-track projects instead of its durable five-stage SIMPL process. As Dietmar Bressau, corporate leader for Innovation Diamond management, explained, "When you open the door to two to three processes, then along comes four, five, and six. Ultimately, anything goes. We want to keep one common *Stage-Gate* process [called SIMPL] that will be tailored, based on the risk profile of an individual initiative—otherwise each team, functional area, or business does its own thing."[17] Nonetheless, the firm has developed a value-driven process for innovation that requires invention: It's called FEI, or Front End Innovation; the argument is that when one brings a project into SIMPL without the invention in place, the project spends forever in the design phase. Thus, the technology development must be handled in advance.

Hewlett-Packard recognized that its traditional phase-review process, while excellent for mature markets requiring product improvements and extensions, was not so well suited to emerging, fast-moving markets. To meet the needs of these different types of markets, HP now defines three development processes:

1. An emergent model for start-up developments, such as cloud computing;
2. An agile model for growth sectors, such as blade servers; and
3. The traditional phase-review system to deliver lower costs or new features for mature markets, such as laptop computers.[18]

Omicron Electronics GmbH, a highly innovative Austrian producer of hardware and software for testing electrical power networks, has a very well-constructed *Stage-Gate* system called ATOM (Accelerate to Market), which handles traditional projects well. But for *breakthrough projects*, when the project is ambiguous or what the project will even lead to is unknown, the firm uses a different process: BTOM (Breakthrough to Market). The BTOM system provides some *breathing room for ill-defined, risky projects*, giving them space to get through the "valley of death" in the early stages, and to the point where something can be shown to management and to a customer.

Here's how BTOM works: If an idea generates enough excitement within the senior-management team, the project is approved as a BTOM project, and resources are provided for a six-month period. The small project team is unfettered, with no rules and no project reviews—in effect, a six-month "protected iteration." At the end of the six months, the project team must have something to show that has been seen and tested by a customer. At that point, there are three possibilities for the project:

1. Termination
2. Transition to the traditional ATOM process with all the normal rules and procedures
3. Continuation of the BTOM project for another six months

The method is still quite new, but has shown very promising results with several breakthrough new products launched—projects that never would have been possible with the traditional ATOM system.

Suggestion: If your business undertakes many different types of development projects—from major high-risk initiatives with many unknowns through to simple modifications and extensions, and even process developments—you've probably discovered that a single-version *Stage-Gate* model does not suit them all. Look at the examples above from leading firms, and do consider adopting several versions or sizes of *Stage-Gate* to better handle your diversity of development projects.

Stage-Gate-TD for Technology Development Projects

A number of firms, such as 3M, Kellogg's, Exxon, and many others, undertake *technology and technology-platform development* projects. Here the "deliverable" is not a new product per se, but *a new technological capability or technology know-how* that ultimately will be used in many new products (or in a new production process). These technology-development initiatives, although more experimental and uncertain, can be effectively managed with a stage-and-gate system, although a *very different model* than that used for product development.

A typical *Stage-Gate* system for technology developments and technology platforms (TD) is shown in Figure 5.5; it consists of three stages and four gates across the top of the figure:

Discovery or idea generation (Stage 1) is the trigger for the process. Idea generation is often done by scientists or technology people, but it can also be the

Figure 5.5: The Technology-Platform and Technology-Development System—*Stage-Gate*-TD

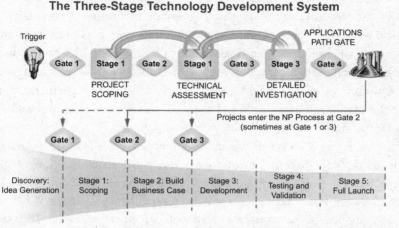

The Three-Stage Technology Development System

The Usual Five-Stage, Five-Gate *Stage-Gate*® New-Product System

Artwork courtesy of Dave Caissy

result of other activities, such as a strategic-planning exercise, technology fore-casting, or a technology road-mapping exercise.

Idea Screen: The first gate is the idea screen, the initial decision to commit a limited amount of time and money to the TD project. This gate is a *gentle screen* that poses the question: Does the idea merit expending any effort at all? Criteria for Go are largely qualitative—strategic, potential impact, leverage, and tech-nical feasibility. The Gate 1 gatekeeper group is typically composed of senior R&D people—the corporate head of technology, other senior R&D people, and representatives from corporate marketing and business development—to ensure commercial input.

Stage 1, Scoping: The first stage is Project Scoping, whose purpose is to build the foundation for the technology-development project, define the scope of the project, and map out the *forward plan* or action plan for the next stage. The effort is limited, typically not taking much more than several weeks. Stage 1 activities are conceptual and preparation work, and include a technical literature search, a patent and IP search, assessment of competitive alternatives, identification of resource gaps, and a preliminary technical assessment.

Second Screen: Gate 2 is where the decision is made to begin limited experi-mental or technical work in Stage 2. Like Gate 1, this gate is also a relatively gentle screen and poses the question: Does the idea merit undertaking limited

technical and physical work? Gate 2 is again largely qualitative and does not require financial analysis (because the resulting product, process, or impact of the
technology are still largely unknown). The gatekeepers are the same as at Gate 1.

Stage 2, Technical Assessment: The purpose of Stage 2 is to demonstrate technical
feasibility under ideal conditions. This stage entails preliminary experimental or
technical work, but should not take more than one to two person-months' effort
and should last no longer than three to four months. Activities here typically
include undertaking a thorough conceptual technical analysis, executing feasibility experiments or definitive technical work, developing a partnership network, identifying resource needs and solutions to resource gaps, and assessing
the potential impact of the technology on the company.

Gate 3: This is the decision to deploy resources beyond a few person-months
and opens the door to a more extensive and expensive investigation, Stage 3.
This gate thus involves a more rigorous evaluation than at Gate 2 and is based on
new information from Stage 2. Gate criteria resemble those for Gate 2, but with
more and tougher subquestions, answered with benefit of better data. The Gate 3
gatekeepers usually include the corporate head of technology, other senior technology or R&D people, corporate marketing or business development, and the
heads of the involved businesses who will commercialize the technology. Very
often the businesses pay for part of the upcoming Stage 3 costs.[19]

Stage 3, Detailed Investigation: The purpose of Stage 3 is to implement the full
experimental- or technology-development plan, to prove technological feasibility, and to define the scope of the technology and its value to the company.
This stage could entail significant expenditures and potentially person-years of
work. Besides the extensive technical work, other activities focus on defining
commercial product or process possibilities; undertaking market, manufacturing, and impact assessments on these possibilities; and preparing an implementation Business Case. Sound project-management methods are employed
during this lengthy Stage 3, including periodic milestone checks and project
reviews with management. Note that the project could be terminated in this
stage if prospects become negative, or it could cycle back to a previous stage
for a reset.

Applications Path Gate: This is the final gate in the TD process, the "door
opener" to one or several new-product or process-development projects (see
Figure 5.5). Here, the results of technical work are reviewed to agree on the
applicability, scope, and value of the technology to the company, and next steps
are decided. Note that this Gate 4 is often combined with an early gate in the
usual product-development process (for example, with Gate 1, 2, or 3, as shown

across the bottom of Figure 5.5). Gatekeepers are typically the senior corporate R&D people, corporate marketing, or business development, plus the leadership team from the relevant business that will assume ownership of the resulting commercial-development projects.

Suggestion: If your business undertakes technology or technology-platform projects—projects that are closer to fundamental science projects—then look what other leading firms do. Install a specially designed *Stage-Gate-TD* process as in Figure 5.5. Don't force these more creative and experimental projects through your traditional product-oriented *Stage-Gate* system: Forcing will do much damage to the project, require unnecessary paperwork and reports, frustrate the project leader, and potentially kill an otherwise excellent project!

Transferring the technology to the business: One of the big challenges is transferring the technology from the corporate lab (or lab where the basic or technology research is done) to the business unit that will eventually commercialize it; this transfer is shown in Figure 5.5. As one executive said: "These aren't smooth hand-offs. It's more like throwing it over the wall, or very often just 'dropping the ball.'" Parachuting a corporate technology project into a business unit is *a major killer of great technology projects*. Why? Once into the business unit, there's no ownership or passion for the project; the technology project doesn't align with the business's current priorities; there's no process or mechanism for handing off the new project; and there's no one available in the business to continue the work. And so another potentially significant project and product simply dies!

Suggestions from firms who have successfully tackled this challenge include:

1. Map out the transfer process clearly, as in Figure 5.5, linking the TD process to the business's existing gating or new-product system (check that the business really does have an effective idea-to-launch system!).
2. Ensure that the business-unit gatekeepers are at the TD gates in Figure 5.5. This promotes early buy-in of the technology project by key people within the business unit. And try to get commitment of some resources from the business's key people to the technology project, even before it's transferred, for example, in Stage 2 in the top part of Figure 5.5. The business's folks can do the exploratory business case or a preliminary market analysis, and most important, the business unit will then have "skin in the game."
3. Merge the final Applications Path Gate with Gate 1, 2, or 3 of the business unit's gating system, as shown across the bottom of Figure 5.5.

4. Ensure that the gate criteria used in the TD process are consistent with and agreeable to the business unit's.

5. Set up portfolio management for TD projects, inviting the business unit's key people to be part of the portfolio-decision process.

6. Transfer some of the people who worked on the TD project from the corporate or technology lab (where the TD project was done) to the business as the project is transferred—that is, some people *transfer with the project*, on a temporary basis. Transferring people is perhaps the most important way to ensure that the new technology development finds a home within the business, according to one major study of larger firms globally.[20] Such a personnel transfer creates accountability, momentum, knowledge retention, ownership, and enthusiasm.

The Risk-Based Contingency Model

The notion of a rigid, lockstep process is dead.[21] Today's fast-paced *Stage-Gate* is flexible, as opposed to a rigid "book of rules and procedures" to be religiously followed. *No activity or deliverable is mandatory. Stage-Gate* is a guide that suggests best practices, recommended activities, and likely deliverables. But the project team has much discretion over which activities it wants to execute and which it decides against.

Every project *is unique and merits its own action plan*. The project team presents its proposed *action plan*—its best attempt at defining what needs to be done to make the project a success—at each gate. At these gates, the gatekeepers commit the necessary resources, and in so doing, approve the action plan. But note that it is the *project team's plan*, not simply a mechanistic implementation of a standardized process!

> No activities are done simply because they are "on a list" in some SOP manual, or deliverables prepared because there is a template that must be completed.

Perhaps the most significant departure from standard gating systems is the *ability to custom-tailor the process to each and every project*—the polar opposite of an SOP approach. In this new approach, the entire new-product process, from idea to launch, is viewed as a *series of steps* and activities designed to *gather information* to reduce uncertainty and thereby *manage risk*.[22] Thus the *nature of the uncertainties and risk* specific to a project should determine *what actions are needed* in that project. But note that information only has a value to the extent that it can improve a decision (reduce project uncertainties or validate assumptions) that has economic consequences—see Figure 5.6.

Figure 5.6: In the Risk-Based Contingency Model, Key Assumptions and Unknowns Define the Knowledge Gaps to Be Closed, and thus the Needed Stage Activities

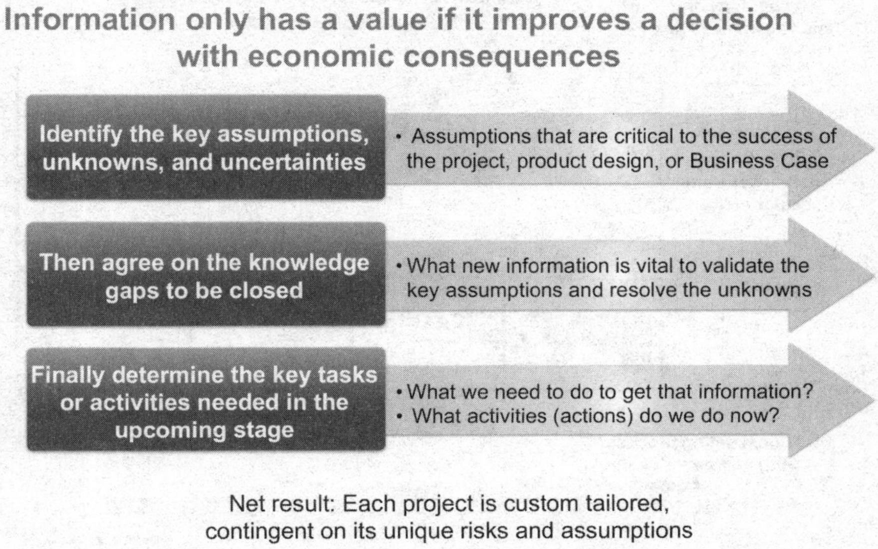

Information only has a value if it improves a decision with economic consequences

Identify the key assumptions, unknowns, and uncertainties	• Assumptions that are critical to the success of the project, product design, or Business Case
Then agree on the knowledge gaps to be closed	• What new information is vital to validate the key assumptions and resolve the unknowns
Finally determine the key tasks or activities needed in the upcoming stage	• What we need to do to get that information? • What activities (actions) do we do now?

Net result: Each project is custom tailored, contingent on its unique risks and assumptions

Artwork courtesy of Dave Caissy

Thus, the project team begins with a blank canvas, and then . . .

- identifies key unknowns and uncertainties,
- pinpoints the critical assumptions ("critical" in the sense that the assumptions have economic consequences), and
- determines what information is needed to validate these assumptions.

This information needs in turn to define the *knowledge gaps to be closed* before the next project review, and hence *determine the activities required* in that stage. In this way, the project team maps out *its own set of activities or tasks* it will undertake next, and thus defines *the deliverables*, but specific to its own project. No activities are done simply because they are "on a list" in some SOP manual, or deliverables prepared because there is a template that must be completed.

The process is very flexible and efficient; every project has its own custom-tailored action plan with no work included that does not add value. The downside, however, is that project teams must be very experienced to make this work.

Figure 5.7: Key Assumptions and Unknowns Are Identified to Help Determine What Information and Next Actions Are Needed

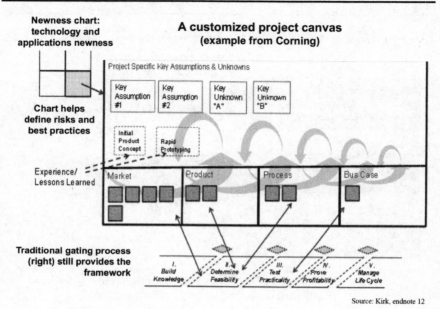

Source: Kirk, endnote 12

An example: Corning developed and piloted a contingency model based on project risk using a blank canvas, shown in Figure 5.7. Key assumptions and key unknowns are identified in each stage. And given these key assumptions, critical activities are defined: "Here is what best-practice project teams have done, and thus what best practices apply to your project, given its assumptions and risks." So the key assumptions help to define the required activity set for the project. Experienced team members have no problem identifying what is important to do, what tasks are critical, and what best practices to do—not every project requires everything. Gorilla® Glass was one of the first products developed by such a team using this method.[23]

The Innovation Project Canvas[24]

How does a project team effectively map out *its action plan or next steps* in their project? Corning uses a "blank canvas" (it really is *not blank* as noted in Figure 5.7; there are headings as a guide). But the company restricts the use of this new model to only 20 percent of its projects—the largest, more critical, and bolder ones. Further, management notes that "these are very smart people."

Figure 5.8: The Innovation-Project Canvas Is a Tool That Helps the Project Team Map Out Their Next Steps (Action Plan)

- Team's "customized project plan"
- Flip-chart canvas is subdivided into sections with headings:
  - Customer needs
  - Market trends
  - Competition
  - Value proposition
- The team discusses the project, moving through the chart, trying to provide the information in each topic section on Post-Its
- They also identify unknowns, assumptions, risks, knowledge gaps, information needs, and thus actions or tasks needed
- It's highly effective and efficient:
  - Accelerates the early stages of the innovation process

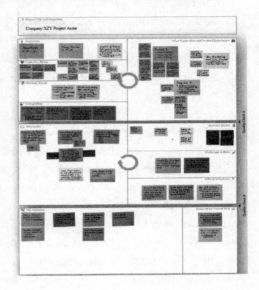

Source: Fürst, endnote 24

But what about "ordinary projects" and "ordinary people"? The Innovation Project Canvas is a blank-canvas process that provides more guidance that may be needed by a less-experienced team; it is shown in Figure 5.8. When the project team meets to map out the action plan, team members list their project hypotheses in a number of areas mapped out on the canvas using Post-Its. Topic areas on the canvas include:

- Customers: Who are the customer target group(s) (segments) for our product?
- Customer needs: What are the standard requirements and important unsolved problems or unfulfilled wishes?
- Market trends: What future developments could influence the demand for our product?
- Competition: Who are the most important competitors (along with their solutions and market positions)?
- Value proposition: What will we offer and why is it attractive to the customer or user?
- Solutions: What solutions should be considered?
- Business Model: How do we achieve value for our company from this project?

- Challenges and risks: What could seriously endanger the success of the project? (One could also list the critical assumptions key to the success of the project, as Corning does in their canvas model in Figure 5.7).
- Critical unknowns: What knowledge gaps must we close?
- Priority issues: What tasks should be given high priority to reduce the unknowns and increase the odds of success?
- Key activities: What are the next steps (by whom, time-to-completion, and resources needed)?

When trying to list on Post-Its what they know about the product, market, and competition, the team quickly sees *what items are fact based,* and others that are really untested assumptions, highly uncertain, or pure guesses. This realization in turn leads to a discussion of what *knowledge gaps* must be closed and ultimately to the *priority issues* and *key activities needed.* It's a *very logical and practical way to get to an action plan for the project.* In the example in Figure 5.8, different color Post-Its were used to denote the different market segments; but different colors could also indicate *different levels of uncertainty and unknowns.* This team process is usually a facilitated one.

Suggestion: Instead of relying strictly on a "standard list of actions" or SOP for each stage resulting in a standard list of deliverables, try letting the project team map out its own action plan—especially for more innovative projects where the "standard model" might not work so well. Use the risk-based contingency approach (Figures 5.6 and 5.7), where the team identifies the key unknowns, assumptions, and risks; defines what knowledge gaps must be closed; and finally moves on to their action plan. Try the Innovation Project Canvas, which provides more guidance to the team as they develop their action plan. The benefits are that this *customized plan* is likely to be more suited to the specific project; that tasks that are in the "standard list" but add no value are deleted; and it's the project team's plan—they have more commitment to it.

Flexible Criteria for Go/Kill Decisions

Most gating processes rely heavily on financial criteria to make Go/Kill decisions. The extension of context-based models, however, requires rethinking the investment criteria for these Go/Kill decisions. Research evidence shows that financial criteria do not yield the best portfolios, not so much because the financial models are theoretically wrong, but because *reliable data are missing.* In short, Business Cases are wrong, especially for the most innovative initiatives, and often by orders of magnitude.

Progressive firms thus are adopting more flexible Go/Kill criteria for the gates. This flexibility may be most important for technology-development projects, which must rely more on strategic criteria than financial, since it is often difficult to predict the longer-term economic impact of the technology. Exxon Chemical was one of the first firms to develop a *Stage-Gate* system for research-based products, and the firm selected nonfinancial criteria (such as strategic fit, competitive advantage, and market potential) as Go/Kill criteria rather than traditional profitability metrics.[25]

Similarly, models proposed for highly innovative projects, where financial projections are likely to be highly unreliable, use scorecard approaches consisting of a mixture of strategic, competitive, leverage, and financial criteria. Scorecards tend to give better decisions when it comes to new-product projects where the situation faced is more ambiguous and less certain. Additionally, more appropriate financial approaches are employed to deal more effectively with project risk, such as options pricing theory, Monte Carlo simulation, and Expected Commercial Value (we'll get into these different Go/Kill and prioritization techniques, useful for more innovative and less certain projects, in Chapter 8).[26]

Finally, the gates and their Go/Kill decisions are no longer stand-alone. *Stage-Gate* was developed before portfolio management became popular in the 1990s, but now leading firms have successfully integrated gates with portfolio management. Portfolio management has become increasingly vital because of concerns arising over the mix and balance of projects in firms' development portfolios, and in particular, the trend to smaller, low-risk projects and away from larger, more venturesome initiatives (recall Figure 1.1 in Chapter 1). Gates occur in real time and look at individual projects in depth; gates are often where a project in trouble is killed after a thorough review. By contrast, portfolio reviews occur periodically (typically four times per year) and look at the entire set of development projects—examining the mix, balance, and prioritization of projects. More on portfolio management in Chapter 8.

AN AGILE PROCESS

A second goal of next-generation idea-to-launch systems is to create a more agile and nimble process: *Agile-Stage-Gate*! Agile Development (hereafter called "Agile") is a set of software-development methods based on the Agile Manifesto and designed to promote teamwork, collaboration, and process adaptability.[27] Two key principles of Agile are:

> Firms have integrated key elements of the *Agile Manifesto* into their *Stage-Gate* processes.

- Working software is delivered frequently (in weeks rather than months); and
- Working software is the principal measure of progress.

In the software world, Agile breaks the development process into small increments with minimal planning. These increments, known as "sprints," are *time boxed*, limited to very short time frames, typically from one to four weeks. Each short sprint is kicked off by a *sprint planning meeting*, and ends with a *sprint review*. Each day during the sprint, the team meets quickly in their morning "daily stand-ups" or *daily scrums* to plan the day (the term "scrum" is derived from rugby—the scrum is similar to, although somewhat more physical than, American football's huddle; Hirotaka Takeuchi and Ikujiro Nonaka introduced the term in this context).[28] At the end of each sprint, the development team must deliver a working product or product features—executable software code—that has been demonstrated to stakeholders. Multiple iterations or sprints might be required to release a product or new features.

Recently, Agile has begun to attract serious interest from *developers of physical products – firms such as Honeywell, LEGO, Danfoss, and Tetra Pak.*[29] In manufacturing firms, Agile was first adopted by IT departments, or by R&D groups in which software development was a key part of hardware projects (for example, telecommunications systems). The results of these initial projects encouraged R&D groups working on hardware or physical product development to experiment with Agile, and to modify the method to fit their needs.[30]

Physical product development, however, is much different from software development. For one thing, software development is almost *infinitely divisible*. A software development consisting of one million lines of code can be broken down into one hundred increments of roughly 10,000 lines, each increment yielding a working feature. But the development of a new machine, a new food product, or a new polymer cannot be incrementalized in this way, and thus the notion of short time-boxed sprints and being able to deliver something that works at the end of each sprint does not apply quite as well.

In spite of these differences, leading firms have integrated key elements of the Agile Manifesto into their *Stage-Gate* processes and created an *Agile-Stage-Gate hybrid model*—see Figure 6.3, next chapter. They have built in time-boxed sprints for which the deliverable is something physical that can be demonstrated: The emphasis is on results rather than on documentation. At the end of each "done sprint," actual results—for example, a validated working model or design drawings—are checked against what was planned in that sprint.

An example:[31] Chamberlain, a large US manufacturer of electromechanical control devices, such as garage door openers for homes, has increasingly moved into remote control devices, for example, to control driveway gates, the lighting, and even the front door lock, via smartphone connectivity. Thus, an ever-larger percentage of each new-product project entails software development. To no one's surprise, the perennial conflict between the hardware and software developers arose: *Stage-Gate* or Agile?[32]

In response, Richard Peterson, the company's vice president for new-product development, introduced the concept of Agile within *Stage-Gate*, integrating the two concepts to improve development efforts across all groups and all project types. "We developed a modified Agile approach that requires a rigorous *Stage-Gate* process, and continual end-to-end assessment."[33] The firm now uses Agile sprints and scrums for both physical and IT development within *Stage-Gate* phases. Agile is employed in particular in the development and testing stages of the *Stage-Gate* process. A scrum master oversees daily scrums, about twenty minutes in length; the firm also builds design reviews into some scrums and even brings in peers and outsiders for a peer review. Sprints are about two weeks in length. For this firm's remote-control devices, it is usually not possible to produce a potentially releasable product every two weeks, but the project team must show something physical at the end of a sprint that was defined at the start; this is *the result of completed tasks in that sprint*—and not just a slide deck. The result of a sprint could be, for example, a set of completed design drawings or a prototype or an early working model of the product.

In Chamberlain's system, project teams have dedicated team members for each project. Because dedicated teams are not feasible for every project, the firm uses this *Agile-Stage-Gate* approach only for the larger, major revenue-generating projects—about 20 percent of the projects in their development pipeline.

Chamberlain has been using this hybrid process on all major new-product initiatives for about four years. The process has worked well, according to senior management, and has driven down cycle times. Also, there is much better communication within development teams, and a heightened sense of community. David Schuda, business transformation leader, described a complex program to develop automated gate operators: "I don't know how we would have got this project done without this Agile-Stage-Gate approach." He went on: "We achieved a 50 percent reduction in field returns in a product that was difficult to get right." Schuda estimates "a 20 to 30 percent cycle-time reduction in new-product projects because there is much less 'redo' in projects now." Productivity is up too: "Anytime you can reduce cycle time, there will be a reduction in work!"

A few challenges have arisen at Chamberlain. Project leaders and teams tended to become so focused on the sprints—the next few weeks and their objective for that sprint—that the team lost sight of the ultimate goal. Senior management now meets with hybrid teams periodically (more frequently than just at gates) to ensure that the longer-term view is considered and the ultimate goal is clear. The problem was resolved.

Additionally, senior leaders were initially somewhat skeptical of the new Scrum system. Thus, they were not required to "speak Agile," and the firm did not change the new-product development language used in the business. Moreover, the gates remained as they had been in the firm's gating system: Deliverables from the previous stage were checked, and a Go/Kill decision was made to move to the next stage. The changes took place at the project team level—multiple sprints were employed within the Development and Testing phases, and program managers (project leaders) were subjected to much pressure to learn how to facilitate the Agile process and to become scrum masters.

The method is very resource intensive: The project team is 100 percent dedicated to the project, and senior management is very much engaged in the many sprint reviews. A project can be killed or redirected at any milestone if important assumptions are not validated; it does not wait until the next gate for the Go/Kill decision.

Integrating Agile with Stage-Gate: The Agile-Stage-Gate Hybrid Model

Adopting Agile doesn't mean abandoning *Stage-Gate*. Indeed, as Daniel Karlstrom and Per Runeson note in their case studies of high-technology firms using agile and gating systems, the *Stage-Gate* framework can provide important support for Agile development processes: "Software development projects are not isolated activities.[34] They usually exist as subprojects in an environment composed of hardware development, marketing, production planning, etc. which all must be managed and coordinated concurrently . . . [A *Stage-Gate* system] gives support not only for the communication within the project, but also for decision-makers sponsoring the project or acquiring the outcome of the project." Similarly, Barry Boehm and Richard

> Adopting Agile doesn't mean abandoning *Stage-Gate*. Indeed, the *Stage-Gate* framework can provide important support for Agile development.

Turner, discussing the contrasts between plan-driven software development and Agile approaches, conclude that future projects will need both agility and discipline, which can be achieved by containing the agile development methodology within the gate model.[35]

Firms are arriving at this conclusion on their own. Corning still uses its *Stage-Gate* framework even for these Agile projects. "After more than 20 years with *Stage-Gate*, people are very familiar with it—it's a common reference point, and a good communication tool across marketing, production, and R&D,"[36] says Bruce Kirk, former director of Corporate Innovation Effectiveness. L. M. Ericsson, maker of telecommunications equipment (hardware and software), has also integrated Agile methods with its *Stage-Gate* system, relying on time-boxed iterations with physical deliverables throughout the development and testing stages. More detail on the *Agile-Stage-Gate* hybrid model is *provided in the next chapter*: results, challenges, solutions, and illustrations.

AN ACCELERATED PROCESS

A third goal of next-generation idea-to-launch systems is to accelerate projects. Often, taking simple steps, such as removing the time wasters and blockages through "lean methods," notably *value-stream analysis,* cuts the time-to-market dramatically. Firms are employing a *range of methods* to accelerate development projects, including overlapping stages and concurrent activities, dedicated teams assigned to properly resource projects, efforts to sharpen the fuzzy front end, and automated systems to support project management.

Overlapping Stages and Concurrent Activities

An important way to accelerate projects is *simultaneous or concurrent execution.* Here, key activities and even entire stages overlap, allowing projects to move ahead when information is reliable and stable; that is, not waiting for perfect information (Figure 5.9). Project teams can move activities forward by executing them in parallel rather than in series. The rule is this: Move forward when the information is reliable and stable (in other words, don't wait to start the next task until you have all the information from the previous task). In this way, the project can be accelerated—a rugby approach with multiple parallel activities, rather than a relay race, with activities strung out in series in a painfully slow fashion. In some cases, it is even acceptable to move activities from one stage to an earlier stage and, in effect, *to overlap stages*: starting one stage before the previous stage is finished, much as was shown in Corning's model, bottom of Figure 4.1.

Figure 5.9: Overlapping Activities Within Stages, and even Between Stages (Overlapping Stages) Saves Time, but Increases Risk

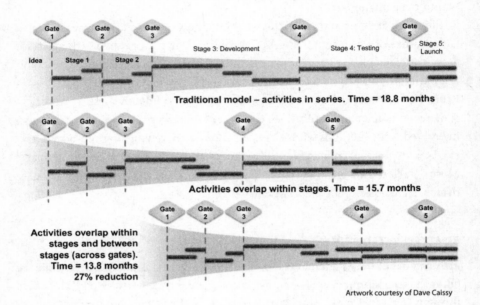

Artwork courtesy of Dave Caissy

> *Stage-Gate* must be agile, adaptable, and flexible. Spirals, along with moving activities forward—overlapping stages and activities (concurrent activities)—are the way to do this.

Note the time savings in Figure 5.9. The upper diagram is the traditional model (18.8 months to market), but by overlapping activities within stages (middle diagram), the time is cut by 3 months, or 16.5 percent. But by overlapping stages—Stages 4 and 3, and Stages 5 and 4—time is reduced by 5 months, or 27.6 percent.

An example: Toyota has long used this approach; the rule in the firm's development process is to *synchronize processes for simultaneous execution.*[37] That is, each subsequent function maximizes the utility of the stable information available from the previous function as it becomes available. Development teams must do the most they can with only that portion of the data that is not likely to change. Each function's processes are designed to move forward simultaneously, building around stable data as they become available.

Concurrent engineering has been around for some time; less well practiced, however, is concurrency across multiple cross-functional activities in order to accelerate the new-product process. When it is acceptable to move activities forward depends in part on the *quality of information available.* The information the project team has should be judged in terms of:

- Reliability—is the information fact based or is it hearsay, speculation, and opinion?
- Stability—is the information likely to change, or is it relatively stable over time?

A word of caution: As noted in Toyota's principles of lean development, only use that portion of the data that is *not likely to change.* Working with early and fluid data will result in much waste—you think you are saving time, but it will actually take longer than the traditional linear process. So, review the available data (example: design requirements), noting that which is fact based and solid versus that which is speculative and fluid.

Simultaneous execution usually adds risk to a project. For example, the decision to purchase production equipment before field trials are completed, thereby avoiding a long order lead-time, may be a good application of simultaneous execution. But there is risk, too—the risk that the project may be canceled or change direction after dedicated production equipment is purchased. Thus, the decision to overlap activities and stages is *a calculated risk*—so calculate the risk! That is, the *cost of delay* must be weighed against the *cost and probability of being wrong*—see Table 5.1.

Suggestion: Take a look at your typical major projects and see how much time can be saved by moving to a concurrent process, as in Figure 5.9. Overlap activities and even overlap stages. But there is risk, so do calculate the risk and see if moving activities and stages forward makes sense. Table 5.1 provides a guide.

Leaning Down the Process

Another facet of Agile development that many firms have embraced is the drive to make the system more lean and nimble. The definition of bureaucracy is "work that adds no value," and getting rid of such work in your idea-to-launch system is certainly consistent with yet another Agile principle: "Simplicity—the art of maximizing the amount of *work not done*—is essential." Here are some typical issues:

Demanding much non-value-added work: Some companies' processes build every possible activity into each stage, and long lists of required tasks and activities per stage are the result. Moreover, many *Stage-Gate* processes over time become far too bulky as more and more make-work gets added to the system.

TABLE 5.1: CALCULATE THE RISK OF MOVING FORWARD

First, determine the Cost of Delay (the actual cost in dollars per day of delay). It has five components:

1. The cost of the deferred income stream:

    - Money has a time value!
    - Look at your projected cash profit stream after launch.
    - Determine its present value (PV in $000).
    - Multiply the PV by your annual cost of capital (%) and divide by 365 days.

    That's the *daily cost* of deferring or postponing your income because of delay.

2. The lost window of opportunity:

    - If your product has a limited window of sales opportunity:
    - Determine the cost of these lost sales (on a per-day basis).

3. The extra development and testing costs:
    - Any project that lasts longer invariably ends up costing more than it should.
    - Estimate the *marginal cost* per day of the project for "hanging around" longer than it should (this marginal cost is less than the full cost per day of development, but more than zero).

4. Loss of competitive advantage:

    - In fast-moving and competitive markets, where being first-in really matters.
    - This is an estimate—the impact of lost market share.

5. Other costs—examples are:

    - The costs of delivering late to a key customer (sometimes there are contractual penalties and certainly other intangible costs).
    - The cost of delaying a partner's launch of their product.

Add up items 1–5 above. Use this cost-per-day of delay ($000) in your calculations when you determine whether or not it makes sense to move forward.

Moving forward in an accelerated fashion is a calculated risk—so do calculate the risk!

Cost of delay = number of days saved x cost-per-day of delay
versus
Cost of being wrong x Probability of being wrong

The cost of being wrong can usually be determined—for example, having to cancel an order on production equipment or write off development of some marketing and launch materials. If the cost of delay far exceeds the cost and probabilities of being wrong, move forward! Move the long lead-time items ahead!

Deliverables overkill: Most companies' new product processes suffer from far too much information delivered to the gatekeepers at each gate—long reports and PowerPoint presentations. The project team screams "too much bureaucracy and too much work to prepare for gates," while the gatekeepers complain that they must plow through pages of materials, much of it not relevant to the decision. Several factors create this deliverables overkill:

- Because the project team is not certain what information is required, they overdeliver—they prepare an overly comprehensive report, and in so doing, *bulletproof* themselves. What is needed is a better understanding between project teams and gatekeepers regarding just what information is needed at each gate: Expectations must be made clear on both sides.
- The fault can also be the design of the company's gating system itself. The system often includes very elaborate templates that must be filled out for each gate, regardless. Some experts argue that templates are mind numbing and encourage unneeded work; others argue that in any process, templates are a useful guide and help to structure the data. Either way, overly detailed templates, replete with pages of fields to be filled in, can lead to deliverables overkill.

Although some of the information that gating systems demand may be interesting, often much of it is not essential to the gate decision. Detailed explanations of how the market research was done, or sketches of what the new molecule looks like, add no value to the decision. Restrict the deliverables and their templates to the essential information needed to make the gate decisions. Some examples:

> Johnson & Johnson has revised its idea-to-launch process to eliminate bureaucracy—work that doesn't add value—using Lean Six Sigma methods. In the company's Ethicon Surgery group, Business Cases that had been thirty- to ninety-page documents that took weeks to prepare are now down to four pages and a lot less work.[38]
>
> P&G's SIMPL process has been similarly trimmed as the company moved to much leaner gates, cutting the volume of deliverables packages to a mere six pages.[39] And at Praxair, the process manager uses lean methods (value-stream analysis) to see where the problems and time wasters are.[40] For example, a chemical reactor for R&D work is typically designed for the task, not for the turnaround. But it takes three days to do the task, and then twenty-one days to turn the reactor around for the next task. A reactor designed for both turn-around and task removes a big time waster in the development stage.

Confusing bureaucracy with useful work? Living any system requires some effort, and indeed *Stage-Gate* makes certain demands on project teams, leaders, and gatekeepers. For example, project teams are expected to meet a certain standard in terms of front-end homework and get the facts on their project—something that may be challenging to people who are used to pulling numbers out of the air. Similarly, gates do take a bit of effort and represent demands both for gatekeepers and project teams, especially in a company used to casual or intuitive decision-making or one-person executive-edict gate meetings.

All of these demands may seem like extra work to those new to *Stage-Gate*. The argument voiced is that "all this extra work is bureaucratic—we can skip over these tasks and save ourselves lots of time and money." This argument would be convincing, if it weren't for the evidence: The extra work is well worth the effort and pays for itself many times in terms of increased success rates, greater project profits, and often shorter times to market in the long run. The point is that one must be very careful not to confuse *avoiding bureaucracy* (defined as doing work that adds no value) with *intellectual laziness* or *sloppy execution* (skipping key tasks that do add much value, but do take a little more time and effort to do them right). Many project teams and companies are guilty of the latter.

Using "Lean Techniques" to Remove Waste

Smart companies have made their next generation *Stage-Gate* process *lean*, removing waste and inefficiency at every opportunity. They have borrowed the concept of *value-stream analysis* from lean manufacturing and have applied it to their new-product idea-to-launch process.

A *value stream* is simply the connection of all the process steps with the goal of maximizing customer value.[41] In product development, a value stream represents the linkage of all value-added and non-value-added activities associated with the creation of a new product or service. The tool known as the *value-stream map* is used to identify and document value streams in product innovation and is critical to identifying both value-added and non-value-added activities, hence is an essential tool to improving your idea-to-launch process.

> Smart companies have made their next generation *Stage-Gate* process *lean*, removing waste and inefficiency at every opportunity. They have borrowed the concept of *value-stream analysis* from lean manufacturing and have applied it to their idea-to-launch process.

In employing value-stream analysis, a task force creates a map of the value stream for typical development projects in your business—the way your current idea-to-launch process really works (an abbreviated example is shown in Figure 5.10). All the stages, decision points, and key activities in a typical project are mapped out, with typical times for each activity and decisions indicated. Use a long roll of paper on a wall, and large Post-Its to show the key activities and decisions along the way. Usually, in undertaking this mapping, it becomes clear that there is often a difference between the way the process is supposed to work, and the way it works in reality.

Once the value stream is mapped out, the task force lowers the microscope on the process and dissects it, critically assessing each step and activity in the process and posing four key questions:

1. What work gets done at this step, stage, or activity?
2. How well do we execute this activity? How long does it typically take?
3. Is this step or activity really needed?
4. If so, how can it be made better? How can it be made faster?

All procedures, required deliverables, documents and templates, committees and decision processes are examined, looking for time wasters. Once problems, time wasters, and non-value-added activities are spotted, the task force then works to remove them. Such a disciplined approach invariably spots non-value-added work in the system, and steps can then be taken to modify the system to remove it:

An example: Acme Company (disguised name) develops important components for paper machines in the pulp-and-paper industry. (Paper machines are huge $100+ million machines that make paper continuously, occupying a

Figure 5.10: Construct the "Value-Stream Map" of Your Idea-to-Launch Process and Look to Remove Waste

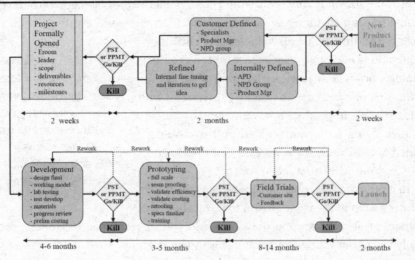

Value-stream map from a manufacturer of process equipment. Disguised and abbreviated. The process chart was drawn on a ten-meter length of paper, but reduced to show here. Times to complete each task are noted, along with recycles and rework (deficiencies in the process are also noted on the original chart—not shown here).

space the size of an aircraft hangar.) The value-stream map in Figure 5.10 is an abbreviated map from this firm.

One particularly troublesome aspect of the process in Figure 5.10 centers on field trials: It takes eight to fourteen months to undertake field trials on a real paper machine; and often the trials don't work, so they must be repeated. Field trials can thus add months, even years, to projects!

The task force undertook a *root-cause analysis*, which revealed the following: Field trials are done at customers' plants—a paper mill—so Acme must wait until a scheduled customer plant shutdown. The field trial is fairly expensive for customers, so they are somewhat reluctant to do these all the time. Besides, there's no real incentive for customers to undertake field trials for Acme. More insights: The frequent recycles, which really slow the project and add cost to the customer, are largely due to a lack of understanding of users' needs and applications, or serious technical flaws in the solution.

Additional analysis revealed that the main competitor does not have the same problem, as it does initial field trials on an in-house *pilot plant paper machine* owned by that company. The pilot machine replicates a full paper machine very well and thus reduces the field trial risk to the customer: The trial product is almost proven on the pilot machine and so recycles are largely eliminated—the competitor gets the product right before conducting a full customer field trial.

Then the task force worked hard to find solutions to the defined problems. Here are the solutions as a result of this value-stream and root-cause analyses that the task force proposed and implemented:

- *Get access to a pilot plant paper machine:* The task force investigated this option and found several pilot machines available; for example, several institutes at universities had such machines and they were available for a fee.
- *Better upfront homework and VoC work:* A VoC Task Force was set up, sponsored by the chief marketing officer, to probe how to do this. VoC methods were investigated and some recommended; and VoC became a mandatory step in their idea-to-launch process: time and actions devoted to determine needs, application requirements, operating conditions, customer benefits sought, and so on.
- *More incentive for the customer:* Project teams were directed to seek a better understanding of the value-in-use for customer (the result of better VoC and front-end homework). Further, incentives for the customer were built in (for example, some degree of exclusivity regarding product use).
- *More selectivity on new-product projects:* Management put some tougher gates and policies in place: "Don't do every customer request—only those projects with a demonstrable, visible benefit to the customer and with a strong incentive to cooperate."
- *Technical issues:* The firm's technical skills were rated number one in the world. But a better understanding of the customer problem, benefits sought, and operating conditions would help focus the R&D work.

These five action items were implemented. They dramatically reduced the field trial problem and greatly accelerated the innovation process—another value-stream analysis success!

Suggestion: Get rid of the waste, bureaucracy, and excess baggage! If it does not add value, cut it out. Use methods borrowed from the field of lean manufacturing, including *value-stream analysis,* to identify non-value-added activities; and use root-cause analysis to rectify problematic steps and tasks in your process.

Properly Resourced Projects with Dedicated Teams

One of the major impediments to fast delivery of new products is *a lack of focus and inadequate resources*—spreading resources too thinly across too many projects and other work.[42] We saw in Chapter 3 that a lack of focus and inadequate resources are *the number one weakness* in businesses' new-product development efforts; Figures 3.7 and 3.8 reveal the magnitude of the deficiency.

If you want speed to market, then focus—resource your projects properly. *Fully dedicated teams* are a must in order to maximize speed, especially for critical and bold projects. Benchmarking studies show that best-performing innovators are considerably more focused than others—not spread too thinly across too many development projects. They also have dedicated resources for product innovation: Half of the top firms have dedicated product-development teams (project team members not working on a lot of other tasks), and more than half have a fully dedicated product innovation group that works on new products full time (see Figures 3.7 and 3.8 in Chapter 3). The Agile method introduced above also stipulates that the development team be 100 percent dedicated to the project, and even colocated (in the same room)!

> If you want speed to market, then focus—resource your projects properly.

Suggestion: You *cannot duck the issue of adequate resourcing* if speed to market is the goal. First, get the facts on your new-product resource situation: Undertake a resource capacity analysis as outlined in Chapter 3. Address the two questions:

1. Do you have enough resources in place (and on project teams) to execute the projects in your development pipeline according to their proposed timelines or launch dates?
2. Do you have enough resources in place to get the right projects executed to achieve your business's new-product development goals (for example, annual sales objectives from new products)?

Once you have the facts, then work on solutions: perhaps singling out 20 percent of "top priority projects" as in examples above and dedicate resources to these. Or maybe undertake a tough pruning exercise and get rid of marginal projects that offer minimal value to the company, thus freeing scarce resources to go to more deserving projects. Or how about just putting the necessary resources in place—a dedicated innovation group, or simply the addition of new people and skills?

Sharpening the Fuzzy Front End

More thoughtful scoping—better front-end homework to anticipate challenges in advance and get projects requiring new technology on the right track—can do much to save time downstream. A sharper, earlier definition of project needs and solutions can help steer downstream decision making and clarify assumptions and risks:

> *An example:* P&G addresses this issue in the design of their Agile Innovation Management (AIM) system,* instituted to build capabilities in project leaders and bring the agility of the system to the next level. AIM forces a very deliberate focus on the scoping of the project, placing an emphasis on the front end of the SIMPL process and making the fuzzy front end a little less fuzzy. This scoping is accomplished through a set of questions that must have clear answers before the project moves forward:
>
> - What is the risk of the project and what are the true requirements for success?
> - What do you want and when?
> - What is possible and when?
> - Do you need invention?
>
> If the answer to the last question is yes, the project moves into P&G's technology development system (FEI, front-end innovation, similar to *Stage-Gate-TD*).

Automated Systems Via Software

An increasingly popular way of accelerating projects is the use of automation software in support of *Stage-Gate* and new-product development generally. The benefits of automation are several. Less time is required to complete stage activities and deliverables, and the administrative load associated with process execution is reduced. For example, project team members can more easily create gate deliverables, search for documents, and perform other routine tasks when they have ready access to embedded templates and best-practice content. Some systems prepopulate templates for key deliverables (such as status reports, presentations, and resource charts) with project information recorded elsewhere in the system. As a result, documents that previously took hours or days to prepare can be completed in minutes.[43]

---

* Nothing to do with the Agile methodology from the software world.

The templates further serve as how-to references that project team members follow as they complete tasks, helping to ensure that key process steps are followed. Automation can also help project leaders by providing them with preformatted models for the creation of new projects, including definitions for each stage and gate and listings of corresponding deliverables. Such preformatted models also help to ensure consistency in process execution.

Senior management and project leaders get the information they need: They can see how a specific project is moving along, or gain a perspective of the entire portfolio of projects. Any number of dashboards and views are available to provide the type of information that both management and the project leader could desire.

Finally, such software tools make positive contributions to many different facets of product development, including resource management, portfolio management, idea management, product roadmapping, and others—all of which help to improve the efficiency and effectiveness of the innovation process.

INTEGRATING THE NEW METHODS INTO A NEXT-GENERATION IDEA-TO-LAUNCH SYSTEM

This chapter has provided many insights into what leading companies are doing to reinvent their *Stage-Gate* systems, and in some cases move beyond it. Integrating these various improvements and changes—some evolutionary, such as fast-track versions, some more revolutionary, such as the risk-based contingency model and the *Agile-Stage-Gate* hybrid model—produces a framework for next-generation idea-to-launch systems. This new framework can be contrasted with traditional *Stage-Gate* development in terms of context, system design, the role of gates, and the organization of project teams, as summarized in Figures 5.11 to 5.12.

> To my knowledge, no company has yet implemented every element of the next-generation system. But some have come close.

The traditional process is *well suited to known and traditional product developments*, which are the majority of projects for most firms. But the newer process is generally designed for more innovative and bolder projects targeted at less well defined but growing markets and relying on newer technology with technology risks.

The next-generation system is *adaptive and flexible, agile, and accelerated*. Projects move quickly and nimbly, sprint to sprint, and feature frequent experiments or spirals, with the evolving product regularly exposed to customers in a

Figure 5.11: The Context or Situation—Traditional *Stage-Gate* and Next-Generation System

	Traditional *Stage-Gate*	Next-Generation *Stage-Gate* System
The Situation	Mature market. Well-known market, customers, and needs. Well-known technology. Few market or technical uncertainties and risks.	Existing and rapidly growing market. Large potential market: "If we can do this, it's big." Many market uncertainties, some technical risks.
Project Type	New item in an existing product line, product improvement, modification, renovation.	Innovation: bigger, bolder project.
Example	New model of an HP ink-jet printer.	Apple's i-Pod.
Customer Needs	Well-known and stable over time.	Some known, some unarticulated. Many unsolved problems and unresolved needs.
Market Size	Large and defined; may be maturing, flat, or even declining.	Existing, not necessarily large, but growing rapidly; large potential; in the "growth phase" of Product Life Cycle.
Competition	Red ocean; many capable competitors; undifferentiated products, even commodity.	Some early competitors, who may not have the right or dominant solution yet.
Technology Maturity	Mature, well-known, in-house.	Newer technology, but largely existing. Technology may be new to company but familiar.
Technical Risks	Few risks; technical hurdles can be overcome easily. Can already envision a solution.	Some risks and technical hurdles; hurdles can likely be overcome. Technical solution is largely envisioned.

Figure 5.12: The Idea-to-Launch Methodology—Traditional *Stage-Gate* and Next-Generation System

	Traditional *Stage-Gate*	Next-Generation *Stage-Gate* System
Idea-to-Launch System	Well-defined traditional *Stage-Gate* process (Figure 4.11). Fairly repeatable and predicable activities. Stages laid out in a linear fashion. Activities specified in each stage, like an SOP manual. Standard gate deliverables, prespecified. Clear Go/Kill criteria, largely financial. Rigorous gate reviews. Monitor the project versus the plan.	Agile, adaptive, and flexible, accelerated *Stage-Gate* system. Stages divided into fast, short time-boxed sprints. Move quickly and nimbly, sprint by sprint. Include frequent "design-build-test" iterations. Overlapping stages. Lean, all waste removed. Custom-tailored action plans—Innovation-Project Canvas. Risk-based contingency approach.
Product Definition	Established in detail up-front (>90% specified) based on well-understood customer requirements and defined technical solutions.	Partly established up-front (40%–70% specified pre-Development). Updated via spirals—feedback on design and on changing or new customer needs.
Under-standing the Market and Customer	Use traditional market research: VoC including site visits and ethnography. Determine needs, wants, desires, problems.	Create mechanisms to work with real customers who represent the market. VoC early to determine needs, problems, market potential. Then iterations with users via rapid prototypes, protocepts, early beta versions, etc.
Building the Right Technical Solution	Follow dominant design by adding customer-valued features (visible improvements). Emphasize process and cost-focused innovations (getting costs down).	Define product, technical choices, and features through early or rapid prototypes, protocepts, and beta-products to customers. Seek customer confirmation of design, value, and sales volume through spirals.

Figure 5.13: How the Gates Work—Traditional *Stage-Gate* and Next-Generation System

	Traditional *Stage-Gate*	Next-Generation *Stage-Gate* System
Go/Kill Criteria	Largely financial: NPV, IRR, Payback Period Financial Risk vs. Return assessment.	More qualitative and strategic. Based on a scorecard with both non-financial and financial criteria. ECV to deal with risk and options.
Gatekeepers	Senior and mid-management from the Business Unit.	Senior and mid-management from the Business Unit. Gatekeepers (sponsors) are senior people—to ensure adequate resourcing.
Emphasis	Gate deliverables are mostly information and documentation (may overemphasize reports, often too volumous).	A focus on results, not on documentation. Being able to show something that works (or something physical) to stakeholders.
Deliverables Required	Well-defined list of deliverables for each gate (relying on standard templates). Fairly disciplined.	Deliverables templates do exist, but used only as a guide. Higher level, less detailed, leaned down.
How Are Deliverables Decided?	Fairly standard and a broad list for every project and each gate, much like an SOP.	Team and gatekeepers identify key assumptions and unknowns, then define knowledge gaps, tasks, and deliverables. Project specific—customized deliverables.
Portfolio Management	Most Go/Kill decisions are taken at gate meetings. Portfolio reviews are a check.	Gates are integrated with portfolio reviews (Go/Kill decisions made at both reviews).

Figure 5.14: Managing and Organizing the Projects—Traditional *Stage-Gate* and Next-Generation System

	Traditional *Stage-Gate*	Next-Generation *Stage-Gate* System
Project Management	Traditional plan-based approach: Gantt Charts or Critical Path Plans are developed and approved for the entire stage	Agile project-management methods: Start with tentative plan, then "plan on the fly" Stages broken into fast, short sprints
Organizational Structure	Organized by specialized functions or as a cross-functional project team.	Organized by project—cross-functional project team. Can be a venture team. for major projects, team may operate outside the organizational structure, e.g., a skunk works or an off-site team.
Resources	Team members are on multiple projects concurrently; projects often understaffed. Time and resource allocation decisions made at gates.	Team is dedicated: 100% (or a high percent of their time) to this project. Properly resourced: "What do you need to get this project done…?"
Team Structure	Balanced Matrix: Project leader is assigned to oversee project. Team members assigned from functional departments.	Project Matrix: Project leader is assigned to oversee project and has primary responsibility and authority for project. Has control over his/her resources.
Relation to Functional Departments	Project Leader shares responsibility and authority with functional managers. Joint approval and direction.	Functional managers assign personnel as needed and provide technical and marketing expertise to project.

series of build-test-revise iterations. Product definition is far from 100 percent at the beginning of development, but evolves as customers confirm the product's value proposition through protocepts, rapid prototypes, and early beta versions. And the team uses Agile project-management methods: stages divided into fast, short sprints, and the team plans "on the fly," sprint by sprint.

Stages and activities overlap—a rugby approach! And the process is customized to each project via the risk-based contingency approach: Starting with the Innovation Project Canvas, teams identify the uncertainties and risks, define the critical assumptions, and identify the information gaps and the activities needed to close the gaps and to validate the key assumptions.

Gates are still part of the next-generation system, but are integrated with portfolio management and portfolio reviews. Go/Kill and prioritization decisions may be made at any of these points, as well as reviews (milestones) at the end of some sprints, for example, if an important assumption is not confirmed. Go/Kill criteria are less financially based, emphasizing more strategic, competitive, and leverage factors; when the criteria are financial, they employ more appropriate financial models to account for risk and options buying. Senior management is more engaged in the investment decision process, ready to commit the necessary resources to execute the project in an accelerated fashion.

Organizationally, the next-generation system requires *dedicated cross-functional project teams* with the resources needed to move the project forward quickly—dedicated people for important projects, not spread over multiple projects and other tasks. Functional managers become resource providers. The project team may be organized as a project matrix or venture team, or may even operate outside the official bureaucracy of the company (for example, as a skunk works).

To my knowledge, *no company has yet implemented* every element of the next-generation system described here. But some have come close. Private discussions with executives in these firms reveal dramatically positive results.

So perhaps it's time to rethink your idea-to-launch system, borrow some of the methods outlined in this chapter, and strive for more a more adaptive, agile, and accelerated stage-and-gate system.

6

THE *AGILE-STAGE-GATE*®
HYBRID MODEL

Intelligence is the ability to adapt to change.
—STEPHEN HAWKING, English Physicist

THE BEST OF BOTH: AGILE AND *STAGE-GATE*
Agile versus Stage-Gate?[1]

One of the most heated meetings I have ever facilitated was between software and hardware developers in a large US instrument firm whose products included both hardware and software components. The question was, for the development of the software component, can or should Agile development methods—designed for software projects—and *Stage-Gate*—designed for hardware projects—be used together or only separately? But more: Can or should hardware developers employ aspects of Agile, for example, the sprints and scrums that are central to the Agile-Scrum method? In other words, are the two approaches *complementary* or *mutually exclusive*? Can Agile be *integrated* with a traditional stage-and-gate model? And can the resulting *hybrid model* also be used for the development of physical products?

> Can Agile from the software world be integrated with *Stage-Gate* and yield faster, more adaptive developments for physical or manufactured new products? Or for service-sector products?

Agile was created in response to the particular problems facing software developers. Its relevance is clear when a firm's products include *both hardware and software*, and the two development efforts must be integrated: A hybrid Agile-Stage-Gate approach can both respond to the specific needs of each component of the project and help integrate the two efforts. Moreover, Agile methods promise to improve speed to market and increase development productivity, something that all hardware developers strive for.

As they face increasingly fluid markets, where nothing is stable for long, manufacturers have also begun looking at development methods that are more adaptive, allowing for faster response to changing customer requirements. Some manufacturers, struggling with these challenges, found Agile quite attractive. But Agile alone isn't sufficient to support new product development for manufacturers. As a result, some manufacturers of products from food to machinery are turning to *hybrid development processes that integrate Agile with Stage-Gate*, even when no software development is involved. And some of these early adopters are finding that the benefits of adopting a hybrid *Agile-Stage-Gate* approach can be significant.

The Evolution of Agile

Agile software development is a group of software development methodologies based on an iterative and incremental process in which requirements and solutions evolve through collaboration between self-organizing, cross-functional teams.[2] When Agile emerged in the late 1990s and early 2000s, its methods were seen as the solution to many problems in software development that traditional *waterfall** or *plan-based development processes* then used by the software industry could not deal with.[3]

These traditional waterfall processes tend to focus on a big, long-term goal—a final product and its major features. But requirements tend to change rapidly in software projects; the features and schedule defined when the project was initially planned often were no longer valid by the end of a twelve- to eighteen-month development cycle. And, as Reagan puts it, "it's hard to alter course when you're being swept down a large waterfall . . . too much upfront planning means too much change management downstream."[4] Committing early to features and schedule means that compromises will be needed late in the game; early commitments to large features, long schedules, long feedback loops, and the replanning inherent in traditional product-development processes create inefficiencies and slow the development cycle.

---

* "Waterfall" is the term used to describe the *plan-based* software-development process. A typical Gantt chart (timeline chart) looks like a series of cascades or waterfalls.

Figure 6.1 The Twelve Principles in the Agile Manifesto that Underlie Agile Development in the Software World

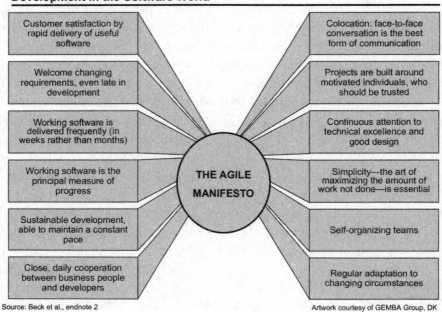

Source: Beck et al., endnote 2   Artwork courtesy of GEMBA Group, DK

Agile emerged in the late 1990s in software development, developed by software project managers who needed smarter ways to execute projects. The trend was global, and more than fourteen different Agile methodologies or frameworks were proposed and implemented. Finally, in 2001, the Agile masters met in a cabin in Utah to discuss their methodologies and find a common ground. From this meeting came the *Agile Manifesto*, which today still binds the Agile methodologies together with a joint set of values. The Agile Manifesto emphasizes:

- individuals and interactions over processes and tools;
- working software over comprehensive documentation;
- customer collaboration over contract negotiation; and
- responding to change instead of following a plan.

The Agile Manifesto elaborated a set of twelve supporting principles, among them an insistence that (1) working software be delivered quickly and iterated frequently (in cycles of weeks rather than months), and that (2) working software be the principal measure of progress—see Figure 6.1.[5]

A Quick Look at Agile

Agile development is designed specifically to help product developers rapidly create working software with *continuous validation from the customer*. Once a development project has been approved and its initial requirements mapped out, Agile provides *a focus on execution*—that is, writing lines of code. In practice, Agile breaks the development phase of the project into a series of very short time-boxed iterations or *sprints*, each typically about two to four weeks long. The goal of each sprint is to deliver working software code that can be demonstrated to stakeholders—that is, software that is potentially releasable to the market (although it usually takes several sprints to produce a market-ready product).

> Agile breaks development into a series of short time-boxed sprints, typically two to four weeks long.

The dedicated development team, which is colocated in one room, meets every morning for their daily stand-up or *daily scrum* to discuss progress and issues, and what they will accomplish that day. Sprint-planning meetings at the beginning of each sprint decide what can be realistically accomplished in the next two- to four-week sprint. Customer feedback and required product changes are introduced at the end of each sprint for action in the next sprint. Thus the Agile process is very fast and responsive—it is *not plan based, but more "plan on the fly,"* sprint by sprint. Note that Agile is usually used initially for the "technical phases" of the project, namely the equivalent of the Development (Alpha) and Testing (Beta) stages of the typical gating system in Figure 4.11.

> The Agile process is very fast and responsive—it is not plan based, but more "plan on the fly," sprint by sprint.

Where Agile and Stage-Gate *Each Fit In*

In their book, Barry Boehm and Richard Turner aptly summarize the differences between plan-driven software development (based on waterfall models) and Agile approaches. Gate models, they explain, are generally "plan-driven models," whereas Agile is more about *planning as the project moves along*.[6] The authors discuss the contrasts between plan-driven software development and Agile approaches at length, complete with successful case examples from the software industry where the two models have been integrated. For instance, plan-driven approaches emphasize verification (working products that reflect the original requirements) and validation (the final product satisfies its intended mission), while Agile emphasizes simple designs based on YAGNI (you aren't going to

Figure 6.2: Where Agile and Plan-Driven Gating Models Fit

Characteristics of Project or Setting	Agile Home Ground	Plan-Driven (Gating System) Home Ground
Criticality of project	Low	Extreme
Developers' Experience	Senior (experienced)	More junior
Product Requirements	Change often during project	Stable requirements and specifications
Project Team Size	Small	Large
Company Culture	Culture that responds to change	Culture that demands order

Adapted from: Boehm & Turner, endnote 6

need it), a concept of not designing anything that is not needed currently—because, as things change, it may never be needed.

The authors propose a means of balancing agility and plan-driven approaches to suit the needs of a given project: The balance depends on looking at the risks of swinging too far in either the plan-driven or the Agile directions. One of the conclusions drawn in their book is that future projects will need *both agility and discipline*, which can be implemented by containing the Agile development methodology within the gate model. The authors note the types of projects best suited to each approach—see Figure 6.2—and since no project is 100 percent one extreme or the other on all five dimensions, a balanced approach appears to be best.

The argument for adopting an *Agile-Stage-Gate* hybrid is that both models bring benefits; that there are circumstances where one model works better than the other; and finally, that senior management has proven somewhat skeptical of Agile, and thus is reluctant to discard the tried-and-proven plan-driven model.[7]

Important Differences Between Agile and Stage-Gate

The differences emerge from the two systems' different intents: *Stage-Gate* is a comprehensive idea-to-launch system and a *macroplanning process*, whereas Agile is a *microplanning project-management* methodology (see Figure 6.3).

Figure 6.3: Characteristics of *Stage-Gate* versus Agile

Characteristic	*Stage-Gate*	Agile
Type of model	Macroplanning	Microplanning, project management
Scope	Idea to launch, end-to-end	Usually for Development and Testing stages; can be expanded to pre-Development and Launch stages too
Organizational: project team and breadth	Cross-functional: RD&E or technical people, Marketing, Sales & Operations	Largely technical (software developers, engineers, IT people); dedicated team
End point	A launched new product in the market	Developed and tested working software product
Decision model	Investment model: Go/Kill decisions Involves a senior governance group	Largely tactical: the actions needed for the next sprint; decisions by the self-managed team

In the IT world, Agile and *Stage-Gate* are not substitutes nor mutually exclusive, but rather complementary, by building Agile into *Stage-Gate's* stages

Source: Cooper, endnote 1

Stage-Gate is cross-functional (that is, involves people from marketing, sales, and operations alongside technical personnel) and it has multiple stages spanning the entire idea-to-launch process, from idea generation through the Business Case, development to market launch. It is also a guide to action, building in specific best practices at each stage—doing voice-of-customer (VoC) work, building a robust Business Case, designing an effective launch, and so on. In this way, it's more like a football playbook than a project-management approach. The decisions in *Stage-Gate* follow an investment decision model; a Go decision at a gate commits the resources for the next stage, so that resources are funneled to the best projects as their potential emerges. *Stage-Gate* thus provides guidance for *what projects to do* and then *what to do within each project.*

While gating methods have proved very effective in most development applications, especially in manufacturing and service industries, there have been criticisms as well.[8] As noted in the last chapter, such models are seen as being too linear, too rigid, and too planned to deal with today's fast-paced and often quickly changing world. *Stage-Gate* is not adaptive enough (although more recent versions do include iterative spirals) and does not encourage experimentation; and the system is too controlling and bureaucratic in some firms, loaded with paperwork, checklists, and too much non-value-added work. Some authors

Figure 6.4: In Traditional Project Management, the Scope of Work (Product Definition) Is Fixed, and Time and Budget Are Flexible. In Agile Time-Boxed Methods, Scope Is Flexible, but Time and Budget Are Fixed

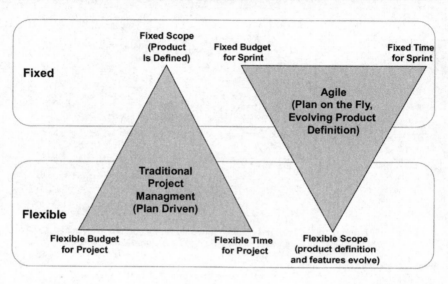

Source: Fürst, endnote 10

have taken issue with these criticisms, arguing that most are due to faulty implementation,[9] while some deficiencies have been corrected in more recent evolutions of *Stage-Gate*.

By contrast, Agile development is designed specifically to help product developers rapidly create working software with continual validation from the customer. Once the software project is approved, then Agile kicks in for the execution of the project—that is, writing lines of software code. As noted above, Agile development typically consists of a number of short development cycles, known as sprints, with each sprint undertaken by a dedicated project team. A sprint iteration typically lasts two to four weeks.

The outcome of each sprint should be *a working product* (executable software code) that can be demonstrated to stakeholders (management and customers). An iteration may not produce enough functionality to warrant a market release, but the goal is to have a *potentially available release at the end of each iteration*: Multiple iterations are usually required to bring a product or major new features to the point of market release, however. Each iteration *validates the product with stakeholders* and may identify new required features. In this way, product requirements, which are not totally known at the start, are *revealed and validated through iteration*, and requirements that are initially thought to be important but turn out not to be are weeded out: The *product's design evolves during development!*

Another conceptualization of the differences between the two systems is from *Agile-Stage-Gate* expert Peter Fürst: "In project management, there are three variables: scope of work, budget, and time. In traditional gating methods, scope of work is fixed (the product requirements), and budget and time are flexible. But in a time-boxed system, *time and budget are fixed*, and *scope of work is flexible*, at least for each sprint [emphasis mine]" (see Figure 6.4).[10]

To sum up, Agile is a *microplanning project-management tool* designed to engage a development team, including the customer, in getting to a working end product quickly. Agile is used mostly during the *Development and Testing stages* of a new-product project, at least initially—that is, for two stages out of the five or six included in the typical *Stage-Gate* process in Figure 4.11. And it is principally used first by the *technical people* doing the actual development work.

Discounting all the hype—Agile has received significant attention since the emergence of the Manifesto—Agile does appear to offer some important benefits for software companies. In their study of its implementation in software contexts, Andrew Begel and Nachiappan Nagappan identified three primary benefits: improved communication and coordination, quicker product releases, and faster responses to changed customer requirements or technical challenges. With these important benefits, Agile, not surprisingly, began to be adopted and embraced by much of the software-development industry.[11]

INTEGRATING AGILE AND *STAGE-GATE*
First Integrated in the IT Sector

As Agile took root in the software industry, a few larger IT firms that had formal development systems already in place began to build Agile into their existing gating processes, thus creating hybrid models. Their experience suggests that Agile and *Stage-Gate* can be used *together to advantage*. For instance, Daniel Karlstrom and Per Runeson studied three large, European high-technology firms where *Stage-Gate* and Agile were integrated for IT projects.[12] The three firms that took part in this Swedish study—Ericsson, ABB, and Vodafone—already had *Stage-Gate* systems; they simply built Agile methods (the XP version) into their existing processes from the development-approval gate onward.

The researchers found first, that the integration did work—the two models were indeed compatible—and second, that this hybrid approach yielded several major payoffs:

- *Better internal team communication*, leading to the team feeling more in control (and also to better and more visually intuitive progress metrics for management, for example, the burn-down chart).
- *More efficient planning*, based on early customer feedback on the really important product features (avoiding inflexible, fixed plans that lead to delays on important features, and "requirements cramming" at the end of development).
- *Improved customer feedback*, as Agile processes seek continuous feedback from customers (making the technical project manager a good candidate for the role of customer representative).
- *Clearer resolution of documentation issues,* as priorities are resolved between documentation and code.
- *Improved attitudes,* as developers are more motivated by the improved communication and sense of control.

There are, of course, also some challenges: Teams communicate better internally, but the dedication of full-time teams to the project may lead to more isolation from other parts of the organization; long-range planning tends to be ignored in favor of a focus on the current sprint; and conflicts and resistance may remain, particularly among managers who must give up some control during the Agile portions of the development process.

Overall, though, the researchers conclude, "Agile methods give the *stage-gate* model powerful tools for microplanning, day-to-day work control, and prog-ress reporting."[13] The daily face-to-face meetings called for by Agile methods provide more powerful communications than written documents, and the fast and continuous feedback from customers on product features make for a better prod-

> Agile methods give the *Stage-Gate* model powerful tools for microplanning, day-to-day work control, and progress reporting.

uct and a more efficient project. Conversely, they note that "software development projects are not isolated activities. They usually exist as subprojects in an environment composed of hardware development, marketing, production planning, etc., which all must be managed and coordinated concurrently . . . [Stage-Gate] gives support not only for the communication within the project, but also for decision-makers sponsoring the project or acquiring the outcome of the project."[14] Thus, Agile offers greater efficiency and focus, and *Stage-Gate* provides a means to coordinate with other development teams and communicate with functions such as marketing and senior management.

Figure 6.5: A Typical Four-Stage, Four-Gate System, with Agile Built into Each of the Stages—an *Agile-Stage-Gate* Hybrid Model

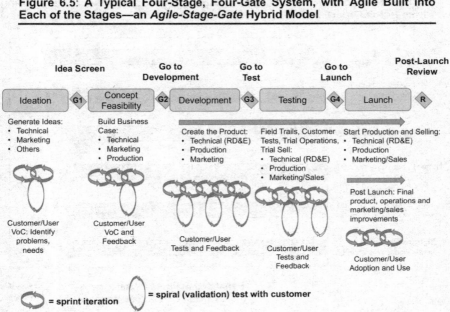

APPLYING THE *AGILE-STAGE-GATE* HYBRID MODEL TO PHYSICAL PRODUCTS

Dramatic Results

Recently, Agile has begun to attract serious interest from developers of physical products, including notable firms such as Honeywell, LEGO, Danfoss, Chamberlain, Tetra Pak, and John Deere.[15] A typical *Agile-Stage-Gate* model is shown in Figure 6.5. Recent evidence is that the *Agile-Stage-Gate* hybrid model has *significant potential benefits for manufacturers* of physical products, from heavy industrial equipment to food and toys, yielding surprisingly and dramatically positive results.[16]

Many R&D managers, familiar with Agile from their internal IT departments, are skeptical about whether Agile can be used with gating approaches or for hardware or physical product development.[17] Development of software, after all, is clearly quite different than new-product development in the manufacturing world. So can Agile work in a manufacturing context? The evidence is limited, but early results from lead users in the manufacturing world suggest that Agile methods can be indeed combined with traditional stage-and-gate or plan-based models and does *work very well for manufactured products*, from consumer food products to heavy B2B equipment.

Figure 6.6: Payoffs from Implementing *Agile-Stage-Gate* in Five Manufacturing Firms (Rank Ordered)

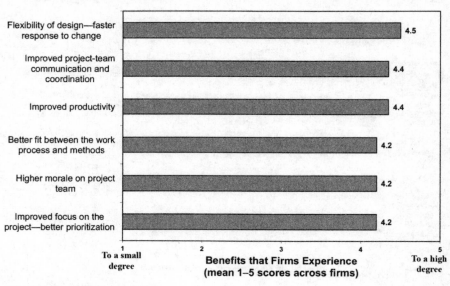

Adapted from: Cooper & Sommer, endnote 19

In lead-user manufacturing firms, Agile was first adopted either by internal IT departments, or by R&D groups in which software development was a key part of hardware projects (for example, telecommunications systems). The results of these initial projects encouraged R&D groups working on hardware development to experiment with Agile and to modify the method to fit their needs.[18]

A study of five major Danish manufacturing firms that built Agile into their existing *Stage-Gate* systems—thus creating an *Agile-Stage-Gate* hybrid model— revealed very positive results. The companies, in a range of industries from B2B heavy equipment to professional products to one strictly consumer goods firm, reported many of the same results found in the software world, namely:

- Design flexibility (faster responses to change).
- Improved productivity, communication, and coordination among project team members.
- Improved focus on the project leading to better prioritization.
- Higher morale among team members.

Figure 6.6 shows performance results quantitatively;[19] note how very strong the positive responses are. Similar results were reported in case studies of other firms.

Figure 6.7: Challenges Faced in Implementing *Agile-Stage-Gate* in Five Manufacturing Firms (Ranked Ordered)

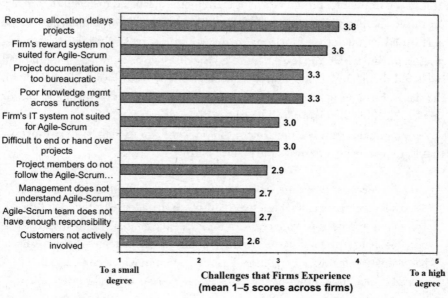

Source: Cooper & Sommer, endnote 19

The Danish study also revealed some negatives, namely, delays due to the difficulty of finding dedicated team members, difficulties in linking project teams to the rest of the organization, mismatches between the requirements of Agile and the company's reward system, and a sense that the system was still too bureaucratic (see Figure 6.7). But these negatives are quite subdued when compared to the enthusiastic positive feedback in Figure 6.6 above.

Other challenges for manufacturers adopting Agile have been identified, including a *lack of scalability, challenges for global project teams*, a *proliferation of meetings*, and a *lack of management buy-in* due to the differences from the familiar gating systems. Management resistance may also be attributed to some common misconceptions: Implementing Agile, for instance, does not mean abandoning *Stage-Gate*: Agile can be added to *Stage-Gate*, creating a hybrid that incorporates positive features of both.[20]

How Agile-Stage-Gate *Works for Manufacturers*

Although there are reported to be at least twenty-six different versions of Agile, the Scrum method seems to be the most popular Agile variant among the handful of firms employing Agile for new manufactured products. Scrum was first identified by Hirotaka Takeuchi and Ikujiro Nonaka in 1986 as "a flexible, holistic product development strategy where a development team works as a unit to reach a common goal" as opposed to a "traditional, sequential approach."[21] This new commercial product development method, labeled the *rugby approach*, promised increased speed and flexibility: The whole idea-to-launch process is performed by one cross-functional team working across multiple overlapping phases, during which the team tries to go the distance as a unit, passing the ball back and forth, similar to the way in which a rugby team moves the ball down the field. In rugby, a *scrum* is the manner of restarting the game after a minor infraction, somewhat like a huddle in North American football; in new-product development, a scrum is a meeting of the project team to plan its next moves—that is, to decide how to move the ball forward.[22]

> *Example: Scrum-Stage-Gate in the construction equipment sector.* A global Swedish manufacturer (automotive industry, B2B) adopted a hybrid *Agile-Stage-Gate* approach when faced with the challenge of accelerating the development of vital mechanical, electronic, and software subsystems. The company had employed for years a traditional gating system in which considerable effort was spent in the front-end work to avoid entering full-scale development with many knowledge gaps. But it was difficult to define tangible, distinct tasks for these front-end phases, and so project teams ended up focused on the technical side, namely on designs and drawings. As a result, there were many knowledge gaps in VoC data, market requirements, and technical concept capabilities. Thus teams were rushing into the development stage without knowing how the concept would perform technically or if it would meet customer requirements.
>
> Scrum was introduced to increase the speed of development and make the front-end work crisper. Four-week sprints were defined, scheduled consistent with calendar months to make planning and time reporting easy. Each project was assigned a visualization room with the scrum board on the wall on one side and a number of alternative designs on the other side. Each team held scrum meetings in front of the board twice a week.
>
> The clear focus and tight follow-up created by the Scrum approach ignited a strong drive on the project teams: Peer pressure within the teams was considerable, with team members pushing each other to deliver on the sprint list. The burn-down curve, updated after each scrum meeting, provided the team with an indicator of progress toward the sprint goals. Teams also learned to be more realistic in work planning after a few sprints.
>
> The concept of time-boxing was also introduced to improve efficiency in some tasks—for example, concept evaluation. The time limit, expressed as

a task requirement to "make the best possible use of ten hours to evaluate concept X," helped the team avoid overengineering. Agreed-on definitions of "done," which included results documented as a single-page report, formatted for posting, reviewed by a colleague, and checked into the document repository, also helped teams know when to move forward. Demonstration meetings with the major stakeholders outside the project team were held after every sprint, and sprints were closed with retrospective meetings at which outcomes were reviewed and next steps determined.

Lars Cederblad, the "consultant and coach," describes his experience with the hybrid process, and its results: "I was acting as scrum master and independent change agent during the first fifteen months of the project. The results really exceeded our expectations, with a speed increase of around 30 percent. With that comes more motivated staff and higher employee satisfaction. We also showed that Scrum is excellent for closing knowledge gaps, the focus of the front-end phases of a project."[23]

Four years after implementation, most of the business's projects now follow the Scrum method within the gating system, and with the same positive effects. The burn-down curves from all projects are now reviewed at the senior level Project Pulse meeting, allowing management to identify potential problems and act before they occur.

Agile-Stage-Gate works much the same for manufacturers as it does in the software world (but there are some *important differences too*, outlined later in this chapter). For manufacturers, *Agile-Stage-Gate* is also based on a series of short time-boxed sprints, each lasting about two to four weeks. At the end of each sprint, the project team produces "something physical" that can be demonstrated to stakeholders, often to customers. Each sprint is planned in real time—on the fly— and thus the process is highly responsive and adaptive. And the rapid, iterative, and incremental releases of concepts, designs, and rapid prototypes provides fast and timely feedback—this constant feedback gets the product right and improves the odds of market success. The voice of the customer thus becomes a dynamic driver throughout the project, as customers also better define their own needs through their active involvement (for example, via frequent user tests or the customer codesigning). The project team itself is dedicated to the one project (not spread too thinly) and is colocated in one team room, thereby ensuring better communication and

> *Agile-Stage-Gate* works much the same for manufacturers as it does in the software world, but there are some important differences too.

faster developments. And the entire process is very visual, with novel visual metrics that display plans, progress, and results in real time.

Gates and stages remain very much part of the process, with gates being the vital Go/Kill decision points—culling out the weak projects and providing focus within the development pipeline, and also enabling senior management to thoroughly review the project at the completion of each major phase. Stages provide a high-level overview of the main phases of the project, and also a guide to the activities required or recommended within each stage and the expected deliverables at the end of each stage.

THE DETAILS OF *AGILE-STAGE-GATE*

Agile execution has *nine distinct elements*: three artefacts, three roles, and three tools, namely the "Power of Nine."[24]

The Three Artefacts

The artefacts generate the framework for fast, incremental product developments. The first artefact is the *sprint*: This is a time-boxed work effort lasting between two and four weeks, where a small part of the project is executed. Sprints begin with a *sprint planning meeting*, where the project teams determines what can be realistically accomplished in the sprint, and maps out the tasks and a plan for their execution. The aim is to have a product increment completed at the end of each sprint. At the end of the sprint, the *sprint review* presents the sprint results to relevant stakeholders, usually customers and management. In practice for manufacturers, not all sprints produce a product increment or prototype; some may yield a design, a concept or a rapid prototype or even the results of a VoC study—"something tangible."

Some manufacturers employ sprints that are longer than the normal two to four weeks, particularly where their products are complex. This longer sprint allows the team more time to create something physical and more useful that they can demonstrate to stakeholders. In other firms, the customer feedback is lengthened to more than the very quick sprint review at the end of the sprint; rather the entire sprint—perhaps the full two weeks—is devoted to getting customer feedback to versions of the product.

The second artefact is the *daily scrum* or daily stand-up meeting. This is a short meeting, where the project team meets at the start of each day for ten to fifteen minutes to review and update. Each team member in turn states what they accomplished yesterday, what they expect to do today, and what problems they

Figure 6.8: The "Starfish Chart" Used at Siemens' Sprint Retrospect Meeting Serves as a Guide to Help the Team Improve

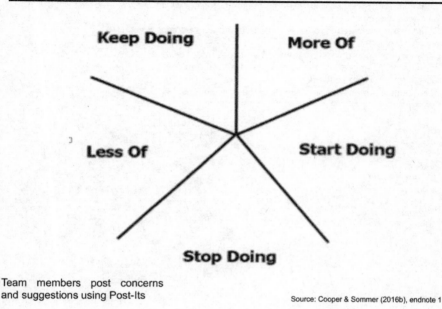

Team members post concerns and suggestions using Post-Its

Source: Cooper & Sommer (2016b), endnote 1

may have. After the meeting, the flagged problems are dealt with through continued within-team collaboration. The benefits of this daily stand-up are both instant knowledge-sharing and increased team motivation.

The final artefact is the *retrospect meeting* at the end of the sprint. The purpose of this meeting is not to review the sprint's results (this is done in the *sprint review*), but for the team members to improve how the team functions. In this retrospective meeting, the team members challenge their own performance, highlight their successes in internal cooperation, and try to improve their ways of working together. This meeting thus helps to institutionalize continuous improvement: solving key issues that arise in order to evolve to a high-performance team.

An illustration: Siemens (Motors Division) uses the retrospect meeting at the end of each sprint to self-evaluate, and to improve team cooperation and utilization of Agile principles. Their *starfish chart* helps to structure the meeting to cover the topics in Figure 6.8. Using Post-Its, each team member notes their concerns and suggestions on the chart; a dialog ensues on how to self-improve

Figure 6.9: The Heartbeat of an Agile Project

Customer feedback and unfinished product features are prioritized, and drive the sprint cycle.
Sprint planning meeting produces a realistic and achievable action plan for the sprint.
Daily scrums ensure constant team communication as the team executes the planned tasks, and produces the next product increment—working software.
Team empowerment is a side benefit of the daily scrums.

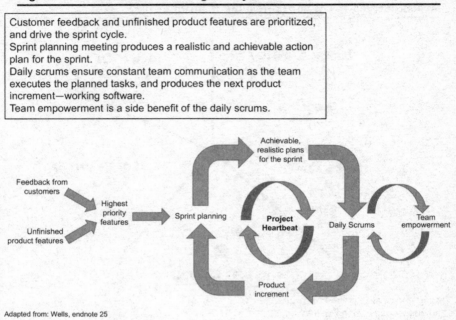

Adapted from: Wells, endnote 25

for the next sprint. This retrospect meeting is facilitated by the scrum master who ensures adherence to the starfish model and sees that all team members participate equally.

The regular sprints thus generate a "project heartbeat" for working productively and creatively.[25] A *steady heartbeat* has a fixed-length iteration, as short as can be. A *strong heartbeat* produces working software ready for deployment. A *responsive heartbeat* creates a new plan for each iteration, based on feedback from the previous iteration and changing customer needs, not just based on what was left unfinished. This measurable, predictable, sustainable, and constant pace or rhythm helps the team plan and meet its commitments.[26]

This analogy of a *project heartbeat* suits the process well (see Figure 6.9): Each short sprint, with a defined plan, permits work to proceed *without interference or change for two to four weeks*, but also without planning activities too far into the future (plans that would invariably get changed). Changes to product requirements are introduced to the project much like oxygen into the body; and the heart is the Agile methodology itself, pumping at a regular pace and keeping the project alive and revitalized. So rhythm and a steady pace or heartbeat are keys

Figure 6.10: The Diamond Pattern of Communication in Agile Teams Fosters Much Better Within-Team Communication

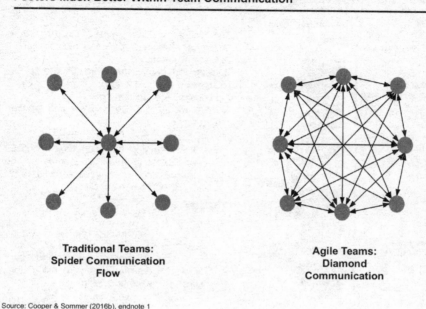

Traditional Teams:
Spider Communication
Flow

Agile Teams:
Diamond
Communication

Source: Cooper & Sommer (2016b), endnote 1

to the team's success, much like *takt time* and the steady rhythm in the world of lean manufacturing.

Three Distinct Roles

The most important role in Agile is the *individual member* of the development or project team. In Agile, the team is empowered to take responsibility for the project's execution: It is the team, and not management, that defines, selects, and allocates activities or tasks among the team members. Based on the agreed target outcome of the sprint, the team's job is to define the necessary activities to achieve the sprint goals, to decide on who does what, and then to undertake the tasks during the sprint.

Agile also has a *process manager,* called the "scrum master," a servant-leader and facilitator of the project team whose role is to support the team as they undertake each sprint. The scrum master facilitates the daily scrums, as well as the sprint planning and post sprint meetings; he or she ensures that the team adheres to the Agile methods and that they use the artefacts and tools properly. The scrum master is also responsible for removing impediments to the team, so that they are able to execute quickly and without roadblocks.

Figure 6.11: The Product Backlog Is Similar to the "Product Definition" Except More Dynamic (Can Change) and Broader (Includes More Items and Tasks)

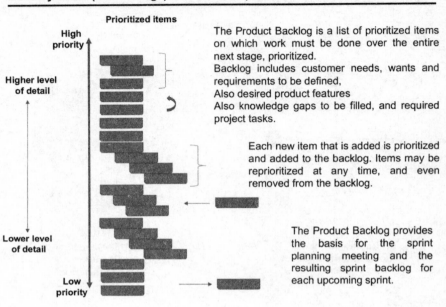

Prioritized items

The Product Backlog is a list of prioritized items on which work must be done over the entire next stage, prioritized.
Backlog includes customer needs, wants and requirements to be defined,
Also desired product features
Also knowledge gaps to be filled, and required project tasks.

Each new item that is added is prioritized and added to the backlog. Items may be reprioritized at any time, and even removed from the backlog.

The Product Backlog provides the basis for the sprint planning meeting and the resulting sprint backlog for each upcoming sprint.

The third distinct role is the "*product owner,*" who is responsible for the product backlog (the product requirement): The owner is not a project team member per se, but is a member of management (often from marketing) who works closely with the development team to ensure that the right product requirements are built into the sprints. The product owner also has some of the same responsibilities as those of a *project leader* in traditional product development (the product owner focuses on stakeholder management in order to ensure management support, input, and resources to the project, and also manages customer involvement) and the *executive sponsor.* Note that not all *Agile-Stage-Gate* user-firms adopt all three roles, and in some cases, remain with one or more of the familiar roles and responsibilities of project leaders, project managers, team members, and executive sponsors.

Improved within-team communication and knowledge sharing is reported as one of the major positives of *Agile-Stage-Gate,* and is illustrated by the spider versus diamond diagrams in Figure 6.10.[27] This figure highlights how having a project manager or leader limits the amount of communication between project members, and how the removal of this role and the resulting creation of many more communication paths enables increased knowledge sharing and team learning. The belief by Agile proponents is that when the responsibilities are appropriately

Figure 6.12: Flexible Sprint Backlog Developed at the Sprint Planning Meeting, Showing Tasks to Be Completed in the Upcoming Sprint

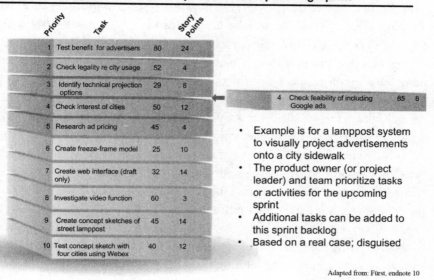

- Example is for a lamppost system to visually project advertisements onto a city sidewalk
- The product owner (or project leader) and team prioritize tasks or activities for the upcoming sprint
- Additional tasks can be added to this sprint backlog
- Based on a real case; disguised

Adapted from: Fürst, endnote 10

divided among the product owner, scrum master, and development team, the project has a better chance of success than traditionally organized projects.

The Three Tools

Agile-Stage-Gate features three important visual tools to help manage and monitor projects. The first is the *product backlog*, which is the Agile equivalent of the traditional product definition or requirements specifications. Unlike a product definition, however, the product backlog does not contain detailed specifications (such as desired materials or performance requirements), but rather *customer requirements, needs, wants, and preferences* (see Figure 6.11), providing freedom for the project team to experiment with the product's design, but within the guidelines in the backlog. (In some firms, the product backlog is broader, and also includes *knowledge gaps to be filled* and *key tasks required* for the next stage, thus is more a "project backlog" than product backlog per se.) Items in the backlog are prioritized, the optimal sequence determined, and the most important tackled first. The backlog is a very dynamic document and is continuously updated and reprioritized as new information and learnings are integrated. At the beginning of each sprint, the sprint planning meeting takes the top priority items from the product backlog and translates them into well-defined activities or tasks for that sprint: the *sprint backlog* (Figure 6.12).[28]

Firms in some industries employ *user stories* in their product backlog. Rather than requirements for the product, user stories describe how users will engage with the final product and how it fulfils the user's needs in practice. User stories are assigned *story points* to indicate how much work is required—expected resource requirements—to create the feature or performance characteristic needed to accommodate that user story. Scales to gauge story points vary widely by company, but a simple measure is T-shirt sizes (S, M, L, XL).

The second tool is the *sprint board* or kanban board. This board contains the sprint backlog, namely the list of activities or tasks to be done during the current sprint. In practice, these are placed as Post-Its on a physical board or as activity cards on a virtual board. There are many ways to set up the sprint board, but the most common format is to use three columns: "to-do," "doing," and "done." During the sprint, the activities are initiated by moving a task from "to-do" into the "doing" column, and when finished, moved into the "done" column. This progression creates a continuous flow of activity cards from left to right across the board during the sprint. If the sprint has been well planned, there will be just enough activities for execution for that sprint.

To keep track of the activity or task flow during a sprint, a *burn-down chart* is used, which displays the number of days in the sprint versus activities finished (see Figure 6.13). Ideally, this chart should be a straight line (the dashed line in Figure 6.13), ending with zero remaining tasks on the final day of the sprint. In practice, deviations occur, which are captured on the burn-down chart on a daily basis—the solid line in Figure 6.13. The development team thus can readily see if they are behind or ahead of schedule. The goal here is to have a constant flow and the ability to plan this flow well. Initially, a team struggles to plan the sprint accurately—they usually overestimate what they can accomplish during a sprint—but over time their ability to plan improves, and so does their performance as gauged by the burn-down chart.

> Most manufacturing firms initially utilize the *Agile-Stage-Gate* method for only the very technical phases of the project—for example, for the Development and Testing stages. As they gain confidence, they then use *Agile-Stage-Gate* for more than just these two technical stages, such as Ideation, Building the Business Case, and even Launch.

An Integrated System

While the *Agile-Stage-Gate* system consists of a number of elements—the nine artefacts, roles, and tools—*the whole is much greater than sum of its parts*. The key to making it work is the change in mindset required by both management

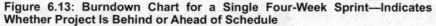

Figure 6.13: Burndown Chart for a Single Four-Week Sprint—Indicates Whether Project Is Behind or Ahead of Schedule

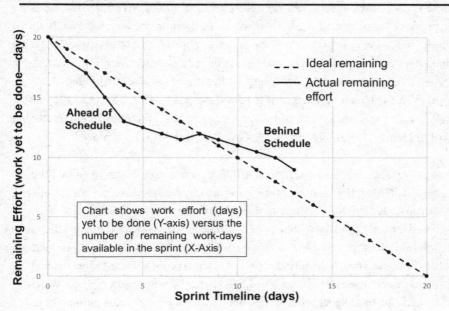

and project teams, and the application of the *entire system* in an integrated fashion. While the elements of the system are useful, experience suggests that they do not bring significant performance improvement unless they are employed together and with the appropriate change in the "way of working."

IMPLEMENTING *AGILE-STAGE-GATE*

When Agile and *Stage-Gate* are integrated, and then utilized for manufactured or physical product development (hardware), Agile is normally applied as the project-management method within the stages in *Stage-Gate*. That is, *the stages remain*, and Agile is *applied within some stages*. The Scrum method is the particular Agile method that seems most appropriate for hardware development, and indeed, is the method used for *all the physical product case studies* uncovered so far in industry.

Next, most manufacturing firms at first utilize the *Agile-Stage-Gate* Scrum method for only the very technical phases of the project—for example, for the Development and Testing stages in the typical stage-and-gate model in Figure 6.5. As firms gain confidence, they then use *Agile-Stage-Gate* for more than just these two technical stages, as shown in Figure 6.5. The method can be employed in the predevelopment stages, to develop the concept and assess feasibility. In these early phases, *open knowledge gaps* become analogous to desired software or product features, and Agile then works in the normal way, with each sprint aimed at resolving a particular gap or set of gaps. Additional implementation challenges exist here, however, and thus more adjustments are required for these earlier stages (for example, defining a "done sprint" and securing dedicated resources in the Concept Stage or Business Case stage). Here's an example of how Agile-Scrum was integrated into *Stage-Gate* in a fairly advanced manufacturing firm in Denmark, namely the LEGO Group, and the results achieved:

An example:[29] LEGO Education is a B2B business unit in the LEGO Group, responsible for development of software and physical products for educational purposes for children in preschool and higher. In 2011, LEGO Education initiated a highly innovative new-product project, *Story Starter*—an educational solution whose purpose was to create confident writers and readers in elementary schools. Due to the introduction of digital components into the product, management tried a totally new-to-LEGO hybrid development method, which turned out to have significant advantages to the project, and ultimately resulted in the launch of this highly successful and innovative new product just twelve months later!

LEGO management saw this *Story Starter* initiative as a radically new business opportunity; but the journey was explorative and the process complex, involving customer trials from early in the project. Initially, the project was managed using LEGO's tried-and-proven but traditional stage-and-gate model. This model, however, did not fit well with the design iterations required by intensive customer interaction (this was a very ambiguous development, with schools and teachers not sure what they wanted or needed). But the team had no alternative, and so had to work with the traditional gating model available to them.

By pure chance, the team was offered a unique alternative that both sped up the customer iterations and improved overall project productivity. It was decided to incorporate a digital-documentation tool in order to document children's learning experiences. The Digital Solutions group at LEGO were already using Agile methods for software development; thus, when project team members from Digital Solutions joined the *Story Starter* team, they brought Agile with them.

After seeing the advantages of Agile for software development, the *Story Starter* team decided to try this new approach for managing the entire project. Management did not want to lose the strategic benefits of their stage-and-gate model, however, so they chose to keep it while implementing Agile within the gating system. As a consequence of this merger, an *Agile-Stage-Gate* hybrid emerged which was applicable for software as well as for physical components.

The *Story Starter* development team began using this new *Agile-Stage-Gate* hybrid model complete with sprints, fifteen-minute daily stand-up meetings (scrums), visual scrum boards, daily activity logs (the requirement for burndown charts), a prioritized project backlog, and sprint planning meetings. The Agile method was incorporated into the project during the development phase and continued into the implementation phase in LEGO's gating model. Throughout the development phase of the project, teachers from more than fifty schools participated in product trials. Sprint reviews were conducted using internal representatives for customers, and pilot studies involving the primary customers (schools) and tests with children were conducted regularly. The number of active team members changed during the project depending on needed expertise, but remained between five and ten throughout; however, they were not dedicated to this one project.

After the implementation of this new *Agile-Stage-Gate* hybrid model, the *Story Starter* project experienced a remarkable acceleration, and within a short period of time, was doing much better than comparable projects. The most dramatic change for the team was the immediate increase in productivity. In hindsight, team members indicated that the productivity increase was caused mainly by much better team communication and a decrease in misunderstandings. Also, team members experienced improved workflow each day, partly due to feeling secure in the knowledge that their current problems would be readily solved at the next morning's scrum meeting. Finally, *Agile-Stage-Gate* helped the team to remain in excellent communication, despite frequent travel and unforeseen activities and tasks.

Following the successful piloting of *Agile-Stage-Gate* with *Story Starter*, a second and large new-product project, *More to Math*, was similarly developed using the new hybrid model, and also proved to be a winner (*More to Math* is an elementary-level teaching solution for mathematical problem solving).

This new and experimental *Agile-Stage-Gate* method, initially piloted because an alternative project-management approach was needed for radical and highly uncertain projects, has proved so effective that an *Agile-Stage-Gate* standard was developed for widespread use in the business. Since 2016, all of LEGO Education's new-product releases have been developed using this novel hybrid approach.

NEEDED ADJUSTMENTS FOR PHYSICAL PRODUCTS

Agile-Scrum methods from the software world cannot be directly implemented for manufactured products *without some important modifications.* Here are some examples:

Defining a Done Sprint

The concept of a "done sprint" is critical, given the tightly time-boxed nature of the process. One important point of difference between Agile for software products and *Agile-Stage-Gate* for physical products is the *definition of a sprint* and what constitutes a *"done sprint."* Software development is almost infinitely divisible: A software development consisting of multiple product features can be broken down into multiple, small subprojects—for example, writing several thousand lines of code and producing a few screens—which can each be completed in a single sprint. A "done sprint" is a working product (executable software, a completed feature, potentially releasable) and can be demonstrated to stakeholders (management and customers). Thus, each increment or sprint yields a working, *albeit feature-limited, product.*

> Agile-Scrum methods from the software world cannot be directly implemented for manufactured products without some modifications and adjustments.

By contrast, the development of a new medical device, machine, or polymer cannot be so easily incrementalized. If your product is an engine or a scanning device, you cannot build part of the engine or part of the scanner and demonstrate it working within a few weeks, nor will it be releasable to the market. Thus, the notion of short time-boxed sprints and the software definition of "done" do not apply so neatly to physical products.[30]

Firms have made the adjustment, however; here are some examples of definitions of a "done sprint" in manufacturing firms:

- Chamberlain, the US-based remote-control systems manufacturer (example in Chapter 5): A "done sprint" is "something physical, the result of completed tasks in that sprint (and not just a PowerPoint show). This could be, for example, a set of completed design drawings, or a rapid prototype, or an early working model of the product."
- Siemens industrial motors: A "done sprint" is when the development team decides the sprint is done. However, the sprint results must be approved by the product owner to become "done done," which marks the actual close-out of a sprint.

- The Swedish construction equipment manufacturer above: A "done sprint" is "results of work done, documented as an A4 (12x17 inch) templated report, easy to read and easy to post on a wall, reviewed by an expert colleague, and checked into the document repository."
- LEGO Education: A "done sprint" is when a ten-element checklist (the "definition of done") is completed by all team members, quality assurance, and the product owner, declaring that all product acceptance criteria have been met, and that all open actions have been completed, handed over, or closed. Sample checklist elements at LEGO include:

  ❏ development documentation created;
  ❏ all open actions completed, handed over to others responsible, or closed; and
  ❏ the Project Handover document updated with relevant product life cycle information.

When Agile-Scrum is applied to earlier stages of the project, for example, the Concept and Business Case stages in Figure 6.5, then the definition of done is relaxed even further to include *anything tangible* that can be reviewed by an expert. For example, the results of a market study or technical feasibility analysis would count as a "done sprint."

Something That Can Be Demonstrated

Newer versions of *Stage-Gate* built in "spirals" or iterations more than a decade ago in order to make the traditional 1990s gating model more adaptive and responsive—see Chapter 5. These spirals were typically a series of "build-test-feedback-and-revise" iterations, usually weeks, sometimes several months apart, to confirm the product's design with the customer and to get the product right, in spite of fluid market conditions and changing customer requirements, as outlined in Chapters 2 and 5.

Here, each iteration builds a *product version* somewhere between a concept (usually drawings and words) and a ready-to-trial prototype—we labelled this in-between version a "protocept." Unlike in Agile in the software world, the result of a sprint may not be a working product, but is still something that can be demonstrated—to test a

> Each iteration builds a *product version* somewhere between a concept and a ready-to-trial prototype—we label this in-between version a "protocept." Unlike in Agile in the software world, the result of a sprint may not be a working product, but is still something that can be demonstrated—to test a market-facing hypothesis (to seek customer feedback), and coincidentally to seek technical proof of concept as well as management buy-in.

Figure 6.14: Successive Iterations of the Product—Various "Protocepts" Through to Prototype

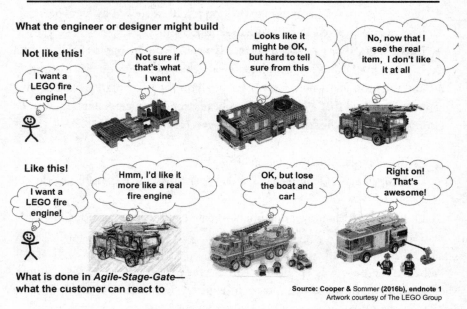

What the engineer or designer might build

Not like this!

I want a LEGO fire engine!

Not sure if that's what I want

Looks like it might be OK, but hard to tell sure from this

No, now that I see the real item, I don't like it at all

Like this!

I want a LEGO fire engine!

Hmm, I'd like it more like a real fire engine

OK, but lose the boat and car!

Right on! That's awesome!

What is done in *Agile-Stage-Gate*— what the customer can react to

Source: Cooper & Sommer (2016b), endnote 1
Artwork courtesy of The LEGO Group

market-facing hypothesis (to seek customer feedback), and coincidentally to seek technical proof of concept as well as management buy-in, as in Figure 6.14. These product versions, or *protocepts*, can be computer-generated 3D drawings, virtual prototypes, crude models, rapid prototypes (3D printed), working models, or early prototypes. The result of a done sprint, in this context, may not be a working product, but it is something physical that the customer can respond to and which management can see.[31]

An example:[32] ThermoValves (disguised name) is a business unit within a major corporation that provides heating solutions ultimately targeted at the residential construction sector (HVAC). The company is a global manufacturer with headquarters in Europe, annual sales of $7 billion, and an R&D spend of 4 percent of sales.

The development of heating solutions is highly innovative, entailing both hardware and software development using novel technologies. The product-development process has for many decades been successfully managed using a traditional *Stage-Gate* model with clear stages, milestones, gates, and deliverables. In recent years, the Agile-Scrum framework had been used to develop the software components within ThermoValves' heating solutions, but these two approaches had never been integrated.

The pilot implementation: In mid-2015, the head of R&D at ThermoValves decided to invest in a pilot project to try an *Agile-Stage-Gate* hybrid model for development of physical products. He realized that market needs were changing faster and faster, partly due to increased global competition, thus necessitating frequent and continuous confirmation of market needs to ensure market success—even after the Development stage was well underway. Thus, he decided to experiment, applying Agile-Scrum to the business's gating process for *physical product developments* as well as for software. A pilot project was selected, and sufficient funding was provided for training on Scrum, to cover the extra costs of the frequent market validations, and for other extra project costs. So successful was this pilot project that the company decided to try this novel approach on several other projects. Early results are positive.

How Agile-Stage-Gate works in this firm: Agile-Stage-Gate at ThermoValves allows for early and frequent customer validations of physical and virtual product designs. The main change from the previous method is that design specifications are *no longer fixed up front,* but are continuously adapted through the design iterations: No longer is there a pre-Development design-freeze!

While ThermoValves' *Stage-Gate* system remains in place and unchanged at the senior management level, a compromise version of Agile-Scrum is used at the operational (project-team) level. The new method is deployed from the earliest stage of the project throughout the entire new-product process for all stages of their *Stage-Gate* model. Two-week sprints are employed to execute both design developments and customer validations (user tests).

As the project progresses through gates and milestones, some design choices are locked-in as manufacturing decisions are made. That is, due to long lead times in manufacturing, some hardware choices must be frozen earlier than software choices; the latter tend to stay open for longer, allowing more iterations with customers on software and after the physical design is decided.

Project teams have so far been dedicated and colocated, with their own project rooms, and use visual, physical scrum boards. Stand-up meetings or scrums are conducted daily within the teams at their scrum boards, facilitated by the scrum master. ThermoValves chose to not employ a "pure" product backlog, but rather *a flexible list of product requirements* in prioritized order *without story points or user stories.* Using product requirements here has worked well, since it better suited a development pipeline consisting of both Agile and traditional projects. And rather than a product owner, ThermoValves decided to keep the existing role of the *project leader* as owner in order to avoid role confusion with roles in other projects.

Customer reviews are conducted regularly, but not as part of the sprint review at the end of each sprint. Rather, conducting user tests is deemed a significant task, lasting an entire sprint, with test results merely presented at the sprint review. These ongoing reviews have also worked successfully and are perceived as a core benefit from this modified Agile-*Stage-Gate* system, permitting more in-depth tests and design iterations.

The gates in the system remain the same as in the traditional *Stage-Gate* model: the regular Go/Kill decision points. The main difference at gates is management's willingness to accept a higher level of ambiguity regarding the final product. But Go/Kill decisions now are thought to be more fact based, the result of frequent user tests which provide better insight into customer acceptance and ultimate product success.

Benefits and challenges at ThermoValves: The pilot project lived up to expectations in terms of being more adaptive to market needs via customer validations. The product design indeed underwent significant alterations to accommodate customer inputs. The project team leader indicated that market success would have been more difficult to achieve without these product modifications made during the early product design phases, and that these changes were made possible by using the *Agile-Stage-Gate* system.

The team leader also realized some unexpected benefits when interacting with internal stakeholders (management) who normally provide inputs to the product specifications. These stakeholders were relieved not to have to provide and approve the entire product specification at the outset, but they too were able to adapt and learn with the development team as they went through the design iterations.

The greatest challenge came from developers who were frustrated by not having a frozen product specification. Some disliked having to iterate and involve people outside the team, rather than being able to lock themselves in a room for six months and come out with a final product!

Learnings and advice from ThermoValves: The resounding advice from the business's leaders at ThermoValves is simple: "Just try it!" They recommend that one begin with a selected pilot project that receives the right level of management attention and resources. Other recommendations include adapting the model to suit the context of the organization (some modifications to the system may be necessary, as happened at ThermoValves) and to provide for open dialog throughout implementation to deal quickly with issues and challenges.

Suggestion: Consider the advice from ThermoValves. The name is disguised, but they are a world-class firm with a solid track record in product innovation. I've worked with them over the years, and they always seem to be a bit ahead of the wave. So I listen closely when they indicate a new direction.

RESOLVING THE DIFFICULT ISSUES[33]

Tough questions often arise at *Agile-Stage-Gate* conferences that identify thorny issues and *apparent inconsistencies* in merging the Agile and *Stage-Gate* approaches for manufactured products. These inconsistencies and issues are partly the reason for management's initial skepticism. Some issues are based on misinformation or a lack of understanding of the new system; others are more profound and require adroit actions. In this section we deal with *ten of these common implementation issues* and *their solutions*.

1. Either or Both Systems?

Agile and *Stage-Gate* have been found to be quite compatible for manufacturing firms, and *are not substitutes* for each other *nor mutually exclusive.* Thus it's not a matter of "either/or": The hybrid model integrates the *best of both systems*. In practice, Agile is typically implemented into an already proficient *Stage-Gate* system, as at ThermoValves. Agile is *not a solution* to a poorly designed or badly implemented gating system; rather, Agile supports an already functional system by providing faster response to change, increased visibility, and increased flexibility.

> Tough questions often arise that identify *apparent inconsistencies* in merging the Agile and *Stage-Gate* approaches for manufactured products. Some issues are based on a lack of understanding of the new system; others are more profound and require adroit actions.

2. For Which Projects?

Agile-Stage-Gate is designed to handle *dynamic development projects facing fluid markets and changing customer needs* and requirements; information uncertainty and ambiguity is also well handled by the new system. Thus, not every development project may be a candidate for *Agile-Stage-Gate*. Moreover, the requirement of dedicated resources also precludes many projects. Most firms limit the application of *Agile-Stage-Gate* to their most important, larger, more innovative, or riskier development projects. For example, at Corning, only the major and critical projects go through the new agile system—about 20 percent of projects—and have dedicated teams. But the majority of Corning's new-product development projects still have team members spread across multiple projects.[34] Similarly, in Chamberlain's case cited in Chapter 5, because dedicated teams are not feasible for every project, the firm uses this *Agile-Stage-Gate* approach only for the larger, major revenue-generating projects—about 20 percent of the projects in their development pipeline.

3. For Which Stages?

Agile is most often implemented *first in the technical stages* of Stage-Gate, for example, for the Development and Testing stages in Figure 6.5. Usually it is the technical people that first hear about Agile: Often companies report that positive results achieved from using Agile in their software-development projects initially inspired technical people to try the system for physical products, as in the LEGO case above. Additionally, the fact that Agile iterations result in working or demonstrable versions of the product suits the technical phases of a new-product project. Finally, the fact that technical people are more likely to be dedicated to a single project makes implementation easier here from a resourcing standpoint.

Beyond the obvious technical stages, *Agile-Stage-Gate* has also been found to work well in *other phases of the project*, as at ThermoValves. Indeed, early adopters report that this new approach should be applied *across the entire project* in order to achieve maximum benefit, including the earlier stages, Ideation, Concept, and Business Case in Figure 6.5, and even for the Launch stage; for example, GEMBA Innovation in Denmark utilizes both ideation and concept sprints in their version of *Agile-Stage-Gate*.[35]

Other functional areas, such as marketers or manufacturing engineers, may find it more difficult initially to adapt to the Agile way of working and to commit dedicated effort to the project; but given solid training, an effective change management effort, and proper project prioritization and resource allocation, the benefits of using *Agile-Stage-Gate* across the entire project soon become evident. Dedicated time is clearly an issue for some departments: For example, marketers, who always seem to over-multitask, might commit to a dedicated effort for a two-week sprint on a project (that is, spend 100 percent of their time on the one project, perhaps doing a market analysis or voice-of-customer study).

4. Is the Testing Stage Still Needed?

Some would-be users of *Agile-Stage-Gate* question whether the Testing stage in Figure 6.5 is still required. They argue: "*Agile-Stage-Gate* builds in lots of iterations and customer validations all the way through the Development stage, so why the need for a separate testing stage?" A good point, and indeed for smaller, less expensive, and shorter projects, it makes sense to combine the Development and Testing stages. In traditional *Stage-Gate*, this has been done for some decades (in *Stage-Gate-Lite* for example).

When *Agile-Stage-Gate* is employed for larger, more expensive, and longer projects, however, the recommendation is that the Testing stage and its "Go to Test" gate in Figure 6.5 both remain. First, far more than just customer validation takes place in this Testing stage—it's *not just a continuation of customer iterations*. Larger projects could have *production trials* here, including the purchase and commissioning of production equipment (with the associated CAPEX[*]); formal and extensive field trials or Beta tests (potentially with legal commitments); and even test markets or trial sells. Thus, it makes sense for senior management to *undertake a full project review before commitment* to production equipment or to going "semicommercial" with the product. Peter Fürst, new-product expert in Europe, also points out: "Contrary to best practice, the R&D people in some firms quit the project when the development is done, especially when the next stage is 'launch.' In their minds, 'launch' is the stage for the sales people. A robust testing phase, including technical, market, and sales tests, keeps the team on board where their development result is really tested in the market. This increases *their commitment to the whole project* (and not just for their development stage) [emphasis mine]." Further, for these larger projects, often the Development phase is quite long, and thus it's prudent for senior management to take *a hard look again* at the project and its Business Case after so many months.

Building in a gate at the end of Development—the "Go to Test" gate in Figure 6.5—is good management practice. So for such larger *Agile-Stage-Gate* projects, this "Go to Test" gate does indeed play a key role, and hence Testing in Figure 6.5 remains a separate and distinct stage from Development.

5. Project-Team Composition

In some firms, the project is handed off to a "commercialization team" partway through the project. But in so doing, one loses momentum, knowledge, accountability, and ownership or passion for the project! By contrast, in *Agile-Stage-Gate*, the core team remains intact from beginning to end of the project: That is, the team remains on the field from beginning to end of game, an approach that is also *consistent with current best practices in Stage-Gate* (see success driver #6 in Chapter 3).

---

[*] Capital Appropriation Request: request for approval of capital expenditure for purchasing manufacturing equipment.

As the project progresses, new people may join the project as needed, for example, manufacturing and sales people may be added towards the commercialization phases. Work intensity by functional area will obviously shift during the project—product designers or developers have a more intense role during the middle phases of the project—but in order to ensure continuity, ownership, and accountability, the team members remain "on the team" throughout the project and up to the post-launch review.

Team members in *Agile-Stage-Gate* have a desired profile: They are experts in their functional area but also have a broad set of general capabilities; for example, a product designer (one's expertise) who is also able to provide support in product testing. Working together, such team members function as a true team: They are able to "play each other's position on the field" rather than each team member just doing their own finite piece of the project alone. In practice, however, people with such profiles are much in demand, and a team of such experts with generalist capabilities may be hard to find. But this ideal team-member profile remains the goal in order to foster a true team approach.

6. The Role of Gates

A commonly asked question by people new to *Agile-Stage-Gate* is: "Are there still gates in the system?" One might expect that because the notion of a gate is "quite rigid," it contradicts the Agile mindset of "being flexible." But not so: Agile is very consistent with tough Go/Kill decisions on projects—*gates with teeth*. The flexibility of the Agile system lies with the product deliverable; that is, there is flexibility about *what* is delivered, not in the Go/Kill decision structure!

The main difference and the *flexibility in Agile-Stage-Gate* versus traditional gating systems is recognizing and dealing with the reality that many projects, especially more innovative ones, have *high levels of ambiguity and uncertainty* at their beginning—that it is often impossible to know everything up front. Thus, uncertainties about *product deliverables* are managed by accepting and even supporting product and project-scope changes, as long as these changes do not affect the overall project plan, budget, and project's financial attractiveness. If they do, the project may be flagged for reevaluation and possibly terminated. Recall that the product backlog (product definition) is very dynamic; indeed, the product may be only 20 percent defined at the point of project approval (the often-cited range is 20 to 90 percent defined at project approval, but 40 to 60 percent defined is more typical). Thus the project team is allowed to learn and adapt during the project, but within limits.

Gates continue to play a vital role in *Agile-Stage-Gate*, however, as at ThermoValves. They allow senior management to periodically review the project, to kill weak projects and reallocate resources to better initiatives, and most important, to ensure that the necessary resources are committed so that the project can move forward. Note that gates are not only a quality checkpoint; they are also a *resource commitment decision*. In this way, the project team secures the needed personnel, time, and funding to continue their work in an accelerated fashion. Note that insufficient resources and project team members spread too thinly is one of the major causes of long times-to-market (see success driver #5, Chapter 3).

Gates also allow senior management to track the progress and on-time performance of the project: When to deliver the product on the "long-term horizon" scale thus remains defined and a key part of *Agile-Stage-Gate*. While each sprint has its own "plan" and time frame and thus is flexible, *the longer-term timeline or plan for the entire stage remains relatively stable*. For example, in one process-control firm, the Agile project leader was asked by senior management: "When will this product be done—when will it be on the market?" The answer the executive received was: "It will be done when it's done!" This answer is clearly unacceptable and inconsistent with *Agile-Stage-Gate*. Indeed, projects within this new system are managed with timelines complete with milestones that clearly define the progress of the project over a predetermined longer-term time horizon. Admittedly this forward plan (or action plan) and the timeline are *fairly high level*, and the *plan's details may change over time*, but the longer-term plan and timeline remain more or less intact.

Hardware versus software gates? Another common gate-related question is: "Should there be different gates for different deliverables, for example, have separate software and hardware gates?" Most users find that having multiple gates for different facets of the same project is troublesome and not beneficial: Such structures only add complexity and ambiguity to the project. And consider the possible and ridiculous consequence of a new product involving both hardware and software, where the software gatekeepers kill the software part of the project at their gate meeting, when a few weeks earlier the hardware gatekeepers gave it a positive decision. Both parts of the project depend on each other, hence the need for a common gate structure. The only instance that a separate gate structure may be warranted is where the two developments are not totally interdependent.

7. Plan Based versus Plan-on-the-Fly and Fixed or Flexible Budgets and Times?

An apparent contradiction within *Agile-Stage-Gate* is typified by the question: "How can a project be approved for Development if you don't know the product definition and consequently don't have a solid development plan (Gantt chart)—

and without a development plan, there is no development cost estimate? Surely an executive cannot be expected to approve a development project when the development cost is unknown!" This question, in one form or another, is the result of trying to reconcile planned-based approaches (traditional gating) with plan-on-the-fly methods (Agile).

The "product backlog" partly fills the role of the traditional "product definition," says Peter Fürst.[36] Note that the product backlog is not locked-in early in the project—it varies depending on uncertainty. And the product backlog (product definition) evolves over time as the project progresses. Nonetheless, a higher level, albeit somewhat tentative product backlog is required at the outset, and provides sufficient definition for planning and project approval. (Note that ThermoValves retained their traditional *list of product requirements*, but a more flexible list.)

The project plan presents a similar dilemma: One goes from a product backlog to a "schedule" of tasks for the entire stage (both are created at the beginning of Development, based on best estimates at the time). The schedule is similar to a traditional product-development plan (a Gantt chart); but it must *necessarily be a very tentative and high-level* schedule or forward plan at the "Go to Development" gate in Figure 6.5, as noted in item 6 above. From this schedule, a budget or estimated development cost is determined. And it too will be somewhat tentative, an estimate. Given the high probability of change, the tasks within stages and thus the project's budget are *certainly variable during the early phases* of the project. Thus management must learn to live with approving projects when costs and times are only estimates, and likely will change. But as one executive said: "There's nothing really new here. We're always approving projects where costs and times change—they always come in over budget and behind schedule!"

> The product backlog (the equivalent of the product definition) and the project plan or schedule are both high level and fairly tentative when approved. Once the project moves into the next stage, for example, Development, the product definition and the plan are constantly updated and validated—they evolve as the project moves forward rather than being fixed at the beginning of the stage when the project is approved.

As uncertainty decreases over time, however, the schedule or timeline and the budget both become increasingly fixed or stable. A rule of thumb is that one can lock-in the final budget by the end of the Development stage in Figure 6.5.

8. The Need for Up-Front Homework and Early-Stage Voice-of-Customer Work

A worrisome potential consequence of *Agile-Stage-Gate* is the *mistaken belief* that the front-end homework and voice-of-customer work is no longer needed—

that one can move a significant project into the Development stage without the traditional due diligence in place. The usual argument is that "things change," that *Agile-Stage-Gate* allows for change, and that attempts to rigorously define the product and the plan in advance—only to see them change later—are a waste of time:

> *An illustration of how things might go wrong (words of the scrum master):* The major Swedish construction-equipment manufacturer (example above) "had employed for years a traditional gating system in which considerable effort was spent in the front-end work to avoid entering full-scale development with many knowledge gaps. But it was difficult to define tangible, distinct tasks for these front-end phases."[37]

> When *Agile-Stage-Gate* was introduced in this firm, the project team members *no longer had to spend as much time struggling*, often in vain, to do due diligence and VoC work before project approval. Taken to an extreme, and being design engineers who did not feel comfortable doing VoC and market-analysis work, the new system might provide *a convenient excuse not to do any of the needed and valuable homework*—that is, to promote ill-conceived shortcuts and intellectual laziness. The temptation to omit front-end homework was certainly an issue here. Were it not for the tough-minded scrum master, who ensured that his project teams still did the due diligence within their abilities, no doubt vital actions would have been skipped.

Indeed, there are often questions about whether market analysis and VoC in the early stages of *Agile-Stage-Gate* are still needed in order to understand the customer. The suggestion is that early VoC studies, which ask customers what they want or need, *can be replaced by product iterations* and customer tests much later in the project. Thus, one view is that these early stage VoC tasks are unnecessary, and even early stage technical assessment may no longer be warranted, simply because the product definition is likely to change dramatically as the project moves along.

These arguments, while intuitively appealing, *are quite wrong*: Agile actually encourages *multiple approaches* to understanding customer and user value and to getting the product right. Thus, the new system still requires proper market analysis and VoC in the early stages in order to provide the necessary foundation for the project and to steer the project in the right direction. And VoC is the basis for developing the vital "product backlog" (see Figure 6.11; also items 6 and 7 above), which in turn leads to the "schedule" (the project *forward plan* or *action plan*) and development cost estimates, all essential items to securing project approval.

Agile-Stage-Gate also requires early stage technical assessment, even though the product definition may change, so that developers can be appraised of technical options and technical risks before charging into the Development stage.

One benefit of *Agile-Stage-Gate* is that the homework—both technical and marketing—*need not be excessive*, thus avoiding the frequent complaint of "paralysis by analysis." That is, the information gleaned predevelopment does not have to be perfect! The initial information available and assumptions at the beginning of the Development stage in Figure 6.5, the result of early stage homework, will be verified many times via the sprint iterations in the stages that follow—by building versions of the product and testing them with users or customers, and also testing for technical proof of concept.

9. New Roles versus Old Roles

Agile introduces some new roles and role terminology. But some users of *Agile-Stage-Gate* stay with traditional roles and terms. For example, some user-firms, such as ThermoValves, do not use the Agile role "product owner" as highlighted above. Rather, they have a "project leader," a member of the project team responsible for *leading* the project. Larger and more complex projects also might have an on-team "project manager," whose role is similar to that the "new" scrum master (see also Chapter 3, success driver #6).

In *Agile-Stage-Gate*, both project leader and project or process manager are valuable and necessary roles, and are preferably delegated to two different people: a product owner or a project leader, and a scrum master or a project manager. The project manager or scrum master is generally able to support more than one project at a time, depending on the project size and complexity. For smaller projects, sometimes the team leader fills both roles—leader and project manager.

10. Managing the Development Pipeline

With projects progressing so quickly, and so much happening fast, the potential for chaos or anarchy exists; so how does a senior manager stay on top of the entire development pipeline of projects? One very positive facet of *Agile-Stage-Gate* is its very *visual nature*: The system generates excellent visibility of the progression of tasks within and across projects. The visual boards contain the details of exactly what activities or tasks are to be conducted during the sprint or iteration, which activities are underway and by whom, and which tasks are done. At any time, the portfolio owner can enter a project room and instantly see the progress within the sprint, and the status of the product backlog and prioritized requirements—and can do this for all projects in the development pipeline.

Even more dramatic is where a *virtual-software tool* is used to create the visual boards. Such software not only enables companies to manage individual projects, but permits one to view the full project portfolio instantly and in real time. With such a setup, managers can run analytics across the portfolio of all projects, for example:

- to reveal differences in the flow of activities across projects, showing all activities that are delayed by more than a week, thus pointing to the need for immediate action;
- to show the types of tasks undertaken by which people and departments, information useful for employee development; and even . . .
- to explore real-time resource capacity and usage (if using story points or similar weightings of probable resource consumption by tasks) in order to improve capacity planning in the portfolio.

As a result, in *Agile-Stage-Gate*, the portfolio owner becomes *more proactive*, and takes action with the project leader when something troublesome is spotted or where an intervention might be needed. Traditionally, the portfolio owner responded reactively, and this reaction was based on periodic updates from project managers or at monthly project reviews. Such a reactive information flow can delay the necessary intervention by weeks. By contrast, with the enhanced visibility inherent in *Agile-Stage-Gate*, problems are immediately pinpointed and interventions take place right away. Sometimes interventions occur before the problem even materializes: for example, intervening when a trend indicates problems are inevitable, such as when project velocity decreases or key activities are delayed.

WHY THE HYBRID *AGILE-STAGE-GATE* SYSTEM WORKS[38]

The benefits of *Stage-Gate* have been well researched and its widespread use documented. Less well-known to manufacturers are the benefits of Agile. The limited experience with *Agile-Stage-Gate* hybrid-development models suggests that manufacturers can indeed benefit greatly from this new hybrid approach; and although there are no studies yet of *Agile-Stage-Gate* in the service sector, there is no reason why it should not work there as well. Here are some conclusions about why and how:

> Understanding product requirements and envisioning a technical solution does not occur before Development, but in *Agile-Stage-Gate* is done *as part of the Development and Testing stages* of the project—learning on the fly.

Deals with Uncertainty and Validates Assumptions for Very Innovative Projects

Most firms' new-product processes emphasize extensive front-end homework to define the product and to justify the development project, *before* Development gets underway. Indeed, robust upfront homework and VoC work early in the project are consistently cited as keys to new-product success. But not all projects are quite so definable. Indeed, in some highly uncertain and ambiguous projects—those in new markets and using new technologies—no amount of VoC work, technical assessment, or market analysis will deal with all the uncertainties and validate all the assumptions prior to the Development stage. Understanding what the customer values and what will work technically only comes about through experimentation.

The rapid sprint-iterations in *Agile-Stage-Gate encourage experimentation and testing*—build something, test it with the customer and in the lab, and then revise one's thinking. The product may be only 40 percent defined on entering the Development stage, as is the case in Hewlett Packard's Agile model cited in Chapter 5[39] (or as noted in the next-generation system in Figure 5.12), but evolves and solidifies via these iterations. In this way, *key assumptions are validated and major uncertainties dealt with, but in real time* and as the project moves along. Thus, understanding product requirements and envisioning a technical solution does not occur before Development, but in *Agile-Stage-Gate* is done *as part of the Development and Testing stages* of the project—learning on the fly.

At the same time, it's a learning process for the customer too. Needs are often difficult for customers to articulate, especially at the outset of a development project and in the case of more innovative products and solutions. But seeing and critiquing *protocept products* along the way helps customers to understand and define their own needs.

Adaptive—Deals with Changing Requirements

When customers' needs change, or a new product requirement becomes evident partway through Development, traditional gating models, with fixed product definitions, fail to respond easily and quickly: They are simply not very adaptive. For example, once product specifications are "frozen," any design change request is viewed quite negatively.

By contrast, by building very early product versions or *protocepts* via the sprints—a model, computer-generated graphics, or a rapid prototype—*Agile-Stage-Gate* is *more adaptive*: If product requirements change, then needed modifications to the product's design can be made *earlier during the Development stage* when the cost of change is lower, much like a *strategic pivot* in the Lean Start-Up method.[40] For example, in Chapter 2 we saw that a study of major B2B European manufacturers revealed that on average, between 3 and 4.5 versions of the product—from early model through to prototype—were presented to validate the design with customers through the Development and Testing stages (while product ideation-and-design contractors, such as IDEO, iterated on average fifteen times with the customer per project!).[41]

Focuses Teams, Accelerates Development, Improves Communication

Agile-Stage-Gate project teams are *dedicated to the one project* to ensure adequate resources to get the work done. In traditional new-product development, only 11.4 percent of average firms have focused (dedicated) project teams (see Figure 3.8), and only for some projects. But Agile-Scrum places such emphasis on this dedicated team facet that teams *really are dedicated for every major project*. This one step alone increases development speed dramatically and may also improve quality of execution of key tasks.

Additionally, time-boxed sprints, and even time-boxed tasks within sprints, bring a sense of urgency to the development project. In Agile-Scrum, all events are time boxed such that every event has a maximum duration: That is, once a sprint begins, its duration is fixed and cannot be lengthened.[42] Project teams commit to certain deliverables at the beginning of each sprint, and then are expected to deliver within the time frame agreed. And it's vital to have exactly the right time available (including a buffer) to undertake the required tasks. (In practice, the project team estimates the times for all tasks at the beginning of a sprint, allowing six hours per person per day available, which assumes 75 percent efficiency).

The key here is to have a *steady flow*, and to avoid doing things in haste or in a last-minute panic (the negative term "feature cramming" is used in the software world). Additionally, the notion of a *steady, strong, and responsive heartbeat* creates a rhythm for the project team, and keeps moving the project along at a sure and steady pace—momentum is maintained.

Finally, dedicated teams (not spread across other work or other projects), a dedicated team room where the entire team resides, and face-to-face daily scrums all contribute to much-improved team communication. Every study of Agile (whether for software or physical products) reports this benefit. Firms practicing *Agile-Stage-Gate* with globally located teams function much the same way as a colocated team, but use superb IT so that team meetings (daily scrums) almost seem as though they take place in the same room.

MOVING FORWARD

The early evidence, albeit quite limited, is encouraging. Lead users of this new hybrid system are enthusiastic. In all the cases cited, the companies have expanded their use of the hybrid model, which speaks for the results it has delivered. Indeed, integrating Agile-Scrum methods into *Stage-Gate* to yield this new *Agile-Stage-Gate* hybrid model may be the most exciting and significant change to the new-product process since the introduction of *Stage-Gate* more than thirty years ago. [43]

> Integrating Agile-Scrum methods into *Stage-Gate* to yield this new *Agile–Stage-Gate* hybrid model may be the most exciting and significant change to the new-product process since the introduction of *Stage-Gate* more than thirty years ago.

Suggestion: If your business faces dynamic markets with high ambiguity—where things change quickly and customers aren't even sure what they want—then take a hard look at this new *Agile-Stage-Gate* approach. The early results are very promising: faster, more productive, and more responsive product developments. True, the method might contradict some of your current ways of working and thinking, and it's certainly is not for every firm nor every project. And it's not quite so easy as parachuting Agile from the software world into your current gating system: A number of adjustments and modifications—many have been highlighted above—will be necessary.

First ensure senior management commitment! *Agile-Stage-Gate* involves a significant cultural change, and so management—middle and senior—must be on board. Next, set up a task force to investigate the new model, and how it would and could work in your business. Let your task force propose the changes needed: how you'll reconcile planning-on-the-fly with a planned-based approach, what your "project definition" at the beginning of Development should look like, or the "definition of done." Then make the commitment and undertake several pilot projects, and in the Agile tradition, making improvements to the new system as you move forward. And if you're like other firms that took the first step here, you'll reap the benefits too.

7

DISCOVERY—THE QUEST FOR BREAKTHROUGH IDEAS

Lack of money is no obstacle. Lack of an idea is an obstacle.

—KEN HAKUTA, American inventor, author, and TV personality

A SHORTAGE OF BLOCKBUSTER NEW-PRODUCT IDEAS

Most companies don't lack for ideas—*they lack for big ideas*! In spite of the desire for breakthrough new products, recent data suggest that quite the opposite is occurring. We saw in Chapter 1 that the nature of new-product development portfolios has shifted dramatically—away from bolder, larger, and more innovative projects to smaller, lower-risk projects (recall the trends in Figure 1.1). Clearly, companies cannot achieve their aggressive product-innovation goals if they continue to focus on small, incremental development products and projects.

The quest for competitive advantage and achieving significant increases in sales and profits though product innovation means that the portfolio of projects must change. Making that happen will require new, bold, and innovative product ideas—*some real game-changers* and *blockbuster ideas*. Of many management practices studied in a major investigation of innovation, five top best practices were identified, including having an idea-to-launch process, resource management, an innovation strategy, and market insights—see Figure 7.1. But of

Figure 7.1: The Five Most Important Drivers of New-Product Performance

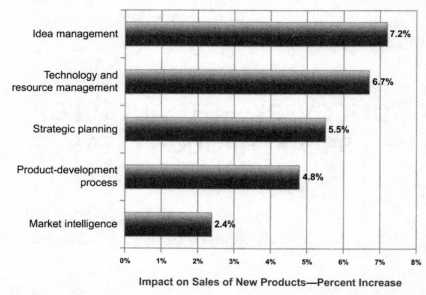

Impact on Sales of New Products—Percent Increase

Source: A.D. Little Innovation Excellence Study, endnote 1

Artwork courtesy of Dave Caissy

these five important drivers, *idea management has the strongest impact*.[1] Having effective idea management results in a dramatic extra 7.2 percent of sales from new products!

Feeding the Innovation Funnel

The trigger for your *Stage-Gate*® system is a new-product idea: In other words, when technological possibilities are matched with market needs and expected market demand. A good new-product idea can make or break the project: Ideas are the *feedstock for the innovation process*. But don't expect a well-oiled new-product process to make up for a shortage of quality ideas: If the idea was mundane to start with, don't count on your *Stage-Gate* process to turn it into a star!

> Of the five most important drivers of businesses' new-product performance, idea management has the strongest impact.

So important is idea generation that I now treat it as a separate stage in the *Stage-Gate* system, namely, the "Discovery stage" in Figure 4.11. In the earlier editions of this book, "coming up with good ideas" was treated as a given and portrayed as a lightbulb in the gating model: It was always assumed that there are lots of ideas sitting around waiting to be worked on. This assumption may be true for some firms, but even here, the *quality of these ideas is often lacking*—lots of little ideas. So a vital facet of a successful new-product effort is designing and installing an effective idea-generating system.

Suggestion: Review your new-product pipeline. Is there a shortage of really great projects—products that promise major revenues or will have a high impact on your business? If so, maybe it's because you're neglecting the Discovery stage of the process. Ask yourself some questions: Where do new-product ideas come from? Where should they be coming from? Are the ideas good ones? How does your company actively solicit new-product ideas? Do you have a new-product idea-generating system? If the answers to these questions make you uneasy, don't worry: This chapter suggests some concrete actions that can be taken to improve idea generation.

WHERE TO START? A PRODUCT-INNOVATION AND TECHNOLOGY STRATEGY

A prerequisite to effective idea generation is having a *product-innovation strategy for your business*. This strategy, among other things, defines the *arenas of strategic focus* or "strategic arenas"—in short, where you want to focus your R&D efforts and thus where you want to hunt for ideas. The development of a product-innovation and technology strategy for your business is thus vital to ideation.[2]

The goal is to define and select *strategic arenas* that are both attractive (large, growing markets; weak competition; good opportunities to develop new products) and where you can leverage your core competencies in technology, marketing, and production to advantage. The hope is that you select arenas that will be *your next engines of growth*—"oasis arenas" in an otherwise sterile desert—rich with fruit and full of many big new-product ideas!

These arenas become your idea "search fields." Delineating *search fields* or *strategic arenas* is important for idea and opportunity identification, because it specifies what's inbounds, and perhaps more important, what's out-of-bounds. This specification makes the quest for great new-product ideas much more directed and focused, and hence more effective—you avoid a scattergun approach often found in traditional idea search. Your innovation strategy also helps to provide validation to new ideas. The first question at every gate meeting is: "Does this idea (or project) align with our innovation strategy?" Without a well-defined innovation strategy, it's hard to make the right choices in project selection. More on innovation strategy and on how to uncover and select the right strategic areas in Chapter 10.

Figure 7.2: Install an Idea-Management System—A Systematic Idea Capture and Handling Process

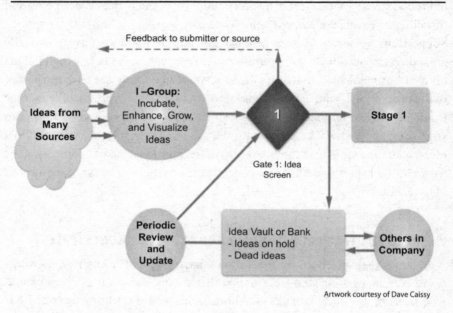

Artwork courtesy of Dave Caissy

SET UP AN IDEA CAPTURE AND HANDLING SYSTEM

Ideas are like grapes on a vine! Unless they are picked, they wither and die. How many times have I heard, "There's no shortage of ideas in our company," but when I ask, "Where are they?" I get blank looks. They're in people's heads, on their laptops, in a file—but not moving ahead. Thus, no matter the source of the idea, there must be *a mechanism in place to capture the ideas*, evaluate them, and then move the promising ones forward. Figure 7.2 shows a typical idea-handling model. So, the place to begin is to install such an idea-management system like the one in Figure 7.2—it's a high-impact best practice, as we see in Figure 7.1!

Reach out to many sources of ideas, both inside and outside the company, establishing communications or "idea flow lines" to stimulate the flow of ideas. These "flow lines" can be connecting with universities, undertaking formal market research, or having an internal idea contest for employees. More on the best sources and methods later.

Next, consider installing *an incubation group*, as shown in Figure 7.2, where ideas get a chance to breathe and "grow legs." One problem with submitting ideas directly to a business review or gate meeting is that many good ideas are too raw and will be instantly killed: *The best ideas are often the most fragile ones!* The I-Group denoted in Figure 7.2 works on the ideas, massages them, and puts some meat on them prior to a gate review. So when they reach the idea screen, these raw ideas are a little more robust.

Next is the decision gate or idea screen: Gate 1. Here, the best ideas are selected for work and to move forward into Stage 1, and the rest go into the idea vault—they are the dead ideas or on-hold ideas. Some firms have purchased idea-management software that allows others in the company to see the ideas in the vault and make suggestions—an open system much like an online blog.

THE SOURCES OF THE BEST IDEAS

Now the task is to *identify potential sources of ideas to reach out to*: Where do the good ideas come from? And more important, where should they be coming from, and which valuable sources are you missing? We do have some relevant data on eighteen different sources of new-product ideas that show the *most popular* versus the *most effective sources*—see the ideation effectiveness chart in Figure 7.3.[3] (Popularity is measured by percentage of firms that extensively use each method, shown on the horizontal axis; rated effectiveness of each method in generating breakthrough ideas is shown on the vertical axis in Figure 7.3, but only for users of that method.)

VOICE-OF-CUSTOMER METHODS

Eight voice-of-customer (VoC) methods are highlighted in the ideation diagram of Figure 7.3, including ethnography, focus groups, and lead-user analysis.[4] Some VoC methods are very extensively used, notably, customer visit teams, focus groups to identify customer problems, and the lead-user method, as noted by the diamonds inside the upper circle in Figure 7.3. Other methods, such as ethnography, forming a community of enthusiasts, or letting the customer help design the product, are less popular, but some are very effective.

> Voice-of-customer ideation methods are among the most popular and are rated the most effective sources of new ideas.

Regardless of popularity, however, *VoC methods generally are rated highly* by users in terms of effectiveness in generating breakthrough new-product ideas and constitute *the top five best-rated methods*. Indeed, most of the VoC methods

Figure 7.3: The Ideation Effectiveness Chart—Effectiveness versus Popularity for Each of Eighteen Ideation Methods

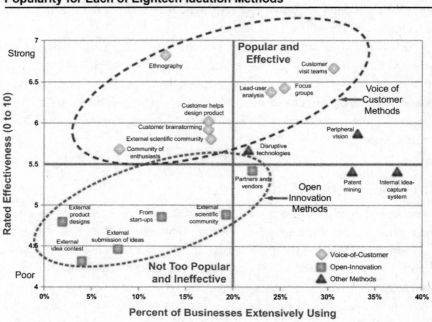

Artwork courtesy of Dave Caissy

fare very well, receiving solid effectiveness scores from users—all in the top half of the ideation quadrant diagram in Figure 7.3. In rank order of effectiveness—best to average—let's look at some of these VoC methods.*

1. Ethnographic Research, or "Camping Out"

If you want to study gorillas, a few focus groups is probably not the answer, nor is asking your salespeople about gorillas, or sending out an online survey. What is required is *real field research*—buy a tent and a backpack and move into their village, much like the anthropologist Jane Goodall did.

Ethnography, the term used in marketing for cultural anthropology, involves camping out with customers or observation of customers for extended periods, watching and probing as they use or misuse products. Although ethnography has become a popular topic in product-innovation

---

* For a more complete list and description of each method, see Cooper and Dreher (2010), endnote 3.

literature, the method is not so popular among practitioners, as seen by its unique location in the upper left quadrant in Figure 7.3. The method sees limited use for ideation, ranking number thirteen in popularity with only 12.9 percent of firms extensively using ethnography. In spite of its lack of popularity, however, this method gets *top marks for effectiveness*, with the highest effectiveness rating:

An example: Gojo, makers of Purell hand-sanitizer, identified a major potential market for sanitizing (antibacterial) products, namely the US Army. The Army faces many challenges in maintaining health of soldiers: Poor personal hygiene results in illness and disease which can impact the ability to perform the mission. The initial sale to the Army was the portable version of Purell (the familiar purse-sized version, with a clear plastic bottle and white cap). The thought was that soldiers could easily tuck the bottle into a vest pocket, and thus cleanse their hands in the field and without requiring water. A good opportunity, but not the right product—once deployed, very negative reports came back from the field!

> Of all the VoC methods, ethnography provides perhaps the greatest insights into the user's unmet and unarticulated needs, applications, and problems, according to users, and hence is a very powerful source of breakthrough ideas.

So a better idea was needed. To study the problem, members of the project team undertook *an ethnographic study*—no, they weren't allowed to observe troops in the front lines in the Middle East, but they did attend Army boot camp in the United States. Soldiers-in-training were asked to use the current product. And the observers from Gojo saw many problems: First, the bottle was not crush-proof, so when a fully-equipped soldier fell flat to the ground, the bottle broke and squirted the hand-cleaner all over the soldier's vest. Next, the square bottom did not fit easily into the snug vest pockets, so packing up was a nuisance. Additionally, the white cap was a dead giveaway when on patrol at night. And finally, the product did not "look and feel Army."

Understanding the problem through in-the-field observation enabled the project team to come up with a *better idea* for the Army product: the Purell FST Military Bottle. It looks and feels like standard military issue (embossed, with a foliage-green design that blends in with uniforms), and is built tough enough for military use; its flexible, V-shaped and lightweight design fits pockets or vest pouches easily; and it comes with special side grips for easy one-handed dispensing. Other features include a low-infra-red signature for night operations and the ability to withstand temperature extremes. The product was perfect for the solder and went on to become a great success.

Ethnography is a relatively new method for identifying unmet needs, although this general type of research—cultural anthropology—has been around for many decades. The main advantage is the depth of knowledge that one gains. Thus, of all methods, ethnography provides perhaps the greatest insights into the user's unmet and unarticulated needs, applications, and problems, according to users, and hence is a very powerful source of breakthrough ideas.

The main disadvantage is exactly that: Because it is so deep, it takes much time and is expensive to undertake. On the other hand, look at the payoffs and the fact that it is rated number one in terms of effectiveness! The time can be reduced by shortening the length of visit per customer site; for example, Fluke, a manufacturer of handheld instruments, spends about one day per customer site in its "day-in-the-life-of" research.

Another word of warning is that this observational method relies very much on the skill of the observer. If your people lack observation and listening skills, or are poor at drawing inferences and integrating information, then the method loses effectiveness. Some talent and training is needed.

Additionally, the method does not suit all product types and markets. For example, employing ethnography at a construction site, or in a factory or hospital is quite feasible; but camping out in someone's kitchen or bathroom is a bit more of a challenge. In spite of low usage and some of these limitations, the method is proven to work and is *definitely recommended*!

2. Customer Visit Teams

Here, teams visit customers or users; and they employ in-depth interviews based on a carefully crafted interview guide to uncover user problems, needs, and wants for new products. The method is ranked number four in popularity, with 30.7 percent of firms extensively using this method. Note, however, that in terms of popularity *and* effectiveness, this method is number one—in the far upper right corner in Figure 7.3.

In practice, customer sites are identified and agreement with the customer for such a visit is obtained. If a business-to-business (B2B) customer, the interviewers try to arrange for a small group of customer people to be available, namely, the *key purchase influencers*. The typical interview team is about three people, and is cross-functional—from marketing, sales, and technical. Technical people must be involved so that they can acquire face-to-face learning, too (rather than receiving the information secondhand and filtered).

When conducting the interviews, a structured and well-crafted conversation guide is essential. This guide lays out the questions and topics, ensures completeness and consistency across interviews, and provides a place to record answers. *Customer problems and "points of pain," needs, functions, and benefits sought by users* are explored, not just features and specifications, and thus the best questions are *indirect and inferential*:

> *Example:* "When you lie in bed at night and think about this product, what keeps you awake?" Or, "What really annoys you when you use this product?"

Once the interview is complete, the interview team should do a walkabout, spending time with the customer where the product is actually used. Often, by watching people use, misuse, and abuse the product, further insights into unmet needs are gained.

> *An example:* VoC using visit teams uncovered multiple ideas that led to a new product in the specialized field of hard-surface drills and saws. The company, Dr. Fritsch GmbH, is a small German firm with annual sales of about 12 million euros. It manufactures production machinery that is sold to producers of diamond-hardened tools—grinding wheels, saw blades, and drill bits. The task was to seek input for a new product in the firm's core market. One of the goals of the VoC study was to find out more about customers' products, their processes, and *their customers'* requirements, and thus their requirements for new production machinery.
>
> First, the team defined hypotheses about the expected results. This was vital, especially because sales people had often said: "We already knew all of what came out of the VoC research." One of the hypotheses was that a new product and technique for setting diamonds, introduced by a Taiwanese customer (called Arix*), would not succeed commercially.
>
> Thirty customer visits were undertaken by cross-functional teams of two to three people globally. A "manual" or protocol for the customer visits was created, and everyone on the visit teams was trained before going out to see customers. Questions focused on needs, problems, issues, and challenges faced by customers and users. Many insights and "ahas" were gained: One

important revelation was that the setting of the diamonds within cutting segments is critical for customers, and that the new Arix technique was indeed making believers out of skeptics in the marketplace.

The VoC results were then condensed in a workshop involving eighteen people, and an ensuing creativity (brainstorming) session took the VoC input and generated about eighty ideas; these ideas were subsequently pared down to seven "hot topics" and rough concepts. Preliminary work was done on the concepts, and a second evaluation reduced the set to three best bets. The firm finally elected the "ideal product" (now called Diaset), a technology to set diamonds automatically to yield the desired diamond arrays for the new product. With the product defined conceptually, the technical challenge now was to develop a production technique that could be integrated into the company's sintering machines to help their customers produce preset diamond-cutting segments efficiently. But by *first understanding the customer needs* and requirements, the technical work proceeded more effectively toward a clear target and solution!

There are several points to note in this example: First, this is a relatively small company, thus VoC using field visit teams is not just for larger firms. Second, this is a very technical product category: Effective market research can and should be done for such products, and not just restricted to simple consumer products. Third, the study was done globally—it did not focus just on a few nearby and convenient customers. Next, a broad-based workshop was held to interpret the results and insights of the VoC study (too often, when the researchers alone interpret results, they get it wrong). Finally, note that the team had an open mind, so that when VoC results came back that contradicted the original hypothesis, they did the needed 180-degree turn (too often, when VoC results are inconsistent with the views of the product managers or sales force, the research is attacked as "bad research"). One final point is that this small German firm did reach out and get professional help in designing and conducting the study and workshop.[5]

> Customer visit teams are valuable for gaining real insights into the customer's world: the ability to identify and focus on customer problems and unspoken needs, a vital source of product ideas.

In-depth customer interviews have a number of strengths as a VoC technique. Because customer visits are a *field-research technique*, they are valuable for gaining real insights into the customer's world. Users claim that the major advantage is the ability to identify and focus on customer problems and un-spoken needs during these interview sessions, a vital source of product ideas. Additionally, closer relationships can be developed with customers. And because the interview structure is flexible and the questions are open-ended, they create an opportunity for surprises, which might not be gained by other tools such as quantitative research. Finally, using cross-functional interview teams promotes a shared vision and understanding of what customers need and expect.

The *main challenge* is getting customers to cooperate: to agree to the session, to take the time, and to provide honest answers. The hope is that your sales-force and distributors have strong relationships with customers, and can lever-age this relationship to set up the session. Further, if the "problem area" under discussion is *really important to the customer,* then the interview can be pitched as a "win-win" for both your customer and you (note: If your customer does not see it that way, that's a strong hint that maybe you're *focusing on the wrong problem*!). Your customer becomes a valued partner in the project—they solve their problem too.

A second challenge is *finding the time and money* to do this valuable study (in-depth interviews at multiple customer sites do take more effort than most of the methods and do involve travel), to train the interviewers, and to design a robust interview guide with the right questions. I often hear developers say, "I don't have the time or money to do this study—I can't afford it." My reply: "You cannot afford not to do it!" The irony is that these same developers are prepared to spend person-months and many dollars developing the new product, but can't seem to find a fraction of that amount to build the right foundation—to do these vital customer visits to understand needs and problems.

A final challenge is dealing with the skeptics that "already know the an-swers, so we don't need the study," as was seen in the example above. Do what this small German firm did: Write down the expectations or "hypotheses" be-fore the study begins. Every time we have written these down, there are always significant ahas and changes in direction, the result of the VoC study. In spite of these tough challenges, however, this VoC visit team method is *definitely recommended*!

3. Lead-User (Innovative User) Analysis

This VoC method has been around since the 1980s but has only really caught on in this century.[6] The theory is this: First, your customer has ideas for your next new product. Second, if you work with the *average customer*, you'll get *average ideas*. But, if you identify a select group of *innovative* or *lead users* and work closely with them, then expect much more innovative new products. Research by Eric von Hippel reveals that many commercially important products are initially thought of and even prototyped by users rather than by suppliers. He also found that such products tend to be developed by "lead users"—innovative companies, organizations, or individuals that are well ahead of market trends and even have needs that go far beyond the average user. The trick is to track down lead users, who are by definition rare—those who are *ahead of the wave*.

The lead-user method has four main steps:[7]

1. Identify the target market and company goals for innovation in this market.
2. Determine the trends: Talk to people in the field who have a broad view of emerging technologies and leading-edge applications.
3. Identify lead users, either via a networking process or a survey. In networking, begin by briefly explaining the quest to people with apparent expertise on the subject: For example, research professionals or people who have written about the topic. Then ask for a referral to someone who has even more relevant knowledge. It's usually not long before one reaches the users at the leading edge of the target market. In a survey approach, customers and users are identified and then contacted, for example, by phone. A cleverly crafted questionnaire asks questions to try to identify more innovative users—for example, for a tool company, one might use questions such as "Have you ever modified this tool?" or "Have you ever tried to build a better tool or jig for this application?"
4. Develop the breakthroughs: Host a workshop with the identified lead users and key in-house technical and marketing people. Participants work in small groups at first, then as a whole, to define final product concepts. Normal group techniques such as brainstorming and inverse brainstorming are used, but the difference is that you are working with abnormal people—folks who are very innovative and creative.

The method is positioned very close to customer focus groups in Figure 7.3 and proves to be quite popular, with 24.0 percent of firms extensively using the approach. And the method is very effective, ranked number four on average by users.

An example: At Hilti, a leading European manufacturer of demolition, fastening, and concrete drilling equipment, lead-user analysis is extensively used. First, lead users are identified—leading edge, innovative customers in the construction or demolition field. Hilti's direct sales force provides guidance here. Hilti's innovation-management department then invites a group of these lead users for a weekend retreat—they watch and they listen, attempting to understand lead users' problems. Suggestions and possible solutions from lead users are fashioned into tentative new-product concepts. Hilti management claims that this lead-user technique has been used with great success across a wide variety of product groups within the company.v

> Innovative customers are quite likely to have the industry's next new product, and this *lead-user method* is one way to uncover what it is.

The advantage of the method is that innovative customers are quite likely to have the industry's next new product, and this method is one way to uncover what it is. And the method works, according to results in Figure 7.3. The major challenges are identifying who the innovative users are, getting them to participate in an off-site workshop, and then structuring and running the workshop session properly. Using referrals is one approach to identifying possible participants, but this can be tedious and problematic. This lead-user method is also used by 3M in North America with positive results, leading to major breakthroughs;[8] it is *definitely recommended*.

4. The Customer or User Designs

This novel method has received much attention in recent years and has been made possible in part because of IT and Internet tools. Here, customers or users are invited to help the product developer design the next new product,[9] and in so doing, provide many ideas for significant product improvements. The "customer designs" method has not caught on widely, but in spite of its limited popularity, *ranks number five in terms of effectiveness* in Figure 7.3.

An example: Witness LEGO's web-based "Digital Designer," which permits you and your child to log on and develop your own LEGO designs.[10] Your children download a simple CAD software package from the Digital Designer webpage so that they can design their own LEGO model. It's a win-win for everyone. Young designers become "master builders" just like in *The LEGO Movie*, and create their own designs. They can share their ideas with other "enthusiasts" in the LEGO Gallery—a showcase of products created by kids—and get feedback. The real payoff is this: The LEGO product-design team gains access to unlimited numbers of good ideas—ideas based on what their target customers *really do want!* At last count, there were over 2,300 pages in the LEGO Gallery, each page showing twenty submitted designs—that's almost fifty thousand designs for LEGO to consider as new product ideas!

One major study found that consumers in aggregate are 2.4 times *more efficient* at developing significant innovations than producers, with an average consumer-per-innovation cost of only 42 percent of that of producers. And consumers were found to be much more prolific and efficient product developers than producers when the field is in its early stages (that situation reverses as the field matures).[11]

The big advantage of this method is that informed users are in the best position to design the next breakthrough new product simply because they know their own needs *and* what they want. But the method can only be applied to certain categories of products. For example, allowing users to design products where the science is beyond the knowledge of the user—pharmaceuticals or aerospace equipment—generally won't work. But it does work for some categories. Additionally, there is the challenge of creating effective web-based tools to allow users to create product designs.

Nonetheless, in spite of only modest popularity, "the customer designs" method is *definitely recommended* for certain industries and product types.

5. Community of Enthusiasts, Social Media

By monitoring social media and blogs, often insights to customers' and users' concerns and needs are identified, which can lead to an aha idea. Additionally, social-media tweets to a business's online community can be used to solicit suggestions for new products, solutions to problems, or even to test very early stage concepts or ideas. "Netnography" or "cyber-ethnography" are formal methods applied here.

Netnography, for example, is a twist on ethnography, except it's done online—"listening" to people as they blog, post items on bulletin boards, or tweet. By undertaking content analysis, one can identify themes, problems, and potentially new ideas for products:

An example: Del Monte (US) Foods (pet-foods division) found a winner via Netnography.[12] Step 1 was the "I love my dog" initiative. The firm gathered and analyzed data from online blogs, forums, and message boards, identifying themes and trends in the pet-food marketplace. Most important, they identi-fied one key segment: "Dogs are people, too"—the dog owners who treat their dogs just like real people.

Next, Del Monte built an online community, "I Love My Dog," designed for continuous consumer interaction. This community was by invitation (five hundred consumers in this "dogs are people" segment) and password pro-tected. The community enabled Del Monte to undertake deeper consumer listening and understanding: Consumers discussed issues, blogged, chatted, shared photos, found resources, and participated in surveys. Dog owners in this segment, it was discovered, treat their dogs like real people, dressing them up, strolling them in baby carriages, and even purchasing dog furniture. They also give their dogs real people food; so if steak is on the adult menu, the dog gets some steak, too! But content analysis of the online community discussions revealed that breakfast was a problem—bacon, sausage, and eggs for the dog? The result was a new product: *Snausages Breakfast Bites*, which filled the need.

This community-of-enthusiasts method is not popular at all as a source of ideas, with only 8.0 percent of firms extensively using it. Similarly, the method is rated the least effective of the eight VoC methods (ranked number nine in effectiveness), but that's still above average. The major advantage is that once set up, this community can be maintained fairly inexpensively. By analyz-ing the comments and messages, as Del Monte did, one gains insights into what is really going on in the user community, learning about users' problems and desires. The challenge is that this method requires considerable skill, in-sight, and time to undertake content analysis. A second challenge is that the method likely only applies to a handful of product classes, for example, sports equipment, computer software, pets—high-involvement product categories in which customers are likely to band together into enthusiast groups or clubs. In spite of very low usage, the method *should be considered for applicable product categories.*

6. Design Thinking

Design Thinking pulls a number of proven approaches together. It's a discipline that uses the designer's empathy and methods to match people's needs with what is technologically feasible and what can be converted into customer value and market opportunity.[13] Design Thinking innovation is powered by a thorough

Figure 7.4: The Current Situation in Most Firms—Strategic Arenas Are Identified, but then There's a Gap Getting to Solid, Tested, Robust Ideas for Development

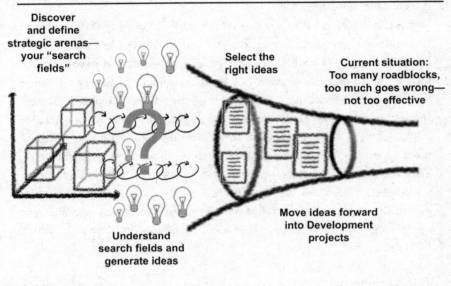

Source: Dreher, endnote 14

understanding, through direct observation, of what people want and need in their lives and what they like or dislike about the way particular products are made, packaged, marketed, sold, and supported.

In practice, Design Thinking simply applies the logical approach of *studying customers or users to determine their needs and wants*, and then applying one's technical or design skills *to create a series of testable prototypes* in an iterative fashion. The result is a validated and robust product concept ready for development.

In most firms, however, this "logical approach" doesn't work quite so well: Strategic arenas may be identified—areas of focus—and market research, including ethnography, is done to identify customer needs; but problems arise when getting to a pretested, robust concept ready for development, as shown in Figure 7.4. There are roadblocks along the way!

The answer: "Superimpose the Designing Thinking model atop the early stages of *Stage-Gate* and the result is much better," argues new-product expert, Dr. Angelika Dreher:[14] One moves more effectively from strategic arenas to needs to testable prototypes (or protocepts) and finally to a robust, tested and partially validated concept ready for development, as in Figure 7.5.

Figure 7.5: A Way to Bridge the Gap—Build "Design Thinking" into Your *Stage-Gate* System in Order to Move More Effectively from Strategic Arenas to Robust, Tested Ideas Ready for Development

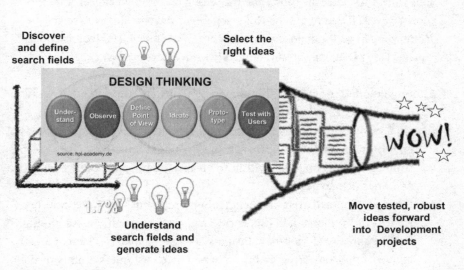

Source: Dreher, endnote 14

An example: Getting an MRI scan is not pleasant for anyone, especially for kids. Design Thinking was applied by GE Healthcare to come up with a better solution. The team worked with kids and parents, and learned that the anxiety curve starts with finding out that the child has to have the scan; it gets worse at the hospital, so the kids and parents are already upset by the time they see the scanner.

The plan was simple: Offer an environment that was so welcoming that children would feel like being scanned is an adventure. To do so, they asked customers and children about what they would like. The result was a *series of adventures*. Pilot kids rooms were then constructed at the University of Pittsburgh Medical Center, which offered a variety of adventures for the kids: Kids are transported to another, more imaginative world, and simple commands to get the scan done become part of the adventure.

Examples: In one of the Adventure Series, children get into a canoe and lie down inside. Children are told to "hold still so you don't rock the boat, and if you really do hold still, fish will start jumping over the top of you." In the Pirate Adventure, children "walk the plank" to be scanned. The Coral City Adventure gives children an underwater experience: They get into a yellow submarine and listen to the sound of harps while the procedure takes place. The Cozy

Camp gives children the chance to be scanned in a specialized sleeping bag, under a starry sky in an impressive camp setting.

The results speak for themselves: Children pick up on their parent's reactions when they enter the room, and the setting makes them all feel at ease. "I know for sure, if you've got the child, you've got the parent. If you've got the parent, you can get the child, because they are always looking for that reaction," explains Doug Dietz, the creator of the MRI Adventure Discovery Series.[15]

Although models for Design Thinking vary,[16] the main steps in Figure 7.5 are:

1. *Understand*: Explore the topic and task. Research the status quo (the task, environment, target groups, what success might look like). Use available sources, such as dialogue within the team, the Internet, outside experts, and one's own experience.

2. *Observe:* Contact users in their real environment—observe, ask, experience, and understand. This is essentially ethnographic research, highlighted above. Develop new insights and gain expertise. Here, empathy is most important—the ability to experience customers' points of pain. And that can only be achieved by firsthand observation, not by a survey questionnaire or a focus group.

3. *Review the insights from the previous two steps.* Select the standpoint: Define the typical user and their characteristics, and define questions and topics for idea generation.

4. *Ideate:* Create as many ideas as possible (use creativity techniques such as brainstorming). Select the most promising ideas.

5. *Prototype:* Translate the idea into something visible and tangible—perhaps a simple model made from paper or cardboard, or molding clay or LEGO blocks. Improvise—the model is simply a representation of the product, a protocept—it does not have to be perfect or elegant.

6. *Test:* Test your rough prototypes with target users or the customer group. Think of this as the first of a series of spirals or validation iterations with customers. Observe users' reactions and behavior. Then improve, adapt, and refine the concept and repeat the prototype and test iteration.

One might argue that these steps are well-known methods, and that Design Thinking is merely a bundling together of ethnography, brainstorming, and spiral development (build-test-feedback-and-revise iterations). True enough, but Design Thinking *does so in an integrated, seamless, and methodological fashion*, and thus the results are better than employing some or all of these methods alone. Design Thinking also has the advantage that it is a recognized "school" and hence is part of some universities' curricula; thus, students who graduate can actually use this method in business.

STRATEGIC METHODS FOR GENERATING IDEAS

Let's now turn to *strategic methods* or "top-down" methods for generating new-product ideas. These approaches are much more strategic in nature and rely on methods used to help fashion a business's innovation strategy (outlined in Chapter 10); but they are *also useful in identifying new-product ideas* and opportunities.

1. Look for Big Problems and Disruptions in Your Market

Big ideas solve big problems! And big problems often come from major shifts or disruptions in an industry. Strategic ideation approaches can be used to identify shifts, dislocations, or disruptions in the industry or marketplace, which often signal an emerging market or a major new-product opportunity. Begin by assessing your customers' industry—your marketplace. Unmet or unarticulated needs are often the result of changes and shifts in a user industry.

Start by developing a map of the *value chain*, identifying the various types of players all the way down to the end user. Next, *assess their futures*: their changing roles, who will gain, and who might be disintermediated (cut out). And always be on the lookout for "ahas" and "wows"— are there opportunities for you? Next, *identify customers' industry drivers* and potential shifts in these drivers. That is, try to assess what factors make them (or their competitors) profitable and successful. Is it cost of materials or low-cost production? Or response time to customer requests? And how are these changing—especially in a way that might open up opportunities for you? And finally, can *you* provide solutions here to help your customers be more profitable?

> Assessing your customer's industry, when coupled with face-to-face VoC research and working with lead users is a powerful technique. It leads to the identification of emerging or unmet customer needs, and new opportunities for new products and solutions.

Then *analyze historical trends* and *estimate future trends*; spell out a scenario (or alternate scenarios) of where your customer's industry—your marketplace—is heading. Next, *follow the money*! Market Maps is a good tool to see where the profits can be made: This is simply a chart that shows which types of players have what piece of the revenue in the industry. A similar and useful tool is Profit Pool Maps, which identifies the activities in an industry, percentage of revenue by each, and profit margins in each.[17]

Figure 7.6: Disruptive Technologies Create New Products which Underperform Current Products—but Note the New Performance Dimension

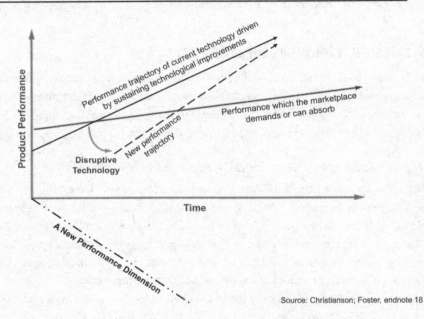

Source: Christianson; Foster, endnote 18

The result of this assessment of your customer's industry should be the identification of the most attractive arenas (segments in the marketplace where you should focus your search for ideas). Assessing your customer's industry, when coupled with face-to-face VoC research (above) and working with lead users (above), is a powerful technique: It leads to the identification of emerging or unmet customer needs, and new opportunities for new products and solutions.

2. Employ a Core-Competencies Assessment

In parallel, conduct an internal assessment on your own business—a strengths, weaknesses, and *core-competencies assessment*. Core competencies are skills and knowledge that differentiate you from your competition in a way that gives you a significant competitive advantage. This competencies assessment helps senior management decide which arenas they wish to focus on for innovative new products and solutions, and often *directly identifies new-product ideas* that build on your strengths.

Suggestion: Undertake a thorough industry and market assessment. Analyze the value chain; identify the industry drivers; and review historical trends and develop scenarios of the future. Look for gaps, emerging needs, and disruptions in your market or your customer's industry. These gaps and problems may signal your next major new-product opportunity. Take a close look at your own core competencies to determine where you have strategic leverage, which might lead to new-product opportunities.

3. Exploit Disruptive Technologies in the Search for Ideas

Periodically, radical or step-change innovations occur that dramatically alter the landscape of an industry. These *disruptive technologies* often yield products with inferior performance initially, and so the new products based on the disruptive technologies are not usually adopted quickly by the mainstream market. But they do pose a potential threat or opportunity for the future: Witness the impact that the digital cameras, the Internet, cell phones, and hybrid cars have had on their industries.

Figure 7.6 shows the situation. The current technology in most industries usually advances over time, driven by a number of small improvements—sustaining innovation—as noted by the solid inclining line (left) in Figure 7.6. Such was the case for 35 mm cameras, the dominant technology prior to digital cameras. Performance of the existing products (vertical axis) can be measured in a number of ways—for example, picture resolution. What usually happens is that the dominant technology improves so much over time that it exceeds the needs of many users (the gently sloping solid line in Figure 7.6).

Along comes a new disruptive technology, denoted by the dashed inclining line (right), whose initial products are inferior to the dominant technology when measured on the traditional performance metrics—picture resolution (remember the first digital pictures—not exactly award winners). So at first glance, it appears that the new technology is doomed!

What is missing in this two-dimensional diagram is the third dimension—the new performance dimension—shown as the Z axis in Figure 7.6. This new dimension here is "a digitized picture." For most camera users, this was not a relevant dimension; but for a handful of very specialized users—for example, commercial-property salespeople, or property-insurance adjusters—who needed to get pictures (not award winners) to their client or to their head office, the new performance dimension was critical; and they were prepared to endure the pain of inferior performance on other dimensions (picture quality) to get the new performance benefit: a digitized picture.

The conventional competitors making 35 mm cameras and film unfortunately were living in a two-dimensional world—a "flat-world"—and either did not see the third dimension or underestimated its impact. But the new digital camera producers had the advantage of living in a three-dimensional world. The rest is history.

The point is that disruptive technologies create *huge threats to the dominant firms* in an industry and *great opportunities* for others. In the last century:

- Digital watches almost destroyed the Swiss watch industry.
- Handheld calculators devastated mechanical calculating devices.
- Ballpoint pens, the Xerox machine, and the jet engine created great dislocations.

When disruptions occur, the dominant firms beforehand are most often no longer the dominant firms afterward. The phenomenon is called the *tyranny of success*.[18] What made firms successful in the first place then sows the seeds of defeat: confidence that leads to arrogance; constancy of purpose, leading ultimately to the inability to change; and huge investments in their technology (now the "old technology") that become golden handcuffs. Even more dangerous, these disruptions are also *stealthy*. They often occur almost unnoticed: Because their first products have inferior performance, the industry experts, forecasters, and market researchers dismiss the new products and the new technology.

So much for the theory! But *how does one predict* whether or not an emerging technology will be disruptive? And how does one seek ideas from the new technology?

1. First, continually monitor the outside technology landscape in your own industry. And identify technologies that might address your current customers' needs better than your own technology does.
2. Next, monitor the technologies in those industries working on related problems. Again, look for new technologies there.
3. When an emerging technology is spotted, assess its likelihood of success. Understand the dynamics of innovation and substitution—there are reasons that new technologies emerge:

   - An unmet customer need that the current technology cannot meet; or
   - A new customer need, the result of shifts in the external environment.

   Determine whether the new technology is likely to satisfy that need better. In order to anticipate disruptive technologies, *don't start with the technology;* start with customer needs and an understanding of what the customer sees as having value.

4. Look beyond what customers ask for, and look further than the mainstream market and users. Try to identify the handful of *potential customers who stand to benefit the most from the new solution*—the insurance adjustor or property salesperson in the digital camera example.
5. Finally, be sure to do lots of fieldwork: face-to-face discussions with early adopters and potential users, so that your people can learn firsthand about applications and users' potential for adoption.

Once a potential disruptive or radical and step-change technology is identified, then shift to assessing its impact on your industry, market, and products; and if needed, begin to identify what new products you will need and when (see the IOTA—Impact of Opportunities and Threats Analysis—later in this chapter).

In spite of all the hype, exploiting disruptive technologies is ranked only number ten out of eighteen in terms of effectiveness in generating breakthrough ideas and is about equal to the least effective of the VoC approaches—see Figure 7.3. Predicting the impact of a new technology remains difficult: Why were cell phones so successful, when an equally excellent, perhaps even better technology, satellite phones, met with limited success? Some argue that analyzing disruptive technologies is a *better tool to explain the past* than to predict the future! Further, disruptions do not occur on a regular basis in most industries, so one might wait decades to see such product ideas come about. The method is *definitely recommended* but with the caveats noted above—disruptions are difficult to predict, and they occur infrequently.

4. Develop Peripheral Vision as an Idea Source

The biggest dangers are *the ones you don't see coming*! Understanding these threats and anticipating the opportunities requires strong peripheral vision.[19] A sad story of the failure of peripheral vision—they didn't see it coming—is DuPont's inability to recognize and deal with the threat of low-cost polymers. DuPont invented many of the polymers that today we take for granted: nylon, Orlon, Dacron, Lycra, and Teflon, to name some. In spite of DuPont's technology prowess, patents had run out and other chemical companies built Asian and Middle Eastern plants with access to lower-cost feedstock and lower-cost labor. DuPont did little: Instead of taking bold action—for example, building Asian or Middle Eastern polymer plants with the advantage of DuPont's superior technology, or joint-venturing with an Asian firm—DuPont slowly retreated from its polymer markets, which led in turn to underutilizing of its production capacity, higher costs, and thus even greater vulnerability. DuPont's polymer business today is a shadow of its former self.

Most companies are blindsided by unexpected events: In a strategic survey, two-thirds of companies were surprised by up to three high-impact competitive events in last five years. And 97 percent lack an early warning system![20] Because most firms are blindsided by major external events, they miss opportunities for new products. Peripheral vision is simply a strategic method for generating new-product ideas: It is a deliberate and formal strategic exercise whereby you assess the external world, identifying trends and threats, and in the process, define potential new products.

Peripheral visioning proves to be a very popular approach to generating new-product ideas (perhaps also under a different name), and is ranked number two out of eighteen, with 33.1 percent of firms extensively using this strategic approach, as shown in Figure 7.3. Effectiveness is also positively rated—a number seven ranking from users. *Definitely recommended!*

5. Assess the Mega-Trends[21]

This method is a *lens for defining an opportunity space*. Here, a team analyzes the major trends in society and in their industry. With foresight, the group is able to identify the "grand challenges" in the industry that may open up great opportunities and ideas. The team looks for the big, inevitable trends and then asks the money questions: Where do we have to play? Where might we play?

> *An example:* If your firm is in the automotive industry—a parts supplier, in finance or insurance, or in manufacturing—the inventible trends mean that you have to play in certain spaces: the electric car, the connected car, and the self-driving car, for example. Then look at potential market and technological disruptions, for example, highly efficient engines, electric cars, nano-coatings, smart cars, self-driving cars, new materials (new composites), smart roads, wireless connectivity, new consumer electronics, changes in financing (such as fin-tech), changes in insurance, and new government regulations. Given these trends and disruptions, and with that foresight, what are opportunity spaces for you?

6. The Value of Future Scenarios

One of the most significant strategic decisions ever made was when AT&T turned down a free offer to take control of the Internet. In the late 1980s, the National Science Foundation (US government) wanted to withdraw from its role of administering the Internet and offered AT&T a free monopoly position. But AT&T had a mental map of the future—namely, a scenario or picture of the future in which their centrally switched technology would remain dominant. The notion of a packet-switched, decentralized switching technology (what the Internet uses) would never be the future. The technical experts at AT&T concluded that the Internet was insignificant for telephony and had no commercial significance in any other context.

What AT&T should have done—and indeed what your company should do— is to develop *alternate scenarios of the future*. Yes, develop the scenario of the "official" or expected future . . . in AT&T's case, a world with centrally switched architecture remaining dominant. But develop an alternate scenario, too—in this case, an alternative in which new markets for Internet services and new kinds of telephony challenge the dominant AT&T architecture. Such a scenario at minimum would have given decision-makers a sense of the Internet's potential and might have led them to consider alternate courses of action. But developing alternate scenarios also helps decision-makers become much more *sensitive to signals of change*. As Peter Schwartz, who advocates the use of scenarios in planning, declares: "What has not been foreseen is unlikely to be seen in time."[22] For example, AT&T executives, by defining the alternative scenario, might have been more alert when increasing numbers of users began to go online, when webpages began to mushroom, and when PC sales to home users grew by leaps and bounds in the early 1990s.

Developing alternate scenarios of the future usually involves senior people taking part in extensive discussions and work sessions. Because your purpose is to arrive at new-product opportunities, restrict the discussion to scenarios that are relevant to your business and deal with the external (or extended market) environment. For a bank, this might be: "Describe the future of financial and related markets, and the financial industry as a whole."

Questions to work on include:

1. What is the best future scenario? Try to describe in as much detail as possible what your (company's) world will look like in the future (five to ten years), given the best-case external environment assumptions.
2. What is the worst possible scenario of the future for your company's external environment?
3. What are some relevant dimensions that characterize these scenarios (for example, in AT&T's case, a relevant dimension was "centralized versus decentralized switching": The best scenario was at one end—namely, centralized switching; the worst case was at the other—decentralized or packet switching dominant).

Then identify the *primary decisions* that you face. In order to identify new-product opportunities from scenarios analysis, the questions are:

- Should you launch new businesses or business models?
- Should you invest in new technologies or technology platforms?
- What types of new products should you be seriously looking at?

Scenarios are utilized by imagining that one or another "future scenario" will be true and then assessing the consequences of making each decision, assuming each alternate future.

Finally, markers or signals of each scenario occurring should be identified, so that managers can spot telltale signs over the next months or years as to which way the world is moving. For example, one banking scenario is that there will be almost no retail bank branches in the future—that bricks and mortar will be history. Telltale signals over the next decade might be: the number of new e-banks launched; the proportion of users in various age groups moving to e-banking; and the development of new communication devices and aps that make the Internet more portable and functional. If such trends, aps, or devices gain rapid momentum, then look for near branchless banking around the corner.

Suggestion: Develop scenarios of the future, but do more than just developing the most likely scenario or your "official future." Develop *alternate scenarios*—best case and worse case. Imagine what would happen if each alternate scenario came true—how would it alter your new-product decisions? And what would be the financial consequences of making decisions assuming the official scenario, if indeed one of the alternate scenarios were to come true (as AT&T's did). Assign just a small probability to these alternate scenarios occurring, and reconsider your new-product investment decisions! And use brainstorming and creativity techniques to uncover imaginative ideas, given that each scenario—official and alternate—occurs.

7. Competitive Analysis

A final strategic approach to ideation is to take a hard look at your competitors. The goal here is to understand their strengths and weaknesses, why they are winning or losing, and what you can learn. Inverse brainstorming competitors' products—ripping them apart and identifying their weaknesses—is a useful tool. And be sure to build questions on competitor products—what customers like or dislike about them—into your market research.

An example: Rust-Oleum, a major US supplier of paint, coatings, and related renovation products, undertakes a "brand deconstruction exercise" in order to generate new product ideas.[23] Marketers in the company pick a competitive brand in their category, one that is doing something right, and get into this competitor's shoes. They do a SWOT (strengths, weaknesses, opportunities, threats) analysis. Questions include: What is the competitor thinking? What keeps those folks up at night? They also shop competitors' products and ask customers about them. They take their competitor's product apart in the lab and also pose questions in consumer and customer research about the competitive brand. Management then takes the findings and acts on them, often coming up with new strategies or new-product ideas.

Putting Your Strategic Exercises to Work

To wrap up your strategic exercises—strategic analysis, forecasting market and technology disruptions, peripheral visioning, creating alternate scenarios, and competitive analysis—hold an *integration session* or *workshop*. Here you review all the trends, events, threats, opportunities, and forecasts that you have identified (the left column of Figure 7.7, the IOTA summary chart). Next, indicate the timing and likelihood of these events or trends: Are they here and now, with 100 percent likelihood of occurring? Or perhaps they're sometime in the distant future and should be ranked as a "maybe." Next, discuss the impact—for example, the impact of carless cities would be disastrous to an "assemble yourself" furniture retailer . . . unless they create a new product, new service, or new business model.

> Put your strategic exercises to work. Review all the trends, events, threats, opportunities, and forecasts. Next, understand their timing and likelihood. Then, forecast their impact. And finally, address the "so what" question—what new products or business models do these trends point to?

Now for the final column in Figure 7.7—so what? What can you do about it? Here you identify the new products or new businesses that this IOTA exercise points to.

OPEN INNOVATION AS A MAJOR SOURCE OF IDEAS

Major corporations face a major threat—the fact that their own internal R&D has not been the engine of innovation in their industries and that they have missed opportunity after opportunity. Indeed, many of the breakthrough ideas, products, and technologies over the last decades have come from outside major corporations.[24] For example, lots of ideas, inventions, and innovations come from smaller, entrepreneurial start-ups funded by venture capitalists;[25] and

Figure 7.7: Summarize Your Strategic Exercises in an IOTA Chart— Impact of Opportunities and Threats Analysis

Area for scanning	List: Threats, major changes and trends, disruptions, danger signals, key issues, and events	How likely?	How imminent (timing)?	Impact on your business— so what does it mean?	What opportunities: new products, new services, new businesses, new business models?
Market changes and shifts—your customers					
Changes in your competitors and their strategies					
Changes in members of your value chain (e.g., suppliers, distributors)					
Technology trends, changes, and disruptions					
Legislative and political changes, events, dangers					
Social and demographic trends, changes					
Economic changes, threats, dangers					

Artwork courtesy of Dave Caissy

many of these start-ups create breakthrough technologies and ideas and new business models that disrupt established product categories and markets. Thus, competitive advantage now often comes from leveraging the discoveries of others. And the implication of that trend is unavoidable.

Does your organization suffer too much from NIH—the "not invented here" syndrome? Leading companies have recognized the need for *open innovation*— for a healthy balance between internally and externally generated ideas and new products. And they have put in place the processes, IT support, teams, and culture to *leverage external partners and alliances* in the quest for new ideas, inventions, and innovations from outside the firm.

In spite of all the talk about open innovation, when it comes to idea generation, it is surprising that these open methods prove not to be very popular, nor are they perceived to be particularly effective as sources of new-product ideas. Indeed, as a group, most are in the lower left quadrant in the ideation quadrant diagram of Figure 7.3 (the solid boxes inside the lower circle). But a major study into open innovation reveals that large companies consider open innovation to be *very important* and are *expecting it to grow even further*:[26] "Companies are increasingly drawing on the innovative potential of external parties: They are cocreating innovations with customers, cultivating informal networks, and collaborating with universities. [But] approaches that have been widely discussed in the media—such as crowdsourcing, in which firms work with unknown outsiders to solve problems—are rated lowest in importance by large companies."

Six different open-innovation approaches to getting new-product ideas are outlined here. There are others. Note that the most popular approach—ideas from partners and vendors—has been around for a long time, and though it is an open-innovation method per se, it certainly is not a new method. The three *most effective open-innovation methods* (as judged by users, see Figure 7.3) are ideas from partners and vendors, ideas from the external scientific community, and ideas from start-up businesses. None of these open innovation approaches is as effective as an idea source as the eight VoC methods are, however, perhaps because of their newness, or perhaps because of their limited applicability.

> Leading companies have recognized the need for *open innovation* and are *leveraging external partners and alliances* in the quest for new ideas, inventions, and innovations from outside the firm.

Open innovation has the advantage of tapping into inventors, scientists, designers, vendors, consumers, and small businesses for ideas, IP, technology, and even finished products—a huge number of sources well beyond the limited capabilities of your own engineering or R&D departments. The major disadvantage is that as a source of new-product ideas, many of the open methods only apply to certain product categories (for example, Procter & Gamble endorses the method strongly, as evidenced by their effective "Connect + Develop" webpage, whereas GE argues that seeking ideas for locomotives or jet engines from the outside world is a little impractical). A second challenge is the amount of time and work it takes to scan, solicit, handle, and process the ideas or IP.

The reasons for the lack of popularity and perceived effectiveness may be that some of the open-innovation approaches are relatively new, and thus many companies have yet to experiment with them. And being new, it's too early to evaluate their effectiveness. Others dispute this claim and argue that open innovation is *not so new*—that "firms have always been open to some degree and that the benefits differ depending on their line of business."[27] Those in industries with simpler technologies and

> "Open innovation" is a relatively new source of innovation ideas. In spite of limited popularity and rated effectiveness, it's recommended for certain product categories.

B2C (business-to-consumer) products, such as P&G, are good candidates for open innovation, with millions of consumers and would-be inventors the target; but companies in advanced technology and complex products may find inviting ideas from the outside world less fruitful.

Yet another critique comes from capital-intensive industries, where products take a long time to develop and remain on sale for years. GE's CEO Jeff Immelt observes that his firm is a leader in a number of fields, such as making jet engines and locomotives, which requires "doing things that almost nobody else in the world can do" and where intellectual-property rights and a degree of secrecy still matter. Mark Little, head of GE research, is even more skeptical and notes that outside ideas "don't really stick well here." He professes great satisfaction with the output of GE's own research laboratories: "We're pretty happy with the hand we've got."[28] From most effective to least, here are the open innovation methods for idea generation:

1. Partners and Vendors

This open-innovation method entails seeking new-product ideas from outside partners and vendors. It is not a new approach, and it is quite popular, with 22.1 percent of firms extensively using it to generate ideas. In terms of effectiveness, the use of vendors and partners as a source of ideas is down the list at number eleven out of eighteen.

The advantages are that vendors and partners bring technical capabilities that may be beyond your scope of expertise. Buried within these capabilities are the seeds of your next great new product. The trouble is that vendors or partners may be equally as uncreative at ideation as you are, so don't expect a plethora of great ideas from this source. Nonetheless, because it is a tried-and-proven approach, is quite popular, and yields decent effectiveness ratings, the approach is recommended; it is also the only open-innovation method even close to the desirable upper right quadrant in Figure 7.3.

An example: Swarovski, the Austrian crystal and jewelry company, actively seeks existing technologies, emerging technologies, and other innovations from suppliers and partners that can be applied to their business.[29] Examples of "search fields" include new surface treatments, new application techniques, new materials, new manufacturing methods, and even new businesses and business models. The firm has established a network of over one hundred key suppliers and potential partners to provide the inputs. Swarovski works hard at setting up and managing the relationships through workshops, regular meetings, and cooperative development initiatives. The thought process employed is logical: First, define the areas for open innovation (the "search fields"); then leverage the global network and find potential partners; and then establish relationships and work with them.

Although managed much more deliberately and professionally today, open innovation with vendors is not new to Swarovski. One of their major open innovation breakthroughs came as early as 1956: Together with Christian Dior, Swarovski developed the "Aurora Borealis" effect, a shimmering finish that enhanced the sparkle of cut crystal by transferring thin-film physical vapor deposition technology from the optical industry into the fashion industry.

2. Accessing the External Technical Community

This open-innovation approach solicits ideas and technology solutions from the external scientific and technical community. A number of online tools, such as NineSigma, Yet2.com, and InnoCentive, make this access much easier today. The method is fairly popular, with 19.5 percent of firms extensively using it. Note, however, that the method tends to be used more for *seeking technology solutions* during the Development stage than for seeking new-product ideas.

3. Scanning Small Businesses and Business Start-Ups

This open-innovation approach accesses small and start-up businesses and gets ideas from these entrepreneurial firms. The argument here is that you can bet that somewhere today there is a scientist or designer with the great next new product in your industry. The trouble is, that person probably doesn't work for you, but is employed in a small business or start-up firm. Indeed, the track record of large and dominant firms in commercializing breakthrough innovations in most industries has been dismal, with many of the true innovations coming from newer or smaller firms. One challenge is that there are hundreds, perhaps thousands, of smaller enterprises that could be sources here, and accessing and vetting all the potential sources is no small task. A second challenge is the protectiveness often exhibited by the start-up entrepreneur— an unwillingness to give up "his baby" or even 50 percent of it in exchange for much higher profits.

4. External Product Designs

This open-innovation method involves using the Internet to invite the general public—customers, users, and many others from the external world—to submit *finished-product designs* (not just ideas). The method is sometimes called "crowdsourcing." Examples are Threadless, a T-shirt company in Chicago that runs online contests for T-shirt designs; Muji, a Japanese furniture company that asks its catalogue members to submit furniture designs;[30] and LEGO's Web-based Digital Designer, aimed at kids and their parents, mentioned above.

Letting outsiders design products is a very novel and step-out method, and I included the customer-focused aspect of this method in the VoC section above. As an open-innovation method, it goes beyond customers and lets the *whole world* participate, and as a result, it seems that both popularity and effectiveness drop off, as noted in Figure 7.3.

The advantage of the method is that the world becomes your product design house—you can capitalize on people's desire to design and develop products, often for little or no financial gain. The example of open-source software is often cited by proponents. Once again, however, this method has limited applicability: It is restricted largely to consumer products and relatively simple and creative goods (note that the examples given above are all creative-design products about which outsiders are likely to have creative insights).

5. External Submission of Ideas

In this open-innovation approach, your customers, users, and others in the external world are invited to submit their new-product ideas, often via the Internet and your webpage. P&G's Connect + Develop system is an example.[31] But few companies have tried this: The popularity of this method ranks number sixteen out of eighteen, with only 7.9 percent of firms extensively using it. Surprisingly, and in spite of the positive review in articles written about P&G's system, the effectiveness of external submission of ideas ranks almost dead last.

On the positive side, users of this method indicate that the entire world becomes your source of ideas, greatly magnifying the possibilities beyond your own employees' creative abilities. The major weaknesses are that the technique probably only applies to the world of consumer and technically simple products. Further, it takes "an army of internal people," as one executive commented, to review the ideas, assess and evaluate them, and get back to the submitter with a business proposal. For example, one major European consumer-goods company tried the approach for a while but then gave it up as far too time-consuming—"a lot of work for the very few good ideas we obtained."

6. External Idea Contest

Hosting an ideation contest and inviting the external world to submit ideas is another open-innovation method. This method is an extension of open method #5 above—external submission of ideas—and shares the same positives, except there is the added incentive (and a little excitement) of a contest with prizes for the submitter. But like #5 above, the method is limited to simple consumer goods. Additionally, there is the added cost and time of setting up a professionally managed contest—all the rules, administration, and awarding of prizes. In summary, external-idea contests are not popular at all, but they do get good reviews from heavy users. This method is worth a look but clearly is not the ideation method of choice for most firms.

Suggestion: You cannot ignore the world of *open innovation* to generate new-product ideas (and perhaps even secure technology and finished products ready to license). There are numerous ways to access ideas through open innovation:

- Scouting teams that investigate small businesses, inventors, and start-ups by visiting conferences, trade shows, and also tracking developments online and in publications—globally.
- Webpages inviting the public to submit ideas, technology, and finished products, as does P&G.
- Interfaces with university technology transfer centers (go with a shopping list!).
- Regular sessions with suppliers and their technical people, and involving your R&D and marketing people, as does Swarovski.
- Webpages that allow customers to design their own products, as does LEGO's Digital Designer.

Open innovation ideation takes effort, however: You must put the resources in place—a *scouting, connect, and develop team*—to work with the external submitters; and you must strive to establish the right climate and culture for open innovation, ensuring that your existing employees are not threatened by the new business model.

Stage-Gate *for Open Innovation*

Leading companies that have moved to *open innovation* have modified their *Stage-Gate* process—built in the necessary flexibility, capability, and systems—in order to enable this network of partners, alliances, and outsourced vendors from idea generation right through to launch. For example, P&G's SIMPL 3.0 version of its *Open Stage-Gate* system is designed to handle externally derived ideas, IP, technologies, and even fully developed products; and some GE companies have also reinvented *Stage-Gate* (GE's Toll-Gate system) to handle open innovation, both outbound and inbound.[32]

In the traditional or *closed-innovation model*, inputs come mostly from internal sources. Then, the R&D organization proceeds with the task of inventing and developing new products—a *fairly closed system*.[33] By contrast, in open innovation, *companies look inside out* and *outside in*, across all aspects of the

Figure 7.8: *Open Innovation Stage-Gate* **Features External Interfaces (Inbound and Outbound) at Multiple Points in the Process—From Ideation Onward**

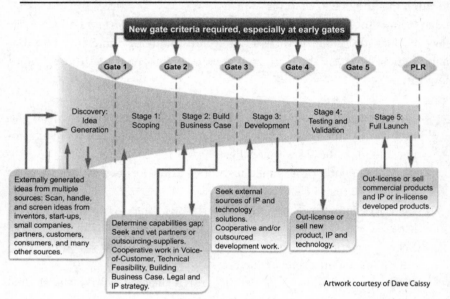

Artwork courtesy of Dave Caissy

innovation process, including ideation, development, and commercialization. Thus *Stage-Gate* must be substantially modified to handle ideas, inventions, and IP from outside the firm, and facilitate working with partners and outsiders on these developments. See Figure 7.8 for a typical *Stage-Gate* system designed for open innovation.

TECHNOLOGY DEVELOPMENT AND FUNDAMENTAL RESEARCH—CHANGING THE BASIS OF COMPETITION

> Be sure to leverage your technology development and basic research effort. Ensure that this research is directed by your innovation strategy.

Do you have a central research facility? Most firms cannot afford a "corporate lab," but if your company does fundamental research or develops new technology, be sure to engage this research unit in your Discovery stage. Fundamental research and technology development will often lay the seed for a great new product, product family, or platform, and hence is a vital source of new-product ideas. The trouble is that much fundamental research is *undirected, unfocused,* and *unproductive*—which is why so many CEOs have shut it down. If fundamental research is not yielding the breakthrough projects it should, then provide direction via your *innovation strategy*, and introduce a little *Stage-Gate* discipline.

I outlined *Stage-Gate TD* in Chapter 5, specifically designed for new technology, knowledge-build, or fundamental-research projects. Some scientists may scream their disapproval, but remind them that this is not a university where curiosity-based research is the rule—this is a business. Other scientists will welcome the opportunity to become more engaged in value-producing research for the corporation.

Suggestion: If fundamental research, science projects, or technology developments are undertaken in your business, try introducing a stage-and-gate process similar to that in Figure 5.5 in order to provide a little more direction and focus. Here, the Applications Path gate should be the trigger for new-product ideas. But note that the TD process—its stages, gates, activities, and gate criteria—will differ substantially from your normal *Stage-Gate* system!

PATENT MAPPING

Patents are an outstanding but all too often overlooked source of valuable information, including ideas for new products.[34] The amount of knowledge contained in patents is enormous, but somewhat overwhelming to access and interpret. Patent mapping involves the distillation and interpretation of large amounts of often complex patent data into one or more high-value representations useful in making business decisions. The goal is to generate actionable intelligence from raw patent information, enabling timely, informed decisions.

For innovators, patent mapping helps the user to conceptualize the IP space and serves as a trigger for new-product ideation and selecting development areas to focus on. For example, if considerable patent and filing activity is noted in a particular field or area, that is a signal—a signal that technologists somewhere are onto something, and more important, that management sees that this area is sufficiently interesting to spend the time and money to file a patent.* Thus, *hot areas in technology* can be spotted—emerging areas, and areas that are seen as having potential.

Patent mapping and patent mining are well known and quite popular, as seen in Figure 7.3. Although the techniques are useful for identifying areas of competitive activity and hence potential areas of focus, they do not generate

---

* Note that patent filing is expensive and consumes scarce IP people resources; therefore, most companies are selective about what they file, thus revealing what they consider important.

new-product ideas per se. As a result, effectiveness is ranked lower, at number fourteen on average, well below the VoC methods.

GETTING GREAT IDEAS FROM YOUR OWN EMPLOYEES

Your own employees are excellent potential sources of new-product ideas. Yet all too often, internally generated ideas are either mundane or not acted upon. Here are some ways to change that.

Internal Idea Capture

Setting up an internal idea capture system is, not surprisingly, the *most popular ideation method.* This typically involves formally soliciting new-product ideas from your own employees (often via an internal webpage or using purchased software), and then screening and handling these ideas via some form of formal and structured process. It is number one overall in terms of extensive usage, but effectiveness is disappointing, ranked number twelve. *But there is wide variation in perceptions of effectiveness* here, suggesting that some firms get it right.

> Your own employees are excellent potential sources of new-product ideas. Yet all too often, internally generated ideas are either mundane or not acted upon. But there are ways to change that.

Suggestion: Implement a professional internal idea-suggestion system to tap into the creative juices of your own employees . . . but with some important caveats. The problem is, like everything else worth doing, the details do matter. And many businesses get the details of internal idea generation wrong. Here are some tips from the firms that got it right:

- Put someone *in charge* of your internal idea-suggestion scheme. The problem is, ideation is everyone's job and no one's responsibility, so it falls between two stools.
- Publicize the idea-suggestion scheme widely—it's surprising in how many firms I visit, folks are not sure whether there is such an internal ideation system in place!
- Separate the "ideas for new products" system from general purpose "idea-suggestion boxes." The latter tend to attract lots of minor cost- and time-saving ideas; but you don't want your innovation ideation scheme mixed in with that!
- Welcome all ideas and do not belittle people for submitting offbeat ideas. And make it easy for employees to submit ideas—virtual suggestion boxes

work for most people (an internal webpage), but paper-based submissions may still be a route for some.

- Provide guidance: On your internal webpage, outline the "search fields" where you are actively seeking ideas; and then provide some background and data to characterize some of the search fields.
- Provide a fast response—on average two to four weeks. People get tired of waiting and soon lose interest and stop submitting ideas. And provide some feedback: Use a scorecard and give feedback on the relevant dimensions—where the idea scored high and low.
- Provide incentives—rewards or recognition. Recognition works best, according to some studies, and is less problematic.[35] Some rewards, instituted with the best of intentions, have the opposite effect. For example, one firm established significant prizes for good ideas, with the rule that in the event of two identical submissions, the first submission took the prize. Sharing ideas among employees dropped, and thus creativity suffered!
- Annually review the system and track the ideas—numbers of ideas, sources, and what happened to them.

Run an MRG or Off-Site Idea-Generating Event

MRG means *major revenue generator*. And an MRG event is an off-site company event designed to produce or scope out at least several major ideas at the end of a few days' tough work. It's fun and it works!

The principle is that your own people, including senior people, often have the seeds of great new products within them. By harnessing the creative energy of the entire group, unexpected outcomes are often the result. An MRG event is a way to stimulate creativity but in a structured fashion. Here's how to proceed:

> An off-site MRG event is a way to stimulate creativity but in a structured fashion. By harnessing the creative energy of the entire group, unexpected outcomes—and great ideas—are often the result.

An annual off-site company conference of senior and middle people is the venue. We've all been to these—two or three days of assorted speakers, some from inside the company, others from outside. A nice event, but not much happens as a result.

This year, make the event yield a different result. Invite fewer speakers, but instead, build in a series of MRG exercises. Let's assume a two-day meeting:

Morning of Day 1: After the usual opening speech, split the attendees into breakout teams. Here's the assignment: "You have ninety minutes to identify the major trends, shifts, changing customer needs, and potential disruptions that are taking place in our marketplace." Be sure to challenge teams to answer the money question: "So what? Do these shifts suggest any major new opportunities?" After the breakout session, teams report back. Pick some teams at random to present their conclusions.

Afternoon of Day 1: Same breakout teams but a new assignment: This time, they identify the major technology shifts in their industry and their customers' industry that will impact the market, and might change the way you do business. Again pick teams at random to report back.

Other breakout sessions over the first 1.5 days deal with similar topics, including an assessment of internal company strengths and core competencies that might be leveraged to advantage; and also shifts in the industry and value chain structure—what new players and competition are there, and what old ones may disappear? But always the challenge to all breakout teams and sessions is: "So what—what opportunities do these changes suggest to you? Do you see any ahas?"

By noon of Day 2, shift to *opportunity mapping*. That is, task the teams with mapping out some of the opportunities that their assessments have suggested— this usually means identifying and listing some of the bolder ideas and ahas. Then, ask each team to present its list of major opportunities or ideas—post these on flip-chart sheets on the wall. Finally, the large group votes on the ideas, using scorecards, and then put "green dots" on the top-scoring ideas. Before the event ends, be sure to identify the "best bets" and have teams put together a go-forward plan on each—the next steps and a team to work on the idea—as the final exercise of the two-day event.

It's a great exercise and it works! To make it even more effective, I recommend some prework. Teams meet in advance to undertake a few tasks: VoC study, a technology forecast, and a market-trends forecast. And during Day 1, interspersed among the exercises, teams present the results of their prework to stimulate discussion.

The result of such MRG events is usually five to ten major opportunities identified and partially defined, a core of enthused people willing to work on each, and the beginnings of an action plan.

Set Up an Internal Innovation Show

Leading firms stimulate creativity and move good ideas forward by hosting innovation shows, much like a trade show, but internal. Here, employees set up booths and display their capabilities, technologies, and hot ideas for the future.

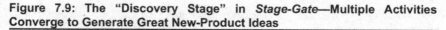

Figure 7.9: The "Discovery Stage" in *Stage-Gate*—Multiple Activities Converge to Generate Great New-Product Ideas

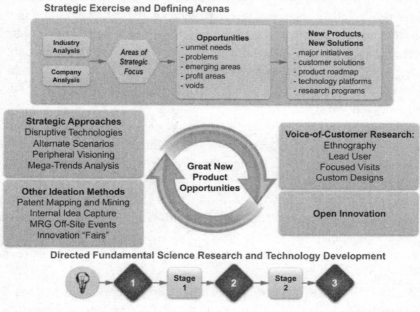

Artwork courtesy of Dave Caissy

An example: Kellogg's (a US-based food company) hosts "moonlighting" events, essentially innovation shows where employees and units set up booths, much like a country fair, to display their ideas and technologies.[36] The show is attended by huge numbers of employees, and also senior executives. Attendees vote on the best ideas, and there are "people's choice" winners. This kind of show has proven to be an effective way of communicating ideas within a large corporation, and also for highlighting winners and gaining visibility for them.

Suggestion: If you seek breakthrough new products, try rethinking your idea stage using the proven Discovery approaches above. Figure 7.9 shows the activities that flow and converge to generate great new-product ideas. Use strategic approaches, in which you undertake a thorough analysis of your external environment, looking for shifts and disruptions that signal new opportunities (top part of Figure 7.9). Concurrently, undertake an internal core-competencies assessment. Pinpoint arenas of strategic focus where you can concentrate your idea-hunting activities—your "search fields." Develop alternate scenarios of your future, and identify the opportunities for new products (left of Figure 7.9)—but don't get caught in the "official futures trap" that AT&T did!

Next, lower the microscope on customers and users in these arenas (right side of Figure 7.9). Employ VoC research, with a particular emphasis on understanding customer problems. Then, seek solutions leading to great new products. There are varied examples here from all industries—from GE's MRI Adventures through to Del Monte Snausages and the small German firm's Diaset machine. Working with lead users, as practiced at Hilti, may be right for you—it's VoC with a different twist.

Fundamental technical research is also a source. But harness your technical talent by engaging them in your Discovery stage: Introduce a tailored *Stage-Gate* approach—*Stage Gate TD*—to your technology development people (bottom of Figure 7.9).

Tap into the creativity of your own employees with an internal idea-capture system, but in a professional way, using the tips outlined above. Hold a major revenue-generating (MRG) event, described above, instead of your annual conference—that's time much better spent! Finally, host an innovation show as at Kellogg's.

An effective Discovery stage, as shown in Figure 7.9, is fundamental to coming up with great ideas to feed your product-innovation system. Seeking extraordinary ideas sometimes means doing some extraordinary things!

8

INVESTING IN THE RIGHT PROJECTS—PORTFOLIO MANAGEMENT

Take calculated risks. That is quite different from being rash.

—George S. Patton, US general

IT'S TOUGH TO MAKE THE RIGHT INVESTMENT DECISIONS

There are two fundamental ways to win big at product innovation:[1]

1. The first way is *doing projects right*: Ensure that an effective cross-functional team is in place and that its members do the front-end homework, build in the voice of the customer, strive for a differentiated superior product, be time driven, and so on. Having a first-rate idea-to-launch system to guide how projects should be executed and building in the many best practices outlined thus far in the book—the topics of Chapters 2 through 7—is the solution that many firms have adopted.

2. The second way is *doing the right projects*. As one executive put it: "Even a blind man can get rich in a gold mine, simply by swinging a pick-ax. You don't have to be a good miner—just be in the right mine!" Thus, *project selection* becomes paramount to new-product performance. And that's

the topic of this chapter—picking the right new product and development projects to invest in: *portfolio management*.

For most businesses, development resources are too valuable and scarce to waste on the wrong projects. But many projects in firms' development portfolios are weak: Either they fail commercially, underperform in the marketplace, or they are canceled prior to product launch; only *one in seven concepts* actually becomes a commercial winner (Figure 1.4). Project selection—the ability to pick the right projects for investment—therefore becomes a critically important task for the leadership team of your business in order to *maximize productivity from your development spending*.

Many Challenges in Project Selection

Making the right investment decisions is one of the most problematic facets of product innovation. The majority of firms undertake project selection in a haphazard, unprofessional way and fail to utilize many of the best-practices approaches available. Look at the benchmarking results in Figure 8.1 (Figure 8.1 is simply the data from Figure 3.2, but shown in reverse format to point out deficiencies):

- More than three-quarters of businesses have *too many projects underway* for the limited resources available. Overloading the development pipeline is a result of not knowing *how to say no* or a *failure to prioritize effectively*. And it has many serious side effects—projects take too long; project teams cut corners and quality of execution suffers; and projects get "dumbed down"—products are de-featured and de-specified.
- Eighty percent of firms have *very unbalanced development portfolios*: They undertake too many small, insignificant projects—tweaks, modifications, minor updates, small sales-force requests—to the detriment of higher-payoff, more innovative, and longer-term projects. Look at the breakdown in Figure 3.3 back in Chapter 3, which reveals that 43 percent of developments are very minor projects and only 10 percent are true "new products." Recall in Chapter 1 (Figure 1.1) seeing the disturbing trend toward less-significant development projects. One result is that almost 90 percent of businesses have "few or no high-value projects" in their development portfolios (Figure 8.1).
- Almost 90 percent of firms *lack effective project prioritization*. And the great majority of businesses (79 percent) have *no professional portfolio management* or project-selection methods in place. Even more astounding is how abysmal the *worst-performing businesses* fare on these same five

Figure 8.1: Challenges Exist in Portfolio Management and Project Selection

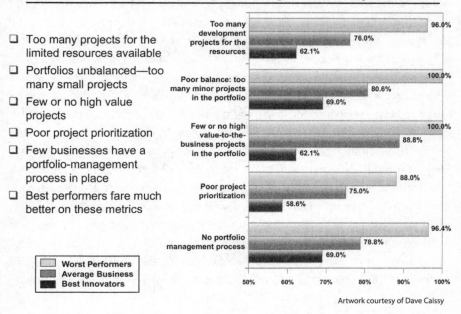

- ☐ Too many projects for the limited resources available
- ☐ Portfolios unbalanced—too many small projects
- ☐ Few or no high value projects
- ☐ Poor project prioritization
- ☐ Few businesses have a portfolio-management process in place
- ☐ Best performers fare much better on these metrics

Artwork courtesy of Dave Caissy

criteria: 100 percent of worst performers have too many minor projects and no or few high-value projects underway; 96 percent have too many projects and no formal portfolio management system; and 89 percent have poor project-prioritization. No wonder these firms perform so badly!

The result of such poor practices is that many of the projects currently in businesses' development portfolios are weak—they are simply bad projects with limited potential. Indeed, in typical portfolio reviews undertaken within firms, we usually find that *about one-third of the projects underway should be killed.* Many should never have been approved in the first place; and others, though fine at the outset, have deteriorated over time, yet nobody had the guts to shoot them. The bottom line is that you've got to learn to be tough—to make the difficult decisions to cull the weak projects from your development portfolio.

> Project selection and portfolio management are among the weakest facets of new-product management.

A second major issue is that most firms face *a serious resource deficiency* when it comes to product development. Businesses generally lack the necessary resources to undertake projects properly or on time:[2] Only 10.7 percent of firms were judged to devote sufficient resources to their new-product projects—that is, in 89 percent of firms, projects are typically underresourced![3]

The *simplistic solution* is to rank all your development projects from best to worst—with the high-value ones at the top of the list. Next, go down the list, and *lop off the bottom third* of projects; then, reallocate those resources to the top two-thirds—the best projects—and get them done faster! The trouble with this solution is that you'll have to make some tough decisions and kill some projects—which no management group seems comfortable doing. So most senior managements elect the default option—*do them all! And so people are spread thinly, projects are underresourced, and they take forever to get to market!* Another problem with this simplistic solution is just *how to rank projects* from best to worst—it's no small feat to define and measure "best" or "value-to-the-company." **Suggestion:** Before becoming too critical of the worst performers in Figure 8.1, take a look at how your business compares on these five criteria. Do you have *too many projects* for your limited resources—are your projects underresourced? And what side effects does overloading your development pipeline create? Does your development portfolio suffer from *too many small projects*, while the more innovative, larger, and longer-term projects suffer? If yes, read on: It's time to install a professional project selection or portfolio-management system in your business.

PROJECT SELECTION IS BUT ONE COMPONENT OF PORTFOLIO MANAGEMENT

Project selection—making the right Go/Kill and investment decisions on development projects—is part of the broader topic of "portfolio management." Portfolio management is a term borrowed from the financial community. In product innovation, every development project is viewed as an "investment"; and these investments can be managed using decision tools and techniques fairly similar to those used in financial markets. One component of portfolio management is the gates—the decision points in your *Stage-Gate®* system where the vital Go/Kill decisions are made and where resources are committed to projects. More on making gates work in the next chapter.

> Project selection is part of the broader topic of *portfolio management*. It's necessary to look at the broad topic—portfolio management—in order to be effective at project selection.

What Is Portfolio Management in Product Innovation?

Portfolio management is about *resource allocation*. That is, which new-product and development projects from the many opportunities the business faces should the business fund? And which ones should receive top priority and be accelerated to market? It is also about *business strategy*, for today's new-product projects decide tomorrow's product-market profile of the firm. Finally, it is about *balance*:

about the optimal investment mix between risk versus return, maintenance versus growth, and short-term versus long-term development projects.

Portfolio management is formally defined as follows:[4]

Portfolio management is a dynamic decision process, whereby a business's list of active new-product (and development) projects is constantly updated and revised. In this process, new projects are evaluated, selected, and prioritized; existing projects may be accelerated, killed, or de-prioritized; and resources are allocated and reallocated to active projects. The portfolio decision process is characterized by uncertain and changing information, dynamic opportunities, multiple goals and strategic considerations, interdependence among projects, and multiple decision-makers and locations. The portfolio decision process encompasses or overlaps a number of decision-making processes within the business, including periodic reviews of the total portfolio of all projects (looking at all projects holistically, and against each other); making Go/Kill decisions on individual projects on an ongoing basis; and developing a new-product strategy for the business, complete with strategic resource allocation decisions and strategic product roadmaps.

Two Decision Levels in Portfolio Management

Portfolio management and resource allocation can be treated as a hierarchical process, with two levels of decision-making. This hierarchical approach simplifies the decision challenge somewhat (see Figure 8.2):[5]

- *Level 1—Strategic portfolio management:* Strategic portfolio decisions answer these questions: Directionally, where should your business spend its development resources (people and funds)? How should you split your resources across project types, markets, technologies, or product categories? And on what major initiatives or new platforms should you concentrate your resources? Establishing Strategic Buckets and delineating Strategic Product and Technology Roadmaps are effective tools here (Strategic Buckets is outlined next in this chapter, while Strategic Product Roadmapping is a topic in the final chapter on innovation strategy).
- *Level 2—Tactical portfolio decisions (individual project selection):* Tactical portfolio decisions focus on individual projects, but obviously follow from the strategic decisions. They address these questions: What specific new-product projects should you do? What are their relative priorities? And what resources should be allocated to each? Such tactical decisions are shown at the bottom part of Figure 8.2 and are handled at both gate meetings and portfolio reviews. These Go/Kill tactical decisions are the main topic later in this chapter.

Figure 8.2: Portfolio Management Is a Hierarchical Process Driven by Your Business Strategy and Your Product-Innovation Strategy

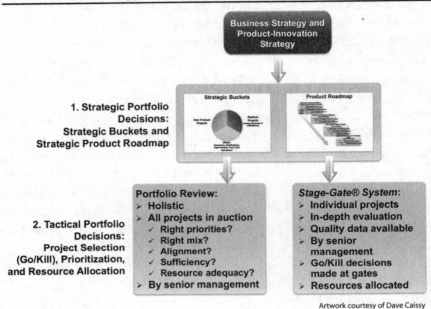

Artwork courtesy of Dave Caissy

STRATEGIC PORTFOLIO MANAGEMENT

From strategy, all else flows! (See Figure 8.2). A business's *product innovation and technology strategy* defines its *goals and objectives* for product innovation and development; it specifies the *strategic arenas*—where innovation and development will be focused; and it maps out *attack plans*—for example, how the business intends to win in each strategic arena. The attack plans also specify the *major initiatives* that must be undertaken in order to win, and thus entails strategic product and technology roadmapping. More on roadmapping in Chapter 10.

The next strategic issue is resource allocation, for example, getting the right mix and balance across project types, or product lines or strategic arenas. And here most firms face issues! They suffer from a poorly balanced portfolio, as noted in Figure 8.1: too many small projects, few high-value projects in the portfolio, and too many projects overall!

USE STRATEGIC BUCKETS TO GET THE RIGHT MIX OF PROJECTS

Strategic Buckets is a powerful method for translating strategy into reality in your development portfolio. It's premised on the fact that *strategy becomes real when one starts spending money*! Unless resources are deployed, "your strategy" is merely *nice words in a document*. Strategy comes alive, however, when resources are committed and spending begins. Using a military analogy, strategy becomes operational through deployment—when there are boots on the ground! So make the strategic spending decisions—establish Strategic Buckets!

Strategic Buckets operates from the simple principle that *implementing strategy equates to spending money on specific initiatives*. In new-product development, for example, should you devote all your development resources* to *defending the base*, your current products? Or take a discrete percentage— perhaps 10 to 15 percent—and apply that to a new emerging area? A tough decision. But that's a strategic spending or portfolio decision! Thus, when translating your business's strategy into strategic portfolio decisions (middle part of Figure 8.2), a major challenge faced is your *spending breakdown or ideal deployment:* That is, where does senior management wish to spend its product-innovation resources—what's the best split across product, market, or technology areas? And what proportion should go to innovative projects versus defensive or renovation projects? And how much should be spent in each strategic arena or area of focus? Thus, operationalizing your strategy really means "setting spending targets."

How Do Buckets Work?

The Strategic Buckets method begins with the business's innovation strategy and requires senior managers to make *forced choices* along each of several dimensions—choices about how they wish to allocate their scarce development resources. This enables the creation of "envelopes of resources," or "buckets."

> Strategy drives your portfolio. Strategic Buckets is one tool to translate your innovation strategy into reality.

Next, existing projects are *categorized into buckets*. Then senior managers determine whether actual spending is consistent with desired spending for each bucket. Finally, projects are *prioritized within buckets* to arrive at the eventual portfolio of projects—one that mirrors management's strategy for the business.

An example: Traditionally, Honeywell leadership teams within business units had reviewed the breakdown of development projects *at the end of each year*— asking where resources had been spent by project type, market, product line,

---

* Note that "resources" includes dollars as well as people, hence resource allocation is for financial expenditures and/or person-days (or full-time equivalent people).

and so on. But that was like driving a car by looking through the rear-view mirror. The information was backward looking rather than forward looking. In the "new approach," the leadership team sits down *at the beginning of the year* and makes strategic choices about where the money will go for *the upcoming year*. As one executive stated, "If we don't make the decision, it will be made for us—and the default option is usually wrong!" A rather simple breakdown is used at Honeywell: its "Mercedes star" method of allocating resources (Figure 8.3). The leadership team of the business begins with the business's strategy and uses the Mercedes emblem (the three-point star) to help divide up the resources. There are three buckets:

1. platform development projects (which promise to yield major break-throughs and change the basis of competition);
2. new-product developments; and
3. maintenance (product improvements and enhancements, extensions, renovations, fixes, and cost reductions).

Management makes strategic choices and splits its development resources across these three buckets. Next, the projects are sorted into each of the three buckets, and then management ranks projects against each other within each bucket. In effect, three separate portfolios of projects are created and managed. The result: Followed with discipline, over time, the spending breakdowns across buckets and project types mirror the business's strategic priorities. Management does the same splitting exercise using other pie charts—by product lines, markets, and geography—as well.

Note: As at Honeywell, resources should be split along multiple dimensions, such as by project type (Figure 8.3), product lines or markets (Figure 8.4), and even by strategic arenas.

Determining the Size of the Buckets

Sounds simple in theory. But how does one decide the *size* of these Strategic Buckets in the first place? For example, how does one determine the appropriate distribution of resources across project types? No magic answer exists here, any more than there is a single optimal split among stocks, bonds, and bank deposits in an individual's personal investment portfolio. But the decision must be made. Failure to make a strategic decision here will result in a split based on a series of ad hoc tactical decisions made as the need arises. As noted in the Honeywell example, "The default option is usually wrong!"

Figure 8.3: Strategic Buckets Ensure the Right Mix and Balance of Projects and that Spending Mirrors Your Strategic Priorities

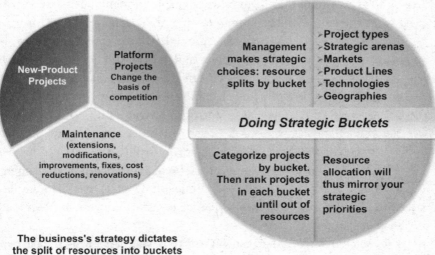

The business's strategy dictates
the split of resources into buckets

Artwork courtesy of Dave Caissy

Figure 8.4: Strategic Buckets Can Also Guide Resource Breakdowns by Product Lines and by Markets

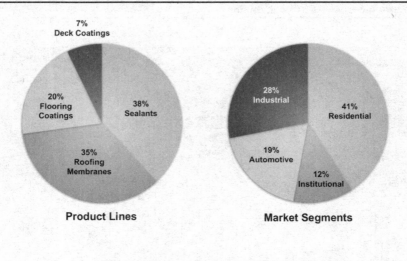

Use two or three dimensions for Strategic Buckets:
Project Types, Product Lines, Market Segments, etc.

Artwork courtesy of Dave Caissy

Start with the current breakdown: In deciding the optimal split for your company, start with the current breakdown of resources, as determined by your current-state assessment: the "what is." Merely knowing the current resource split—something that is not always visible in many businesses—will suggest what the split should be, for example, that certain areas or project types should have increased resource allocations and others should be decreased. The *direction* is perhaps as important as the absolute spending amount. As the CTO of Emerson Electric said, "Our business unit executives are pretty bright—if they see these current splits, they should have a good idea of what the spending split ought to be!" Emerson Electric has also implemented Strategic Buckets; there, this practice is "a core concept of Emerson's portfolio-management process."

> Start with the current breakdown of resources: the "what is." Knowing the current resource split will suggest what the *split should be*, for example, that certain areas or projects types should have increased resource allocations and others should be decreased.

Move to the desired split: Management can go beyond reviewing the current splits and move towards the *desired split* in resources—the "what should be," as follows (the decision inputs are noted in Figure 8.5):

Figure 8.5: The Inputs in Deciding the Right Split of Resources Across Strategic Buckets in Your Business

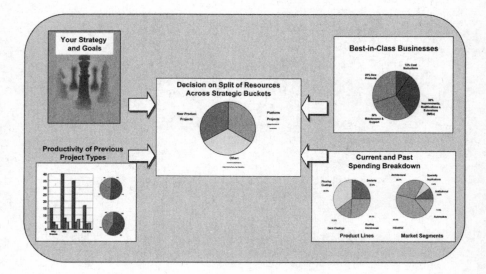

1. *Undertake an historical review:* Where were the resources spent for the last twelve to twenty-four months (typically a review of pie-chart splits across markets, strategic arenas, project types, and perhaps geographies, as in Figures 8.3 and 8.4).
2. *Assess results from recent projects:* How well have you done? Which types of spending and projects yielded the best results (the highest productivities)?
3. *Review the current split in resources:* Determine the "what is" along with a listing and quick review of major projects currently underway.

Example: What is the current breakdown of your development projects by project type? Where are the resources going? And where are the sales coming from? Figure 8.6 shows a chart from a Mars Petcare (pet-foods) business, showing three current views of the portfolio (the far right chart shows expected net incremental sales, the increase in sales, for year one, based on the data in each project's Business Case). Management reviews this and similar charts—breakdowns by product line and market segment—to gain a quick insight into the health of the current development portfolio.

A quick look at the three charts in Figure 8.6 reveals major issues where action is sorely needed:

❑ First, three quarters of the projects and more than half the resources go to very minor *tactical projects*—why? (It turned out that an overzealous sales director kept submitting many "must do" minor-modification projects in order to "get the order"; many of these "sales requests" were very low value.)

❑ Next, *disruptive projects* are only 4 percent of the total, but likewise get only 4 percent of the resources. One might have expected more like 10 or 12 percent of resources here, as these projects are much larger. (It turned out that these projects, potential big hits, were being starved—each very underresourced.)

❑ The most productive projects (highest sales output per R&D dollar input) are the more innovative types, which receive the least resources. And why are the *least productive projects— tactical*—getting more than half the resources?

This chart provides an excellent starting point to a fruitful management discussion about the right split in resources.

Figure 8.6: Begin with the "Current Situation"—Three Different Views of the Current Portfolio Breakdown by Project Types (Charts Reveal Major Problems)

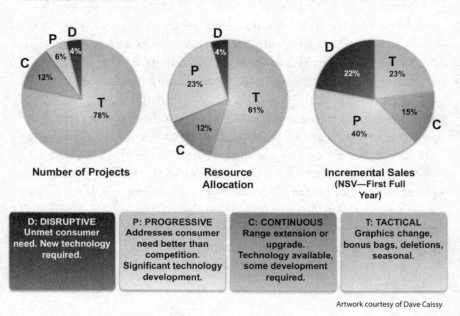

| | Number of Projects | Resource Allocation | Incremental Sales (NSV—First Full Year) |

| **D: DISRUPTIVE** Unmet consumer need. New technology required. | **P: PROGRESSIVE** Addresses consumer need better than competition. Significant technology development. | **C: CONTINUOUS** Range extension or upgrade. Technology available, some development required. | **T: TACTICAL** Graphics change, bonus bags, deletions, seasonal. |

Artwork courtesy of Dave Caissy

4. *Look at best practice firms and their splits:* One *Harvard Business Review* article claims that "outperforming firms typically allocate about 70 percent of their innovation resources to core offerings, 20 percent to adjacent efforts, and 10 percent to transformational initiatives. As it happens, returns from innovation investments tend to follow an inverse ratio, with 70 percent coming from the transformational realm. The ideal balance will differ from industry to industry and company to company."[6] Our own research (Figure 3.3) suggests that the optimal breakdown, based on our 20 percent best innovators, should be:

    ❏ 35 percent: Incremental developments and renovations, fixes and modifications.
    ❏ 25 percent: Significant product improvements and updates, replacement products . . . the so-called "new and improved" products.
    ❏ 25 percent: Genuine new products—products that *really are new to the business.*
    ❏ 15 percent: Innovations—new to the market (which are also new to the business) products.

As noted above, this optimal split will vary greatly with the nature of your company and your industry. But it's a guide.

5. *Next comes a strategic review:* The leadership team considers the business's overall strategy and its innovation strategy—goals and objectives, the targeted strategic arenas, and strategic thrust—as well as data that went into this strategic analysis. During this analysis and discussion, with the inputs shown in Figure 8.5, those buckets that are underresourced, and those that receive perhaps too much becomes clear.

6. *Then the decision is made:* One effective way is a modified Delphi approach, in which senior managers simply write down what they believe the *correct split of resources should be* across several different dimensions. They post their "votes" on a Post-It on a flip chart (or onto a large-screen projected display), and discussion ensues. Often there is agreement by the "first round"; and it rarely takes more than three rounds (three votes) to come to an agreed decision.

An example: At one major tool manufacturer, one dozen key executives take part in the Strategic Buckets session. The current splits in resources, along with a list of current major projects, is presented; so are the overall business strategy and the strategies for each of the firm's four major product lines. Then the executives vote by *allocating resources as percentages* across product lines, across project types, and across geographic regions of the world. These votes are immediately displayed on a large-screen spreadsheet, are debated, and consensus is reached. The buckets are decided.

Choosing the Right Dimensions for the Buckets

What dimensions should be used in the Strategic Buckets splits? One R&D executive explained: "Whatever dimensions the leadership team of the business finds most relevant to describe their own strategy." Some common dimensions you might consider are:

- *Strategic goals:* Management splits resources across the specified strategic goals. For example, what percent should be spent on defending the base? On diversifying? On extending the base? and so on.

- *Types of projects:* Most firms have too many of the wrong kinds of projects, as

> A best-practice way to *integrate the collective wisdom* of a group of well-informed managers to make *an informed decision* is the modified Delphi approach (based on the Oracle of Delphi's effective decision-making ability back in ancient Greece).

seen in Figure 8.1, so decisions or splits should be made in terms of *types of projects*. Given its aggressive product-innovation strategic stance, at EXFO Electro-Optical Engineering (a highly innovative company making fiber-optic test equipment), management targets 65 percent of R&D spending to genuine new products; another 10 percent to platform developments and research (technology development for the future); and the final 25 percent goes to incrementals (the "support-folio," namely, product modifications, fixes, and improvements). In this way, management tilts the portfolio in favor of bolder innovation projects.[7]

- *Across strategic arenas:* As part of your innovation strategy-development exercise, you have assessed the attractiveness of each strategic arena—areas where you wish to focus your R&D efforts—and defined the priorities of each. Optimal spending splits across arenas is a logical outcome of this exercise.

Other commonly used dimensions or splits include:

- *Product lines:* Resources are split across product lines: For example, how much should be spent on Product Line A? On Product Line B? On C? A plot of product-line locations on the product life-cycle curve is used to help determine this split.
- *Technologies or technology platforms:* Spending splits can be made across technology types (for example, base, key, pacing, and embryonic technologies) or across specific technology platforms: Platforms X, Y, and Z.
- *Familiarity Matrix:* What should the split of resources to different types of markets and to different technology types be in terms of their *familiarity to the business*? You can use the popular "familiarity matrix"—technology newness versus market newness—to help split resources, as in Figure 8.7.
- *Geography:* What proportion of resources should be spent on projects aimed at North America? At Latin America? At Europe? At Asia Pacific? Or at all regions (global)?
- *By stage of development:* Some businesses distinguish between early stage projects and projects in Development and beyond. Two buckets are created, one for development projects, the other for early stage or "seed corn" projects.

Categorizing Projects by Bucket

Following this splitting or voting exercise, existing projects are categorized by bucket, and the total current spending by bucket is added up (the "what is"). By "existing projects," I mean projects actively under development, or heading into development—in short, anything that has passed Gate 2 in Figure 4.11

Figure 8.7: Split Resources Across the Nine Cells in the Familiarity Matrix—New Markets and New Technologies

Product or Production / Market	Uses our existing operations/ technology processes	Operations/ technology processes new to us but exist externally	Product or operations technology are totally new, don't exist
Sells into existing market and/or customer, one we are familiar with	**Low Risk Overall**	**Moderate Risk:** Moderate Technical Risk; Low Market Risk	**High Risk:** High Technical Risk; Low Market Risk
Sells into a new market and/or customer, but one we are familiar with	**Moderate Risk:** Low Technical Risk; Moderate Market Risk	**Moderate-High Risk Overall**	**Very High Risk:** High Technical Risk; Moderate Market Risk
Sells into a new and/or unfamiliar market/customer for us	**High Risk:** Low Technical Risk; High Market Risk	**Very High Risk:** Moderate Technical Risk; High Market Risk	**Exceptionally High Risk Overall**

(before Gate 2, there is very little data on the project; thus one normally treats these as "early stage projects," not really consuming resources and hence not really "in the portfolio" yet).

Spending gaps are then identified between the "what should be" and "what is" for each bucket. Spending gaps usually indicate that there are *too many projects for a given resource allocation* to a bucket. Sometimes, there are too few projects—for example, for the "breakthrough projects" bucket—so the call goes out to generate some big ideas and "fill the bucket."

Ranking the Projects Within Buckets

Finally, projects within each bucket are rank-ordered until you are out of resources in that bucket. Recall the voting exercise above allocated specific resources to each bucket—this is the *resource limit* in a given bucket. To do this ranking within buckets, as a first attempt, you can use a financial metric such as NPV. You list the projects from highest value or highest NPV to lowest value—from 1 to N—noting the resources required for the time period (quarter or half year). Then draw a line when the resource limit is reached. Those projects "below the line" are either killed or put on hold, and those above are resourced and moved forward. (Later in the chapter, we introduce other metrics, such as Project Attractiveness Scores from scoring models and other financial criteria, such as the Productivity Index, which are better than the NPV for ranking the projects.)

The result is a list of "Go" projects, prioritized within each of several optimally resourced buckets.

The Benefits of Strategic Buckets

At first, Strategic Buckets seems like a rather simple, almost simplistic model. But don't be fooled! Its implications are much more profound than one might think—there are many benefits! First, resource allocation over time *will mirror your strategic priorities*. The first year, there will be some resource shifts—the needle moves slightly, since people are not infinitely fungible. But as one reaches steady state, the outcome is remarkable: Resource allocation and stated strategy really are aligned! For example, you'll finally be doing the right numbers of small versus large projects, or devoting the right percentage of effort to different strategic areas of focus.

This method also puts a *limit on the numbers of projects* within each bucket: Rank projects until out of resources! So not only do you achieve the right balance across project types, markets, and product lines, you also get the right balance in terms of *resources versus numbers of projects*—supply versus demand for resources. The numbers of projects are capped!

Next, and this is critical, you are not *comparing apples and oranges*. When doing the ranking within buckets, you do not compare projects *between buckets*, only *like projects within a bucket*. For example, you rate new products against other new products, but not against minor modifications. When all projects are tossed into one bucket and compared, the result is predicable: The small, low risk and low hanging fruit initiatives always win, which is one reason most firms have too many minor projects underway.

Finally, you use *different criteria for different types* of projects (investments). If you were considering your personal investments—stocks, bonds, and bank deposits—you certainly would use different criteria to rate and evaluate these. So you should when it comes to development projects! For example, for the "new products" bucket, you might use financial criteria (such as NPV) and a scoring model; but for cost-savings projects, a metric that captures "savings for every day worked on the project"—an easy-to-calculate productivity metric—might be better.

Suggestion: Implement Strategic Buckets. This is an excellent method for ensuring that your new-product spending or deployment mirrors your business's strategic priorities. And it's a way to *set aside resources for more strategic and bolder innovations* (so that all the resources aren't consumed by the smaller, shorter-term projects). Further, *the method works*, and it seems to suit management's style in most businesses!

By breaking the decision process into two levels—first decide the strategic breakdown of your resources via Strategic Buckets, and then decide which projects to do—your portfolio mix and balance of projects will ultimately reflect your business's priorities in terms of project types, markets, and product types. And via Strategic Buckets, you take steps to prevent the problem that many firms suffer from, namely,

> Strategic Buckets ensures that spending mirrors your strategic priorities, puts a limit on the numbers of projects, makes the correct comparisons (compares apples to apples), and allows the use of different criteria for evaluating different project types.

an overabundance of small, incremental, low-value projects, and a real lack of major innovations.

VISUALIZING YOUR PORTFOLIO—THE MANY VIEWS

A picture is worth a thousand words! Some firms have not adopted Strategic Buckets per se, but use similar charts to *portray their portfolio in a strategic way*. For example, various charts can show the mix and balance of projects in your portfolio—the "what is"—in a number of useful views. These charts are helpful both *at gate meetings and at portfolio reviews*, and often move the leadership team toward a Strategic Buckets way of thinking.

Numerous parameters, dimensions, or variables exist across which you might wish to view the balance of projects in your development portfolio:

- *Resource breakdown by project types:* What is your spending on product innovation versus product renovation? And what should it be? Pie charts effectively capture the current spending split across project types. Pie charts that show the resource breakdown by project types are a particularly useful sanity check, as in Figure 8.6, left and center pie charts.
- *Markets, products, and technologies:* These provide another set of dimensions across which managers seek balance. The question is: Do you have the appropriate split in R&D spending across your various product lines? Or across the markets or market segments in which you operate (see Figure 8.4)? Or across technologies? Pie charts are again appropriate for capturing and displaying data of this type.
- *Size of projects:* Some managements are interested in seeing the distribution of projects by size—do you have too many small projects? Figure 8.8 shows such a breakdown, using cumulative three-year sales as the size metric. Note here that of the twenty-four projects, far too many (twenty) were identified as "small," with three-year sales of less than $500,000!

Figure 8.8: Check Your Distribution of Projects by Project Size

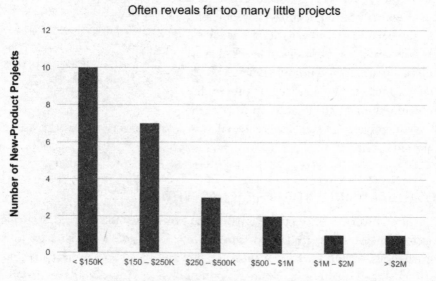

Project Size (Expected Sales: Cumulative Three Years)

- *The risk profile of the portfolio:* The familiarity or newness matrix provides a sense of the risk distribution of the project portfolio. Projects are plotted as bubbles on two newness dimensions: how new the market is to the company, and how new the technology is (use the newness matrix in Figure 8.7 and show projects as "bubbles" or circles; the bubble size denotes resources per project).
- *Risk-reward diagrams:* Many businesses employing a systematic portfolio-management method use the *risk-reward bubble diagram* in Figure 8.9, or one like it. Here, the horizontal axis is some measure of the *reward* to the company, the vertical axis is the *success probability*:

  ❑ In Figure 8.9, the NPV is plotted versus the probability of technical success. Note that all projects on this chart are into Development, so that an NPV had already been determined. Alternately, three-year cumulative sales could be used as a proxy for reward.
  ❑ Another approach is to use a *qualitative proxy for reward*, ranging from "modest" to "excellent." The argument here is that too heavy an emphasis on financial numbers can do damage, notably in the early stages of a project. The vertical axis is the probability of over-

all success (probability of *commercial success* times probability of *technical success*).

❑ Finally, *scores from the gate scorecard* can also be used to create the risk-reward bubble diagram. Scorecards are outlined later in this chapter, but two scorecards factors rated by the gatekeepers—risk and return—are crossplotted in Figure 8.10 to give yet another view of the risk-reward profile.

An example: A bubble diagram is shown in Figure 8.9 for a high-technology business unit of a major chemical company. Here the size of each bubble shows the annual resources committed to each project (dollars per year; it could also be people or work-months allocated to the project). Given that this business unit is a "star business" seeking rapid growth, a quick review of the portfolio map in Figure 8.9 reveals many problems: too many *White Elephant* projects (it's time to do some serious project pruning!); too much spent on *Bread and Butter*, low-value projects; not enough *Pearls*; and some heavily underresourced *Oysters*.

One feature of this bubble diagram model is that it forces senior management to deal with the resource issue. Given finite resources, *the sum of the areas of the circles must be a constant*. That is, if you add one project to the diagram, you must subtract another; alternatively, you can shrink the size of several circles. The elegance here is that the model forces management to consider the resource implications of adding one more project to the list—that other projects must pay the price!

Also denoted in the bubble diagram is the product line that each project is associated with (via crosshatching, not shown). A final breakdown is timing (shown as shading or color). Thus, this apparently simple risk-reward diagram shows a lot more than simply risk and profitability data—it also conveys resource allocation, timing, and spending breakdowns across product lines.

Suggestion: Charts that display the current mix and balance of projects in the portfolio are popular at portfolio reviews and at gate meetings. This section has revealed a number of different displays and formats. Pie charts are quite popular (Figures 8.3, 8.4, and 8.5), and lead nicely into Strategic Buckets. They are often used to display the current situation—the current breakdown in resources by:

- Project type: new products, improvements, sales-force requests, platforms, and so on.
- Market: market segment, market sector, or geographic market.

Figure 8.9: Assess the Risk-Reward Profile of Your Development Portfolio

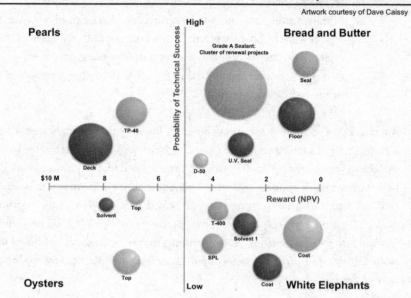

The bubble sizes denote the resources committed to each project.
The shading shows the stage in the firm's Stage-Gate® system (light = early stage).

Figure 8.10: Another Version of a Risk Reward Bubble Diagram, Which Uses Scores from the Firm's Scorecard Model

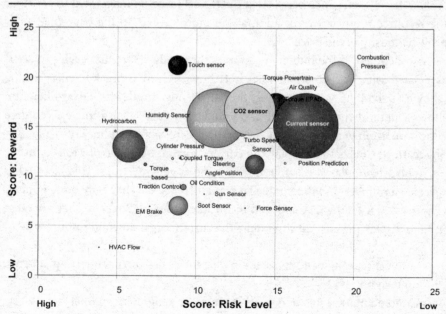

- Product: product line or product category.
- Technology: technology types or technology maturity (embryonic, pacing, base).
- Project size (by cumulative sales or spending level).

In addition, consider your portfolio's risk profile (the familiarity matrix—Figure 8.7) or risk-reward profile (via bubble diagrams—Figures 8.9 and 8.10).

Pick the dimensions that are most relevant to your business and your leadership team. Hint: Don't use too many different charts—they tend to overwhelm people at meetings. As one executive declared in frustration after acquiring portfolio-management software, "We have a case of bubble-itis in our company!" Consider using a maximum of three pie charts (as in Figures 8.3–8.5) along with one risk-reward bubble diagram (as in Figures 8.9 or 8.10). For the risk-reward diagram, use quantitative axes such as "probability of success" versus "reward" (where "reward" can be measured in terms of profitability, such as NPV in Figure 8.9; or cumulative three-year sales; or scale values from a scoring model as in Figure 8.10).

TACTICAL DECISIONS: PICKING THE RIGHT PROJECTS
Gates and Portfolio Reviews

Two decision processes must be in place in order to handle the tactical portfolio decisions well: *gates*, part of the *Stage-Gate* system, coupled with periodic *portfolio reviews* (both shown in the bottom part of Figure 8.2). Note that many of the tools and methods introduced in this chapter see double duty—they can be employed at gates as well as at portfolio reviews, but used slightly differently at each. Let's look at what gates and portfolio reviews are, and then delve into the best-practice methods for project selection and prioritization:

1. *Gates* (bottom right of Figure 8.2): Embedded within your idea-to-launch system are Go/Kill decision points called "gates." Gates provide an in-depth review of individual projects, and render Go/Kill, prioritization, and resource-allocation decisions—hence gates must be part of your portfolio-management system. Effective gates are vital to product innovation: They weed out the bad projects early, and they commit the needed resources to the deserving projects.

   But gates are not quite enough! Many companies have a gating process in place, but they confuse that with a comprehensive portfolio-management system. Doing the *right projects* is more than simply individual project selection at gate meetings; rather, it's about the *entire mix* of projects and new-product or technology investments that your business makes:

- Project selection *deals only with the "trees"*: Go/Kill decisions are made on individual projects, each judged on its own merits.
- Portfolio management *deals with the "forest"*: It is holistic and looks at the entire set of project investments together.

2. *Portfolio reviews:* The second decision process is the periodic *portfolio review* (bottom left of Figure 8.2). Senior management meets about four times per year to review the portfolio of all development projects. Here, senior management also can make Go/Kill and prioritization decisions, where *all projects* are considered together, and all or some could be *up for auction*. Key issues and questions at the typical portfolio review are:

- Are your projects strategically aligned (do they support your business's innovation strategy)?
- Do you have the right priorities among projects?
- Are there some projects on the active list that you should kill? Or perhaps accelerate?
- Do you have the right balance of projects? The right mix? Or are there too many small, insignificant ones?
- Do you have enough resources to do all these projects? Or should some be cut or put on hold?
- Do you have *sufficiency*: meaning, if you do these projects, will you achieve your stated product-innovation goals—for example, your annual sales objectives from new products?

Both decision processes—gating and portfolio reviews—are needed and must work together harmoniously. Note that the gates are *project specific and provide a thorough review of each project*, in-depth and in real time. By contrast, the *portfolio reviews are holistic:* They look at all projects together, but in much less detail on each project. In many businesses, if the gates are working, not too many decisions or major corrective actions are required at the portfolio review. Some leadership teams indicate that they don't even look at individual projects at the portfolio review, but only consider projects in aggregate! But in other businesses, the majority of decisions are made at these quarterly or semiannual portfolio reviews.

Suggestion: Establish a hierarchical or *two-level approach to portfolio management,* as in Figure 8.2. Recognize that there are strategic decisions (directional and high level) and tactical decisions (project selection and prioritization). For the tactical decisions, two decision processes complement each other here: your idea-to-launch *gating process,* which focuses on individual projects; and your *portfolio review* approach, which looks at the entire set of projects. Use both!

FINANCIAL TOOLS FOR GATES AND PORTFOLIO REVIEWS

At gates and portfolio reviews, a number of tools can be used to help achieve your portfolio goals, namely, to maximize your portfolio's value, achieve the right balance and mix of projects, and ensure portfolio sufficiency without overloading the development pipeline.

Maximizing the value of your development portfolio is a principal goal for most businesses. It's analogous to "buying low and selling high" on the stock market. You invest a certain amount of money or resources in development, and desire that the value of the resulting portfolio of projects be maximized. An admirable goal, but often difficult to achieve! For one thing, how do you measure the *value of your portfolio*? When I ask the question, most senior managers cannot tell me the value of their development portfolio; but they can tell me how much it cost!

The methods used to achieve this goal range from financial tools through to scorecard models. Each has its strengths and weaknesses. The end result is a rank-ordered or prioritized list of "Go" and "Hold" projects, with the projects at the top of the list scoring highest in terms of achieving the desired objectives: The portfolio's value in terms of that objective is thus maximized. Here are the specific methods:

Select and Rank Projects by Their NPVs

The simplest approach is merely to calculate the NPV (net present value) of each project on a spreadsheet. Most businesses already require the NPV and a financial spreadsheet as part of the project's Business Case, so the NPV number is already available. If the NPV is positive, the project is a Go at the gate; and at portfolio reviews, you can rank-order your projects—best to worst—by the NPV. Sounds easy!

The NPV is a proxy for the *economic value* of the project to the business and is generally accepted by financial people as the correct economic indicator of the shareholder value of any investment within the corporation. Additionally, popular spreadsheet programs (such as Excel) come with the NPV calculation built in as a standard routine, so finding and using the technique should be no problem.

Three financial numbers—the NPV in dollars, the Payback Period in years, and the IRR as a percent—capture the profitability of the project, and are useful inputs to Go/Kill and prioritization decisions. Also, consider risks using sensitivity analysis (identifies the key assumptions; shows results with best-and-worst case scenarios) and the risk-return ratio (a "downside-upside" risk ratio).

NPV is a form of discounted cash-flow analysis (DCF). DCF analysis requires a year-by-year cash-flow projection of the project's incomes and expenditures; further, in the DCF method, the net cash flows for each year are discounted to the present using a discount rate. This stream of future cash earnings, appropriately discounted to the present, is then added and initial outlays are subtracted to yield the Net Present Value (NPV). Explaining the details of how the NPV works—the fine points of the formula and calculation—is beyond the scope of this book, but good explanations of the theory and calculations underlying NPV are available from a number of sources.[8]

The NPV can be used in two ways:

1. First, make Go/Kill decisions at gates based on the NPV. Require that your project teams use the minimum acceptable financial return or *hurdle rate percent* for projects of this risk level as the discount rate when calculating their projects' NPVs. If the NPV is positive, then the project clears the acceptable hurdle rate. So NPV is a key input to Go/Kill decisions at gates. Additionally, the project's NPV can be compared to other active projects' NPVs right at gate meetings in order to gain insight into the relative position or prioritization level for the new project.

2. Second, at portfolio reviews, rank all projects according to their NPV. The Go projects are at the top of the list. Continue adding projects down the list until you run out of resources. Draw a line across when you hit the resource limit: Those projects above the line are Go, and those below the line are put on hold or killed. In this way, you end up with a prioritized list of projects, which logically should maximize the NPV of your portfolio.

DCF analysis has certain advantages as a profitability indicator:

- It recognizes that money has a time value, and it penalizes those projects with more distant launch dates and distant future revenue streams.
- It is a cash-flow method and avoids the usual problems of accounting and accrual techniques.

- It places much less emphasis on cash-flow projections that are many years into the future (that is, the result is not particularly sensitive to estimates made for many years out, particularly if the discount rate is high).

    In addition to determining the NPV, you can also calculate two other numbers using the same data, so they're an easy addition to your spreadsheet:
- The *internal rate of return,* or IRR, which is simply the value of the discount rate that forces the NPV to zero; it gives the project's true return-on-investment (ROI) as a percent.
- The *Payback Period,* namely, how many years before you get your initial investment back. This is a useful metric, and although not a DCF method per se, it is often used by entrepreneurs, because it answers the question: "When can I start sleeping well at night?" Shorter paybacks are obviously highly desirable: The return-on-investment (ROI) is approximately proportional to the inverse of the Payback Period; and with short paybacks, you don't have to count on earnings far into the future, hence lower risk. So the Payback Period captures both risk and return.

These three numbers—the NPV in dollars, the Payback Period in years, and the IRR as a percent—denote the profitability of the project well.

The Right Discount or Hurdle Rate?

In determining the NPV, normally, the discount rate used is the firm's cost of capital adjusted for the *risk level* for that type of investment. Normally, a business's finance department provides different discount rates for different types of investments, from capital equipment to a new-product project. These rates, although accepted internally, are usually fairly arbitrary, however.

An interesting twist to the NPV is to use a discount rate equal to the *lowest rate achieved by projects* of this type currently underway in your portfolio (that is, use the IRR of the lowest-return project of that type). This rate will be a higher rate than the minimum acceptable hurdle rate, and thus raises the cut-off bar: Any project with a negative NPV means that its return is less than the worst project of that type in the current portfolio, and thus should be killed. By only accepting projects with rates higher than this rate, this method thus automatically improves the value of the portfolio with each additional project.

More: Because the "lowest rate" is *above the minimum acceptable hurdle rate,* the method thus introduces the notion of an "opportunity cost"—the best return available from an alternate investment. If all your other projects are earning quite low rates, barely above the minimum acceptable rate, then that's the hurdle rate to use. But if all your other projects are earning high returns, use the lowest of those—that's what your new project is competing against for investment resources. The method also eliminates the need to set *arbitrary minimum hurdle rates* for different types of projects: The existing portfolio of projects is the basis for establishing the hurdle rate.

Identifying and Handling Risks

To help identify project risks, *sensitivity analysis* is recommended. This procedure is quite easy to do, especially if your project data are already in a spreadsheet format. In sensitivity analysis, key assumptions are tested: For example, what if the revenue drops to only 75 percent of projected; what if the manufacturing cost is 10 percent higher than expected; or what if the launch date is a year later than projected? Spreadsheet values are changed, one at a time, and the financial calculations are repeated. Some managements require best-case and worst-case calculations, also done via sensitivity analysis.

If the returns are still positive under these different "what if" scenarios, the conclusion is that the project justification is *not sensitive to the assumptions* made. However, if some "what if" scenarios yield negative returns, then the associated assumptions become critical: Key project risks have been identified.

Another useful financial calculation is the *risk-return ratio*—a "downside-versus-upside" metric. Here, take the maximum amount that could be lost (the project's most negative cumulative cash flow position) divided by the value of the project (the NPV).

$$\text{Risk-return ratio} = \frac{\text{Maximum negative cumulative cash flow}}{\text{NPV}}$$

Often the maximum possible loss is shown as a curve over time: the cumulative cash flow from the beginning of investment. Increasing investment over time takes the project deeper and deeper into a hole—negative cumulative cash flow. Then the product is launched, revenue begins, the cash flow turns positive, and the cumulative cash position begins to improve. The maximum negative cumulative cash position is the number to use when calculating this downside-upside risk-return ratio; high ratios denote high risk projects.

Suggestion: Ask your finance department to develop a *standardized spreadsheet* for the NPV, IRR, and Payback Period calculations, so all project teams produce consistently calculated profit figures. Also, ask your finance department to develop a table of *risk-adjusted discount rates* for project teams to use to determine the NPVs for different risk levels of projects: low risk (for example, a cost reduction) to high risk (genuine new product, first of its kind. (The IRRs for current projects of each type is the minimum acceptable return,

Figure 8.11: Rank Projects by Value to the Company Within Buckets (by NPV)

1	2	3	4	5	6	7
Project	PV (present value of future earnings)	Development Cost	Commercialization Cost	NPV (net present value)	Ranking Based on NPV	Decision
Alpha	30	3	5	22	4	Hold
Beta	64	5	2	57	2	Go
Gamma	9	2	1	6	5	Hold
Delta	3	1	0.5	1.5	6	Hold
Echo	50	5	3	42	3	Hold
Foxtrot	66	10	2	58	1	Go

Artwork courtesy of Dave Caissy

Shown for one Bucket only: Major Projects. All figures are $ M.
Ranking projects by NPVs, the top four projects are Foxtrot, Beta, Echo, and Alpha.
There is a resource limit of $15M Development budget, however.
Thus, only two projects are Go: Foxtrot and Beta, yielding a portfolio value of $115M.

hence a guide to the appropriate discount rate to use). Higher discount rates appropriately discount (or penalize) future earnings well into the future, much more so for higher-risk projects; and the further into the future, the higher the discount.

Additionally, request that a *fairly standard sensitivity analysis routine* be built into the spreadsheet to yield best-case and worst-case scenarios, and also to identify the most critical assumptions. Also include the cumulative cash-flow curve, and the calculation of the "downside-upside" risk-return ratio.

Prioritization in Practice: Ranking Projects Using NPV

An example: Using the NPV to rank and prioritize projects is shown in Figure 8.11, using disguised data from a large materials company. Here, six fairly comparable projects are shown with disguised names, Alpha through Foxtrot, in the first column. In column two, the PV, or present value, is the sum of the future earnings of the project, taken out five years and discounted by the firm's discount rate for major development projects (this company uses Strategic Buckets and thus groups projects into buckets—these six projects are in the "major projects" bucket, hence the large dollar values for PV).

Also shown are the development costs and commercialization costs (this is a capital-intensive business—most major projects require capital equipment, hence large dollar values for commercialization costs), shown in columns three and four. The NPV is shown in column five, simply the income stream (PV) less the development and commercialization costs. For project Alpha, for example, the NPV is 30 less 3 less 5, equals $22 million.

Now the decision rule: Rank the projects according to their value-to-the-business, namely, the NPV. This ranking is shown in column six, with Foxtrot being number one with an NPV of $58 million. Beta is a close second at $57 million, and so on through to Delta, which is last. As in most firms, there is a limit to how many projects can be done. The firm has two constraints—the capital budget (equipment budget) and the R&D budget (full-time equivalent people, but expressed as a dollar figure).

I'll only show the calculation for the R&D budget constraint, which is $15 million (but recognize that this firm redoes the numbers, the second time with the capital budget constraint, and then merges the two sets of results).

The total time to do any one of the six projects is about one year; but if we decided to do all six—the comfortable "default option" that many of us would be tempted to elect—we see that the total development costs (add up column three) come to $26 million. This means we could start all six projects, but *it will take almost two years to get all six done.*

Perhaps doing all of them is a wise option, because it means we don't need to make a decision on which projects not to do—*just do them all!* On the other hand, the astute financial person recognizes that this approach guarantees that all projects move at half the speed they could, and defers our income for an extra year . . . a considerable cost, since money has a time value. So the more professional executive says, "Let's focus—let's pick our 'best bets' and get them done!"

So let's focus! Based on this NPV method of ranking projects, do the number one project, Foxtrot—this consumes a whopping two-thirds of the budget; next do Beta, which consumes the rest of the budget. So the decision is: "Do two projects—Foxtrot and Beta; consume all the $15 million on these two; put the other four projects on hold; but get the two 'best bets' done and into the market in one year." These decisions are shown in the last column, column seven. Note that the total value of the portfolio is $58 + $57 = $115 million, which is quite good for R&D spending of $15 million!

"But just a minute!" you say: "Isn't that a bit risky—putting all your eggs in one basket? Shouldn't we try to 'hedge our bets' and spread the risk by doing more projects than just two? And surely we can find some combination of 'more efficient' projects." You're right on both counts, but I come to that in the next section where the topic is the Productivity Index method.

Pros and Cons

Using NPV to make Go/Kill and prioritization decisions is fine in theory, but there are some real problems. First, the NPV method assumes that financial projections are accurate. This is a bad assumption in product innovation: Indeed, internal studies reveal that financial estimates are usually quite unreliable—in error by orders of magnitude—especially for higher-risk, bolder projects; and particularly at the earlier gates when the first Go/Kill decisions must be made! Next, NPV assumes that only financial goals are important—for example, that strategic considerations are irrelevant. Finally, the method generally ignores probabilities of success and risk (except by using a risk-adjusted discount rate). A final objection is more subtle: NPV assumes an all-or-nothing investment decision, whereas in new-product projects, the decision process is an incremental one—one buys the project a piece at a time—more like buying a *series of options* on an investment.[9]

This NPV method has a number of attractive features, however. First, it requires that the project team members submit a financial assessment of the project: That means they must do some research, make some fact-based projections, and think through the commercial implications and outcomes of the project. One always learns something from doing a solid financial analysis, often how unreliable the data are! Second, a discounted cash-flow (DCF) method is used, which is the correct way to value investments—as opposed to the ROI, EVA (economic value added), or Payback Period. Thus, income streams years into the future—which are uncertain at best—are automatically heavily discounted. Finally, all monetary amounts are discounted to *today* (not just to the launch date), thereby appropriately penalizing projects that are years away from launch. The method is a good one—both for use at gate meetings and at portfolio reviews—and is recommended. But one can do better, especially for ranking projects.

Rank Projects by Their Productivity

Here's an important modification to the NPV-ranking approach in order to maximize the value of your portfolio, while recognizing that you have limited resources.[10] The challenge is that some projects—for example Foxtrot and Beta in Figure 8.11—are great projects and have huge NPVs, but they consume a lot of resources, thus making it impossible to do other and lower value but perhaps far more efficient projects. How does one decide? Simple: The goal is to *maximize the bang for the buck*. To do this, take the ratio of what one is trying to maximize (in this case, the NPV) divided by the

> Use NPV to help make Go/Kill decisions on projects, and the Productivity Index to rank and prioritize them.

constraining resource (the R&D dollars required)—and voilà, the best bang for the buck.* You may choose to use R&D people or work-months, or the total dollar cost remaining in the project (or even capital funds) as the constraining resource. This bang-for-the-buck ratio, or Productivity Index, is shown in column four in Figure 8.12:

$$\text{Productivity Index} = \frac{\text{NPV of the project}}{\text{Resources remaining to be spent on the project}}$$

The example continued: Now it's time to resort the list of projects in Figure 8.11. But first the constraint: The R&D spending constraint is $15 million for new products in this business; development costs per project are shown in column three in Figure 8.12, and add up to $26 million. To select the "Go" projects, simply calculate the Productivity Index—the NPV/Development Cost—as shown in column four. Note that now Beta is the best project, with a Productivity Index of 11.4. This means that for project Beta, every dollar spent on R&D delivers $11.40 of value! By contrast, Delta is far less productive: Every R&D dollar spent there delivers only $1.50 of value. So which project would you invest in?

Now rerank the project list, ranking projects according to the Productivity Index (this reordering is shown in Figure 8.12, with Beta at the top of the list and Delta at the bottom). Then go down the list until one runs out of resources; column five shows the cumulative resource expenditure. One runs out of resources—hits the $15 million limit—after project Alpha. (There is still $2 million left, and being a wise manager, following the rule of "use it or lose it," one spends the last $2 million on project Gamma to use up the entire annual budget.) Thus, the Go decision is now: Beta, Echo, Alpha, and Gamma. The NPVs for these four projects total $127 million, an increase of $12 million versus the ranking in Figure 8.11. Thus, the Productivity Index method gives a better set of projects.

The point to note here is that introducing the Productivity Index and constrained resources dramatically changes the ranking of projects. Compare the ranked list in Figure 8.11 with that in Figure 8.12: Note that Foxtrot, previously the number one project, drops off the list entirely when one uses the Productivity Index. This Productivity Index method yields benefits in addition to those inherent in the straight NPV-ranking approach in Figure 8.11. By introducing

---

* This decision rule of rank order according to the ratio of what one is trying to maximize divided by the constraining resource is an effective one. Simulations with a number of sets of projects show that this decision rule works very well, truly giving "maximum bang for the buck"!

Figure 8.12: Better—Rank Projects by the Productivity Index Until Out of Resources in a Bucket

1	2	3	4	5	
Project	NPV	Development Cost	Productivity Index = NPV/ Dev Cost	Sum of Dev Costs	
Beta	57	5	11.4	5	
Echo	42	5	8.4	10	
Alpha	22	3	7.3	13	
Foxtrot	58	10	5.8	23	Limit reached
Gamma	6	2	3.0	25	
Delta	1.5	1	1.5	26	

The horizontal line shows the bucket's limit: $15M Development Costs is reached.
"Go" projects are now Beta, Echo, and Alpha (above the line) and Foxtrot drops off the list.
Add Gamma to consume the last $2M, and the portfolio value is now $127M…
up from $115M in Figure 8.11.   Artwork courtesy of Dave Caissy

the Productivity Index, the method favors those projects that are almost completed (the denominator is small, hence the Productivity Index is high). And the method deals with resource constraints, yielding the best set of projects for a given budget or resource limit.

Suggestion: Use the Productivity Index for ranking projects, best to worst. It's a relatively simple extension of the NPV method, but gives a higher-value portfolio. The additional calculation is quite simple—it adds another line to your spreadsheet—and all the data are available on the spreadsheet. Note: When considering resources remaining to be spent (the denominator of the productivity ratio calculation), count only the "go forward" costs—the *costs to be incurred from this point forward*, or the person-days to get the project finished. *Sunk costs are not relevant to the decision to move forward!*

Use Success Criteria

Another financial-selection method, and one employed with considerable success at firms such as Procter & Gamble, is the *use of success criteria*.[11] P&G relies primarily on success criteria to help make better Go/Kill decisions on projects. Specific success criteria for each gate relevant to that stage are defined for each project and are agreed to by the project team and management at each gate—that is, *what would the project have to achieve in order that it be considered "a success."* Examples might be: first year sales of ten thousand cases; profit margin of 30 percent; launch by date July 1. These success criteria—and forecasts on them—are then used to evaluate the project at successive gates and are also key evaluation criteria at the Post-Launch Review: Did the project team achieve what was agreed to?

Success criteria typically include metrics on profitability, first-year sales, launch date, and even expected interim metrics, such as test results. The method allows the project team to custom-tailor criteria to suit the nature of its project. The method has the benefit of instilling project-team accountability: At the Post-Launch Review, the project's results are compared against the original projections made by the team. Thus the method motivates the team to make much *more realistic and accurate sales, costs, and time projections*, which in turn provides better data for management to make the Go/Kill decision. A word of caution here: This success criteria method does have risks; and its use should be reserved for businesses with considerable experience with gating systems and a solid track record of making realistic sales, cost, time, and profit estimates.

Caution in Applying Financial Criteria Too Early

Some managers don't understand that, at the early stages of a venturesome project, they are not making an all-or-nothing Go/Kill decision. Rather, they are making a relatively small investment to undertake a preliminary investigation—providing the resources to *test the waters*. Thus, these initial investment decisions do not need the rigor of later-stage decisions. Think of the idea-to-launch process as *buying a series of options* on the project, rather than buying the whole project outright. Buying options is one way to *mitigate risk*. That's one good reason for using a gated approach that breaks the project into stages, with each stage being more costly than the previous one. Gates precede each stage; at each successive gate, the data are more reliable, but the investment is also greater. This gating, or *options approach*, helps to manage the risk of major or breakthrough development projects.

> The best way to destroy true or bold innovation in your business is to have tough early gates and use rigorous financial criteria to make these early Go/Kill decisions.

An example: At ITT Industries, managers had been demanding rigorous analyses even at very early gates in their stage-and-gate process. Project teams arrived at early gate meetings with full NPV and payback calculations, constructed with *far more apparent rigor* than was required for such an early decision. But major projects, which often involved more innovative concepts, technologies, and markets, were plagued by uncertain data, making these financial analyses suspect. As a result, these projects suffered at the early gates; management lacked the confidence to move forward.

Two points are relevant here: First, even though the project might be a potentially large one, the *first stages are not expensive*. Realizing that such an approach was killing all but the sure bets, ITT's management team dictated that the first few gates should be relatively gentle, with qualitative rather than financial criteria. As one frustrated executive told me, "We're not betting the whole farm here—we're making a relatively small decision to spend a little money, have a look-see, after which we'll make another decision to continue." Second, even though project teams had been presenting NPVs and detailed financial analyses very early on, the *sophistication of the analysis far exceeded the quality of the data*; the data upon which the NPVs were based were largely speculative and often wrong—certainly not reliable enough to drive a valid decision.

At some point in the investment process, certainly before moving into the expensive Development stage, financial analysis must be used as part of the Business Case. But product development is not an all-or-nothing decision; as noted above, it should be *a series of options decisions*—invest in a preliminary investigation; check the results; and either kill the project or, if the results are positive, move ahead to a more detailed phase. And the assumptions in an NPV calculation are not consistent with this step-wise approach, as noted next.

Dealing With Risks—Options Approaches

One way to deal with riskier projects was outlined in the section above on NPV and hurdle rates: Simply apply a risk-adjusted discount rate to the NPV calculation, and riskier projects will be appropriately "penalized." In fact, some financial people apply *different discount rates* depending on the degree of risk: For example, if your risk-free discount rate is 10 percent, you might apply a 15 percent discount rate for "moderate-risk" projects and a 20 percent rate for higher-risk initiatives. That way, income earned in the future is heavily discounted in the case of risky projects—a desired way of treating distant but uncertain income.

The NPV method has weaknesses, however. First, it fails to adequately deal well with risk and probabilities of success—for example, the risk-adjusted discount rates that are applied are set quite arbitrarily. Second, NPV is a standard *capital budgeting technique*: It assumes an "all-or-nothing" decision situation, and thus is quite appropriate for capital-expenditure decisions—should we build the factory or not? But new-product projects are not a zero-one decision: They are *purchased a piece at a time*—in increments. That is, the decision to invest in a new-product project really is a *series of options decisions*—invest in a preliminary investigation; check the results and kill the project—or if the results are positive, invest more and move ahead to a more detailed phase in much the way one bets in a game of five-card stud poker. At each gate, management is in effect *buying options on the project*; and these options cost far less than the full cost of the project, hence are an effective way to mitigate risk.

Experts argue that *options-pricing theory* rather than NPV is the appropriate way to evaluate the worth of a new-product project at each gate: Real options analysis deals with step-wise investment decisions under uncertainty. The problem is that the method is quite complex: Black, Scholes, and Merton, who developed the Black-Scholes equation[12] for pricing (valuing) such options, won a Nobel Prize for their mathematics.[*]

The Expected Commercial Value

The good news is that here is a much simpler approach that approximates quite well the complex options-pricing approach, namely, the Expected Commercial Value, or ECV. ECV looks at risks and probabilities, but most importantly, takes the investment a step at a time via a *decision-tree approach*.

An example: Consider a risky major project with a potential payoff over five years of $50 million (based on the present value of a stream of future earnings). The all-in development and commercialization costs are $7 million, for an apparent NPV of $43 million. The project can be broken up into four phases, each with its own probability of success (follow the decision process in Figure 8.13).[13]

The overall probability of success is 0.147 (arrived at by multiplying the chain of four probabilities together), which is unacceptable: *one chance in seven* of winning! And suddenly, the NPV is not so attractive: The "classic" probability adjusted NPV is actually only $350,000—not too attractive (see text in Figure 8.13). Kill the project!

But this reasoning is wrong! Using the ECV decision-tree approach, one sees that the project is actually worth $5.2 million at its beginning when the decision is to spend a mere $300,000. Follow the calculation in Figure 8.13. Further, the project's value jumps to $19.4 million by the time the $3 million

---

[*] Black had passed away by the time the 1997 Nobel Prize for Economics was awarded to Scholes and Merton.

Figure 8.13: The Expected Commercial Value (ECV) Is Determined Via a Decision Tree Approach, a Step-Wise Investment Model

A model of a four-stage investment-decision process: Starting on left, first, invest $300K in a Preliminary Investigation, with 50-50 odds of a positive outcome. Then invest $700K in a Detailed Investigation, with a 60% chance of positive results, and so on, for a total investment of $7M.

If commercially successful, the payoff (PV) is $50M (far right). The unadjusted NPV is thus $43M (i.e., $50K – $7K).

The overall probability of success is (.5x.6x.7x.7) or 0.147

The "usual" probability-adjusted NPV is only $350K (i.e. .147 x 43 – 7 x .853)—not too attractive!

Using the ECV approach, however, one sees that the ECV is a respectable $5.17M. (Work backward from right to left; for example, just before launch, the ECV is $35M; drop back to the beginning of commercialization, subtract $3M, and the ECV is $32M, and so on all the way back to a starting ECV of $5.2M.)

Note that on entering Development, the ECV is $19.4M.

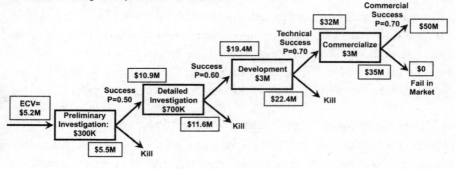

Figure 8.14: Risk Is Managed! Consider the Value of the Project at Each Gate—It's Much Higher than the Required Investment at Each Gate

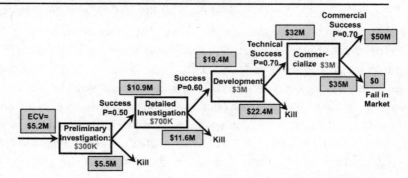

Item \ Gate	Start	Decision to Do Detailed Investigation	Decision to Develop	Decision to Commercialize
Amount to Invest	$300K	$700K	$3M	$3M
ECV (Value of Project)	$5.2M	$10.9M	$19.4M	$32M
Risk = Ratio of Investment / ECV	0.058	0.064	0.155	0.094

Go-to-Development decision must be made. Figure 8.14 shows the increasing value of the project at each stage versus what must be invested. The ECV presents a much more realistic view of the situation and will portray risky and larger projects in a *fairer and thus more favorable light*. The decision now would be Go!

Suggestion: For riskier, bolder, and larger development projects, use the Expected Commercial Value (ECV) method, which approximates the *options-pricing model* used in financial markets. It introduces the notion of *risks and probabilities*—the gates are *a series of incremental purchases of options on the project*. The calculation of the ECV is based on a decision-tree analysis and considers the future stream of earnings from the project, the probabilities of both commercial success and technical success, along with both commercialization costs and development costs (see Figures 8.13 and 8.14 for the calculation and definition of terms). It also provides for the opting out of a project at any point. ECV thus tends to treat risky and bolder investments more fairly and thus more favorably than does NPV.

A Monte Carlo Simulation Model for Major Projects

Another way to introduce risk and probabilities is the use of a Monte Carlo Simulation model. Here's how these models are used: Instead of merely imputing a point estimate for each financial variable in your spreadsheet, such as Year One Sales, Year Two Sales, and so on, input three estimates for each variable—a best case, worst case, and likely case. A probability curve (much like a bell-shaped curve) is drawn through each set of three estimates. So each financial estimate—sales, costs, investment, and so forth—has a probability distribution.

The model begins by calculating multiple scenarios of possible financial outcomes, all based on your probability distributions. Tens of thousands of scenarios are quickly generated by the computer, each one yielding a financial outcome such as the NPV. The distribution of the NPVs generated from these thousands of scenarios becomes your profitability distribution—an expected NPV as well as a probability distribution of NPVs. Use the expected NPV and its distribution to help make the Go/Kill decision at gates; and then take the expected NPV and divide by the costs remaining in the project and rank the projects according to this probability adjusted NPV, much like in the Productivity Index method above.

These Monte Carlo Simulation models are commercially available and relatively easy to use. But there are a few quirks or assumptions in these models that cause problems. For example, the model fails to deal with the *options facet* of a new-product project—the fact that you can terminate the project if things turn negative. Further, it permits the generation of all-but-impossible scenarios that human intervention would have prevented. Nonetheless, it's a fine method, and particularly appropriate for projects that involve large capital expenditures and where probability distributions of input variables can be estimated.

IMPROVING DATA INTEGRITY

The best project-selection system in the world is worthless unless the data are sound. As one executive cynically remarked about his firm's adoption of an elaborate financial-evaluation tool, "They're trying to measure a soft banana with a micrometer," noting that the precision of the tool far exceeded the quality of the data on projects. The lack of good, early information plagues many companies' new-product projects. Major challenges to getting robust data were noted in Chapter 2—a lack of solid front-end homework and weak VoC and market information plague most projects. An ongoing APQC study of portfolio methods reveals that the greatest challenge faced in portfolio management *was not the portfolio tool* or model—it was *the data integrity* (or rather, the lack of data integrity)![14]

> The greatest challenge in project selection and portfolio management is not the selection tool, but getting better data integrity.

Just how serious is the problem of data integrity? Few companies have attempted to measure "the integrity of data in the Business Case"—a multiproject *comparison of forecasted sales and profits versus actual sales and profits* achieved; and to my knowledge no published studies have revealed these results (such data are quite confidential). The few private studies I've seen reveal average errors for genuine new-project projects of about 200 percent—that is, actual sales and profits were about 40 to 60 percent of predicted values, on average. But that's an average, and includes many overestimates and some underestimates too, so the "real error" is much higher than a factor of two!

Data integrity and fact-based decision-making in new-product development pays off! As evidence in Chapter 2 revealed, those businesses that devote more effort to the early phases of a project—for example, seeking and obtaining better market information; front-end loading their projects; and seeking sharp, early, fact-based product definition—are rewarded with much higher performance in innovation. And simply applying a correction factor of 2.0 to sales and profits estimates doesn't work either, because while most sales and profit estimates are overstated, some are actually too low—*the error is in both directions!*

Clear Expectations

The first step to ensuring better data is to ensure that *information requirements are clear*. As one executive put it, "If the expectations are clear, there is a much better chance that project teams will deliver." But too often, project teams are uncertain about just what activities are expected and what information is re-quired—what they should do and deliver—to enable the executives to make ef-fective Go/Kill decisions. If senior management needs to know "expected sales" or the "target price" to plus-or-minus 10 percent, then make that requirement loud and clear to project teams!

One way to make expectations clear is *to install an effective gating system* as out-lined in Chapter 4, and then *practice it*. At minimum, this process should specify:

- The stages, and in particular, *the best-practice activities within each stage* that project teams are expected to execute. Chapters 2 and 4, for ex-ample, sketched out the recommended activities in Stages 1 and 2— the market studies, technical assessment, concept tests, and other key tasks as input to building the Business Case. In your *Stage-Gate* pro-cess, these recommended or mandatory tasks should be a clear guide to project teams.
- The gates, and most important, the *information needs to be defined* for each of these Go/Kill decision points: What information does senior manage-ment need to see in order to make a timely and effective Go/Kill decision? Often these information needs or *gate deliverables* are specified in the form of easy-to-use but short templates.

Project Team Accountability for Forecasts and Projections

A second key to data integrity is *instilling project-team accountability*. This is a best practice that we saw in Chapter 3 in Figure 3.9. In the *team-accountability model*, project teams present forecasts or projections at early gates—for example, in the preliminary and full Business Cases presented at Gates 2 and 3. These projec-tions typically include sales forecasts for the new product, costs, margins, a launch date, and so on.

> Make project teams accountable for the projections they deliver. That way, projections are more realistic and accurate, and data integrity improves.

On the basis of these and other data, senior management approves the proj-ect and commits the resources to move forward. These projections become the *success criteria* against which the project is judged at subsequent gates (outlined above). But most important, the *project team is now responsible for the achievement of these projections:* Following Launch, there is a Post-Launch Review (typically about one year after launch, that is, after a full year of operating results)—see Chapter 4. Here, the project team presents the results it achieved—first-year sales, margins, costs, launch date—versus what was promised at Gates 3 and 5. In short, "winning" means "winning results in the marketplace," not just getting one's project approved: There is no room for "showcasing projects" to get project approval and then "launch and leave." One result of this accountability model is that the project team makes much more *professional and realistic estimates*—data integrity improves!

Validation of the Data with Spirals

Dealing with the high technical and market uncertainties inherent in many larger and bolder projects presents a major challenge to some senior-management teams. The traditional development process requires that all the homework be done upfront, and that answers to most of the key questions, including expected sales, costs, and margins, are found in the Business Case *before* development begins. But reliable data and "all the answers" are often not available for all projects, especially for major innovations with much ambiguity and uncertainty in the earlier stages. For some management teams, this presents too high a risk, and they simply back out of the project.

We saw in Chapters 5 and 6 that leading companies have made their traditional gating system much more agile and adaptive in order to handle uncertainty and ambiguity in development projects. By building a series of build-test-feedback-revise iterations (spirals) into the development process, one gets confirmation not only of the product and its requirements, but most importantly, *validation of financial assumptions and estimates* (see Figures 5.3 and 6.3). For example, by building protocepts and testing them with customers and users, one gains insights into customer liking, preference, and even purchase intent—valuable inputs into estimates of market size, expected sales, and pricing. And by constructing such protocepts or early prototypes, technical issues, including likelihood of technical success and manufacturing costs, can be better estimated. Thus, building these validation spirals into your development process helps to validate the data useful for making investment decisions, and early in the process.

PROFILING PROJECTS TO PICK THE WINNERS: SCORING MODELS

Have you noticed how DNA research has progressed so much of late? Researchers have discovered certain markers on DNA that can actually predict whether a person will get a particular disease. Have you ever wondered whether or not a new-product project *has its own DNA*—a pattern or profile—and whether or not *certain markers* might be used to predict its outcome, success, or failure? Research in the field of new-product development, going back to the 1970s, began to uncover some of these markers.

What are the telltale signs of a winning new-product project? Do you know? Surely there are some key indicators, markers, or descriptors of projects that are very good predictors of success. If we knew what these predictors were, then we could *develop a scorecard* and use that to *rate and rank projects* in a much more professional and predictive way.

The Markers That Predict Success

Sounds great in theory. For decades, people have been trying to develop such "predictive models" to pick winning racehorses, winning dogs at the dog track, winning stocks on the stock market, and so on—without much luck. But the situation is quite different for new products. Indeed, there have been some impressive research investigations that have probed the *key markers* or *predictors of success* in product innovation.[15] Much of this research has been published over the years and now is in the public domain, so we know what these markers are. And some firms have privately done major internal investigations of their past projects and have come up with their own scoring models or scorecards for rating projects; some are now public.

The markers were identified in Chapters 2 and 3—many of our new-product success drivers. These proven and research-based success predictors for new-product projects, which can be used to help predict project outcomes, include factors such as:

1. *Strategic fit and alignment:* Projects that align well with your innovation strategy and are targeted at defined strategic arenas have a higher likelihood of winning. The hope is that your strategy defines arenas that are attractive (large growing markets, good margins, many opportunities) and in which you have the core competencies and strengths to win. After all, that's why you have a strategy—to point you toward more lucrative arenas.

2. *Product advantage:* A unique, superior, differentiated product with a compelling value proposition is the number one driver of new-product success and a key marker or predictor—it alone accounts for about 26 percent of new-product profits (in Figure 2.11). So this one vital driver must be front and center as a factor in your project-selection model.

3. *Leverages core competencies:* Leveraging core competencies is another key to success: Step-out projects that do not build on the business's strengths have a much higher likelihood of failing.

4. *Market attractiveness:* This is another success driver in Chapter 3 that impacts strongly on profitability. Thus, market attractiveness—the size and potential of the market as well as the competitive situation—becomes yet another factor in your project selection model.

5. *Technical feassiblity:* Here, three critical key subquestions probe the size of the technical gap (new science and invention required? Or merely an engineered repackage?); the technical complexity of the project (many versus few technical hurdles, and whether a solution can be envisioned); and technical uncertainty (certainty of a solution, and whether you've done this type of project many times before). The point is that projects with large technical gaps, technical complexity, and technical uncertainty all have much higher failure rates (although they may score high on other important factors, such as product advantage).

6. *Risk and return:* While the financial estimates—NPV, IRR, Payback—are often in error for development projects, they are indeed correlated to success and failure, but not in a one-to-one fashion. Therefore, they too are included in project selection models.

These factors—numbers one to six above—*are strongly correlated with success and financial performance* of new-project projects, and thus can logically be crafted into a *scorecard model* to help pick projects for development: If one can explain success, then one can predict success!

Use a Scorecard Approach to Rate and Rank Development Projects

Smart companies, such as Procter & Gamble, W. L. Gore, 3M, and BASF, have developed scorecards for gatekeepers to use in rating and ranking projects at gate meetings. One goal is to protect more venturesome projects in the early days—to get them partway through the "valley of death"—until the project team has something tangible to show management and customers. Rigorous use of financial models in the early days of a riskier project all but guarantees death. A second goal of these methods is to reduce the overreliance on financial models in general—models which are often based on faulty data.

Scorecards place more emphasis on nonfinancial factors, the theory being that certain projects have a winning profile, and that profiling projects via a scorecard provides an excellent predictor of eventual success. Research evidence

Figure 8.15: Proven, Research-Based Scorecard for New-Product Project Selection at Gate 3—"Go to Development"

Factor 1: Strategic	• Alignment of project with our business's innovation strategy • Importance of project to the strategy
Factor 2: Product and Competitive Advantage	• Product delivers unique customer or user benefits • Excellent value for money for customer/user • Completing Value Proposition • Differentiated product versus competitors • Positive customer/user feedback on product concept (concept test results, spirals)
Factor 3: Market Attractiveness	• Market size • Market growth and future potential • Margins earned by competitors in this market • Competitiveness—how tough and intense competition is (negative)
Factor 4: Leverages Core Competencies	• Project leverages our core competencies and strengths in: - technology - production/operations - marketing (brand name, market presence, distribution, and sales force)
Factor 5: Technical Feasibility	• Size of technical gap (new science and invention?) • Technical complexity (major barriers?) • Technical uncertainty (familiarity, experience) • Technical results to date (proof of concept?)
Factor 6: Risk versus Reward	• Size of financial opportunity • Financial return (NPV or ECV) • Productivity Index • Certainty of financial estimates • Level of risk and ability to address risks (e.g., ratio of max negative cum cash flow vs NPV)

Projects are scored by the gatekeepers at the gate meeting, using these six factors on a scorecard (0–10 scales on each of the 6 factors in bold).
The Project Attractiveness Score is the weighted or unweighted addition of the scores, out of 100.
A score of 60/100 is usually required for a Go decision.
This scorecard is for Gate 3, Go-to-Development. Similar scorecards are used at earlier gates.

also suggests this is true.[16] Moreover, scorecards are generally rated by managers to be more effective and more efficient than financial tools for pre-Development project selection.

In a scoring model system, at gate meetings senior managers each rate the project on a number of criteria on 1–5 or 0–10 scales on a physical scorecard. The scores from the gatekeepers at the gate review are tallied and combined, and the *Project Attractiveness Score* is computed: the weighted or unweighted addition of the question ratings. This attractiveness score is one basis for making the Go/Kill decision at gates and can also be used to rank-order projects at portfolio reviews.

If you do decide to craft your own scorecard, note that it is best to keep the number of questions to ten or less. More than that, and the evaluators tend to tire of doing the scoring. But do *make sure that these are robust questions—proven predictors of success*, and that you can prove it! A best-practice scoring model, research based and proven, for *well-defined but major new-product projects* is shown in Figure 8.15 for Gate 3, Go to Development.

Scorecards work! They yield efficient, effective Go/Kill decisions and suit management's style.

Suggestion: Use scoring models (scorecards) at gate meetings in conjunction with financial models to help select the right projects; and use the Project Attractiveness Score along with the Productivity Index to rank projects at portfolio reviews. Scorecards are especially recommended for bolder projects with more unknowns, and at the earlier gates, where financial data are usually unreliable: Gates 1, 2, and even Gate 3 in Figure 4.11. You can develop your own scorecards, but often the result is not positive; instead, consider adopting one of the tried-and-proven and research-based scorecards, as shown in Figure 8.15. Scoring models are generally praised in spite of their limited popularity: They produce a strategically aligned portfolio that reflects the business's spending priorities; they yield effective and efficient decisions; and they result in a portfolio of high-value projects.

EVALUATE NEW TECHNOLOGY PLATFORMS DIFFERENTLY

Many companies seek a target proportion of breakthroughs, radical innovations, disruptive technology, and technology-platform projects within their development portfolios, perhaps 10 to 20 percent of the total. This is a laudable goal, as evidenced from the portfolio breakdown of top-performing businesses in Figure 3.3. Tactically, however, these same organizations often cannot cope with such projects once they enter their idea-to-launch framework. In Chapter 5, I outlined a special version of *Stage-Gate* to handle these venturesome projects: the *technology development process* or *Stage-Gate-TD* in Figure 5.5.

If you undertake technology-development and technology-platform projects, then be sure to recognize that such projects are less predictable and more loosely defined. Thus, *use different Go/Kill criteria* for these types of projects, criteria that are more visionary and less financial. Figure 8.16 shows a sample scorecard used for *advanced-technology and radical-innovation* projects, again research-based and validated—but a scorecard that is quite different from the scorecard for normal new products shown in Figure 8.15. Note that in this best-practice model, the key factors include strategic fit and importance, strategic leverage, likelihoods of commercial[*] and technical success, and reward. Here, the reward questions are quite broad and require only rough estimates.

> Financial methods really don't work well for technology-platform and advanced-technology projects. Use a scorecard with much more strategic and qualitative criteria instead.

---

[*] For process developments, the "market-focused" questions in Figure 8.16 can be modified to describe an "internal application," e.g., an application or need within a company manufacturing facility.

Figure 8.16: Research-Based Scorecard for Advanced Technology Project Selection

Main Factor	Criterion (19)	Score = 0 (on 0 to 10 scale)	Score = 10 (on 0 to 10 scale)
1. Business Strategy Fit	Congruence	Only peripheral fit with our business strategies	Strong fit with several key elements of strategy
	Impact	Minimal impact; no noticeable harm if project is dropped	Business unit future depends on this project
2. Strategic Leverage	Proprietary Position	Easily copied; no protection	Position protected thru a combination of patents, trade secrets, access to raw materials or components
	Platform for Growth	Dead-end; project is one-off	Opens up many new-product possibilities
	Durability	Quickly leap-frogged; no sustainable advantage	Long product life-cycle; will impact for many years
	Synergy with Company	Limited to a single business unit	Could be applied widely across the company
3. Probability of Technical Success	Technical Gap	Large gap between solution and current practice; must invent new science	Incremental technical improvement; easy to do
	Project Complexity	Difficult to envision this solution; many technical hurdles	Few or no technical hurdles; can see a solution
	Technology Skills	Technology is new to company; almost no skills here	Technology widely practiced within company
	Resources Availability	Must hire people and build facilities	People and facilities immediately available within company
4. Probability of Commercial Success	Market Need*	Extensive market development required; no apparent existing market or need	Product immediately responsive to customer need; a large market already exists
	Market Maturity*	Declining market(s)	Rapidly growing market(s)
	Competitive Intensity	High: many tough competitors in this field	Low: few competitors; not strong
	Commercial Skills	New application to company; must develop commercial application skills	Commercial application skills already in place in company
	Commercial Assumptions	Low probability of occurring; very speculative assumptions	Highly predicable; high probability of occurring
	Regulatory/Social/Political	Project will have negative impact	Positive impact on a high-profile issue
5. Reward	Absolute Contribution to Profit (5 years)	Less than $10 M cumulative over 5 years (estimate)	More than $250 M cumulative over 5 years (estimate)
	Payback Period	Greater than 10 years (estimate)	Less than 3 years (estimate)
	Time to Commercial Start-Up	Will take a long time to commercialize this technology: greater than 7 years (estimate)	Can commercialize this technology quickly: less than 1 year

Suggestion: If you undertake advanced-technology projects or technology-platform developments, then implement a custom-tailored system for such projects. Don't force them through your regular stage-and-gate process, but instead adopt *Stage-Gate TD* as outlined in Figure 5.5. As part of this model, recognize that the gate criteria will be different—much more strategic and less financial. A scorecard is best suited to operationalize these more qualitative criteria (shown in Figure 8.16) and is recommended for evaluating such technology projects.

GOOD GOVERNANCE: INTEGRATING GATING, PORTFOLIO REVIEWS, AND ROADMAPS

Your *Stage-Gate* system manages your currently active projects, where Go/Kill decisions are made on an ongoing, real-time basis. Your Portfolio Reviews look at the entire portfolio of active and on-hold projects periodically. And your product roadmap outlines which projects your business will probably undertake; it has a longer-term horizon—"future projects" with tentative commitments earmarked. All three systems yield decisions on projects—but how do the three tie together? Figure 8.17 shows the interrelations and interaction of the three decision systems to yield a more holistic picture of the innovation governance system:

1. *Roadmaps:* Strategic product roadmaps (and technology roadmaps) are developed (at the top of Figure 8.17), providing a future view of the probable development portfolio—they provide "placemarks" for future projects. Methods for identifying roadmap candidate projects are outlined in Chapter 10.

2. *Stage-Gate:* When the timing is right according to the roadmap, place-marked projects enter your *Stage-Gate* system. They are screened at Gate 1 and start moving through the process, stage by stage, gate by gate (the bottom right of Figure 8.17). Gates are the quality-control checkpoints: Some projects that looked great at the outset, and thus were included in the roadmap, will be spotted as duds at Gates 2 or 3, and are culled. Note: Just because a project is in the roadmap *does not guarantee it will be done.* So the *Stage-Gate* system acts as a check on the visionary roadmap, and provides feedback: The roadmap is appropriately updated as active projects are killed. (Note that other projects enter your *Stage-Gate* system too—for example, serendipitous or opportunistic ideas—not just strategically driven ideas or projects from the roadmap.)

3. *Portfolio Review:* Once projects pass Gate 2* in the *Stage-Gate* system—when resource commitments become considerable, and when there is enough data to characterize the project—they are "in the development portfolio." Once "in the portfolio," that project, along with many others, is scrutinized at portfolio reviews (the bottom left of Figure 8.17). Although many companies consider the quarterly (or semiannual) portfolio review to be "a minor course correction," other firms make numerous Go/Kill decisions here. Thus, portfolio decisions impact both the gating system and the product roadmap, and updates are made to each.

And so the process continues—each decision process in Figure 8.17 feeding the others in a closed-loop system—with the various components of the governance process working in harmony.

PORTFOLIO MANAGEMENT: RECOMMENDATIONS

A number of tools and methods have been described that help you select development projects and visualize and manage your development portfolio. The recommendation is that you use a combination of approaches: *No one approach*

---

* Gate 2 is the typical point where projects are placed "in the portfolio." Gate 1 is likely too early—not enough data. Gate 3, when full development really starts, is the point in some firms where the portfolio process kicks in.

Figure 8.17: The Portfolio Governance Processes—Your Stage-Gate System, Portfolio Reviews, and Product Roadmapping—Are Integrated with Each Decision Process Feeding the Other

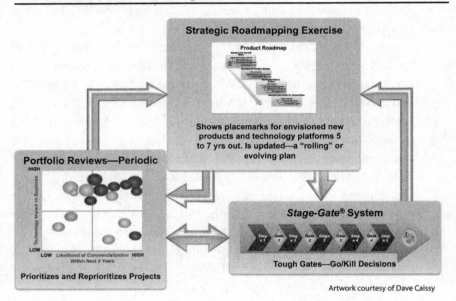

Artwork courtesy of Dave Caissy

works perfectly, so triangulate! Indeed, the best-performing innovators use multiple methods: They recognize that no one method can do it all.

The recommendations are, for *bolder innovations* and *major new-product projects*:

- Use a financial analysis, namely, NPV (and the IRR and Payback Period) along with the Productivity Index, *but not at the early gates.* Too early a financial screen will kill all but the sure bets! However, a financial analysis is usually expected by Gate 3, and you always learn something from undertaking such an analysis. The NPV is generally accepted as the most appropriate financial method to reflect value to the corporation. The Productivity Index, an extension of the NPV method, is best for ranking and prioritizing projects. For large but highly uncertain projects, consider using the expected commercial value (ECV), which builds in risk, probabilities, and options.

- Use the *scorecard (scoring model) method* as well, especially in the earlier gates (Gates 1 to 3) and for bolder projects, also technology developments. Scorecards are well rated for effectiveness, efficiency, and their fit with management's style; they also yield robust portfolios. But use *different scorecards* for different types of projects: Figure 8.15 for *genuine new products* and Figure 8.16 for *advanced-technology* or technology-platform projects, and simpler scorecards for smaller projects.

- Introduce a few well-chosen *success criteria*—for example, first-year sales, launch date, and a profitability metric—by Gate 3. Use these success criteria both at successive gates as Go/Kill criteria, and also to hold the project team accountable for key results and hence to improve data integrity.
- For *lower-risk and smaller development projects*—such as product improvements, fixes, or extensions—*other project-selection methods* are more appropriate and practical. More on these projects in the next chapter.
- Portfolio management is not just about tactical project selection—you must also consider strategic issues. From strategy all else flows, so use Strategic Buckets (above) and Strategic Roadmaps (in Chapter 10) to translate strategy into project-investment decisions.
- Finally, the many charts in this chapter—the pie charts and bubble diagrams—provide useful ways for management to view their firm's development portfolios, and are sensible additions to both gate meetings and portfolio reviews.

Data reliability is also a challenge. All these methods are only as good as the data upon which they are based. Securing more reliable data should be a goal, and indeed is a key outcome of an effective *Stage-Gate* system outlined in Chapter 4. So practice your *Stage-Gate* system with discipline! Additionally, make project teams accountable for the projections (and promises) they make at the critical Gates 3 and 5. Hold a Post-Launch Review, where promised versus actual results is the topic. And build in validation spirals—build-test-feedback-and-revise iterations with customers—to get more reliable data for use in project evaluations.

9

MAKING THE GATES WORK— GATES WITH TEETH

You gotta know when to hold 'em,
Know when to fold 'em,
Know when to walk away,
Know when to run.

—KENNY ROGERS, "The Gambler"

CHALLENGES AT THE GATES

The devil is in the details. Perhaps the greatest challenge that users of *Stage-Gate*®
face is making the gates work.[1] *As go the gates, so goes the process!* In a robust
gating system, poor projects are spotted early and killed and their resources redirected to better projects; and projects in trouble are also detected, then sent back
for rework or redirect—and put back on course. But it seems that as quality-
control checkpoints, the gates aren't too effective in too many companies and
allow a lot of poor projects to proceed.

This chapter delves into the details of making the gates work. The previous
chapter introduced many of the tools that are used in portfolio and project selection. In the current chapter, we take these selection tools, along with other
concepts and approaches, and show how they can be effectively used at gate
meetings to make better Go/Kill decisions.

GATE DEFINITIONS

GATES

"Gates" are project-review and decision meetings—the vital Go/Kill decision points in the *Stage-Gate* idea-to-launch system. At gates, projects are evaluated by management; projects are approved and prioritized, resources are allocated to projects; and poor projects are killed before additional resources are wasted.

GATEKEEPERS

"Gatekeepers" are a management team of decision-makers and resource owners responsible for selecting the best projects for development, and then ensuring that these projects receive committed resources—the gatekeepers thus facilitate the rapid commercialization of selected projects.

GATEKEEPING

"Gatekeeping" is the set of management practices, behaviors, procedures, and rules of engagement that govern decision-making at the gates. These practices are designed to enable project teams to move good projects forward rapidly and effectively through to launch. Note that the emphasis here is on enabling and facilitating projects—not just on judging and critiquing.

Gates are rated as one of the weakest areas in product development, with project evaluations consistently cited as weakly handled or nonexistent: Decisions involve the wrong people from the wrong functions (no functional alignment); no consistent criteria are used to screen or rank projects; or there is simply no will to kill projects at all.[2] Only 49 percent of firms are found to have effective gates throughout the idea-to-launch process.[3] Further, we saw in Chapters 3 and 8 that most firms have too many projects and too many minor projects in their development pipeline—see Figure 3.2. Finally, only 51 percent of development projects meet their profit targets (49 percent do not, as shown in Figure 1.3), which means that gates aren't doing their job: Too many bad projects and too many projects in trouble are sliding through!

Getting on the Same Page

"Gates" are meetings between the project team and senior management designed to assess the quality of the project, make the Go/Kill and prioritization decision, and approve the needed resources for the next stage (see box entitled "Gate Definitions"):

- Gates are specified throughout the idea-to-launch process. Typically, there are about five gates for a major project, from the Idea Screen through to the Go to Launch decision point, as shown in Figure 4.11.
- Gates focus on one project at a time. By contrast, portfolio reviews consider the entire set of projects. Gates tend to provide a much more in-depth assessment of the individual project than do portfolio reviews.
- Gates have defined decision-makers: the gatekeepers.
- Effective gates utilize the various tools seen in the previous chapter to sharpen the decision-making: NPV, Productivity Index, Payback Period, ECV, scorecards, and success criteria.

Gates with No Teeth

Although your company might have installed a *Stage-Gate* system, the gates are often either *nonexistent* or *lack teeth*.[4] The result is that projects are rarely killed at gates. Rather, as one senior manager exclaimed, "Projects are like express trains, speeding down the track, slowing down at the occasional station [gate], but never stopping until they reach their ultimate destination, the marketplace." In short, *the gates have no teeth*: Once a project is approved, it never gets killed.

The reason: Management does not know how to say no; that is, to *drown some puppies*! Thus, even though gate meetings are held with the best of intentions—to provide a critical evaluation of the project and make a Go/Kill decision—the Kill option is rarely exercised. And like the addictive poker player who does not know when to fold his hand and walk away, there are many good (and not so good) reasons for continuing to push the project onward—see the box, "Seven Reasons Why We Can't Seem To Kill Projects."

Even worse, in many firms we have investigated, there was never an intention to kill a project once underway. After the initial Go decision, the gates amount to little more than a project-review meeting or a milestone checkpoint, but not a serious Go/Kill decision meeting.

An example: In one major high-tech communications-equipment manufacturer, once a project passes Gate 1 (the Idea Screen), it is placed into the business's product roadmap. This means that the estimated sales and profits from the new project are now integrated into the business unit's financial forecast. Once into the financial plan of the business, of course, the project is locked in: There is no way that the project can be removed from the roadmap or killed. In

SEVEN REASONS WHY WE CAN'T SEEM TO KILL PROJECTS

1. Momentum:
   - People and enthusiasm—hard to stop the train once it's rolling
   - We've already spent $XX—we can't quit now

2. Difficult to say "no":
   - Nobody likes to "drown puppies"—a difficult and unpleasant task
   - We have a "can do" culture—"no" is not in our vocabulary

3. Political reasons:
   - Executive-sponsored pet projects
   - Executives saving face
   - Executives vying for their fair share of the resource pie

4. The project team won't let go—just too stubborn or determined:
   - "Victory is just around the corner"
   - Stopping now is an admission of defeat
   - It's not career enhancing

5. It's in the plan:
   - The project is already "in" the business's product roadmap
   - It's built into this year's financial plan—we can't take it out now

6. Incomplete or unreliable data:
   - It's difficult to make tough decisions when the data are poor
   - A lack of data integrity, deliverables to the gate are not fact based
   - The *wrong* information

7. No valid method for killing projects:
   - No clear and consistent Go/Kill criteria used by the gatekeepers
   - Wrong people at the gate meeting—not the decision-makers
   - Go/Kill is not discussed: a "vote" is never taken at gate meetings—it's not really an investment-decision meeting.

effect, all gates after Gate 1 are merely rubber stamps! Somehow, management in this firm missed the point that the idea-to-launch process is a funnel, not a tunnel, and that gates after Gate 1 are also Go/Kill points: This should *not be* a one-gate, five-stage process!

In too many firms like this one, after the initial Go decision the gates amount to little more than a project-update meeting, a project-review meeting, or a milestone checkpoint: Is the project on time and on budget? But rarely is the issue of "should we continue investing in this project?" ever discussed. Thus, instead of the well-defined *funnel* that is so often used to depict the new-product process, one ends up with a *tunnel* where everything that enters comes out the other end, good projects and bad. Yet management is deluded into believing that the firm has a functioning *Stage-Gate* system.

The point needs to be made: Gates are *investment-decision or Go/Kill meetings*. Like any investment meeting, the most current information is reviewed, an assessment is undertaken, and a Go or Kill decision is made. Because this is an *options model*—that is, the decision to fully invest is made via a series of Go/Kill decisions—early decisions to move forward can be reversed at later gates: Often, projects look good and are approved at Gates 1 and 2 based on very limited information; but by the time they reach Gate 3, and with the benefit of more complete information, the evaluators determine that the project has turned sour and must be killed. That Kill decision must be made!

> Gates are investment-decision or Go/Kill meetings. Because this is an options model, early decisions to move forward can be reversed at later gates, based on new information.

Hollow Decisions at Gates

A closely connected problem is *hollow gates*. Here, the gate meeting is held and a Go decision is made, *but resources are not committed*. Somehow, management fails to understand that approval decisions are rather meaningless *unless a check is cut*: The project leader and team must leave the gate meeting with the resources they need to progress their project. Instead, projects are approved, but resources are not—*a hollow Go decision*, and one that usually leads to too many projects in the pipeline, and projects taking far too long to get to market. And lacking the resources to get the project done, the project leader is set up for failure!

The Ugly Results

Gates without teeth usually means that there are too many projects in the development pipeline, many of them of limited value. And hollow gates—approving projects without committing resources—means that there is no limit to the number of projects that can be approved! Note, however, that approving too many projects for the limited resources triggers many ailments. First, project team members are spread too thinly over too many projects. Multitasking is a good thing up to a point; but too much multitasking leads to decreased productivity—switching from task to task, with the associated "start-up" and "shut down" costs.

With resources spread so thinly, many projects are in a queue, awaiting people to work on them; thus, projects start to take longer and longer. In some firms, the innovation process is virtually gridlocked—*nothing moves*. Even worse, facing aggressive timelines and without the time to do the job right, some project team members cut corners in order to save time, with negative results. Doing too many projects has a few other negative side effects, as covered in Chapters 3 and 8: Project team members become stressed and start blaming each other for missed milestones, which is not good for team morale; and "clever teams" simply *dumb down their projects*.

Suggestion: Take a look at your gates. Are they working well? Do you actually kill projects at your gate meetings, or are they like gates in too many firms—an information update-and-review meeting? Draw your attrition curve as shown in Figure 1.4 to find out. Do you really commit resources to teams at gates, or is your company guilty of *hollow gates*? If the answers to these questions signal problems, read on and see what can be done.

A FUNNELING APPROACH—LEARN TO DROWN SOME PUPPIES

If "gates without teeth" and "hollow gates" describe your company's gates, then it's time to start drowning some puppies and reallocating (and committing) resources to the deserving projects. Here are some ways:

Prune the Current Portfolio—Major Surgery

One way to kick-start the process is by undertaking a ruthless one-time pruning operation—a tough-minded project-by-project portfolio review:

> *An example:* One major chemical company was suffering from too many projects: over 1,000 active development initiatives in their pipeline. A thorough review of the project list revealed that many were mediocre, of limited value to the company, or lacking strategic impact. A brutal pruning exercise reduced the list to 250 projects. The result: Time-to-market was cut in half within one year, and project execution improved dramatically.

Pruning the portfolio means making difficult choices. A 75 percent pruning rate in this example is extreme; experience suggests that in the typical portfolio, *roughly one-third of the projects should be cut*. Drowning puppies is unpleasant for most managements, however: All projects look good; all are worthy or needed; and no one likes to kill any of them. The other tough issue is this: Even if there is the will to kill, which projects should be killed or put on hold?

Do Fewer But Better Projects—a Decision-Factory Mentality

In the longer run, strive for better new-product focus. Project selection must occur in light of your resource constraints—ensuring that the right number of projects is undertaken for the limited development resources available. It is better to undertake four projects and do them properly, rather than try to do ten badly. Thus, embrace the funneling approach, and know that a certain percentage of projects should be cut at each gate, especially early on, at Gates 1, 2, and 3:

> *An example:*[5] A division of Cooper-Standard Automotive faced a grid-locked product-development system. A chart from that year showed *fifty major projects underway*, time-to-market was "infinite," and there were zero launches. At that low point, a tough-minded executive forced a *decision-factory mentality* into his gate meetings—kill the weaker projects. The result was that seven years later, the number of major projects was down to eight, time-to-market was reduced to 1.6 years, and major product launches were up to five annually. Revenue from new products steadily increased, and has *risen more than tenfold* during the seven-year period.

The Optimal Kill Rate

A tough question at our portfolio management seminars is this: Is there an optimal attrition curve? Or what percentage of projects should be cut or killed at each gate? As an example, in the venture capital business, one rule is: Consider one hundred opportunities, invest in ten, and one will be a big winner.

In the case of product innovation, I know of no such optimal or *magic curve*, although some folks have unsuccessfully tried to calculate the theoretical optimal kill rate at each gate. One rule of thumb is that the number of projects at each stage should be inversely proportional to the cost of the stage. But doing the math leads to an exceptionally steep attrition curve, so it's probably a poor rule.

Another view is to use the *average attrition curve*, shown in Figure 1.4, the theory being that the average decision-maker is optimal. This attrition curve translates into seven projects in Stage 1; five projects in Stage 2; four projects in Stage 3; and 1.5 launches—roughly a five-to-one attrition rate from Gate 1 to Gate 5. Note that this curve is for *true product developments*—innovations that tend to be riskier. More predictable, lower-risk, and minor projects have a more gentle attrition rate than five-to-one. Further, the shape of the curve in Figure 1.4 is wrong—it should be much steeper at the earlier stages in order to optimize spending; that is, the greatest cuts as a percent should come at the early gates—for example, go from seven projects to three to two when moving from Gate 1 into Development—with very little attrition after Gate 3. EXFO Electro-Optical Engineering likens their process to a "funnel leading to a tunnel"; and a major chemical company computes the percentage of projects killed after Gate 3—the percentage of "late kills"—as a negative metric.

Whatever the ideal kill rate at each gate might be, here are some good practices:

- Track the percentage of projects killed at each gate. The percentage should be highest at the early gates, but after Gate 3 (that is, Gates 4 and 5), the percentage of kills should tend to zero—a funnel leading to a tunnel.
- If the kill rate at the early gates is close to zero—with nothing being killed— then *you do have a problem:* gates with no teeth. It is highly unlikely that every project that starts out in your innovation process is a good one, and thus some that pass Gate 1 should be cut later on.
- The kill rate should be higher for venturesome projects (a steeper attrition curve) than for lower-risk, predictable, and short-term projects.
- The average attrition curve in Figure 1.4 is not a good benchmark. Your ideal curve should be steeper at the beginning, and become less steep as it approaches the final stages. Note that the area under the curve in Figure 1.4 is roughly proportional to spending, so it pays to cut projects early rather than late.

SHARPENING THE GATE DECISIONS

Best practices found in various firms as they attempt to sharpen their gate decisions are summarized in the box entitled "Requirements for Gates with Teeth." Some of these practices were highlighted in previous chapters, while others are outlined below. I integrate them here in the box, while Figure 9.1 shows some best practices at gates.[6]

Build Clearly Specified Gates into Your Innovation Process

Gates must be built into your idea-to-launch system, as in a typical *Stage-Gate* process shown in Figure 4.11. But gates are not just project-review meetings or milestone checks. Rather, they are *Go/Kill meetings:* Gates are the occasion when senior management meets to decide whether the company should

> Gates are an irrevocable decision to commit resources to a project leader and team—to complete the next stage of their project.

Figure 9.1: Best-Performing Businesses Build Important Elements into Their Gate Meetings to Improve Effectiveness

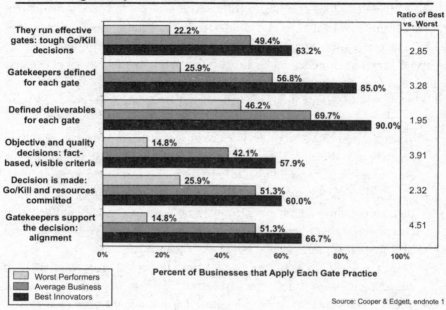

Percent of Businesses that Apply Each Gate Practice

Worst Performers
Average Business
Best Innovators

Source: Cooper & Edgett, endnote 1

continue to invest in the project based on the latest information or perhaps cut losses and get out of a bad project. Note that gates are also *a resource-commitment meeting*, where, in the event of a Go decision, the project leader and team receive a commitment of resources to pursue their project: Projects cannot just be approved without committing the resources; otherwise, the result is hollow gates and too many projects!

Clear Deliverables

To make good decisions, gatekeepers must have the right information available.[7] Defined deliverables specify what information the project team must provide to enable decision-making and also provide a guide for the gatekeepers—what information they can expect. Having defined deliverables for each gate is a clear best practice: 90 percent of best-performing innovators set clear expectations, generally via a standard list of items that the project team is expected to deliver at each gate in the process—see Figure 9.1.

Employ Visible Go/Kill and Prioritization Criteria

Having Go/Kill decision criteria defined for each gate, written down and visible to everyone, is another strong best practice, employed by best innovators

REQUIREMENTS FOR GATES WITH TEETH

1. Clearly specified gates in the process:

   - Shown clearly in your idea-to-launch schematic (see Figure 4.11)
   - Gates defined as Go/Kill decision points
   - Not just project review, milestone review, or status-update meetings
   - Projects cannot continue unless a Go decision is made

2. Data integrity:

   - Quality information to make the Go/Kill decision
   - Reliable information—based on solid front-end homework
   - And validated via spirals or iterations with customers
   - The required homework clearly specified in your *Stage-Gate* system

3. The right deliverables:

   - Relevant information presented to gatekeepers in a useful manner
   - Clear expectations for deliverables from project teams
   - Short and clear templates and guides

4. Project teams accountable for results:

   - Versus the data (forecast) they present at gates
   - "Success criteria" employed to monitor results (Chapter 8)
   - Results checked—a formal Post-Launch Review built in

5. Visible go/kill and prioritization criteria:

   - Made operational via a scorecard and "success criteria"
   - And financial metrics (NPV, the Productivity Index, ECV—Chapter 8)

6. A resource allocation method at the gate:

   - Linked to portfolio management—the big picture
   - The right balance and mix of projects
   - Strategic Buckets and Strategic Product Roadmaps
   - Full portfolio review with senior management: two to four times per year

more than three to one versus worst performers—again see Figure 9.1. Almost all best performing innovators (85 percent) employ specific Go/Kill criteria—often in the form of a gate scorecard—to evaluate the merits of projects, to assist management in making Go/Kill decisions, and to make decision-making more objective and less emotional. In spite of the logic of having gate criteria spelled out in this way, the *lack of such criteria is fairly widespread*, especially among poorer performing businesses, with only one-quarter of worst performers having specified Go/Kill criteria!

Use scorecards: A number of leading firms use scorecards for early stage screening (for Gates 1, 2, and 3 in Figure 4.11); the project is scored by the gatekeepers right at the gate meeting on key criteria. This scorecard method was introduced in the previous chapter as a project-evaluation tool. Recall that scorecards rely on qualitative factors, such as market attractiveness, leveraging core competencies, and competitive advantage (rather than just on financial numbers such as NPV) to assess the relative attractiveness of a project at a gate. Note, however, that financial criteria are also built into the scorecard to be considered along with other criteria for Go.

> Build clearly specified gates into your innovation process. And use visible criteria—scorecards, success criteria, and financial hurdles—to help make the Go/Kill and prioritization decisions.

Use the right financial criteria: Most firms rely heavily on financial criteria to select development projects. Thus it's prudent to spell out exactly what these criteria are—NPV (or ECV), IRR, Productivity Index, and Payback Period—and what the hurdles are for different types of projects.

Employ success criteria: Another selection method introduced in the previous chapter, and employed with considerable success within gates is the use of *success criteria.* These criteria, and targets to be achieved on them, are agreed to by the project team and management at each gate.[8] If the project's estimates fail on any agreed-to criterion at successive gates, the project could be killed. Note that success criteria can be used along with the scorecard method.

Try self-evaluation by the project team: Some companies encourage the project team to submit its own filled-in scorecard—a self-evaluation—prior to the gate meeting. The view is that the project team's judgment of the project's attractiveness is also important information for the gatekeepers. The gatekeepers also score the project as above, but *before seeing the project team's scores* in order to avoid bias. The two sets of scores are then displayed at the gate meeting, and differences in opinion between project team and gatekeepers are addressed.

Alternatively, some companies encourage project teams to submit their evaluation regarding how solid or *reliable the information* is that is contained in the deliverables. That is, instead of rating the project on scorecard criteria, the project team self-rates the "integrity of information" contained in each of the deliverables. For example, in one major firm, the project team indicates the validity of assumptions (data integrity) by *assigning bets against their salaries* in their Business Cases: for example, "Bet one month's salary" on assumption X, "bet one year's salary" on assumption Y, etc.*

Display in-process metrics at gates: In-process metrics are also considered important by some management groups, and hence are displayed at gates. In-process metrics capture how well the project is being executed, and whether it is on course and on target. Poor performance on these metrics is not usually a Kill indicator, but a strong signal that the project and team could be in trouble, and that course corrections are needed:

> *An example:* A noted Austrian electronics firm, Omicron Electronics GmbH, has introduced insightful metrics at gates in their *Stage-Gate* process.[9] They call it their "360-degree feedback at each gate" (see Figure 9.2). Here, three vital metrics are rated and tracked during each stage: meeting project targets, team efficiency, and quality of execution during the stage. The summary 360-degree chart in Figure 9.2 provides the total view of the project on these metrics at each gate meeting and helps indicate whether the project is on track and on course.

Be Sure to Make the Decision!

The Go/Kill and resource allocation decisions must be made.[10] Gates are decision points; the result of a gate meeting should be a Go/Kill and resources commitment decision. But in about half of businesses, gate meetings do not produce decisions—see Figure 9.1. Rather, the meetings tend to be "information sessions" or "project updates." Learn from the best performing innovators: When compared to poor performers, they run their gate meetings as *true decision meetings* that produce one of four or five outcomes: Go, Kill, Hold, or Recycle (or sometimes Conditional Go).

Decisions should be objective and fact based: The majority of businesses we study lack a high-quality approach to decision-making at gates, where decisions are supposed to be fact based and objective and based on visible decision criteria—see Figure 9.1. Even the best-performing innovators are somewhat deficient here, with just more than half claiming high-quality and objective decision-making. Even so, the best innovators still fare much better than the worst performers,

---

* No salary is actually lost—it's a theoretical bet.

Figure 9.2: A Best Practice Is to Display a 360-Degree View of In-Process Metrics at Gates

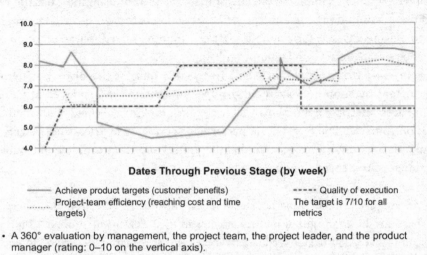

Dates Through Previous Stage (by week)

——— Achieve product targets (customer benefits)   - - - - Quality of execution
.... Project-team efficiency (reaching cost and time   The target is 7/10 for all
         targets)   metrics

- A 360° evaluation by management, the project team, the project leader, and the product manager (rating: 0–10 on the vertical axis).
- These rating data are summarized and shown at every gate meeting for the previous stage.

Artwork courtesy of Dave Caissy   Source: Five I's Innovation Management, Austria.

only 14.8 percent of whom indicate confidence in the quality and objectivity of their gate decisions.

Gatekeepers must support the decision: Gatekeeper unanimity and support for gate decisions is a problem for more than half of businesses, according to results in Figure 9.1. Only the best innovators fare well in this respect: Here, each gatekeeper visibly supports the decisions made at gates, including committing resources from their departments. That is, there is *total alignment between the gatekeepers and across functional areas!* By contrast, less than 15 percent of worst performers report gatekeeper alignment regarding the gate decision and resource commitments.

Employ a Resource Allocation Method at Your Gates

Gates are held in real time—when a project completes one stage and requires resources to proceed to the next phase. Although the gate meeting is largely focused on one or a few projects, the decision to proceed *cannot be made in isolation.* To ensure effective resource allocation right at the gate meeting, consider displaying a list of active projects with their ratings or prioritization level, together with current resource commitments (by department or by person). Sometimes the new project "passes" the gate criteria, but when compared to the other active projects, does not look so strong. And often the entire resource pool is fully allocated to the existing projects, and then tough decisions must be made: where to find the resources for the project under review at the gate. Management cannot keep adding projects to the "active list" without dealing with the resource implications.

Finding resources at gates: How does one find resources at gate meetings? People aren't patiently sitting in their cars in the parking lot waiting to hop onto a new development project! Three approaches are common:

1. In smaller firms, often the *project leader* arrives at the gate meeting with a list of proposed project team members for the next stage. The leader has usually talked with each candidate and with their supervisor to check interests, skills, compatibility, availability, and timing.

2. In larger firms, the stage-gate *process manager (or PMO*)* uses resource-management software. Such software shows the availability and work-day assignments of each person per department involved in product development—and across all relevant departments. Individuals' assignments to all projects are recorded (from previous gate meetings and resource commitments made then), so that the process manager can show immediately who might be available and when for the project under discussion. Many firms develop their own resource model, consisting of a set of spreadsheets—one sheet per month—showing people versus projects, with person-days committed noted (example in figure 9.3). In more advanced software, the skills of individuals are also noted in order to best match people against projects, and also "what if" scenarios are possible—what is the resource impact if projects x and y are dropped and a and b are done instead?

3. Finally, in a few firms, *the gatekeepers* are expected to arrive at the gate meeting with an understanding of who is available in their departments and when they can start work on the project. This requires some discipline and premeeting preparation on the part of the gatekeepers.

The point is, one must assign or commit resources at gate meetings; and there are various ways to track and assign resources at gates. Pick one method, or modify and adopt one of the above, and use it. Without an effective resource-tracking and allocation method, likely you'll end up with hollow gates and too many under-resourced projects!

---

* PMO = Project Management Office, common in many larger firms.

Figure 9.3: Resource Management Chart—Supply-Demand

Project	Marketing Dep't	RD&E Dep't	Operations	Sales Force
K-Lift	8	45	0	2
Propel	7	55	2	2
True-Tone	8	25	18	6
Roller-B	4	18	15	1
Tilt-Table	5	27	5	2
Cursor	4	10	0	2
P-Lift	5	20	2	5
Examinator	7	17	2	10
Demand: Person-Days	48	217	44	30
Supply: No. of people	7	12	12	15
% of time available	30%	80%	10%	10%
FTE people available	2.1	9.6	1.2	1.5
Person-days available per month	46.2	211.2	26.4	33
Surplus (Deficiency)	(-1.8)	(-5.8)	(-17.6)	3

Table shows commitments to projects by department (person-days). Table is simplified for this illustration—normally is shown by person per department. One such chart per month.

Implement a Formal Portfolio-Management System

Your portfolio-management system should be integrated with your gating process. Portfolio reviews are held periodically—typically two to four times per year—and are more holistic than gates, looking at the *entire set of projects* (but obviously less in-depth per project than gates do).[11] Portfolio reviews deal with issues such as achieving the right mix and balance of projects, project prioritization, and whether the portfolio is aligned with the business's strategy.

> *An example*: EXFO Electro-Optical Engineering has implemented both *Stage-Gate* and Portfolio-Management systems.[12] The gates make Go/Kill decisions on individual projects. But four times per year, the business leadership team, chaired by the CEO, evaluates, ranks, and prioritizes the complete slate of development projects during the Portfolio Review meeting. Any project at or beyond Gate 2 is included in this prioritization exercise.

As part of your portfolio-management system, use *Strategic Buckets*. Strategic Buckets was introduced in the last chapter as a way to allocate resources across

Figure 9.4: At Gates, Must Consider the Impact of Adding the New Project on the Existing Portfolio of Projects

If we add this new project to the Active List in this Bucket...
- Does it improve or reduce the value of the portfolio?
  - Use the Project Attractiveness Scores (from scorecard) and Productivity Indexes
  - Compare to other active projects in this Bucket

Project Name	Current Ranking Within Bucket	Scorecard: Project Attractiveness Score PAS (out of 100)	Productivity Index: NPV/person-days of work remaining	Resources Required (Loading— person-days)	Cumulative: Sum of Loadings (person-days)
Murray	1	83	206	120	120
Timor	2	83	194	140	260
Bering	3	75	180	90	350
Elk	4	78	142	180	530
Berlin	5	70	148	100	630
AVERAGE	--	78.0	174.0	--	--

New Project
PI=190
PAS=80

Table shows ranked list of active projects (past Gate 2)
within the "Major New-Product Projects" bucket.
The proposed new project (circle at right) would be about #3 in the ranking if added, and improve the overall value of the portfolio (its PI and PAS exceed the portfolio's average).

various dimensions, such as by project types or product lines. Once resources are allocated across buckets, projects within each bucket are ranked from best to worst until the bucket's resource limit is reached. Buckets, and the ranked list of projects within buckets, can be shown at portfolio reviews to help management prioritize all projects; and the relevant prioritized project list can also be displayed at a gate meeting to help the gatekeepers prioritize the new project under discussion (Figure 9.4).

Suggestion: Take steps to create gates with teeth. Try a one-time pruning exercise—a thorough portfolio review to dump weak projects. Then move to a decision-factory mentality—gates where a certain percentage of projects do get killed. Define required deliverables (information) for gates, and employ clearly visible Go/Kill criteria at gates. Make the decision—Go/Kill and resource commitments—and seek functional alignment and stick by the decision. And build some portfolio thinking into the gate as well—comparing the new project to the list of active, existing projects to determine its priority. Ultimately, implement a formal portfolio-management system with periodic (quarterly or semiannual) portfolio reviews of the entire set of active projects.

HOW EFFECTIVE GATES WORK

Now it's time to start thinking about how to use the various evaluation methods outlined in the previous chapter—scorecards, the Productivity Index, ECV—in a governance model for your business. In short, how do you integrate these models and tools into your *Stage-Gate* system to yield effective gates and gate decisions? For the rest of this chapter, we look at the design of gates: requirements, structure, criteria, gatekeepers, and protocol.

Requirements for Effective Gates

When designing your governance model for project evaluation and selection, and when electing the approach that best suits your business, be sure to consider these points:

Each decision point is only a tentative commitment in a sequential and conditional process. Each Go/Kill decision is only one in a sequence of such decisions. A Go decision is not an irreversible one, nor is it a decision to commit all the resources for the entire project. Rather, gate decisions can be viewed as a series of *options decisions*, beginning with a flickering green light at the Idea Screen, with progressively stronger commitments made to the project at each successive decision point. In effect, you buy discrete chunks of the project at each gate: The entire new-product project is incrementalized—stage-wise commitments—in order to mitigate risk.

The gating procedure must maintain a reasonable balance between the errors of acceptance and errors of rejection. Too weak an evaluation procedure fails to weed out the obvious losers and misfits, resulting in misallocation of scarce resources and the start of a creeping commitment to the wrong projects. On the other hand, a too-rigid evaluation procedure results in many worthwhile projects—perhaps your next breakthrough product—being rejected. This dilemma is especially true at the very early gates, where the project is little more than an idea. Note that great ideas tend to be extremely fragile and vulnerable, and often too easy to kill.

Project evaluation is characterized by uncertainty of information and the absence of solid financial data. The initial decisions to move ahead with a project amount to decisions to invest that must be made in the *absence of reliable financial data*. The most accurate data are not available until the end of the Development stage or even after Testing and Validation and as the product nears commercialization—information on manufacturing costs, capital requirements, and expected revenue. But at the early gates, data on projected sales, costs, and capital requirements are little more than educated guesses (if they exist at all). This lack of reliable financial data throughout much of the new-product system emphasizes the *substantial differences* in the methods needed for new-product screening and predevelopment gate evaluations versus those required for conventional commercial investment decisions.

Project evaluation involves multiple objectives and therefore multiple decision criteria. The criteria used in project Go/Kill decisions should reflect the business's overall objectives, and in particular its goals for its new-product efforts. Obvious new-product objectives are to contribute to business profitability and growth. But there could be other specific ones, including opening up new windows of opportunity, operating within acceptable risk boundaries, focusing on certain arenas of strategic thrust, or simply complementing existing products. Moreover, as was seen in Chapters 2 and 3, many qualitative characteristics of a new-product project—such as product advantage, market attractiveness, and leverage—are correlated with success and financial performance, and hence should be built in as goals or "desired characteristics" as part of the evaluation criteria.

The evaluation method must be realistic and easy to use. Project-evaluation tools must be user friendly. In short, they must be sufficiently simple and time-efficient that they can be used by a group of executives in a meeting setting. Data requirements, operational and computational procedures, and interpretation of results must all be straightforward. At the same time, the evaluation method must be realistic. For example, it cannot entail so many simplifying assumptions that the result is no longer valid. Many mathematical and operations research evaluation tools fail on this point, largely because their simplifying assumptions render the method unrealistic, whereas some of the bubble diagram approaches introduced in the previous chapter are viewed as a little simplistic.

The Structure of Gates

A little structure at gate meetings goes a long way toward improving the effectiveness and efficiency of your business's decision-making. Well-designed gates and gate meetings have a common format, with three main components—see Figure 9.5:

1. *Deliverables:* expectations must be made clear! Too often, project leaders do not understand the expectations of senior management, hence they arrive at gate meetings either *lacking the vital information* that senior management needs in order to make a timely go/kill decision, or produce *too much of the wrong information.* So gates must define *visible deliverables in advance.* These are what the project leader and team must deliver to the gate—they are the results of actions in the preceding stage; these

Figure 9.5: All Gates Have a Common Structure

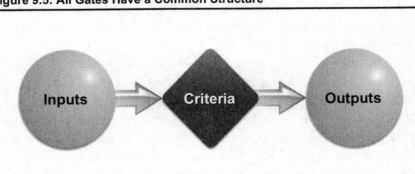

- **Inputs:** A prescribed list of "deliverables" that the project leader and project team present to the gate
- **Criteria:** A set of Go/Kill and prioritization criteria that the project is judged on
- **Outputs:** A decision: Go/Kill/Hold/Recycle
  If Go: approved Action Plan and resources are committed

Artwork courtesy of Dave Caissy

listed deliverables for a gate become the *objectives* of the project leader and team. A *standard menu of deliverables* is specified as the entry to each gate—for example, at gate 3, the deliverables list might be: "a business case along with the proposed project plan with needed resources listed." Often these required deliverables are in the form of templates.

Even for *Agile-Stage-Gate* projects, the *end points of the stage*—the expected deliverables—are still *specified, firm, and clear.* In *Agile-Stage-Gate* as noted in chapter 6, the initial action plan (or schedule or forward plan) for the next stage is *fairly tentative*—both the action plan and the product definition evolve during the stage. But the end-point of the stage is not tentative—it's firm: at the end of the business case stage, for example, the expected deliverable is a "business case"; and at the end of the development stage, the expected deliverables are "a developed product, ready for full field trials; and an updated business case." Each stage's expected deliverables are clear—clear goals for the project team!

> **Gates have a common structure:**
>
> - Inputs (deliverables)
> - Decision criteria
> - Outputs—Go/Kill/Hold/Recycle

2. *Criteria:* in order to make good decisions, gatekeepers need decision criteria—criteria that are operational (meaning, they are really used at gate

meetings), visible, and clearly understood by all. These criteria are what the project is judged against in order to make the go/kill and prioritization decisions. These criteria are usually a standard set for each gate, but change somewhat from gate to gate. They include both financial and qualitative criteria, and are broken down into required (must-meet or knockout) characteristics versus desired characteristics useful for project prioritization (should-meet items).

3. *Outputs:* too often, project-review meetings end with a rather vague decision. Ask any three people who attended the meeting about what decisions were made, and you're likely to hear three different answers. Thus, gates must have clearly articulated outputs. Outputs are the results of the gate meeting and include a decision (go/kill/hold/recycle) and a path forward. There are only four, sometimes five, possible decisions from a gate meeting; the decision cannot be to "defer the decision":

- *Go* means just that—the project is approved, and the resources are committed by the gatekeepers, both people and money, for the next stage; the action plan or forward plan is approved, along with the timeline and interim milestones; and the deliverables for the next gate are agreed to, along with a date for the next gate. (For *Agile-Stage-Gate* projects, the higher level, tentative forward plan for the entire stage is approved, along with an approximate date for the next gate; in some firms, the gate approves the project only for a discrete number of sprints—perhaps two or three—after which management revisits the project via a quick "check-in.")
- *Conditional Go**—the project is approved, and resources committed as above, but subject to a condition being met within a specified time frame. Some companies allow this conditional go decision; but there are risks, too—that the condition is never met and the project continues unchecked.
- *Kill* means "terminate the project"—stop all work on it, and spend no more time or money here. And don't resurrect the project under a new name in a few months' time! Resources are reassigned to better projects.
- *Hold* means that the project passes the gate criteria—it's an OK project—but that better projects are available or resources are not available for it. A Hold decision is a prioritization issue.

---

* Most firms do not allow a Conditional Go decision—it's either Go Forward, Go Back, Hold, or Kill.

- *Recycle* is analogous to "rework" on a production line: Go back and redo or fix some tasks in the previous stage, this time doing them right. Recycle signals that the project team has not delivered what was required. (For *Agile-Stage-Gate* projects, there are no Recycles at the end of sprints within a stage—rather, continue to the next sprint and complete the unfinished or backlogged tasks. But the option of a Recycle decision at a gate remains, even for *Agile-Stage-Gate* projects.)

Gates as Quality-Control Checkpoints

Gates are essentially the quality-control checkpoints in the innovation process, the occasion when you and your leadership team address two fundamental quality questions:

- Are you doing this project right?
- And are you doing the right project?

Thus "right projects right" becomes the motto for good gates. These two quality issues boil down to three main topics for the gate meeting:

Readiness Check:
- Have the steps in the previous stage been executed in a quality fashion?
- Have the project leader and team done their job well?
- Are the deliverables in good shape—is there data integrity?

Business Evaluation:
- Is this a good investment?
- Does the project (continue to) look like an attractive one from an economic and business standpoint?
- How does the project compare to other active projects?
- Are the proposed action plan and the resources requested reasonable and sound?
- Do you have the resources available, or could they be found without hurting other active projects?

Note that these two topics are separate issues and should be debated separately. For example, often a project team does a superb job but has its project put on hold, simply because there are better projects to do. Unless the debate on "quality of execution" is separated from "business rationale," the team may have

Figure 9.6: Gates Are a Three-Part Decision to Commit Resources

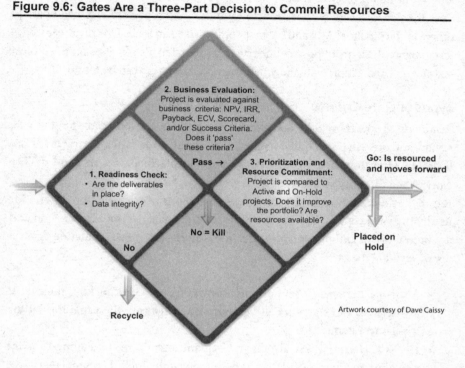

2. Business Evaluation: Project is evaluated against business criteria: NPV, IRR, Payback, ECV, Scorecard, and/or Success Criteria. Does it 'pass' these criteria?

1. Readiness Check:
- Are the deliverables in place?
- Data integrity?

Pass →

3. Prioritization and Resource Commitment: Project is compared to Active and On-Hold projects. Does it improve the portfolio? Are resources available?

Go: Is resourced and moves forward

No = Kill

No

Placed on Hold

Recycle

Artwork courtesy of Dave Caissy

the impression that it is being chastised by senior management for the job it did. And morale suffers needlessly.

A Three-Part Diamond Decision

Gates can thus be viewed as a *three-part diamond decision process*—see Figure 9.6. The first part of the gate meeting is a "readiness check" and deals with the deliverables: The focus is on the content of the deliverables, the quality of work underlying them, and *data integrity*. If the project fails on these readiness-check criteria, the decision is not Kill, but rather Recycle—stop the meeting and instruct the project team to go back and get it right.

Next, the meeting shifts to the *business evaluation*—that is, is the project a worthwhile investment? Here the various models and tools introduced in the previous chapter are used: the financial tools, scorecards, and success criteria. If the project fails these business criteria, then the decision is Kill, as shown in Figure 9.6.

The final part of the gate meeting turns to *prioritization and approval of resources*. Recall that in the event of a Go decision, resources must be committed—no hollow gates allowed! But just because a project "passes" the business evaluation criteria does not necessarily mean it moves forward! Now the emphasis shifts to looking at this project *in relation to the other active projects*—for example, how does the new project's NPV, Productivity Index, and scorecard score compare to others in the pipeline? Mix and balance could also be an issue: Do you already have too many of this type of project underway? Discussion also focuses on the project team's proposed action plan and whether or not resources can be found.

Types of Gate Criteria

Readiness check: These address whether the project is even ready for the gate review and are usually handled in checklist format—one rating per required deliverable. Questions are: Are the deliverables in place? Based on good quality work? Data integrity satisfactory?

Business evaluation: Each gate has its own list of business-evaluation criteria for use by the gatekeepers. These criteria are what the gate decision is based on and are both Go/Kill and project-prioritization criteria. Business-evaluation criteria are of several types:

- *Must-meet criteria:* These are preliminary Yes/No or knockout questions; a single No can signal a Kill decision. Checklists are the usual format for must-meet items.
- *Go/Kill criteria:* These are typically quantitative criteria. Failing to meet any one can signal a Kill decision. These usually include financial criteria and hurdles.
- *Should-meet or prioritization criteria:* These are highly desirable project characteristics—such as competitive advantage—but a "No" or zero on one question won't necessarily kill the project; rather, these questions are scored and a point count or project score is determined.
- Scorecards handle the should-meet questions, and financial criteria (Go/Kill) can also be built into the scorecard.

In the design of a gating system, the must-meet criteria or *checklist business questions* are efficient culling questions to ensure that the project meets minimum standards in terms of strategic alignment, company policies, feasibility, and so on. These questions are designed more to weed out obvious losers, "nonstarters," and misfit projects, especially at the early gates, rather than to give a strong green light. Examples include:

- Is the new project within the strategic mandate of your business?
- Is it consistent with your company policies on ethics, the environment, safety, and legality?

- Are there any evident showstoppers or killer variables (or the absence of these)?
- Are you capable of undertaking the project? Or is the project's scope just too big?

A "no" to these questions—for example, the lack of a strategic mandate or contravention of company's ethics policies—is enough to kill the project.

Next are *Go/Kill criteria*, which typically are quantitative items that are compared to a minimum acceptable hurdle. Financial criteria are typical. Examples might be:

- Is the NPV (or ECV) positive (note that the NPV is calculated at the acceptable hurdle rate for this type of investment; thus a positive NPV signifies that the project clears the hurdle rate)?
- Is the Productivity Index higher than a minimum, or higher than the average in the current portfolio?
- Is the Payback Period less than three years?
- Is the Internal Rate of Return (IRR) greater than 30 percent?

The Project Attractiveness Score based on the scorecard can also be a Go/Kill criterion: This score must clear a minimum hurdle (usually about sixty to sixty-five points out of a possible one hundred). Success criteria, if used, can be introduced here as well: Does the project meet or exceed the success criteria previously agreed to?

> Don't mix the various gate criteria—it gets confusing at the gate meeting. Rather, split them into logical categories:
> - Readiness check criteria (a checklist)
> - Must-meet—culling or knockout criteria (used at earlier gates)
> - Go/Kill and prioritization—financial criteria, scorecard criteria, and success criteria

By contrast, the *should-meet criteria* capture the *relative attractiveness* of the project for purposes of prioritization. Example questions include:

- Is the market attractive—a large and growing one? How attractive?
- Is this familiar technology to us—do we have the technical skills in-house?
- Can the product utilize existing plant and production equipment/technology? How easily?
- Will the product have sustainable competitive advantage? How much?

These should-meet or "relative attractiveness" and prioritization questions are best handled in scorecard format, introduced in the previous chapter (see

Figures 8.15 and 8.16 for examples of excellent and proven scorecards). A *no* or *negative* answer to any one of these scorecard questions usually won't kill the project. But *enough low scores* may indicate that the project is simply not attractive enough to pursue. The Project Attractiveness Score—the weighted or unweighted addition of the scorecard scores—is a key input to the Go/Kill decision and can also be used to judge the relative attractiveness of the new project versus existing projects right at the gate meeting.

Financial criteria can also be built into the scorecard, as shown in Figure 8.15. Here, a zero score on these financial criteria kills the project: The NPV (or ECV), the IRR, and the Payback Period are Go/Kill criteria at gate meetings—these financial numbers must exceed a minimum hurdle, otherwise the project is dead. But these same financial criteria can also be used as *prioritization criteria*—the higher the better—and the financial factor in Figure 8.15 is thus added to the five qualitative factors to yield an overall Project Attractiveness Score. Additionally, when converted into the Productivity Index, the NPV (or ECV) becomes a very useful prioritization criterion and can be used to compare the new project to other projects in the pipeline to determine its relative attractiveness, as illustrated in Figure 9.4.

Suggestion: Most firms do not have a visible list of Go/Kill and prioritization criteria for selecting projects (other than financial criteria, which are probably not the best ones to use in any event, especially at early gates). If you lack visible criteria, develop a set. Consider using a set of *must-meet questions in a checklist format* as culling questions, especially for early gates, and a short list of *Go/Kill and should-meet questions together in a scorecard format* to help make the Go/Kill decision and to determine relative project attractiveness. Be sure to use these criteria at your gate meeting, discussing each question and reaching closure on it. If you do, chances are your gatekeeping group will make more objective, more reasoned, and better decisions.

TIPS AND HINTS IN GATE GOVERNANCE
Prioritizing Projects at Gates

When assessing the relative attractiveness of the new project versus active projects in the pipeline—for example, by comparing the Productivity Index or scorecard score—only assess the new project's relative position. *Don't try to reprioritize all the other projects* in the pipeline. First, you don't have complete data on the other projects at this gate meeting; second, you don't have enough time; and most important, it's poor practice to prioritize another project when that team's members are not in the room to defend their project! The periodic reprioritization of projects takes place at portfolio reviews, not at gate meetings.

Consistent Gate Criteria from Gate to Gate

As much as possible, try to maintain consistency of gate criteria from gate to gate. This makes the gating system *easier to understand* for the gatekeepers; it also means that *projects at different stages can be compared* to each other. This is particularly important from Gate 2 onward, as typically here the project "enters the portfolio" and becomes part of the portfolio—it shows up in the rank-ordered lists, pie charts, and bubble diagrams shown at portfolio reviews.

The financial criteria must obviously change from gate to gate, especially at the early gates. For example, while it makes sense to look at NPV, IRR, and the Payback Period at Gate 3 (after all, a full Business Case is a deliverable to Gate 3), using such criteria at Gate 1, the Idea Screen, is not only impractical—the data are not available—it is also harmful. That's where the scorecard method proves its worth, because here many of the scorecard criteria can be applied from gate to gate. For example, consider the scorecard in Figure 8.15. Note that criteria such as strategic fit, product advantage, and leverages core competencies can be applied at Gate 1 almost as easily as at Gate 3 or 4. And most of the other criteria, such as market attractiveness and technical feasibility, can be estimated reasonably well even at early gates.

Solution: Keep the main criteria—the six factors in Figure 8.15—consistent from gate to gate. If necessary, modify the subquestions for some of the factors. For example, the Financial Reward versus Risk factor essentially asks the question: Can you make money? At Gate 3, the subquestions are very specific and based on hard data:

- The financial return (NPV, IRR, or ECV)
- The Payback Period
- The Productivity Index.

At Gate 1, the fundamental question is still the same: Can you make money? But create a new list of feasible subquestions that are much more qualitative, such as:

- What's the size of the prize (qualitatively, from "modest" to "huge")?
- What are the odds you can make money here (from "really doubtful" to "easily")?
- How likely are the commercial assumptions (from "low probability" to "highly likely")?
- Would you invest your own money in this venture (from "not in a million years" to "here's my check")?

These questions rely on qualitative scales, but they can be addressed at Gate 1 even with limited information.

Different Criteria for Different Types of Projects

Would you use the same criteria to evaluate stocks, bonds, and real-estate investments? Of course not! So it is in product innovation. Thus far, much of the discussion of selection criteria has focused on *major new-product projects*; note that the financial and scorecard criteria outlined above (and in Figure 8.15) are for major and more innovative product developments. But many development projects are smaller, lower risk, and more predictable, and they merit somewhat simpler evaluation criteria. The scalable system portrayed in Figure 5.4 reveals three different versions of *Stage-Gate* that often correspond to three different Strategic Buckets of projects. Gate criteria for the *XPress* and *Lite* projects are usually much simpler than for major new-product projects. For example:

- For smaller, medium-risk projects, namely extensions, updates, modifications—so-called "renovation" projects—use the three-stage *Stage-Gate Lite* system shown in Figure 5.4. Additionally, the Go/Kill criteria should be easier to compute and easier to use than the traditional NPV used for larger projects. For example, use the Payback Period calculation. The advantage of a payback calculation is that the required estimates are less demanding: It's an easier calculation, and you only have to forecast sales, costs, and earnings as far into the future as the payback year—perhaps only a few years forward—rather than the traditional five-year projections required in an NPV calculation.

    A simpler Productivity Index should also be employed—for example, one based on the Sales Impact[*] divided by Person Days of work remaining in the project is common.

$$\text{Productivity Index} = \frac{\text{Sales Impact}}{\text{Person Days of Work Remaining}}$$
(for Lite projects)

    This relatively simple-to-calculate metric can be used at both gate meetings and portfolio reviews, and helps to position (rank) the project against

---

[*] Standardize on two or three years' sales impact. "Sales impact" is the dollar sales created by the new item, or the dollar sales protected by the new item, cumulative over a two- to three-year period. Alternately, use the Gross Profit earned (Sales x Profit Margin percent, in dollars) over a two- to three-year period.

Figure 9.7: Proven Gate 3 Scorecard for Lower Risk *Stage-Gate-Lite* Projects—Improvements, Modifications, Extensions, Renovations

Scoring Criteria	0	5	10	Score (0-10)
1. Strategic Fit and Importance • Degree of fit with business's innovation strategy • Importance of project to the innovation strategy	Is not aligned with innovation strategy; not Important to do: KILL	Moderately aligned with innovation strategy; moderately important to do	Aligns very well with innovation strategy; very important to do	
2. Competitive Rationale • Existence of competitive rationale to undertake the project (e.g., needed update, competitive threat, customer request, etc.)	No competitive reasons exist to do the project	Moderate competitive reasons exist to do the project	Strong competitive reasons exist to do the project	
3. Technical Ease of Execution • Level of difficulty to achieve a technical solution	Technical solution is difficult to achieve; a lot of R&D work	Technical solution is moderately easy to achieve; some R&D work but doable	Technical solution is easy and fast to achieve; straightforward; minimal R&D work	
4. Manufacturing/ Operations Ease of Implementation • Degree of modification required to current manufacturing/ operations process	High level of manufacturing/operations process modification required; new equipment	Moderate modification of manufacturing/ operations process required	No modification of manufacturing/operations process required	
5. Financial Reward vs. Financial Risk • Financial reward based on Payback Period and Productivity Index • Level of financial risk	Payback Period > 5 years Productivity Index (3 yr. Sales Impact/Person-days) < hurdle; a financial risk to do: KILL	Payback Period about 3 years Productivity Index (3 yr. Sales Impact/Person-days) => hurdle; acceptable financial risk	Payback Period < 2 years Productivity Index (3 yr. Sales Impact/Person-days) >> hurdle; very low financial risk	

other similar projects in the same bucket. The acceptable or cut-off Productivity Index is often the average of the other projects underway (bare minimum: the average of bottom third of other projects in this bucket); and thus any new project added improves the overall Productivity Index of the entire portfolio.

Figure 9.7 shows a scorecard for Gate 3 for these medium-risk Lite projects: Fewer criteria, and also simpler financial criteria, are employed than in the scorecard for major projects.

- Scorecards can also be used for *very low risk projects*, for example, salesforce requests. These are often single customer requests, requiring minimal development, and no CAPEX in the plant. Such projects, although individually quite small, collectively often consume a lot of resources, and thus should go through a gated model: the two-stage XPress system in Figure 5.4. The scorecard used is tailored to suit the size and nature of the project, and is substantially different from Figures 8.15 or 9.7. For example, a major paper-products company employs a "Marketing Scorecard" for sales-initiated customer-request projects—a handful of simple questions that gauge the importance of the customer, impact on future business, cost-benefit of the project, and ease and speed of doing the project.

Figure 9.8: Gatekeeper Best Practices in Best-Performing Businesses

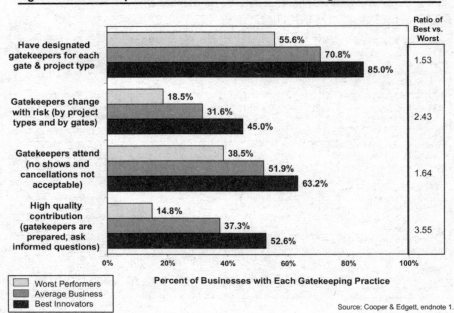

Percent of Businesses with Each Gatekeeping Practice

Worst Performers
Average Business
Best Innovators

Source: Cooper & Edgett, endnote 1.

Another type of project is the technology-development project. Here, traditional financial criteria are next to useless, because so little is known regarding the eventual commercial impact of the new technology or technology platform—see Figure 5.5. Thus, the scorecard in Figure 8.16 is recommended for such technology or science projects—qualitative and strategic questions, with only "guesstimates" of the size of the prize.

> Gatekeepers own the resources required for the project to move to the next stage. They are a cross-functional group of senior people. Consider having different gatekeepers for different gates, and for different types (risk levels) of projects. Best innovators do!

Suggestion: Take note of the tips and hints above. First, don't try to reprioritize all your projects at your gate meetings—that's the role of a portfolio review. Next, try to design criteria that are fairly consistent from gate to gate: They're easier to follow this way, and projects can now be compared even though they are in different stages. The scorecard model works particularly well here. Finally, recognize that different categories or buckets of projects call for different evaluation criteria (scorecards) as well as different *Stage-Gate* systems: Lite, Xpress, and TD.

WHO ARE THE GATEKEEPERS?

Who are the people tending these critical gates—the gatekeepers who make the Go/Kill and resource-allocation decisions and who are essential to making the new-product process work? Sometimes it is unclear just who should undertake project reviews and whose authorizations are needed for a project to proceed. Defining the *locus of decision-making*—the management team that makes the vital Go/Kill decisions at gates—is an important feature of many firms' idea-to-launch processes. Most companies, 70.8 percent according to our research, have clearly designated gatekeepers—see Figure 9.8. This is especially true for best performing innovators, with 85 percent having defined gatekeepers.[13]

The choice of the gatekeepers is specific to each business and its organizational structure. But here are some rules of thumb:

- The first rule is simple: The gatekeepers at any gate must have the *authority to approve the resources* required for the next stage. That is, they are the *owners of the resources* required by the project team to move the project through the next stage.
- Since resources are required from different functions, the gatekeepers must *represent different functional areas*—R&D, marketing, engineering, operations, and perhaps sales, purchasing, and quality assurance. There's not much sense having a gatekeeper group just from one functional area, such as marketing or R&D!

Different gatekeepers at each gate: In some businesses, the gate decision-makers remain the same from gate to gate, throughout the entire project and regardless of project type—for reasons of consistency. But in other firms, especially the best innovators, the *gatekeepers change depending on the risk* associated with the decision. This is true even in larger or more risky projects. More senior people are the gatekeepers at points where significant commitments are required, such as at the "Go to Development" and "Go to Launch" decisions, Gates 3 and 5. By contrast, mid management staffs the earlier gates—for example, Gate 1, the idea screen, or Gate 2—where commitments and hence risks are lower. In 31.6 percent of businesses, gatekeepers completely change from gate to gate, according to our research, and much more so among best innovators (45 percent); but in 26.2 percent of businesses, the gatekeeping group is totally static, with no change at all from gate to gate—see Figure 9.8:[14]

- Gatekeepers can also include people who will be *key to the project's success* at some future point. For example, for technology-development projects, the gatekeepers at early gates are largely from the technology department, but many companies ensure that important people from the business units that will ultimately commercialize the technology attend these early gates, even though they are not committing their resources at these early stages.

- There should also be some *continuity of gatekeepers* from gate to gate. In short, the composition of the evaluation group should not change totally, requiring a total start-from-the-beginning justification of the project at each gate. For example, some members of the leadership team—the heads of marketing and R&D, for example—might be at Gate 2, with the full leadership team at Gate 3 for major projects.

Gatekeepers for different project types: Different types of projects often have *different levels of gatekeepers. Stage-Gate* is scalable—there are Full, XPress, and Lite versions of the system, depending on project size and risk (Figure 5.4). Mid management personnel may serve as gatekeepers at all three gates for lower-risk projects in the Lite version, with more senior people—the leadership team of the business—being the gatekeepers for higher-risk projects. Almost half of best innovators (45 percent) employ this practice, which is far less prevalent among worst performers—see Figure 9.8.[15]

An example: In one major financial institution, there are two levels of gatekeepers from Gate 3 onward:

- A senior Gate 3 to 5 gatekeeping group for larger, riskier projects (total cost greater than $500,000). These are the senior VPs from the bank.
- A midlevel gatekeeping group—for lower-risk or smaller projects (coincidentally, this is also the Gate 2 gatekeeping group for major projects).

Some businesses also consider geography in assigning gatekeepers. Our research shows an almost even split here: 46.9 percent of businesses have gatekeepers with oversight for projects spanning multiple geographic locations, while a slight majority (53.1) percent have not opted for globalized gatekeeping—it's strictly local or domestic gatekeeping. There is no significant difference between best and worst performers here—see Figure 9.8.

HOW TO RUN GATES

Gates must be fair, and be perceived to be fair by the project team. They must also be transparent—there should be no room for politics and "games" by gatekeepers. Gates must also be effective, yielding good decisions and sound resource allocations to the right projects. And gates must be efficient, yielding decisions in a timely fashion and not dragging on for the whole day. Thus, best-practice firms develop *professional gate protocols*, such as the following, a comprehensive set of procedures borrowed from a handful of best-practice companies.

Gate Protocols

Gatekeepers must operate as an effective *decision-making team*. And all teams, even senior people, need *rules of engagement*. A sample list is provided on the following page. It's critical that your gatekeeper group develop a similar list of behavior rules and then commit to abiding by them.

> Learn from the best-innovator companies. Develop a protocol for your gate meetings, including rules of engagement. And make sure there's a process manager in the room with the authority to facilitate the meeting and enforce discipline.

Gate meetings, although held when needed by project teams, are usually scheduled monthly for the leadership team of the business, often in conjunction with another executive meeting that day. Any project leader can "sign up" a project for a scheduled gate meeting with sufficient notice. Usually about sixty to ninety minutes of meeting time is allotted per major project (Gate 3 onward).

The deliverables are sent to the gatekeepers about three working days prior to the meeting. Project teams are asked to use a standard format for their deliverables (for example, templates—but keep these short!) so that gatekeepers can compare projects more easily. When reading the advance material, if a gatekeeper has a major question or spots a showstopper, they should contact the gate facilitator or project team in advance—no surprise attacks at the gate meeting!

Hold the meeting! Cancellations or postponements are unacceptable unless the deliverables are not ready. And hold the meeting even if a Kill decision is imminent, in order to achieve closure, agree on lessons learned, and celebrate a correct Kill. Note: A correct Kill is deemed a success—*you just saved yourself a bag of money and heap of trouble!*

Video- and tele-conferencing are acceptable, but make sure you have the robust telecommunications facilities and that they work! The project team is present where geographically possible (or via video- or tele-conference). Usually the team stays for the entire gate meeting, hears the full discussion, sees the scoring, and listens to the reasons underlying the decision (although some firms allow a private discussion by gatekeepers for which the project team is asked to leave the room for a few minutes).

A gate facilitator should be present—usually this is the *Stage-Gate* process manager. This person is analogous to the referee on a football field—not the

A TYPICAL LIST OF GATEKEEPER RULES OF ENGAGEMENT

1. Gatekeepers must hold the gate meeting and be there:
   - Postponed or canceled meetings are not an option
   - If you cannot attend, your vote is "yes" (or send a designate with full "voting" authority)

2. Gatekeepers must have received, read, and prepared for the meeting:
   - Contact the gate facilitator or project team if there are showstoppers
   - No "surprise attacks" at the gate meeting

3. Gatekeepers cannot request information or answers beyond that specified in the deliverables:
   - No playing "I gotcha"
   - Not a forum to demonstrate your machoism, political clout, or intellectual prowess

4. Gatekeepers cannot "beat up" the presenter:
   - Give the Team an uninterrupted period to present
   - Q&A must be fair—not vicious

5. Gatekeepers must make their decision based on the criteria for that gate:
   - Gatekeepers must review each criterion and reach a conclusion
   - A scoring sheet should be filled out by each gatekeeper at the gate meeting

6. Gatekeepers must be disciplined:
   - No hidden agendas
   - No invisible criteria

7. Decisions must be based on facts and criteria—not emotion and gut feel:
   - All projects must be treated fairly and consistently
   - All must pass through the gate—no special treatment for executive sponsored or "pet" projects
   - All projects are subjected to the same criteria and with the same rigor

8. A decision must be made:

   - Within that working day
   - If deliverables are there, you cannot defer the decision
   - Remember: This is a system built for speed—gatekeepers cannot create unnecessary delays

9. The project team must be informed of the decision:

   - Immediately
   - Face-to-face (not by e-mail)

10. If the decision is go, the gatekeepers support the agreed-upon action plan:

    - Commit the resources (people, person-days, and money)
    - Agree to the release times for people on the project team
    - No one gatekeeper can override the Go decision or renege on agreed upon resources

11. If the decision is hold:

    - The gatekeepers must try to find resources
    - Cannot remain on Hold for more than three months—up or out!
    - This time limit puts pressure on gatekeepers to make tougher decisions (some real Kills) or commit more resources overall

biggest player on the field, but the person with the whistle, and with ultimate control of the meeting.

A head gatekeeper is often nominated or designated, although this is optional. The head gatekeeper's role is to follow up with the project leader on loose ends, for example, making sure that the condition is met in the case of a Conditional Go decision.

How a Typical Gate Meeting Should Work

The gate procedure is typically this: The project team has fifteen minutes to present, uninterrupted. Limit the number of PowerPoint slides to about ten. Further, the team should not regurgitate the deliverables package but deal only with key issues—what the risks are and what decisions are requested by the project team—as well as any new issues. Then follows a question-and-answer session, which the process manager moderates (the process manager ensures that the gatekeepers stay on topic and ask relevant and fair questions; the process manager must have the authority to call a time-out).

Once conversation has died down, the process manager takes gatekeepers through a list of criteria, starting with the readiness check questions, to determine whether the deliverables are in good shape—see Figure 9.6. Use a readiness checklist. Then follows the must-meet or knockout culling questions: Often simply showing these on the projector screen is sufficient, asking gatekeepers to reply by exception only.

The meeting now shifts to the Go/Kill and prioritization criteria. For example, the financial criteria are discussed, and the scorecard is handed out. More discussion ensues and then the project is scored (gatekeepers are asked to keep their scores to themselves during this period of thoughtful reflection). The scorecards are collected and inputted immediately, and results are displayed on the projector screen as in Figure 9.9. (If the project team has done a self-scoring, their results can now be displayed on the screen next to the gatekeepers' scores, as illustrated on the "Team" line in Figure 9.9.)

In the event of major differences of opinion between gatekeepers, as in Figure 9.9, the process manager tries to get the differences on the table and move toward resolution. For example, the process manager identifies the high and low scorers and asks them to explain their positions. One by one, the process manager leads the gatekeepers through the scoring criteria, reaching an understanding and consensus on each.

For the Pass versus Kill decision in Figure 9.6, the process manager leads a review of the financial criteria—the NPV (or ECV), Payback, and IRR numbers versus the hurdles; the results of the sensitivity analysis; and the Project Attractiveness Score. A Pass versus Kill decision is agreed. A Pass does not necessarily mean Go, however; it just means that the project meets minimum standards or hurdles, but it may not be the best project to do.

Now *prioritization* and *resource commitment* become the topic. Often the process manager displays a list of active projects that shows their Project Attractiveness Scores, NPVs, and Productivity Indices, as in Figure 9.4. Gatekeepers then get a feel for how attractive this new project is relative to the others in the pipeline. Pie charts and a bubble diagram showing the current portfolio (previous chapter) can also be displayed, so gatekeepers can see where the new project fits in, and whether it helps to balance (or unbalance) the portfolio. The project team's proposed action plan and resource needs are now reviewed. And issues of resource availability are discussed.

The decision faced now is Go versus Hold, as shown in Figure 9.6. The gate decision is now agreed: Go/Kill/Hold/Recycle. If Go, a project-prioritization level is established and the action plan and deliverables for the next gate are agreed to. The resource commitments are made, and a date for the next gate is

Figure 9.9: Display the Scorecard Scores at the Gate Meeting—Promotes a Rich Discussion and Better Go/Kill Decision

Project: Monty-21

Project Attractiveness Score (PAS): 34.4 out of 60 or 57%					Decision: KILL		

Evaluator	Strategic	Product Advant-age	Market Attract-iveness	Leverage Compe-tencies	Technical Feasi-bility	Reward vs. Risk	Score out of 60
JCC	0	10	4	7	7	10	38.0
MB	10	7	4	4	7	4	36.0
SJC	10	10	7	4	4	4	39.0
NCC	107	7	7	4	7	0	35.0
FK	7	7	4	4	7	0	29.0
FM	7	5	4	4	4	0	24.0
GRT	10	10	4	7	7	4	42.0
HH	7	7	4	7	7	0	32.0
Total:	61	63	38	41	50	22	275.0
Mean:	7.6	7.9	4.8	5.1	6.3	2.8	34.4
Team:	10.0	7.0	4.0	4.0	7.0	4.0	36.0
Std Dev:	3.42	1.89	1.39	1.55	1.39	3.54	

Overview of Project Score

Artwork courtesy of Dave Caissy

set. And the project team is informed in person—immediately (although usually the project team is still in the room).

Hint: Decide in advance how consensus will be reached. This is not the Supreme Court and split decisions are not acceptable—it must be a unanimous Go or Kill. Some firms use the "majority rules" decision rule; in other firms, it's a democratic decision, except the boss or senior gatekeeper has 51 percent of the votes.

> *An example:* In one major bank, the senior executive at the gate meeting made the "split decision rule" very clear: "I let my executive team [at the gate meeting] make the decision. But if they cannot reach a decision within the hour, then I make the decision—this democracy quickly becomes a dictatorship."

I also include a tongue-in-cheek summary of ways to ruin gate meetings—each one is based on real-life experiences. Avoid these behaviors at all costs—see the box entitled, "The Ten Best Ways to Ruin Gate Meetings." Finally, here are a few best practices for gatekeepers that our research has uncovered—details perhaps, but as said above, then the *devil is in the details*:

Gatekeepers schedule and actually attend the gate meetings: Compliance with the process is always an issue, especially for gatekeepers. The fact is that in about half of the businesses we have studied, gatekeeper "no shows" and

THE TEN BEST WAYS TO RUIN A GATE MEETING

1. Miss most meetings. When you do come, start reading the materials (deliverables) as the meeting starts.
2. Don't give the project team a chance to make its presentation. Attack with tough questions as soon as the team puts up its first PPT slide.
3. Always ask for information that has not been specifically requested; this way you keep the project team off-balance.
4. Attack the team with vicious, rude questioning. Make sure these junior people really live in fear of the executive gatekeepers.
5. Ignore the stated criteria at the gates. Make the decision from the gut. And ignore the facts—use your own opinion instead.
6. Dwell only on the financial projections. Spend at least three-quarters of the meeting arguing over numbers. The rest of the information doesn't matter.
7. Your role is that of a judge. Never offer any help or advice.
8. If in doubt, don't make a decision. Keep the project team waiting around for several weeks—it shows who's boss.
9. Don't prioritize projects. Just keep adding projects to the active list. They'll figure out a way to get the project done—and there's always some slack in the organization.
10. Demand that the project team reduce the timelines and resources requested. And resources committed— they can be rescinded at any time. Resource commitments are not firm.

gate-meeting cancellations are common. By contrast, among best-performing innovators, there is more discipline: Virtually all of the key decision-makers invited to participate as gatekeepers attend the gate meetings; gate-meeting cancellations are not acceptable; and when a gatekeeper cannot attend, the meeting still goes ahead (gatekeeper substitutes are often allowed, with full voting authority).

Gatekeepers are prepared—they are engaged and properly contribute to the gate decision meeting: I often witness gatekeepers who arrive at gate meetings poorly prepared and not informed enough to make a good decision. Indeed, almost two-thirds of businesses we have studied indicate that the quality of the gatekeepers' contributions is not high. In best-performing innovators, however, gatekeepers consistently make high-quality contributions. That is, each gatekeeper *comes prepared* for the meeting, has *read the project deliverables*, and asks *insightful questions* to understand the risks, payoffs, and costs associated with the project. This practice is the *weakest area* for the worst performers, less than 15 percent of whom report high-quality participation from gatekeepers—see Figure 9.8.

Red Flags to Spot Projects in Trouble

What happens when a project gets into trouble within a stage—for example, it misses milestones, or its financial outlook changes? Do you wait until the next gate to address the problem and kill or redirect the project? Definitely not! But don't do what some firms mistakenly do: build in a host of additional gates within long stages. That becomes a bureaucratic nightmare.

The simple answer is to employ *red flags*. A red-flag situation is much like a yellow flag at a NASCAR racetrack. When the yellow flag is dropped, everyone takes action—there is an emergency on the racetrack. All the race cars slow down; everyone proceeds with care.

Red flags work the same way. Whenever a project gets into trouble, the project leader is required to "throw out a red flag." The flag is picked up immediately by the process manager, who meets with the team leader to discuss the seriousness of the situation; They alert the gatekeepers, and an *emergency gate meeting* may be scheduled. The notion here is not to wait out the situation but to take immediate action to correct the problem or to kill or redirect the project.

A red flag is triggered by any one of the following conditions:

- *Technical roadblocks:* whenever technical barriers are encountered that increase the development time and cost by more than 10 percent, or reduce the probability of technical success by more than 10 percent (versus the success probability estimate at the previous gate).
- *Project schedule:* if the project falls significantly (more than thirty days) behind the time line agreed to at the previous gate or if two milestones in a row are missed.
- *Product features and specifications:* if the product design or product specifications are revised or relaxed in a way that impacts negatively on meeting a customer need or on the product definition.
- *Sales forecast:* When there is a significant change in the projected sales versus the sales estimates in the Business Case at the previous gate (that impacts on the Business Case by more than 20 percent).
- *Delivered cost:* If there is a significant change in the expected product cost versus the cost in the Business Case at the previous gate (that impacts on the Business Case by more than 20 percent).

- *Resources:* Whenever a major functional department fails to meet its ongoing resource commitments agreed to in the project's approved action plan.
- *Business Case:* If any change occurs that significantly impacts the Business Case and the financial outlook for the project versus the financial forecasts accepted at the previous gate (by more than 20 percent).

Whenever any of the above occur, the project leader throws out a red flag. Action is taken.

Suggestion: The details of the governance system are fundamental to making *Stage-Gate* work. Be sure to define clearly *who the gatekeepers are*—the locus of decision-making. Note that gatekeepers may change from gate to gate, and may be different people, depending on project type, magnitude, and risk level. Think through the *protocol for the gate meeting*, using the guidelines above borrowed from leading firms. Be sure to encourage the gatekeepers to develop *rules of engagement* to minimize bad behavior, and consider the use of *red flags* to spot projects in trouble and take the needed action.

WAYS TO ACCELERATE THE GATES

The protocol and guides outlined above all help to make the gates more effective. But the need for speed and accelerated gates is still paramount, given the desire for shorter times to market and thus faster Go/Kill decisions. If a project is held up awaiting a gate for three weeks, and this happens at all five gates, that's fifteen weeks, or *almost four months of dead time*—unacceptable in today's fast-paced world. We saw in Chapter 5 ways to remove waste and bureaucracy in the idea-to-launch system, and in particular, the concept of *leaning down the gates*.

Using value-stream analysis, defining what information is really required to make the decision (keeping the deliverables lean), and creating clear expectations are some of the ways that leading firms are accelerating gate decisions and removing non-value-added work. Here are other practices that firms employ to accelerate the gates:

Self-Managed Gates

In the case of smaller and lower-risk projects, some gates are now self-managed (for example, Gates 2 and 4 in Figure 4.11). In effect, the project team conducts its own review and makes its own Go/Kill decision. One major telecommunications firm has experimented with this approach (an alternative is simply to adopt the three-stage Lite process, as in Figure 5.4).

Electronic Gates

Global development teams and gatekeeping groups mean that gate meetings in some companies have become electronic, global, and in some cases even virtual. A number of firms now employ remote electronic gates: Here, the gate deliverables are distributed to gatekeepers automatically, electronically, and globally. Then, the video conference begins, much like any other gate meeting, with the project team presenting. Gatekeepers, remotely located, score the projects from their own laptops. All input scores are then displayed on the various screens—in the meeting room as well as on gatekeepers' laptops. The use of IT—for information dissemination, the scoring and integration of scorecard results, and the meeting itself—enables these electronic gates.

Virtual Gates

With virtual gates, there is no actual gate meeting; rather, gatekeepers simply review the deliverables and electronically sign off on the Go/Kill decision, independently of each other—an electronic signature. The goal here is to reduce absenteeism of key gatekeepers, to get input of people normally not at the gate meeting, and to speed up the decision process, especially in the case of remotely located gatekeepers. Although the advantages of virtual gates are obvious, the big negative is that because no meeting actually takes place, the gatekeepers do not have the opportunity to engage in back-and-forth discussion and the learning that ensues. Hence, they make the Go/Kill decision without benefit of full knowledge.

MAKE THE GATES WORK!

I began the chapter with the statement, "As go the gates, so goes the process." Although gates may represent only sixty minutes (times five) in a project's life, they are perhaps the most critical sixty-minute segments—and make all the difference between winning and losing at product innovation. The gates must work! And so it makes sense to spend a little time and effort getting the gates right. By now, you realize that there's more to making the gates work than simply assembling a group of well-intentioned executives for a monthly meeting. There are many approaches, methods, tricks, and protocols that deliver better results, making the difference between the "normal" gate meeting—which is often inefficient and results in poor decisions (too many projects with an overabundance of weak, insignificant projects)—and meetings that are effective and efficient. The result is a stunning portfolio of high-value development projects.

10

A PRODUCT-INNOVATION STRATEGY FOR YOUR BUSINESS[1]

Strategy without tactics is the slowest route to victory.
Tactics without strategy is the noise before defeat.
—Sun Tzu, *The Art of War,* 5th century BC.

A TALE OF TWO COMPANIES

It was the best of times and the worst of times.

In the late 1990s, two large firms were growing by leaps and bounds, driven by the boom in fiber-optic communications:[2] Corning Glass, which manufactured fiber-optic cable, and Nortel Networks, which produced the boxes at each end of the cable to convert the light signal into an electronic signal. Then came the crash of 2000; overnight, both firms' sales plummeted, and their share prices plunged from over one hundred dollars to about one dollar.

Ten years later, Corning was thriving and continues to do so today, whereas Nortel went bankrupt and no longer exists. Why? How did two great and innovative companies, facing the same crisis, end up so differently almost two decades later? One reason for Nortel's demise is that the company lacked direction and an innovation strategy after the crash; instead, it limped along *from one ad hoc decision to the next*. And R&D was cut in order to save money! By contrast, Corning's senior management took charge, developed a strong product-innovation and technology strategy for the firm, and provided leadership and direction to see that strategy through.[3]

How? Corning's management took a hard look at the company's previous one hundred years of successes in innovation and what drove them. They concluded that the "repeatable keys" to success—the elements in Corning's culture and history that they could draw on to face this new challenge—were a leadership commitment, a clear understanding of the company's capabilities, a strong connection to the customer and a deep understanding of major customer problems, and a willingness to take big but well-understood risks. Strongly committed to breaking out of the crisis through innovation, management assessed Corning's core competencies, determined what they could leverage, and matched those strengths to emerging and adjacent market opportunities.

The result was a renewed innovation strategy and a three-pronged strategic attack that called for the company to grow current businesses via product-line extensions, exploit market adjacencies, and create totally new opportunities. The latter two thrusts required a heavy emphasis on exploratory research and new business development, and thus, in spite of financial challenges, R&D spending was maintained at 10 percent of sales revenue. A number of new opportunities and strategic arenas were identified and assessed, and the most promising were exploited.

The results were impressive: In less than ten years, major innovations had been realized in each of Corning's businesses, including the creation of four new business platforms and exploitation of three major market adjacencies. New-product sales had rocketed to 70 percent of annual sales, and profits moved from minus $500 million to more than $2 billion after taxes.

Interesting, both companies have excellent *Stage-Gate* new-product systems (I had helped both firms design and install their gating systems), and both firms certainly devoted the needed resources—big R&D budgets and talented people—to new-product development. But one succeeded, the other failed. The example of Corning offers some important strategic lessons: *Tactics are important, but strategy is vital!* As the Corning case illustrates, an *innovation strategy is essential* for product development and continued growth, especially in difficult times.

WIN THE BATTLE, LOSE THE WAR?

What if . . .

❑ What if your business had implemented a *Stage-Gate*® new-product system to guide new-product projects to market?

❑ And what if all your business's development projects followed the process and were executed well—good upfront homework, solid marketing input, tough Go/Kill gates, and so on?

❑ And what if your business committed the necessary resources to product development—both quality and quantity of resources?

... would the result be top performance in product innovation? Not necessarily, as seen in the two company examples above. One of the four vectors or main drivers of success in product innovation is still missing, and that driver makes the difference between winning individual battles and winning the entire new-product war. Recall the four vectors in the Innovation Diamond in Figure 1.2 in Chapter 1.

The missing vector or driver is the *business's product-innovation and technology strategy*. And it's lacking in too many businesses we have studied (see Figure 3.1 in Chapter 3). The product-innovation strategy charts the strategy for the business's entire new-product efforts. It is the master plan: It provides the direction for your enterprise's new-product efforts, and it is the essential link between your product-development effort and your total business strategy.[4]

What is Strategy?

Before we start into this new topic, do you know what the word "strategy" means? We use (and misuse) it a lot in every day conversation and in business. Today the word is defined as: a plan of action or policy designed to achieve a major or overall aim. Its roots are found in ancient Greece, where the word *stratēgia* (στρατηγία) meant the "art of the troop leader" or "generalship." Indeed, the word *strategy* was rarely used in English language writing until 1900, and even then, largely in a military context.

The first recorded book on strategy was by Sun Tzu (author of the quotation at the beginning of this chapter) who wrote the *Art of War* in the 5th century BC. There have been many military books on strategy since. Thus, much of what we know and practice regarding strategy in business—concepts such as having clear objectives, focusing one's forces (principle of mass), and deployment—have their roots in the military.

This chapter begins with a look at the *need for a product-innovation strategy*, and the hard evidence in support of strategy—facts that make it imperative that you develop a product-innovation and technology strategy for your business. The *components of an innovation strategy* are then defined. Next, *approaches to developing a product-innovation strategy* are outlined—approaches where you define and elect arenas of strategic thrust for your new-product efforts and possible attack plans.

So let's move forward, elevating ourselves above the battle—above the level of the individual new-product project, tactics, and the *Stage-Gate* system—and play the role of the general, looking at strategy and direction for the business's entire new-product effort. Let's go win the war!

Vital for Your Business

Businesses that are most likely to succeed in the development and launch of new products are those that implement a company-specific approach, driven by business objectives and strategies, with a *well-defined new-product strategy* at its core. This was one of the findings of an extensive and early study of new-product practices by Booz Allen Hamilton: The new-product strategy was viewed as instrumental to the effective identification of market and product opportunities.[5]

Our benchmarking studies also reveal that having an articulated product-innovation strategy for the business is one of the four important drivers of new-product performance. Recall the four vectors that drive innovation performance from Figure 1.2 in Chapter 1. Businesses with a defined product-innovation strategy—one that specifies goals and objectives and the role of new products, defines arenas of strategic thrust, and has a longer-term orientation—achieve better new-product results: These businesses meet their new-product sales and profit objectives more so; they boast new-product efforts with a much greater positive impact on the business; and they achieve higher success rates at launch—see Figure 3.1.

WHAT IS A PRODUCT-INNOVATION STRATEGY?

A product-innovation strategy is a *strategic master plan* that guides your business's new-product war efforts. But how does one define or describe a product-innovation strategy? The term "strategy" is widely used in business circles today. The word is derived from the ancient Greek word meaning "the art of the general" and until comparatively recently, its use was confined to the military (see side bar "What Is Strategy?"). In a business context, strategy has been defined as "the schemes whereby a firm's resources and advantages are managed [deployed] in order to surprise and surpass competitors or to exploit opportunities."[6] More specifically, strategic change is defined as "a realignment of firm's product/market environment."[7] Strategy is thus closely tied to product and market specification: Corey argues that strategy is about choosing your *markets to target*, and choosing the *products to target them* with.[8]

Business strategy here refers to the *business'* strategy; and your *product-innovation and technology strategy* is a component of that business strategy (or flows from your business strategy).[9] By *business and product-innovation strategy*,

Figure 10.1. A Framework for Developing a Product-Innovation Strategy—Begins with Goals (top) and Moves Through to Tactics (bottom)

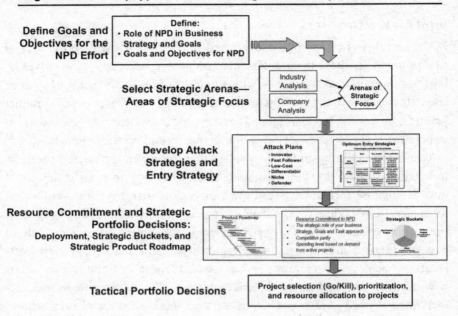

I do not mean a vaguely worded statement of intent, one that approaches a vision or mission statement. Rather I mean operational, action-specific strategies. A business's product-innovation and technology strategy includes:

1. The goals and objectives for your business's total product-innovation efforts.
2. The role of product innovation: how new products tie into achieving your business's overall goals.
3. Strategic arenas defined—arenas of strategic focus: the markets, technologies, product categories on which to focus your new-product or R&D efforts (including priorities).
4. Deployment—your spending allocations (or splits) across these arenas (R&D funds or people, possibly marketing and capital resources for developments)—including the use of strategic buckets.
5. Attack plans—how to attack each arena in order to win: for example, being the innovator or fast follower or low-cost provider. The attack plan often maps out a number of planned assaults in the form of *major new-product or technology initiatives*—your strategic product roadmap and technology roadmap.

These components of an innovation strategy were outlined in Chapter 3 as success driver number 1, and their logical linkages are shown in Figure 10.1.

Doing Business Without a Strategy

Developing a product-innovation strategy is hard work. It involves many people, especially top management. Why, then, go to all the effort? Most of us can probably name countless companies that do not appear to have a master plan for their new-product efforts. How do they get by?

> Your product-innovation strategy consists of the goals, objectives, and role for product innovation in your business; your strategic arenas—where you'll focus your new-product efforts; where and how you'll deploy your resources; and your attack plans—how you'll win in targeted arenas.

Running an innovation program without a strategy is like running a war without a military strategy. There's no rudder, there's no direction, and the results are often highly unsatisfactory. You simply drift. On occasion, such unplanned efforts do succeed, largely owing to good luck, heroic efforts, or perhaps brilliant tactics. But examples are rare.

A business's new-product effort without a strategy will inevitably lead to a number of ad hoc decisions made independently of one another. New-product and R&D projects are initiated solely on their own merits and with little regard to their fit into the grander scheme (portfolio management is all but impossible, for example). The result is that the business finds itself in unrelated or unwanted markets, products, and technologies: There is no focus.

Goals and Objectives: The Necessary Link to Business Strategy

What types of direction does a product-innovation strategy give a business's new-product efforts? First, the goals embedded in your product-innovation strategy tie your product-development effort tightly to your overall business strategy: New-product development becomes a *central part of the business strategy*, a key plank in the business's overall strategic platform.

The question of spending commitments on new products is dealt with by defining the role and goals of the new-product effort. Too often the R&D or new-product budget is easy prey in hard economic times. Development and new-product marketing spending tend to be viewed as discretionary expenditures—something that can be slashed if need be. Establish product innovation as a central facet of your business's overall strategy, and firmly define the role and goals of product innovation, however, and cutting this R&D budget becomes much less arbitrary: There is a continuity of resource commitment to new products.

Finally, new-product objectives for your business provide targets for everyone to strive to achieve, become the criteria to help make difficult new-product and resource-allocation decisions, and serve as benchmarks against which to measure performance.

The Strategic Arenas: Guiding the Innovation Effort

This second facet of the product-innovation strategy, the definition of arenas, is critical to guiding and focusing your new-product efforts. The first stage in the *Stage-Gate* system is Discovery or idea generation. But where does one search for new-product ideas—in which hunting grounds? Unless the arenas or "search fields" are defined, the idea search is undirected, unfocused, and ineffective.

Your business's product-innovation strategy is also fundamental to project selection and portfolio management. That's why I show strategy as the top box in the *portfolio-management process* of Figure 8.2 in Chapter 8—strategy overarches the entire decision and selection process. For example, the first gate in the idea-to-launch process is *idea screening*. The key criterion for this early Go/Kill decision is whether the proposed project has strategic alignment. This usually translates into: "Is this the kind of market, product, and technology that we as a business have decided is *fair game*—or maybe top priority—for us?" Without a definition of your playing fields—arenas of strategic thrust—good luck in trying to make effective screening decisions! The strategic alignment question remains a vital criterion for project selection at almost every gate throughout the *Stage-Gate* process, and also helps dictate spending splits and the desired balance of the portfolio of projects; hence, it is critical to portfolio management.

The definition of arenas also guides long-term resource and personnel planning. If certain markets are designated top priority arenas, then the business can acquire resources, people, skills, and knowledge to enable it to attack those markets. Similarly, if certain technologies are singled out as arenas, the business can hire and acquire resources and technologies to bolster its abilities in those fields. Resource building doesn't happen overnight—one cannot buy a sales force on a moment's notice, and one can't acquire a critical mass of key researchers or engineers in a certain technology at the local supermarket. Putting the right people, resources, and skills in place takes both lead-time and direction.

SETTING GOALS AND OBJECTIVES

Strategy begins with the goals and objectives for the business's product-innovation effort and a clear understanding of how these product-innovation goals tie into the broader business goals. As an aside, it's interesting to note that one of the first principles in military-strategy handbooks, on which business strategy is so heavily based, is this: "Objective—Direct every operation toward a clearly defined, decisive, and attainable objective."[10]

Many businesses lack product-innovation goals, or the goals are not articulated and communicated well. In Corning's case, the goals were ambitious: to innovate their way out of a business crisis and to double the rate of creation of new businesses per decade. These goals were supported by specific sales and profit objectives for product innovation. Note that goals are broad and give general intentions, whereas objectives are narrow, concrete, and precise—see sidebar "Goals versus Objectives."

Goals versus Objectives	
Goals are broad	Objectives are narrow
Goals are general intentions	Objectives are precise
Goals are intangible	Objectives are tangible
Goals are abstract	Objectives are concrete
Goals are generally difficult to measure	Objectives are measurable

Like Corning's, your business's product-innovation strategy should specify the goals and objectives of the business's total product-innovation effort and indicate the role that product innovation will play in helping the business achieve its objectives. Your product-innovation strategy must answer the question: How do new products and product innovation fit into the business's overall plan? Most of us accept the premise that defining goals and objectives for your product-development strategy is essential; however, our benchmarking investigations reveal that many organizations lack written and measurable goals for their innovation effort, as shown in Figure 3.1. Do you?

What types of objectives and goals should be included in an innovation strategy? I use the SMART acronym when trying to establish a set of goals and objectives:

- Specific—targeted at a specific area, such as "new products" or "all R&D developments." One must thus define what is meant by a "new product" or a "development" (see Chapter 1 and Figure 1.5).
- Measurable—so that they can be used as targets to achieve and also as benchmarks against which to measure performance.
- Action oriented—giving both senior management as well as project teams a sense of direction and purpose, and be criteria for Go/Kill gate decision-making.
- Realistic—be reasonable to achieve, and have adequate resources in place.
- Time bound—have a time frame attached.

Additionally, these objectives should tie the business's new-product effort tightly to its business strategy.

High Level Goals and Objectives

One type of new-product objectives focuses on high level or overarching impact that new-product effort will have on the business. Some examples:

1. *Percentage of sales:* a popular objective is the percentage of your business's sales in year x that will be derived from new products introduced in the previous five years. Five years is an historically accepted timespan in which to define a product as "new," although given today's pace of business, two or three years is more appropriate for many businesses. About 28 percent of sales comes from new products launched in the previous three years, on average and across all industries (see Figure 1.3).

    When measuring sales from new products, some firms (notably consumer-goods firms) include only additional (incremental) sales from products launched—the *net sales value*—in order to discount cannibalization sales from replacement and extension products. One can also use *absolute sales* as the objective—dollar sales from new products in year x—rather than relative sales or percentages.

2. *Percentage of profits:* a similar objective is the percentage of your business's profits in year x that will be derived from new products introduced in the previous three or five years. Again, *absolute profit dollars* can be used instead of relative or percent of profits. Profits, of course, ought to be the *real objective* for most firms, not as sales as in (1) above. But profits are not as "clean" a metric—there are many different ways of computing "new-product profits"—leading to problems operationalizing this metric and also to a higher opportunity to game the system when reporting results versus objectives.

3. *New products as a percent of growth:* sales and profits objectives can be expressed as a percentage of business growth over the next y years. For example: 70 percent of growth in your business's sales over the next five years will come from new products introduced in this period.

4. *The strategic role:* these are less quantitative and measurable, and so can be used in addition to objectives (1) to (3) above. They include: defending the base business, defending a market share or market position, exploiting a new technology, establishing a foothold in a new market, opening up a new technological or market window of opportu-

nity, capitalizing on a strength or resource, or diversifying into higher-growth areas.

5. *Number of launches*: the *number of major new products to be introduced* over a given time period can also be used as a call to action for the business. One senior executive proclaimed an objective of "fifteen in five," which meant "fifteen major new products to be launched in the next five years." It was a clear, concise, and actionable objective for everyone in the organization. There are problems with this type of objective, however: products could be large-volume or small-volume ones, so one must define what counts as a "major product launch." Further, the number of products does not directly translate into sales and profits.

Which objective for your business?

- By far the most popular is objective type (1) above: percentage of your business's sales in Year X to be derived from new products. It's the metric that 3M popularized where it is called the NPVI, the *new-product vitality index*.
- Objective type (2) is profit related and thus seems even more appropriate, but may be harder to measure.
- Objective type (3) is closely linked to (1) and (2) and can be used with (1).
- And don't forget to consider goal type (4)—it's more qualitative and merits consideration, but it's best used in conjunction with (1) or (3) above.
- And objective (5) is very action oriented, but again best used alongside objectives (1) to (3).

Criticisms: One of the criticisms of some of the recommended objectives above—namely, new-product sales or profits as a percent of company sales, profits, or growth—is that they *may motivate the wrong actions*.[11] Because a "new product" is often so broadly defined, these objectives becomes all-encompassing so that *anything marginally new* counts as a "new product." The result is that the *wrong kind of development effort* is encouraged: too many tweaks, modifications, and extensions that are renovation initiatives, and not enough significant product development or bold innovation; and *too much churn* in the product line—replacing anything older than three years, regardless, just to "make the numbers."

For bolder innovation: If the overall goal is *bolder innovation*, then change your metrics! Be sure to specify and communicate your business's new-product objectives—but tighten the definition of "what counts as a new product" so that genuine product development, and not just product modification, becomes the objective. For example, one major manufacturer of fluid-handling equipment defines a new product as "any new item offered for sale to the marketplace with new features, functionality, and performance characteristics that are clearly visible to the customer or user, and involves more than fifty person-days of development time." In this way, the definition includes both an external element (visible to the customer) and internal (the minimum investment by the company); it also excludes freebies, tech-service efforts, and minor developments. And some firms simply define a *significant new product* this way: any product that is the result of going through the full five-stage *Stage-Gate** process in Figure 5.4!

Other firms, such as 3M, seeking a balance of bold versus less ambitious new products, define *two metrics*: percentage of sales from bold, innovative new products; and percentage of sales from all new products, including renovations. *Communicate!* Another key best practice is to ensure that the role of new products in your business—goals and objectives—is clearly communicated to all.[12] The whole point of having goals and objectives is so that everyone involved in the activity has a common purpose, something to work toward. Instead, what we observe here are typically very mediocre practices, with less than 40 percent of all businesses defining and clearly communicating the goals and objectives for product development (see Figure 3.1). One rule here is to make sure your objectives and goals are *easy to communicate and understand*: They should be concise and precise!

> *Percentage of sales* derived from new product—the NPVI—is the most popular metric for use as a new-product objective, but also has some problems. To stimulate *bolder innovation,* consider a tougher, narrower definition of what counts as "a new product"; or use two NPVI metrics: one metric for *bold new products,* and a second metric for *all new products.*

Performance Objectives

A second type of objectives deals with the *expected performance* of the new-product effort. Such goals are useful guides to managers within the new-products group. Examples include:

- success, failure, and kill rates of new products developed;
- number of new-product ideas to be considered annually;
- number of projects entering development (or in development) annually; and
- minimum acceptable financial returns for new-product projects.

---

* With renovations, extensions, and minor projects using the three- or two-stage process in Figure 5.4.

Many of these specific performance objectives flow logically from the higher-level goals. For example, if the business wants 70 percent of sales growth to come from new products, how does that figure translate into number of successful product launches annually; number of development projects; success, failure, and kill rates; and number of ideas to be considered annually?

How to Set Product-Innovation Objectives

Setting these objectives is no easy task. The first time through, the exercise is often a frustrating experience. Yet these goals are fundamental to developing an innovation strategy, not to mention a logically determined R&D budget figure. New-product goal-setting usually begins with a strategic planning exercise for the entire business. The business's growth and profit goals are decided; these business goals are then translated into new-product objectives, often via *gap analysis*:

An example: Senior management at Guinness (Ireland) developed an overall strategic plan for their brewing business. Ambitious growth and profit goals were decided, driven by the parent company. A review of current products and markets worldwide revealed that gaps would exist between projected sales and the goals. That is, current markets and products' sales were projected into the future, and expected revenues and profits were compared to the desired level of sales and profits (the business goals). The gaps must be filled by new markets, new products, or new businesses. From this, new-product sales objectives as percent and in euros were determined.

Another example: There are only so many ways to *fill the gap between the probable state and desired state*: market growth, increased market share, new markets, new products, and acquisitions. Figure 10.2 shows an illustration from an automotive-components supplier. Here management starts with the overall growth goal for the business (at top of the figure), and then identifies the sources of growth, along with estimates of each source (in dollars and percentages). Some estimates of growth are fairly predictable, such as market-share increase (small!) and market growth (also small). Others, such as the objective for new products (organic growth), often drop out of the calculation: dollars required to fill the growth-goal gap. These top-level estimates (second row in Figure 10.2) are then used to set specific growth targets for each growth source (bottom row of Figure 10.2).

Figure 10.2: Define Your Innovation Goals and Objectives, Starting with Your Business's Growth Goals

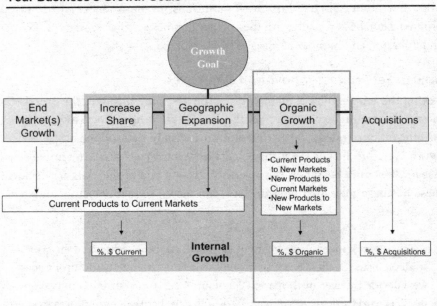

Illustration Is from an automotive Tier I parts supplier

THE TARGET STRATEGIC ARENAS—YOUR BATTLEFIELDS

Focus is the key to an effective product-innovation strategy.[13] Your product-innovation strategy specifies where you'll attack, or perhaps more importantly, where you won't attack. Thus, the concept of targeting strategic arenas—the markets, industry sectors, applications, product types, or technologies on which your business will focus its new-product efforts—is at the heart of a product-innovation strategy. For example, Corning's decision to focus on flat screens for LCD TVs was a bold move at the time, yet in hindsight, it was a brilliant maneuver, marrying the company's technological competencies to an adjacent and emerging market opportunity.

> The specification of targeting strategic arenas—what's "in bounds" and "out-of-bounds" for product innovation—is like the generals mapping out and deciding their battlefields. It's fundamental to spelling out the direction or strategic thrust of the business's product-development effort.

The specification of *target strategic arenas*—what's "in bounds" and "out-of-bounds" for product innovation—is fundamental to spelling out the direction or strategic thrust of the business's product development effort. One of the essential elements of military strategy, from which so much of business strategic thinking is derived, is the notion of concentrating one's effort or forces and hitting specific sectors hard: the principle of mass. In product development, we call these areas of focus "strategic arenas," namely, the markets, sectors or segments, technologies or product types where you will focus your new-product efforts.

So pick your battlefields—select the *target areas of strategic focus* where you plan to focus your R&D and new-product effort. The key word is "focus"—the opposite of a scattergun approach.[14] It is the result of identifying and assessing new-product opportunities at the strategic level. Without defined strategic arenas, the search for specific new-product ideas or opportunities is unfocused. Over time, the project portfolio for new products is likely to accumulate a lot of unrelated projects, in many different markets, technologies, or product types. The result of such a scattershot effort is predicable: a not-so-profitable new-product effort.

> *An example:* A construction-materials firm and producer of OSB (oriented strand board) had defined one area of focus as "the residential construction market in the United States"—so broad that it provided no direction at all. After a rigorous rethinking of its innovation strategy, three very specific arenas were defined in terms of markets or products or both: disaster-related OSB products (fire, flood); panelizers (makers of prefab walls or panels used on-site in residential construction); and finally, a benefit segment, namely, large tract builders seeking innovative solutions to reduce onsite labor costs.

Our research shows that most firms have defined areas of strategic focus for innovation; but the evidence also suggests *they are not the right ones*—that they lack the potential to be your *future engines of growth*. Typically, strategic arenas are the same old areas where the business already operates, or closely related areas—areas that are familiar and easy, but mature, stale, and sterile, offering little prospect for true innovation and growth.

Look For Blue Oceans?

Instead, what is needed is a determined search for *bolder, more productive strategic arenas*.[15] Sometimes these will be "blue ocean" arenas, arenas where *no firm* currently operates (as opposed to "red oceans," which are crowded and highly competitive). The trouble with this theory is that seeking blue oceans has not had the impact the pundits promised: Blue oceans are not in plentiful supply! Moreover, often an arena is a blue ocean for good reason: Nobody really wants to be there!

Find Big Problems in New and Growing Markets

A second approach is to look for embryonic or newer but rapidly growing markets or sectors where customers face many problems. The battle cry is "find big problems, look for big solutions."

Some examples: Apple's iPod, highlighted in Chapter 1 and considered by some to be the most successful new product ever launched, did not create the MP3 portable music market. That market had existed for about ten years before Apple launched in 2001, and there were more than forty competitors selling MP3 players. But users faced many problems: MP3 players were hard to use; they lacked storage capacity; they were bulky; and legally downloadable music was difficult to find. Apple applied its unique design and technology skills and solved the problems, giving the world the iPod and iTunes system solution, and the rest is history.

> Define the strategic arenas where you will focus your R&D efforts. "Find big problems and look for big solutions" is the battle cry.

Corning did much the same thing, emerging from the tech wreck earlier this century, when it targeted the flat-screen TV and monitor market still in its infancy. This bold strategic move led to huge growth and ultimately to products like Gorilla Glass used in the iPad. Ironically, the technology that Corning relied on for screens was not all that new, and could be traced back decades earlier to automotive windshields.

Tackle Large, Established Markets That Have an Itch

"Scratch an unscratched itch" when looking for disruptive innovations, Clayton Christensen points out.[16] "Make it easier and simpler for people to get an important job done." His historical examples include innovations such as Federal Express, Intuit's QuickBooks, and P&G's Swiffer, all of which solved major issues that customers were having with traditional products in well-established markets.

Thus, a third approach is to find large and established markets with considerable long-term potential but facing new or large unresolved problems. The quest for clean drinking water, waste management or disposal, commuting to work (potentially leading to driverless cars), energy conservation, efficient farming, and replacement body parts are examples of such markets or sectors with huge unresolved problems or "grand challenges."

Examples: GE and Siemens are both targeting the potable water and waste-water sectors, but there is lots of room for other, smaller players. For example, Grundfos, a Danish pump-maker, has targeted the complete water-treatment cycle with a series of systems, equipment, and pumps—part of their *sustainable water strategy*. As for body parts, it's not just medical-product firms opening doors here: W. L. Gore, makers of the Gore-Tex textile used in hiking and ski outerwear, is applying its unique technology to develop components in the human cardiovascular system with considerable success.

The pattern is clear: Find large markets with huge problems, and then apply your strengths and core competencies to provide the big solutions.

Don't Miss the Ahas—Walk Heads Up

Many companies claim to employ one or more of the approaches outlined above. But a closer inspection usually reveals they have missed the point. All too often, the set of arenas defined as potential candidates is *too close to home* (a minor extension of their existing business), *too conservative and risk-averse*, and *not very attractive* in terms of long-term potential. Sometimes this myopia occurs because those people leading the strategic effort are simply risk averse and short-term focused. Or maybe they are just blind to opportunities—they lack insight and the vision. And too often those involved in the strategic exercise are in a rush—they have not set aside the time and done the necessary prework, such as voice-of-customer input, megatrends analysis, and technology forecasting. And so, when the off-site strategic session begins, there is nothing new to spark the conversation, and thus the same old ideas, areas, product types, and markets become the focus of the meeting—and the needle never moves!

A jungle trek: I use as an analogy a trek through the upper Amazon jungle I was on. As our group trudged along the narrow jungle path, the fellow immediately ahead of me was fixated on watching the ground—careful that he did not trip over a root or stumble on a rock. His approach was "heads down and cautious"—I don't think he saw much of the jungle's beauty that day. Another fellow seemed impatient and was intent on just reaching the next destination. By comparison, just ahead of him, my wife Linda was walking "heads up" and taking the time to look all around . . . noticing that beautiful orchid in a tree, a monkey on a branch, or that brightly colored bird above us, and taking lots of pictures. She had many ahas that day . . . it was an enlightening experience.

Most companies sadly are like that fellow ahead of me: *heads down and cautious*, with few ahas; others are just in too much of a hurry and don't set aside the time to have a good look around, and so they too miss many opportunities. Thus, when you do undertake this strategic exercise (it's usually a group effort), treat it like a *trek through a beautiful jungle*, and take the time, heads up, and keeping your eyes open for the many ahas. Later, I'll show useful exercises that foster this *heads-up approach*.

The Leaders Must Lead

Leadership by senior management is also what's needed here—a major commitment. As mentioned, the word strategy is derived from the ancient Greek *stratēgia*, which means "the art of the general." And so *the generals must lead!* This leadership begins with a strong statement about marching orders, specifically: "The executive team is going to lead and engage in a serious strategic effort, and the input and work of a number of people in the firm—from marketers and product managers to technologists, salespeople, and operations—will be required if this effort is to succeed."

The execs lead the effort, and they must set aside time dedicated to this endeavor; but many others are required to do the heavy lifting too: all the prework leading up to the requisite robust strategic discussion and decision meetings.

IDENTIFYING THE POTENTIAL STRATEGY ARENAS

The process begins with a *divergent, creative effort* to identify potential strategic arenas where you might play the game, followed by a tough evaluation to narrow down the field to the best bets—the strategic arenas where your business should focus its new-product or R&D efforts. The final decision might be to focus on your current area—on those markets and product types where you currently operate, in short to defend the base. Often, however, new arenas are identified— ones that offer new and exciting opportunities. The thought process—your *trek through the jungle* to seek ahas and then to converge on the best bets—is shown in Figure 10.3.

The first task, then, is to diverge—*to identify potential arenas*, areas that might offer the business some new and profitable opportunities. The OSB construction-materials firm, one of the examples above, identified a total of *twelve new potential strategic arenas* in their strategy development, and ended up choosing only three as target arenas.

Here are some useful ways—exercises or tasks—designed to stimulate the discussion and provoke the ahas. (I make the assumption that your innovation strategy development is a leadership-team exercise—held as an off-site strategic session or retreat—with support from the next level down and others in the business.) The *strategic analysis exercises* below typically involve some prework

Figure 10.3: Define Target Arenas for Product Innovation—First Diverge by Identifying Potential Arenas, Then Converge and Select Target Arenas

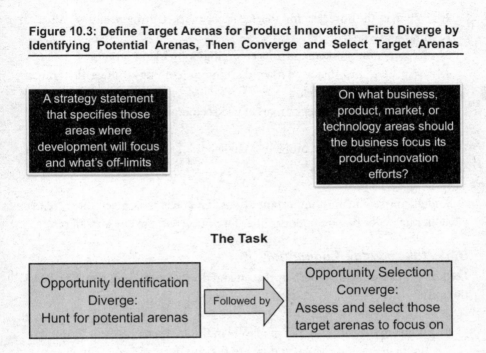

by subgroups, a few presentations at the strategy session, and then discussions to identify possible opportunities and areas that the business could target—potential strategic arenas.

Look at How Your Markets Are Changing

Markets are always changing, and many are in great turmoil, which means new opportunities for you. For example, recently I gave a seminar to suppliers at a mining institute conference in mining country. Mining is a very old, mature industry, but I posed the question anyway: "What are the major trends and problems in the mining industry?" The dominant answer: The major trend is that mines are getting deeper and deeper—some as deep as four kilometers!—and so the temperature is going up: The rock is at 60°C (140°F) in some deep mines! Providing ventilation to that depth, exhausting the "waste" air (some mines still use diesel engines underground!), cooling the air, and enabling workers to work are obvious issues, and offer endless possibilities for product innovation!

Key questions in your market analyses include:

1. What's happening in your marketplace? And in related or adjacent markets?

2. What is the forecast for market size, market growth and significant market trends?
3. Are any new market segments emerging? Why? How large?
4. Are there any major market disruptions coming—things that might change the playing field?
5. Are any new customer or market needs emerging? How fast and certain? What impact?
6. What are the major problems, challenges, and *points of pain* faced by customers?

And of course, the most important discussion question is: given these trends, what are the major market opportunities for you? Are there any ahas here?

Undertake a Value-Chain Analysis

Look at your value chain—both upstream and downstream from you. Key questions are:

1. Who are the various types of players in the value chain—your customers, their customers, and so on down to the end user; and your suppliers?
2. Assess their futures: what are their changing roles? Who will gain? Who might be dis-intermediated (cut out)?
3. And what are the threats or opportunities for your business?

Do these trends suggest any new-product or *new business model* opportunities—for example, performing some of the functions that others in the value chain profit from now?

Undertake a Competitive Analysis

I'm not suggesting that you should copy your competitors' products, although a "fast-follower" strategy is both popular and often successful—more on that topic later. Often an analysis of competitors' successes and failures yields insights into how to win, and what's needed next. Key questions are:

1. Who are the direct and indirect competitors (indirect: firms providing a different product or service, but satisfying the same need as your product does)?
2. Who is winning? Who is losing? And most important, why?
3. Can we learn anything here?

4. Are there opportunities for you?

An example: Thermo-Pipe (disguised name) some years back had developed a novel way to heat insulated pipes in a chemical or petroleum refinery, using a semiconducting plastic strip. After many years, most chemical and petroleum plants had miles of these novel heating strips in their plants. But markets are changing in those industries, and many plants are reducing operating staff dramatically. In recent years, the major heat-strip competitor had seized the opportunity and introduced a line of hardware-and-software automated controls for their heating strips, thereby automating much of the heating control process.

Thermo-Pipe had been slow to act here, and so the strategic decision became: Should Thermo-Pipe also enter the heating controls market? Or simply let their customers buy others' controls? By analyzing their competitor's products as well as other generic controls (their strengths and weaknesses, and competitors did have weaknesses in this application!) and doing VoC work, the answer became a strong "yes"—there was a major unfulfilled need. And Thermo-Pipe was able to launch a "fast-follower" heat-strip-control product line with significant advantages, and do very well!

Three messages: Don't ignore key market trends and get caught napping, as Thermo-Pipe did. Next, when competitors do leap ahead, take a hard look at their products and strategy—learn from their victories and find their weaknesses! Finally, VoC, the next topic, is a key input to the decision and to the eventual new-product strategy.

Undertake Voice-of-Customer Work
Understand customers' and users' needs and challenges—walk in their shoes. Key questions in your VoC strategic assessment are:

1. How do customers or users employ products like yours (or similar products in related markets)?
2. What need are they satisfying? What problem are the solving? What benefits are they seeking?
3. Is there a better way they could think of to meet that need, solve that problem, or deliver those benefits?
4. What are customers (and users) asking for—what are their desires, stated needs, and wants?

5. What major problems are customers and users facing? When they use a product like yours (or related products) what do they complain most about—what keeps them awake at night?

6. If they do mention a specific want—a new product, or a new feature— probe why: why do they want that feature or product? What's the underlying need here?

7. What new needs do or will they have? What are their future plans?

8. For B2B: assess what factors make customers profitable and successful— can you provide help and solutions here?

An example: Aero-Flow (disguised name) is a major European producer of premium vacuum cleaners for the home, marketed globally (except in North America). The vacuum-cleaner market has become increasingly mature and competitive, especially with very innovative players such as Dyson. Aero-Flow had undertaken many "fast-follower" developments, such as cyclone technology and robot vacuums, but were now one among many players, albeit positioned at the quality high end. New strategies were sought, including the possibility of entering new arenas (new markets, new product categories).

As part of their off-site strategic exercise, teams were asked to undertake some pre-event work. One task was to undertake VoC in users' homes—watching customers vacuum the floor and then discuss needs and wants, problems and opportunities. One major aha came from the Chinese team: They brought photos to show users vacuuming the floor in a city such as Shanghai or Beijing (typically in an apartment). The photo-show looked as expected for the first few pictures; but then the aha: The customer finished the job and sat down with the observing team, but *did not turn off the vacuum cleaner*! "Why?" the team wanted to know. "Your vacuum cleaner has a very good HEPA filter that cleans the air," said the customer, "so we clean the floor first and then leave it on to clean the air."* The implications for a strategic thrust into a new-product category are clear: air cleaners or air-filtration units (window mounted or mounted in wall) for an urban apartment.

Try Peripheral Visioning

Most companies lack peripheral vision, according to George Day and Paul Schoemaker—the ability to look to the left and right and see what's coming—and so they are blindsided by unexpected events.[17] These events are often a threat,

---

* Air pollution is a major problem in China's major cities.

but when identified early enough and flipped over, become an opportunity. Recommended questions to address in this exercise are:

1. Who in your industry picks up on advance warnings and acts on them? What are they working on now?
2. What have been your blind spots in the past? What's happening there now?
3. Is there a relevant analogy from another industry—for example, GMO's negative experience with environmental groups and what that might mean to a newer technology, such as nanotechnology?
4. What important signals are you rationalizing away—for example, Nokia's failure to deal with the threat of Apple's iPhone (management there largely dismissed the new entrant as clever design but weak technically)?
5. What are peripheral customers and nondirect competitors saying (adjacent markets, former customers)?
6. What are your mavericks and creative thinkers in your own company trying to tell you?
7. What new futures could really hurt (or help) you—for example, for a ready-to-assemble furniture retailer, the prospect of cities without cars and young people who don't drive.
8. Is there an unthinkable scenario of the future—for example, the near collapse of the world's financial system in 2008?[18]

And again, do your answers suggest new opportunities for your business?

An example: Mattel, one of the world's largest toy-makers and owner of the Barbie doll brand, failed to recognize that preteen girls were maturing at a younger age: They wanted to be more like their older sisters. Thus, they were outgrowing young-girl dolls, such as Barbie, and shifting to more sophisticated, more older-girl dolls, such as Bratz. The shift drove down Barbie's sales dramatically after decades of prosperity, and appeared to catch the company sleeping. How could Mattel's market research have missed this trend? Why were they blindsided so badly? And if they saw it coming, why didn't they take action?

By comparison, LEGO did see the trend coming . . . little boys growing up quickly and playing with electronic devices and games. At one point early this century, LEGO sales and profits did start to suffer! But the company regrouped and identified new strategic arenas—such as building new IT technology into their blocks and products. The result was a series of right-on and exciting new-product launches: Mindstorms (robotics); video games; web-based games; and computer-generated movies for kids. And so by 2014, LEGO had taken the top spot as the world's biggest maker of toys by sales, overtaking Barbie-doll-maker Mattel.

Assess Potential Disruptive Technologies[19]

Be on the lookout for competitive new products based on new technologies that could change the playing field. "Occasionally disruptive technologies emerge: innovations that result in worse performance, at least in the near term."[20] That is, the first products introduced often *have inferior performance* based on traditional performance metrics, and so they don't look very threatening. For example, the first digital cameras yielded poor quality pictures, were expensive to buy, and had limited capacity when compared to the then-dominant 35 mm technology cameras. But on other performance dimensions, the new product excelled: in this case, the ability to digitize a picture, a benefit that was important to only a handful of potential users at that time.

Because the initial products from the new technology have such poor relative performance, initial sales volumes are not huge, and certainly penetration in the mainstream market is limited. But they *do have the potential to change the entire marketplace*! Often, significant improvements are quickly made to the initial products, so the second- and third-generation versions function much better, to the point that they exceed customer expectations on the traditional performance dimensions, yet still provide the extra benefits on new dimensions (Figure 7.6). And so they ultimately win—often in record time—as Kodak and Polaroid both found out to their chagrin.

The point is that you cannot afford to dismiss disruptive technologies, simply because the initial products offer poor performance.[21] Many of the hundreds of major firms that made this mistake are no longer in business. Rather, treat the new technology as an opportunity to be monitored and investigated. Be sure to identify potential disruptive technologies and radical or step-change innovations as part of your strategic analysis. And assess the probability and timing of each, the potential impact, and whether or not this represents an opportunity (or a threat) for your business. And most important, ask "so what?"—what can and should you do about this technology? Six tips for assessing and forecasting disruptive technologies in your industry were outlined in Chapter 7—use them here as well.

Do a Core-Competency Assessment

Always attack from a position of strength![22] Thus, a critical component of strategic analysis is an internal assessment, namely, looking at your own business, trying to identify your unique strengths that can be leveraged to advantage. Many studies repeat the message: Leveraging your strengths and core competencies increases success rates and new-product profitability.[23]

Many strategists misunderstand the concept of a core competency, and think that it is simply a strength. Not so. A company's core competency is defined as something it can do better than its competitors. But more: A core competency is critical to enabling the firm to create new products and services and to achieving competitive advantage with these products. A core competency has three characteristics:[24]

1. It should make a significant contribution to the perceived customer benefits.
2. It can be leveraged widely and applied to many products and markets.
3. It should be difficult for competitors to imitate.

A core competency can take various forms, including technical and IP know-how, a reliable or cost-effective manufacturing process, or close relationships with customers and suppliers. It may also include an effective product-development capability or culture.

The point of undertaking a core-competency assessment is to help you identify adjacencies—for example, adjacent markets, sectors, and product classes—which you can attack from a position of strength. These adjacencies become potential new strategic arenas for your business. Leveraging your core competencies in new and adjacent arenas enables your business to create new products and services, but most important, helps you to achieve competitive advantage there.

> Always attack from strengths! So undertake a *core-competency assessment* and understand what you can leverage to your advantage, much like Corning did.

So take a hard look at your business, and undertake a core-competencies assessment. This means looking at leverageable strengths in all facets of your business, and relative to your competitors:

- Your technology strengths, notably product and development technologies.
- Your marketing, customer-relations, distribution, brand-name, and sales-force strengths.
- Your operations or production capabilities, capacities, and technology.

Figure 10.4. The Product-Market Matrix Shows Potential Strategic Arenas on Which to Focus New-Product Development or R&D Efforts

The product-market matrix for a telecommunication firm

	Voice	Data	Internet	Wireless	Media
Small office Home office		★	★	★	★
Midsized business		★		★	
Large business		★		★	
Multi-national				★	
Residential	★			★	★

Markets (vertical axis label) — **Products** (horizontal axis label)

★ = Target Arena

Identify your core competencies. These are your unique and leverageable strengths, so you can now look for target arenas where you can leverage these strengths to advantage in the development of new products.

List the Potential Arenas

Many firms use the product-market matrix (Figure 10.4) to visualize new areas in which they can operate profitably. Each cell in the matrix represents a potential strategic arena that offers a number of new-product opportunities. Other firms simply make a pragmatic list—markets, segments, product types, and technologies, along with combinations of these. Here are dimensions that we see managements using in order to help identify possible new strategic arenas:

- Customer groups (markets, segments).
- Industry sectors.
- Product categories (for consumer goods) or product classes or product types.
- Customer functions (what function the customer performs, e.g., fabricators, processors, distributors).
- Technologies required to deliver solutions.

TABLE 10.1 CRITERIA USED TO RATE STRATEGIC ARENAS

Criteria used to assess potential strategic arenas cover a range of issues and factors:

1. Arena Attractiveness

   Market attractiveness:
   - Size of the market(s) in the arena.
   - Market growth rates.
   - Intensity of competition and strength of competitors.
   - Margins earned by others here.

   Technological opportunities in this market:
   - Rate of change of technology in the arena.
   - Technological elasticity: If one spends a dollar, how much performance improvement is there (that is, where on the technology S-curve is this technology—embryonic versus mature, steep versus flat)?

2. Business Strength

   Technology leverage:
   - Ability to leverage your development skills in this arena (technology, IP, R&D, or design engineering).
   - Degree of fit between production/operations processes required to succeed here and your production/operations processes, skills, and IP.

   Marketing leverage:
   - Ability to leverage your sales-force and/or distribution-channel system.
   - Ability to leverage your customer relationships and market presence here.
   - Ability to leverage your marketing communications, brand name, and image.

   Competitive advantage—*envision some of the products you could or would develop here . . .*
   - Would your new products be unique (differentiated from) current competitors?
   - Would your new products meet customer needs better than competitors?

SELECT YOUR TARGET ARENAS—YOUR NEXT ENGINES OF GROWTH

The diverging or searching exercises (Figure 10.3) should produce a list of the potential strategic arenas. Then *knock out the obvious misfits* and nonstarters. For the remaining short list, find out what it takes to win in each arena, and how well you can leverage your core competences in each area: Do you have what it takes to win? And determine how attractive the markets are in each arena and whether they are fertile ground for innovation. This *fact-finding does take some work—* small teams are assigned to the various arenas to undertake quick due diligence.

Pick Your Target Strategic Arenas—Your Battlefields[25]

Next comes the task of evaluating these arenas, selecting the battlefields—your next engines of growth. This is a converging or "zeroing in" exercise, shown on the right side of Figure 10.3. Usually two dimensions are used for this evaluation:

1. *Arena attractiveness:* this is an external measure that captures characteristics such as size and growth of markets in the arena, intensity of competition and margins earned, and the potential for developing new products (for example, the technological maturity of the area).
2. *Business strength:* this involves assessing the business's core competencies and strengths and asking whether these competencies could be leveraged if the business chose to enter the new arena.

Usually, a set of six to eight questions is developed for each dimension, which senior management then uses to rate the various arenas under consideration. See Table 10.1 for sample criteria.

The result is the *strategic map* or *"Strat-Map,"* with each arena plotted (Figure 10.5). Arenas in the upper right quadrant—the "good bets"—are those designated as the most promising. These are where the business should focus its product development resources. With strategic arenas selected, idea generation becomes more directed and productive, specific projects within each strategic arena can be funded, and the entire R&D effort gains focus.

Don't be confused between this Strat-Map shown in Figure 10.5 and the old GE-BCG model: the "cash-cows, stars, and dogs" map.[26] The two maps may look similar in that they are both x–y plots with bubbles, but that's where the similarity ends.[27] The BCG map is for *existing businesses*, and was developed as a *capital-allocation model*. The details of the x–y axes are also quite different from the Strat-Map: The original BCG model looked at existing business units in terms of market growth versus market share; by contrast, the Strat-Map in Figure

Figure 10.5: Create Your "Strat-Map"—Plot Potential Strategic Arenas, Choosing Arenas in the "Best Bets" or "Conservative Bets" Quadrants

10.5 shows *new arenas*—markets, technologies, and products or combinations of these—as the circles or bubbles, and with different axes, as shown in Figure 10.5, that are made up of metrics quite specific to innovation and the Strat-Map.

A Blow-by-Blow Description of "Strat-Mapping"

Let's look at some of the details of this method of searching for and prioritizing arenas. For this illustration, I use a simple and real company, Chempro,[*] a medium-sized manufacturer of process equipment (agitators, mixers, and blenders) for the pulp and paper industry:

The illustration: Chempro's major strength is its ability to design and manufacture rotary hydraulic agitation equipment. The company is so focused technically that it has turned this rather narrow agitator-design "art" into a science. The market

> Use a Strat-Map to help visualize and select the target arenas. The two axes are Arena Attractiveness and Business Strength. Potential arenas are rated by senior management and are plotted on the two-dimensional chart as bubbles. Those in the top right quadrant are generally the best.

---

[*] Disguised name; some details have also been disguised. Agitators are simply a propeller on a shaft powered by an electric motor, much like a kitchen appliance, but up to three hundred horsepower for the pulp and paper industry.

Figure 10.6: The "Who, What, How" Three-Dimensional Map Used in the Chempro Illustration to Define Potential Strategic Arenas

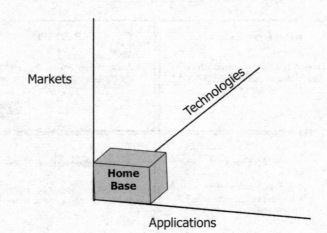

"Home Base" is the business's current market, current technology, and current application. Move away from home base in any direction and identify adjacencies.

served is the pulp and paper industry. The application is agitation and blending of liquids and slurries.

Chempro's management elects "who, what, how" as three dimensions to define potential arenas: customer groups, applications, and technologies; these are shown as the x, y, and z axes in Figure 10.6. Home-base or the current business is located, and other opportunities are identified by moving away from home-base along each axis to other (but related) customer groups, applications, and technologies—to new but adjacent areas.

What potential new-product arenas exist for the company? Clearly, the home-base is one of these, and indeed the firm is active in seeking new-product ideas for agitation equipment in its pulp and paper field. Most of these opportunities, however, are limited to modifications and improvements, and the market is stagnant and, in some geographies, declining.

One direction that senior management can take is to develop new products aimed at related but new customer groups. These customer groups include the chemical, food-processing, petroleum-refining, and hydro-metallurgical fields. Some of the options are shown across the top of the matrix in Figure 10.7.

Figure 10.7: Two-Dimensional Matrix Portray Potential Strategic Areas at Chempro

		Adjacent Markets			
		Pulp and Paper (home base)	**Chemical Process Industry**	**Petroleum Refining**	**Hydro-Metallurgical**
Applications that Build on Current Technology	**Agitation and Blending (home base)**	HOME BASE: Agitators and blenders for P&P industry	Chemical mixers and blenders	Blenders for petroleum storage tanks	Hydro-metallurgical mixers, agitators
	Aeration	Surface aerators for P&P waste treatment	Surface aerators for chemical waste-treatment plants	Surface aerators for petroleum waste-treatment plants	Aerators for floatation cells
	Wet Refining	Pulpers, Repulpers, and refiners			Wet refining equipment
	Specialty Pumping	High density paper stock pumps	Specialty chemical pumps	Specialty petroleum pumps	Slurry pumps

Similarly, new products in related applications can be sought. These related applications include the pumping of fluids, fluid aeration, and refining and repulping, as shown on the vertical or y axis of Figure 10.7.

Considering these two dimensions—different applications and different customer groups—management now proceeds to define a number of new potential arenas. Working with the resulting two-dimensional matrix (Figure 10.7), recognize that, besides the home-base arena, there are twelve other arenas that the company can consider for its new-product focus. For example, Chempro could develop blending and agitation equipment (same application) aimed at the chemical or petroleum industries (new customer segments). Alternatively, the business could develop surface aeration devices* (a new application) targeted at its current customers, namely pulp and paper companies. Each of these possibilities represents a new arena for Chempro.

Chempro could also move on the third dimension in Figure 10.6 by shifting from its home-base of "rotary hydraulic technology" to other technologies. If the

---

* Surface aerators: essentially an agitator propeller, mounted flat at the surface of a pond or tank. The propeller throws water vertically into the air, which captures air on its way back down to the water surface. The air is vital for liquid waste treatment (biological oxidation) in waste-treatment ponds or tanks in many industries.

Figure 10.8: Chempro's Strat-Map Shows How the Various Potential Arenas on Its "Short List" Fare on the Two Key Strategic Dimensions

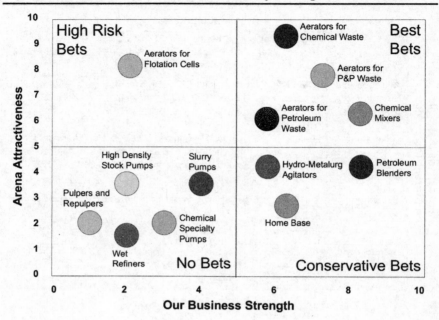

technology options are superimposed along the third dimension, the result is a much larger number of potential arenas. Possible alternative arenas along the "new technologies" axis include magneto-hydrodynamic pumps and agitators for a variety of end-user groups, bio-oxidation reactors in the food industry, and many others.

Assessing the Arenas at Chempro

At Chempro, strategic arena assessment is simplified when management faced the reality of the company's technological and financial resource limitations. Chempro's main core competency is its ability to design and engineer rotary hydraulic agitation equipment. Embarking on new and expensive technologies, such as bio-oxidation reactions, is deemed out-of-bounds. Management thus chooses to *attack from a position of strength*, and so the third dimension, new technologies, is deleted. The result is the two-dimensional matrix in Figure 10.7 (very similar to the product-market matrix of Figure 10.4).

Next, data are gathered on the twelve potential arenas plus the home-base by a handful of small teams. Management also makes available the services of a search company to lend a hand in digging for the data.

At a strategy-session meeting attended by the small teams and senior management, management now rates the twelve potential arenas and home-base on the two key dimensions of Arena Attractiveness and Business Strength. A list of rating questions is employed by senior management, with each arena rated on each question; the list of rating questions is similar to the list in Table 10.1. The 0–10 ratings are added, and both a Business Strength and Arena Attractiveness score are computed for each of the thirteen arenas. Using these two scores for each arena, the thirteen arenas are then plotted as bubbles on an x–y grid to yield Chempro's Strat-Map, shown in Figure 10.8.

Picking the Right Arenas at Chempro

The choice of arenas depends on the risk-return values of management. Selecting only those arenas in the top half of the Strat-Map—the best bets and the high-risk bets—emphasizes the attractiveness of the external opportunities. This choice places no weight at all on the business-strength dimension: It is a high return, but possibly higher-risk strategy. The other extreme is selecting only those arenas to the right of the vertical, the good bets and conservative bets. This is a low-risk, possibly lower-return strategy: selection of only those arenas in which the company possesses the right strengths to be leveraged.

Ideally, one looks for a combination of the two:

- Arenas in which the arena attractiveness and the business strength both are rated high—the best bets in the upper right quadrant of Figure 10.8.
- Some balance of arenas: some attractive but riskier arenas, some lower risk but less attractive ones.

Chempro illustration continued: For Chempro, six arenas fall into the "no bets" sector, including all four pump arenas. These are dismissed immediately. But six other arenas are rated positively on one or both dimensions. In order to quantify or rank-order the arenas, a diagonal cutoff line is drawn on Figure 10.9 (dashed line). Arenas to the right of and above this line are deemed positive; those to the left and below are negative. The distance of each arena from that line is measured: the greater the distance, the more desirable the arena.

Based on this exercise, three "best bets" and one "conservative bet" are defined as target arenas for Chempro – see Figure 10.9:

- Surface aerators for the chemical industry (wastewater treatment).
- Blenders for the petroleum industry.

Figure 10.9: Chempro's Strat-Map Shows the Relative Position of Each Arena—Those Furthest to Top Right Are Strategically the Best

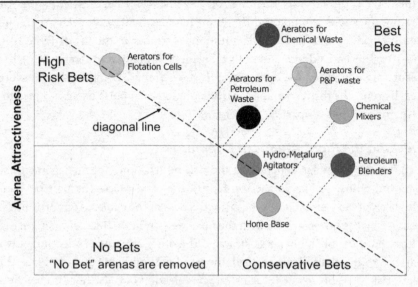

- Agitators and mixers for the chemical industry.
- Surface aerators for the pulp and paper industry.

Management also decides to continue seeking new or improved products in the home-base arena, but fairly defensively. The first stage of strategy development is now complete—management can now focus on the target strategic arenas, and has a sense of their priorities.

How Your Strat-Map Guides Your Innovation Effort

The choice of the right strategic arenas, usually those in the upper right quadrant of Figure 10.9, provides guidance in two important ways, as shown in Figure 10.10:

1. First, your chosen strategic arenas define the "search fields"—those areas where you should focus your search for new-product ideas. If ideation is to be effective, *search fields must be delineated*, partly to help marketers, technologists, and employees in general focus their search efforts,

Figure 10.10: Your Innovation Strategy Delineates the "Search Fields" for Ideation and Helps in Selection of Ideas and Projects for Development

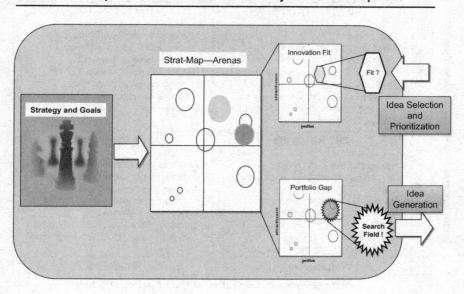

and, perhaps more importantly, to define "what's out-of-bounds" so that search effort is not wasted in the wrong areas.

2. Second, your Strat-Map helps you *select the right projects* for development. The first question for most project-selection scoring systems at the early gates is, "does this proposed project fit your strategy—do you have strategic alignment here?" Without clearly defined strategic arenas, as in Figures 10.5 and 10.9, it's difficult to answer that question!

DEVELOP ATTACK PLANS

Having defined the target battlefields (the arenas), the next questions is: How do you win on that battlefield—the attack plan? One way of looking at attack strategies is via a typology based upon the way that a business responds to changing market and external conditions—a popular model originally proposed by Raymond Miles and Charles Snow.[28] There are two dimensions to this model, as shown in Figure 10.11:

- First, how important is product innovation to your business? Is innovation front and center, and a key part of your overall business strategy? Or does

Figure 10.11: Strategic Thrust Based on Innovativeness

		THE FAST FOLLOWER	THE INNOVATOR

Importance of New-Product Development	**Critical**	▪ The "analyzer"
		▪ Carefully monitors actions of competitors
		▪ Sees growth opportunities and users' problems
		▪ Moves quickly to copy and improve upon the innovator's product—better product or lower cost
			▪ The industry leader or "prospector"
			▪ Values being "first-in" with new products—ahead of the wave
			▪ Responds rapidly to early signals pointing to new opportunities:
			  ✓ new technologies
			  ✓ new market needs

		THE REACTOR	**THE DEFENDER**
	Minimal	▪ Not aggressive in defending its established products and market share ▪ Responds only when forced to ▪ Reacts to competitors and external forces and threats—not proactive ▪ "Slow follower" ▪ An inconsistent or "non strategy"	▪ Attempts to maintain a secure position or niche in a stable area or market ▪ Aggressively protects its domain by offering higher quality products, better service or lower prices ▪ but does not rely on product innovation as main element of its "marketing mix"
		Reactive	**Proactive**

Proactive versus Reactive Market-Facing Strategy

your company mostly rely on other strategies for gaining business, for example: low price, intimate customer relationships, superb service, or broad distribution?

• Second, how proactive versus reactive are you when it comes to innovation? Some firms find the best approach is to let others take the lead, and then to follow. Alternately, a very proactive stance may be best for your business.

The four strategy types, based on these two dimensions, are shown in Figure 10.11:

• *The Innovators*: These businesses are the *industry innovators* or *prospectors*. They *value being first in* with new products and are first to adopt new technologies, even though there are risks. Innovators respond rapidly to early signals that point to emerging or new opportunities. This is a very popular strategy, with *about one-third of firms* engaged in product development considered to be the industry innovators—see Figure 10.12.[29]

• *Fast followers*: These businesses are the *analyzers*. By carefully monitoring the actions of major competitors, and by moving quickly, they often are able to bring *a superior product to market*—more cost efficient or with better features and user benefits than the innovator's product. But analyzers are rarely first to market. The fast-follower strategy is *the most popular of all strategies*, with 37 percent of development firms adopting such an approach. The strategy has also gained in popularity, up from 27 percent in the 1990s, because it is such a viable strategy, and at the same time only moderately risky.

- *Defenders:* Defenders place relatively *little emphasis on product innovation* as a leading edge of their overall business strategy, but they still develop new and improved products. Defenders attempt to locate and *maintain a secure position* or niche in a relatively stable product or market area. They protect their domain by offering higher quality products, superior service, or lower prices. Defenders represent about 27 percent of all companies that develop products, but is declining in popularity as a strategy. One reason is that companies that adopt a strictly defensive position often do not fare well over the long term: They are vulnerable to attack by others; and when markets and technologies change, they are unwilling or unable to change.

> Define your attack plans or strategies for each arena. Consider whether you'll be the innovator, fast follower, or defender. Or how you'll compete: low cost provider, differentiator, or niche marketer. Finally don't forget the international dimension: whether to emphasize domestic products, or global development and new products, or perhaps a more "glocal" approach.

- *Reactors:* These firms are not aggressive in maintaining established products and markets: They *respond only when forced to* by strong external or market pressures—a "slow follower." It is difficult to imagine any business deliberately electing this strategy—some would argue that it's a "non strategy"—although some may fall into this quadrant in Figure 10.11 by default. About *8 percent of product developers* fall into the reactor category, down slightly from previous years.

Other attack strategies might focus *on how one competes.*[30] For example:

- be the low-cost provider—offer products at lowest competitive prices; or
- be the differentiator—offer highly differentiated products at premium prices; versus
- be a niche player—targeted one type of customer, offering highly differentiated products at premium prices.

Figure 10.12: Popularity of Different Types of Strategic Thrusts

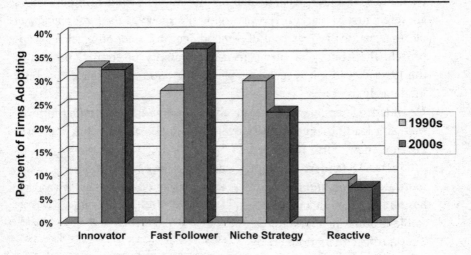

No strong evidence that Innovator, Fast Follower, or Niche works best.
Your choice depends on many factors: your markets, your strengths, etc.
But do the assessment and do select a strategy—don't drift!

Still other competitive strategies emphasize certain strengths, core competencies, or product attributes and advantages. Examples are: having the best service and support, the fastest delivery, the broadest distribution, or the most reliable cell-phone network with the best countrywide coverage.

Attack strategies can also specify the *globality of the innovation effort*, defining whether innovation will be guided by a series of domestic or regional initiatives, or take a more global approach, or be "glocal" in nature (global product concepts and platforms, locally tailored products)—see Figure 2.8. For example, Procter & Gamble has very much a global strategy: R&D is conducted in major R&D centers globally and new products are developed largely for the world (or at least global platforms, with products adjusted for local tastes). In contrast, 3M is much more a domestic US product developer. Much of their heavy R&D work is done in the United States: develop an excellent US product targeted at the US market; then international subsidiaries adjust it to suit their respective local markets. Two different but successful strategies—each right for that company.

An understanding of the business's core competencies (unique strengths that can be leveraged to advantage in the marketplace) coupled with knowledge of industry success drivers (what it takes to succeed in the industry, sector, or arena) are key factors in the selection of the appropriate attack strategies.

Additionally, *entry strategies* should be defined for *new arenas*. The strategy might be to "go it alone" via internal product development; or to *seek alliances* through licensing, partnering, joint venturing, and open innovation as a way to enhance product-development capabilities in new arenas.

DEVELOP YOUR STRATEGIC PRODUCT ROADMAP

Roadmapping has emerged as an effective way of creating and portraying a product-innovation strategy and its elements. Your product and technology roadmaps *logically flow* from your Strat-Map and attack plans. Roadmapping provides a bridge among all the strategic and tactical decision processes, different business functions, and different organizational units though the *common element of time*.[31]

A strategic roadmap is *top-down strategic approach* and is an effective way to plot a series of major initiatives over time as part of the attack plan.[32] A roadmap is simply a management group's view of how to get where they want to go or achieve a desired objective. Although growing in popularity, especially in high-technology businesses, the use of roadmaps is far from universal, with only 27.6 percent of businesses developing product roadmaps (see Figure 3.1). About twice

> A strategic roadmap establishes "placemarks" for major new-product and technology projects envisioned well into the future.

as many best innovators use product roadmaps as worst performers. Note that there are different types of roadmaps: the product roadmap[33] and the technology roadmap. [34]

A *strategic product roadmap* defines your *major* new-product developments along a time line, often for five years into the future. The roadmap is a *tentative plan*, and provides "placemarks"—tentative commitments of resources—for future projects. Five years is a long time to forecast, and thus the roadmap is *updated annually*: It's a "rolling plan," so that *only the first year is ever implemented!* An example is in Figure 10.13 for Chempro:

Chempro illustration continued: Although five arenas, including home-base, were selected in Figure 10.9, not all can be attacked at once, hence the need for a roadmap over time. The decision was to target the less demanding but still attractive arenas first, arenas that could build from the firm's existing agitator technology platform: agitators for petroleum and for the chemical industries (developing

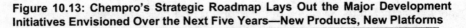

Figure 10.13: Chempro's Strategic Roadmap Lays Out the Major Development Initiatives Envisioned Over the Next Five Years—New Products, New Platforms

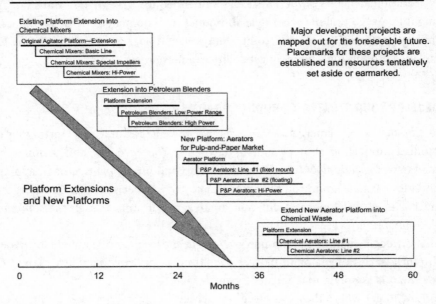

product lines for these two arenas was expected to take almost three years, as noted in Figure 10.13). Further expansion beyond these two will require *a new technology platform*, namely an aeration platform.

Starting in year three, work will begin on the new aerator platform; this development is partially de-risked by focusing on the existing pulp and paper market first. In years four and five, the new platform will yield products targeted at other markets as well. (Note that in this illustration, the strategic roadmap maps out both the major product developments and their timing, and also the technology platform extensions needed to develop these new products).

The *technology roadmap* is derived from the product roadmap. It lays out the technologies and technology platforms that are needed in order to develop and source the products in the product roadmap. The technology roadmap is thus a logical extension of the product roadmap.

Characterizing the products: Most often, the specification of products on the product roadmap is left *fairly general and high level* . . . a few attributes to characterize the new product. For example, designations such as "a low-carb beer for the Atkins diet market" or "ceramic-coated tooling for the aerospace industry" or "low-power petroleum blenders" as shown in Figure 10.13, are often the way these projects are shown on the product-roadmap timeline. That is, *placemarks*

Figure 10.14: Inputs to Developing the Product Roadmap

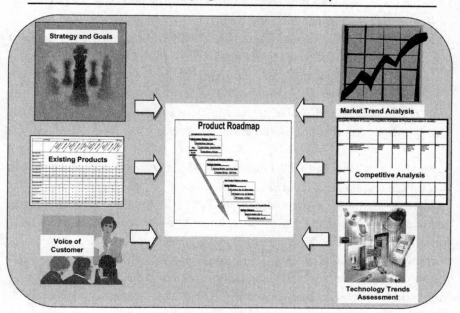

for projects "yet to be well defined" are the norm: The roadmap is meant to be directional and strategic, but not provide detailed product definitions. As each project progresses through the *Stage-Gate* system, however, increasingly the project and product become specified and defined.

Creating Your Product Roadmap

How does one develop a strategic roadmap? Delineating the major initiatives required as part of your product roadmap is a multifaceted task and includes the following inputs—see Figure 10.14.

- *Strategic assessment:* Often, the mere specification of a strategic arena as top priority leads logically to a list of those products and projects that are necessary in order to enter and win in that arena.
- *Portfolio review of existing products:* Here, you take a hard look at your current product offerings and decide which are tired and should be updated, and which should be pruned and replaced.
- *Competitive analysis:* Where are your competitors' products and product lines relative to yours? This exercise often points to the need for new products either immediately or in the foreseeable future.

- *Technology-trends assessment:* Here you forecast technology and its potential impact on your business, and thus what new products (and technologies) will be required and their timing.
- *Market-trends assessment:* Again, this is a forecasting exercise that looks at major market trends and shifts. Often you are able to pinpoint specific initiatives that you must undertake in response to these evident market trends.
- *Voice-of-customer:* What are your customers asking for and what are their needs, wants, and problems? Often these insights lead to defining the products you could or should develop.

Finally, there's the existing list of "to do" projects gathered from other sources that should also be considered here.

Many of the inputs above and in Figure 10.14 are the same types of insights and assessments used in strategy development, for example, the "jungle trek" exercises earlier in the chapter, but are more product focused and granular for purposes of roadmapping. So the strategy prework can also be used for roadmapping, with some refinements and a little more drill down.

Suggestion: Strategic roadmaps that lay out the major initiatives—major product and technology projects over time—are also a powerful concept and can be used in concert with Strategic Buckets in Chapter 8. Note that the roadmaps should be strategic, with placemarks defined for major projects, many of which might be bold innovations. And the roadmaps should be a timeline for the longer term, not just a list of products and projects for this year.

Roadmapping—The Details

Here's how roadmapping might work for you. Roadmapping is a *multifaceted process* and involves a number of multifunctional people, hence the need to assemble a cross-functional roadmapping team. The many and different inputs for developing your product roadmap are outlined in Figure 10.14. From these varied inputs, a list of potential products or *candidates for the roadmap* are developed—a "wish list" of new products and product improvements desired, both "must do" and "would like to do." These desired products can each be described on a simple one-page template as shown in Figure 10.15. Note that this outline is a *very high level description of a product idea*, certainly not a full product definition or Business Case rationale.

Which Are "In," Which Are "Out"?

Next, these "wish-list" projects are presented, one by one, at a "Gate 0" meeting—a *pre-Stage-Gate gate*! That is, right at the Gate 0 meeting, these wish-list

Figure 10.15: Use a Template to Capture Ideas and Product Concepts—The "Wish List" of Projects to Be Considered for the Product Roadmap

Candidate Projects for Roadmap—Project Information for Scoring	
Proposal Name	Pump-in-a-Pipe (PIP)
1. Project scope: provide further details on the project concept	Hermetically sealed (or "canned") in-line centrifugal pump; the magnetic field rotates impeller inside the pipe
2. Target market: What market segment is this aimed at? Which geographies, etc.	Oil and Gas; Chemical; Pharma: dangerous, toxic, polluting, expensive, caustic, potentially explosive
3. What customer problem(s) will the product solve? What benefits to users or customers will product deliver?	Leaking pump seals, especially dangerous or expensive liquids; leaks creating pollution; high seal maintenance costs, space limitations (no room for concrete base); vertical pipes
4. Compelling Value Proposition: When compared to competitors' products, why will people buy this product?	No pump seal! No leaks, no seal maintenance. Fits in tight spaces, no base needed. Maintenance savings pays for premium price over life of pump—positive "value in use"
5. Positioning Strategy: How will product be positioned versus competitors?	Premium priced (about 20% vs. in-line centrifugal pump). A hermetically sealed solution that has no seal, no leaks, and no seal maintenance. Other benefits—better way to handle toxic, dangerous, polluting liquids
6. Product Requirements, Features, Attributes	Estimate: 1-40 HP; Q=1000 gpm; H=500 ft.; 1 inch to 4 inch pipe;
7. High level—indication of opportunity size or revenue generation	Est. in-line centrifugal pump market NA is $400M (target); (in-line=10% of $4B pump mkt) Specific targeted application = 35% of market (est) Assume 20% share = $27M Sale annually after 3 years Moderate to high technical risks

products are scored by senior management using a simplified version of the Idea Screen scorecard, for example, using scales such as:

1. Importance to and fit with our innovation strategy (0–10)
2. Unique customer benefits (0–10):
   - Offers the customer unique benefits (solves a problem, meets a user need better)?
   - A "wow factor" in the product idea—will it excite the customer?
3. Market attractiveness (0–10):
   - Is the market large or growing; does it have good margins or weak competition?
4. Technical feasibility (0–10):
   - Likelihood that this is technically feasible?
   - Technical solution envisioned? Or new science and invention required?
   - Doable by our business?
5. Potential reward versus risk (0–10):
   - Market size and sales potential?
   - Size of prize—potential for profit?
   - Commercial risk level (a negative)?

Figure 10.16: A View of Projects "In" the Roadmap and Those "Out"

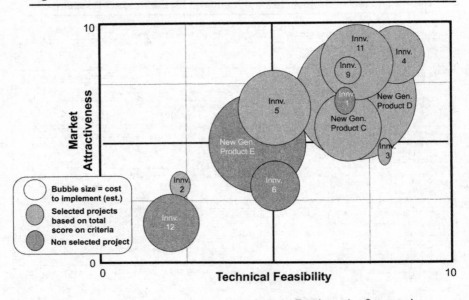

Dimension values are taken from the Roadmapping Scorecard

The scores or votes are collected, and a "first-cut" decision is made on those products "in" and "not in" the roadmap. Some firms create a few bubble-diagram charts based on the rating dimensions, as in Figure 10.16, to portray the results of the roadmapping session: selected and non selected projects. Finally, a few attendees regroup following the Gate 0 meeting (often product managers and technology managers) to check approximate resource requirements for each "in" project, resource availability, and possible timing. The result is a feasible road-map on a timeline, much as in Figure 10.13.

Once you have crafted your product roadmap, be sure to go the next step and develop the *technology roadmap*, outlining what technologies are needed and when, in order to execute your product roadmap.

NO PAIN, NO GAIN!

Our and others' research offers concrete evidence of the importance of a product-innovation strategy and the strong positive impact such a strategy has on performance (see Figure 3.1). This chapter laid out a pathway for developing such a strategy for your business. The journey begins with your business's goals and objectives and culminates with resource-deployment decisions using strategic buckets and strategic roadmaps to put the strategy into practice.

If you're thinking that your business lacks such a clearly articulated innovation strategy, and that maybe now is the time to lay the groundwork for developing such a strategy, you're probably right on both counts. But a word of caution: This does take considerable time and effort. Senior management (and lower levels of management) must be prepared to make the time available and commit to the hard work involved. But the reward is worth the effort, as evidenced by the results achieved by those businesses that have developed a robust product-innovation strategy.

END OF BOOK . . . NOW TIME TO MOVE FORWARD

In Chapter 1, I challenged you and your business to focus on *bold innovation*—not just more of the same old vanilla development efforts that plague so many businesses these days. Getting these bold initiatives to market in record time was a second challenge. As a guide, I introduced the *Innovation Diamond* and the four key vectors that lead to superb performance in product innovation (see Figure 1.2):

1. Crafting an *innovation strategy* that focuses your business on the right strategic arenas.
2. Fostering a *climate, culture, and organization* that promotes bolder innovation.
3. Generating *big ideas* and driving these big concepts to market quickly via an idea-to-launch system, such as *stage-gate* and *agile-stage-gate*.
4. Making the *right investment decisions* via effective portfolio management to pick the winners.

We now have come full circle. The critical tasks of generating blockbuster ideas, picking the winners, optimizing your development portfolio, and designing and executing a world-class idea-to-launch *Stage-Gate* system have been outlined in sufficient detail in previous chapters that you and your colleagues should now be able to move forward. And ways to make your gating system work better—more agile, accelerated, and adaptive, and more flexible—were also highlighted if you want to move beyond *Stage-Gate*. Finally, in this current chapter, your product-innovation strategy—what it is, why it's needed, and ways to map it out—were outlined, culminating in a product and technology roadmap.

This may be the end of the book, but for many readers, it's just the beginning of implementation . . . the next steps are yours!

NOTES

CHAPTER 1: THE INNOVATION CHALLENGE

1. This first section is taken from: R. G. Cooper, "The Innovation Dilemma: How to Innovate When the Market Is Mature," *Journal of Product Innovation Management* 28, no. 7 (December 2011): 2–27. See also R. G. Cooper, "Creating Bold Innovation in Mature Markets," *IESE Insight* 14, no. 3 (2012): 20–27.

2. "Has the Ideas Machine Broken Down?" *The Economist*, January 12, 2013, http://www.economist.com/news/briefing/21569381-idea-innovation-and-new-technology-have-stopped-driving-growth-getting-increasing

3. R. G. Cooper, "Agile-Stage-Gate Hybrids: The Next Stage for Product Development," *Research-Technology Management* 59, no. 1 (January 2016): 1–9. See also A. F. Sommer, C. Hedegaard, I. Dukovska-Popovska, and K. Steger-Jensen, "Improved Product Development Performance Through Agile/Stage-Gate Hybrids—The Next-Generation Stage-Gate Process?" *Research-Technology Management* 158, no. 1 (January–February 2015): 1–10.

4. The iPod case study is based on research in I. Abel, "From Technology Imitation to Market Dominance: The Case of the iPod," *Competitiveness Review, An International Business Journal* 18, no. 3 (2008): 257–74.

5. *Global Apple iPod Sales from 2006 to 2014, The Statistical Portal*, http://www.statista.com/statistics/276307/global-apple-ipod-sales-since-fiscal-year-2006/

6. See L. Kahney, "An Illustrated History of the iPod and Its Massive Impact," *Cult of Mac*, September 13, 2014, http://www.cultofmac.com/124565/an-illustrated-history-of-the-ipod-and-its-massive-impact-ipod-10th-anniversary/

7. Kahney (2014), endnote 6.

8. Taken from Kahney (2014), endnote 6.

9. Kahney (2014), endnote 6.

10. R. Stross, "How the iPod Ran Circles Around the Walkman," *The New York Times*, May 13, 2005, http://nytimes.com/2005/03/13/business/worldbusiness/13digi.html

11. *The Economist* (2013), endnote 2.

12. *The Economist* (2013), endnote 2.

13. R. P. Barpa, "Is American Innovation Dead," *Tech.Co*, February 3, 2016, http://tech.co/american-innovation-dead-2016-02

14. R. G. Cooper, "Best Practices and Success Drivers in New-Product Development," in *Handbook of Research on New Product Development*, ed. P. N. Golder and D. Mitra (Cheltenham, UK: Edward Elgar, 2017); and R. G. Cooper, "New Products—What Separates the Winners from the Losers and What Drives Success," chap. 1 in *PDMA Handbook of New Product Development*, 3rd ed., ed. K. B. Kahn (Hoboken, NJ: John Wiley & Sons, 2013).

15. Source of Figure 1.1: R. G. Cooper, "Your NPD Portfolio May Be Harmful to Your Business's Health," [PDMA] *Visions Magazine* (hereafter *Visions*) 29, no. 2 (April 2005): 22–26. Some data in Figure 1.1 is from M. Adams and D. Boike, "PDMA Foundation CPAS Study Reveals New Results," *Visions* 28, no. 3 (July 2004): 26–29; and *The PDMA Foundation's 2004 Comparative Performance Assessment Study (CPAS)* (Chicago, IL: Product Development and Management Association, 2004).

16. R. G. Cooper, "What's Next? After Stage-Gate," *Research-Technology Management* 157, no. 1 (January–February 2014): 20–31.

17. See Cooper (2014), endnote 16.

18. See Cooper (2011), endnote 1.

19. B. Kirk, "Creating an Environment for Effective Innovation," Proceedings of Stage-Gate Innovation Summit 2009, Clearwater Beach, FL, 2009.

20. Cooper (2014, 2016), endnotes 3 and 16.

21. As reported in J. Surowiecki, "The Short-Termism Myth," The Financial Page, *New Yorker*, August 24, 2015, http://www.newyorker.com/magazine/2015/08/24/the-short-termism-myth

22. R. G. Cooper and S. J. Edgett, "Best Practices in the Idea-to-Launch Process and Its Governance," *Research-Technology Management* 55, no. 2 (March–April 2012): 43–54.

23. Performance data sources: Cooper and Edgett (2012), endnote 22; some earlier data is from R. G. Cooper, S. J. Edgett, and E. J. Kleinschmidt, "Benchmarking Best NPD Practices—Part 1: Culture, Climate, Teams, and Senior Management's Role," *Research-Technology Management* 47, no. 1 (January–February 2004): 31–43.

24. OECD Data, *Gross Domestic Spending on R&D* (2016), https://data.oecd.org/rd/gross-domestic-spending-on-r-d.htm

25. Latest data released in 2016: National Science Foundation, *Business R&D and Innovation Survey, 2013* (Washington, DC: National Center for Science and Engineering Statistics and US Census Bureau, 2016), http://www.nsf.gov/statistics/2016/nsf16313/. This survey was also the source of Table 1.1.

26. D. R. Schilling, "Knowledge Doubling Every 12 Months, Soon to Be Every 12 Hours," *Industry Tap*, April 19, 2013, http://www.industrytap.com/knowledge-doubling-every-12-months-soon-to-be-every-12-hours/3950

27. C. F. von Braun, *The Innovation War* (Upper Saddle River, NJ: Prentice Hall, 1997).

28. T. Higgins, "Apple iPhones Sales in China Outsell the U.S. for the First Time," *Bloomberg Technology*, April 27, 2015, http://www.bloomberg.com/news/articles/2015-04-27/apple-s-iphones-sales-in-china-outsell-the-u-s-for-first-time

29. Figure 1.4 is a composite chart based on a number of studies: for example, Booz Allen Hamilton, *New Product Management for the 1980s* (New York: Booz Allen Hamilton, 1982); and A. L. Page, "PDMA New Product Development Survey: Performance and Best Practices," PDMA Conference, Chicago, IL, PDMA, November 13, 1991. For

mid-1990s data, see A. Griffin, *Drivers of NPD Success: The 1997 PDMA Report* (Chicago, IL: PDMA, 1997); and our own studies: R. Cooper in *PDMA Handbook* (2013), endnote 14.

30. Performance results from several sources: for example, Cooper et al. (2004), endnote 23; and Cooper and Edgett (2012), endnote 22.

31. The original typology of new products was developed by Booz Allen Hamilton; the "all industry" data in Figure 1.5 are from the PDMA best-practices study, Cooper et al. (2004), endnote 23.

32. The PDMA article that provides citations and a review of research into product innovation management is W. Biemans, A. Griffin, and R. Moenaert, "Twenty Years of the *Journal of Product Innovation Management*: History, Participants, and Knowledge Stock and Flows," *Journal of Product Innovation Management* 24, no. 3 (May 2007): 193–213.

Chapter 2: Why New Products Win

1. The success factors outlined in this chapter are based on many studies undertaken by the author, colleagues, and others, and are summarized in two product-development handbook chapters, both by the author; these handbooks' chapters provide many references to the original studies: R. G. Cooper, "Best Practices and Success Drivers in New-Product Development," in *Handbook of Research on New Product Development*, ed. P. N. Golder and D. Mitra (Cheltenham, UK: Edward Elgar, 2017); and R. G. Cooper, "New Products—What Separates the Winners from the Losers and What Drives Success," chap. 1 in *PDMA Handbook of New Product Development*, 3rd ed., ed. K. B. Kahn (Hoboken, NJ: John Wiley & Sons, 2013). See also R. G. Cooper, "Stellar Performer: The Stage-Gate System for New-Product Development," in E. Verzuh, *The Fast Forward MBA in Project Management*, 5th ed. (Hoboken, NJ: John Wiley & Sons, 2015), 65–73; R. G. Cooper, "The Stage-Gate® System for Product Innovation in B2B Firms," chap. 32 in *Handbook of Business-to-Business Marketing*, ed. G. L. Lillien and R. Grewat (Northampton, MA: Edward Elgar Publishing, 2012); and R. G. Cooper, "The Stage-Gate® Product Innovation System: From Idea to Launch," chap. 24 in *Encyclopedia of Technology and Innovation Management*, ed. V. K. Narayanan and G. O'Connor (Chichester, West Sussex, UK: John Wiley & Sons, 2010), 157–67.

2. This section on reasons for new-product failure is updated from a section that first appeared in R. G. Cooper and S. J. Edgett, *Lean, Rapid and Profitable New Product Development* (Burlington, ON: Stage-Gate International, 2011), available on Amazon.com.

3. Some of these success factors are reported in various publications. See endnote 1.

4. The research studies that identified these factors and results are summarized in endnote 1.

5. Parts of this section are paraphrased from: Cooper, *PDMA Handbook* (2013), endnote 1.

6. S. A. Rijsdijk, F. Langerak, and E. Jan, "Understanding a Two-Sided Coin: Antecedents and Consequences of a Decomposed Product Advantage," *Journal of Product Innovation Management* 28, no. 1 (January 2011): 33–47.

7. The new-product performance of businesses was gauged on ten metrics, including percentage of projects meeting sales and profit objectives, percentage of sales from new products, ROI on R&D spending, new-product profits relative to competitors,

and time-to-market and slip-rate. These metrics were then used to identify the top 20 percent of businesses—the "best performing innovators."

8. C. Rainey, "Keurig Says Sales of Its Machines and Coffee Pods Continue to Plummet," *Grub Street*, February 4, 2016, http://www.grubstreet.com/2016/02/keurigs-sales-keep-getting-worse.html

9. Rainey (2016), endnote 8.

10. R. G. Cooper and A. Dreher, "Voice of Customer Methods: What Is the Best Source of New Product Ideas?" *Marketing Management Magazine* (Winter 2010), extended online version at http://www.marketingpower.com/ResourceLibrary /Publications/MarketingManagement/2010/4/38–48_Xtended ersion3.pdf

11. J. Morgan, "Applying Lean Principles to Product Development," SAE International, Society of Automotive Engineers, 2002, http://www.sae.org/manufacturing/lean /column/leanfeb02.htm

12. P. Sandmeier, P. D. Morrison, and O. Gassmann, "Integrating Customers in Product Innovation: Lessons from Industrial Development Contractors and In-House Contractors in Rapidly Changing Customer Markets," *Creativity and Innovation Management* 19, no. 2 (June 2010): 89–106.

13. E. J. Kleinschmidt, U. de Brentani, and S. Salomo, "Performance of Global New Product Development Programs: A Resource-Based View," *Journal of Product Innovation Management* 24, no. 5 (September 2007): 419–41.

14. U. de Brentani, E. J. Kleinschmidt, and S. Salomo, "Success in Global New Product Development: Impact of Strategy and the Behavioral Environment of the Firm," *Journal of Product Innovation Management* 27, no. 2 (March 2010): 143–60; Kleinschmidt et al. (2007), endnote 13; and "Innovation in America: A Gathering Storm?" *The Economist*, November 20, 2008, http://www.economist.com/node/12637160

15. Cooper, both handbooks (2017, 2013), endnote 1.

16. Parts of this section are based on R. G. Cooper and S. J. Edgett, "The Dark Side of Time and Time Metrics in Product Innovation," *Visions* 26, no. 22 (April–May 2002): 14–16.

Chapter 3: Drivers of Success—Why the Best Innovators Excel

1. The success factors outlined in this chapter are based on many studies undertaken by the author, colleagues, and others, and are summarized in two product-development handbook chapters both by the author; these handbooks' chapters provide many references to the original studies: R. G. Cooper, "Best Practices and Success Drivers in New-Product Development," in *Handbook of Research on New Product Development*, ed. P. N. Golder and D. Mitra (Cheltenham, UK: Edward Elgar, 2017); and R. G. Cooper, "New Products—What Separates the Winners from the Losers and What Drives Success," chap. 1 in *PDMA Handbook of New Product Development*, 3rd ed., ed. K. B. Kahn (Hoboken, NJ: John Wiley & Sons, 2013). See endnote 1 in Chapter 2 for a summary of the benchmarking studies, the source of the bar charts in this chapter.

2. See endnote 1. See also X. M. Song, S. Im, H. van der Bij, and L. Z. Song, "Does Strategic Planning Enhance or Impede Innovation and Firm Performance?" *Journal of Product Innovation Management* 28, no. 4 (July 2011): 503–20.

3. R. G. Cooper and S. J. Edgett, "Developing a Product Innovation and Technology Strategy For Your Business," *Research-Technology Management* 53, no. 3 (May–June 2010): 33–40.

4. R. G. Cooper, "The Innovation Dilemma—How to Innovate When the Market Is Mature," *Journal of Product Innovation Management* 28, no. 7 (November 2011): 2–27.

5. See endnote 1.

6. R. G. Cooper, "Your NPD Portfolio May Be Harmful to Your Business's Health," *Visions* 29, no. 2 (April 2005): 22–26.

7. On open innovation, see M. Docherty, "Primer on 'Open Innovation': Principles and Practice," *Visions* 30, no. 2 (2006): 13–17; and H. Chesbrough, "'Open Innovation' Myths, Realities, and Opportunities," *Visions* 30, no. 2 (2006): 18–19.

8. M. E. Porter, *Competitive Advantage: Creating and Sustaining Superior Performance* (New York: Free Press, 1985).

9. "Enduring Ideas: The GE-McKinsey Nine Box Matrix," *McKinsey Quarterly* (September 2008), http://www.mckinsey.com/business-functions/strategy-and-corporate-finance/our-insights/enduring-ideas-the-ge-and-mckinsey-nine-box-matrix

10. See drivers of new-product success in endnote 1.

11. Parts of this section are taken from R. G. Cooper and S. J. Edgett, "Overcoming the Crunch in Resources for New Product Development," *Research-Technology Management* 46, no. 3 (May–June 2003): 48–58.

12. Most of the conclusions regarding new-product problems and failure causes are based on several benchmarking studies (reported in endnote 1 above); but an additional and rich source of information, particularly the anecdotal information that leads to more insight into the problem and possible solutions, is the result of "problem-detection sessions" held in over three hundred businesses over twenty years by the author and colleagues.

13. See endnote 1.

14. See endnote 1.

15. Cooper and Edgett (2003), endnote 11.

16. See endnote 1.

17. This "new game, old game" outline is based on D. Berger, "How Do You Get Those Big Growth Ideas," Proceedings, Beyond Stage-Gate: Bold Innovation for Real Business Growth, Jersey City, NJ, April 22–23, 2014.

18. J. Menn, R. Waters, and D. Gelles, "Jobs Biography Reveals Apple Recipe for Success," *Financial Times*, October 25, 2011, 15.

19. W. Isaacson, *Steve Jobs: The Exclusive Biography* (New York: Simon & Schuster, 2011).

20. Source of P&G quotation in box: M. Mills, "Implementing a Stage-Gate Process at P&G," Proceedings, First Annual Stage-Gate Summit, St. Petersburg Beach, FL, 2007.

21. R. G. Cooper and S. J. Edgett, "Best Practices in the Idea-to-Launch Process and Its Governance," *Research-Technology Management* 55, no. 2 (March–April 2012): 43–54. See also endnote 1.

22. The name "Stage-Gate" first appeared in print in R. G. Cooper, "The New Product Process: A Decision Guide for Managers," *Journal of Marketing Management* 3, no. 3 (1988): 238–55.

23. Adapted from R. G. Cooper, "The Stage-Gate Idea-to-Launch Process—Update, What's New and NexGen Systems," *Journal of Product Innovation Management* 25, no. 3 (May 2008): 213–32.

24. First-generation new-product processes were described in Booz Allen Hamilton, *New Product Management for the 1980s* (New York: Booz Allen Hamilton, 1982).

25. M. Mills, "Implementing a Stage-Gate® Process at Procter & Gamble," Proceedings, American Manufacturing Excellence "Focus on Global Excellence" Conference, Cincinnati, OH, 2004.

26. The impacts of implementing stage-and-gate processes have been reported in numerous publications over the years. See, for example, R. G. Cooper, "The Stage-Gate® Product Innovation System: From Idea to Launch," chap. 24 in *Encyclopedia of Technology and Innovation Management*, ed. V. K. Narayanan and G. O'Connor (Chichester, West Sussex, UK: John Wiley & Sons, 2010), 157–67; and as early as R. G. Cooper and E. J. Kleinschmidt, "New Product Processes at Leading Industrial Firms," *Industrial Marketing Management* 10, no. 2 (May 1991): 137–47.

27. M. Mills (2004), endnote 25.

28. An early *Stage-Gate* study: R. G. Cooper and E. J. Kleinschmidt (1991) in endnote 26.

29. T. Agan, *Renovating Innovation: Why the Best CPG Companies Derive over Six Times More Revenue from New Products vs. the Rest* (k.p.: A. C. Nielsen, 2010).

CHAPTER 4: THE *STAGE-GATE*® IDEA-TO-LAUNCH SYSTEM

1. A quotation describing the quality process, which has equal applicability to the new-product process. See T. H. Berry, *Managing the Total Quality Transformation* (New York: McGraw-Hill, 1991).

2. Section taken from R. G. Cooper, "The Stage-Gate Idea-to-Launch Process—Update, What's New and NexGen Systems," *Journal of Product Innovation Management* 25, no. 3 (May 2008): 213–32.

3. R. G. Cooper, "Best Practices and Success Drivers in New-Product Development," in *Handbook of Research on New Product Development*, ed. P. N. Golder and D. Mitra (Cheltenham, UK: Edward Elgar, 2017); and R. G. Cooper, "New Products—What Separates the Winners from the Losers and What Drives Success," chap. 1 in *PDMA Handbook of New Product Development*, 3rd ed., ed. K. B. Kahn (Hoboken, NJ: John Wiley & Sons, 2013).

4. This chapter is taken from many sources, for example, see endnote 3. See also R. G. Cooper, "Stellar Performer: The Stage-Gate System for New-Product Development," in E. Verzuh, *The Fast Forward MBA in Project Management*, 5th ed. (Hoboken, NJ: John Wiley & Sons, 2015), 65–73; R. G. Cooper, "The Stage-Gate® System for Product Innovation in B2B Firms," in *Handbook of Business-to-Business Marketing*, chap. 32, ed. G.L. Lillien and R. Grewat (Northampton, MA: Edward Elgar Publishing, 2012); and R. G. Cooper, "The Stage-Gate® Product Innovation System: From Idea to Launch," chap. 24 in *Encyclopedia of Technology and Innovation Management*, ed. V. K. Narayanan and G. O'Connor (Chichester, West Sussex, UK: John Wiley & Sons, 2010), 157–67.

5. T. Gehring, "Sustaining an Innovative Culture at 3M," Proceedings, Stage-Gate Innovation Summit, Miami, FL, November 2011.

6. B. Kirk, "Accelerating Time to Market: Using a Next Generation Innovation Framework," Proceedings, Stage-Gate Innovation Summit, Miami, FL, February 2013.

7. R. G. Cooper and A. F. Sommer, "The Agile–Stage-Gate Hybrid Model: A Promising New Approach and a New Research Opportunity," *Journal of Product Innovation Management* (June 2016): 1–14.

8. M. Gerstner, "ITT Way: Lead with Technology—Innovation Diamond and IMS 6P," Proceedings, Stage-Gate Leadership Roundtable 2016, Cape Coral, FL, March 2016.

9. R. G. Cooper, S. J. Edgett, and E. J. Kleinschmidt, *New Product Development Best Practices Study: What Distinguishes the Top Performers* (Houston, TX: American Productivity and Quality Center, 2002); R. G. Cooper, S. J. Edgett, and E. J. Kleinschmidt, "Benchmarking Best NPD Practices—Part 3: The NPD Process and Decisive Idea-to-Launch Activities," *Research-Technology Management* 47, no. 6 (January–February 2005): 43–55.

10. R. G. Cooper and S. J. Edgett, "Best Practices in the Idea-to-Launch Process and Its Governance," *Research-Technology Management* 55, no. 2 (March–April 2012): 43–54.

11. "Stage-Gate" is a term coined by the author—see endnote 22 in Chapter 3. Second-generation processes are what many companies began to implement toward the end of the 1980s; the third-generation processes of the late 1990s and early 2000s have improved time efficiencies and were more adaptive (spirals built in). Now Agile-Stage-Gate is starting to be used.

12. R. G. Cooper, "Agile-Stage-Gate Hybrids: The Next Stage for Product Development," *Research-Technology Management* 59, no. 1 (January 2016): 1–9.

13. R. D. Ledford, "NPD 2.0: Raising Emerson's NPD Process to the Next Level," in *Innovations* (St. Louis, MO: Emerson Electric, 2006), 4–7.

14. Internal document at Emerson Electric.

15. This section taken from Cooper (2008), endnote 2.

16. T. Leavitt, "Marketing Myopia," *Harvard Business Review* (July–August 1960): 45–56.

17. G. Belair, "Beyond Gates: Building the Right NPD Organization," Proceedings, First International Stage-Gate Conference, St. Petersburg Beach, FL, February 2007.

18. Source of checklist: Cooper and Edgett (2012), endnote 10.

CHAPTER 5: BEYOND *STAGE-GATE*

1. Much of this chapter is based on R. G. Cooper, "What's next? After Stage-Gate," *Research-Technology Management* 157, no. 1 (January–February 2014): 20–31; and R. G. Cooper "Idea-to-Launch Gating Systems: Better, Faster, and More Agile," *Research-Technology-Management* 60, no. 1 (January–February 2017): 48-52; and R. G. Cooper, "Best Practices and Success Drivers in New-Product Development," in *Handbook of Research on New Product Development*, ed. P. N. Golder and D. Mitra (Cheltenham, UK: Edward Elgar, 2017).

2. See how Stage-Gate has progressed over the years in Chapter 4. See also R. G. Cooper, "Third-Generation New Product Processes," *Journal of Product Innovation Management* 11, no. 1 (1994): 3–14; and R. G. Cooper, "The Stage-Gate Idea-to-Launch Process—Update: What's New and Next-Gen Systems," *Journal of Product Innovation Management* 25, no. 3 (May 2008): 213–32.

3. See Chapter 3 and Figures 3.14 and 3.15. See also Cooper (2017), endnote 1; R. G. Cooper, "New Products—What Separates the Winners From the Losers and What Drives Success," chap. 1 in *PDMA Handbook of New Product Development*, 3rd ed., ed. K. B. Kahn (Hoboken, NJ: John Wiley & Sons, 2013); and R. G. Cooper and S. J. Edgett, "Best Practices in the Idea-to-Launch Process and Its Governance," *Research-Technology Management* 55, no. 2 (March–April 2012): 43–54.

4. B. Becker, "Rethinking the Stage-Gate Process—A Reply to the Critics," *Management Roundtable* (July 12, 2006); and S. Lenfle, and C. Loch, "Lost Roots: How Proj-

ect Management Came to Emphasize Control over Flexibility and Novelty," *California Management Review* 53, no. 1 (Fall 2010): 32–55.

5. See Becker (2006), endnote 4.

6. See Chapter 4. See also Cooper (2008), endnote 2.

7. S. D. Anthony, M. Eyring, and L. Gibson, "Mapping Your Innovation Strategy," *Harvard Business Review OnPoint* (May 2006): 1–10.

8. See Chapter 2. See also Cooper and handbooks (2017, 2013), endnotes 1 and 3.

9. W. Isaacson, *Steve Jobs: The Exclusive Biography* (New York: Simon & Schuster, 2011), 567.

10. E. Ries, *The Lean Startup: How Today's Entrepreneurs Use Continuous Innovation to Create Radically Successful Businesses* (New York: Crown Publishing Group, 2011).

11. Isaacson (2011), endnote 9.

12. Cooper (2014) in endnote 1. See also B. Kirk, "Accelerating Time to Market: Using a Next Generation Innovation Framework," Proceedings, Stage-Gate Innovation Summit, Miami, FL, February 2013.

13. Cooper and Edgett (2012), endnote 3.

14. R. G. Cooper, "Managing Technology Development Projects: Different Than Traditional Development Projects," *Research-Technology Management* 49, no. 6 (2006): 23–31.

15. M. E. Maley, "Driving Global Innovation: Kellogg Company's Secret Ingredient (People!)," Proceedings, Stage-Gate Innovation Summit, Clearwater, FL, November 2010.

16. T. Gehring, "Sustaining an Innovative Culture at 3M," Proceedings, Stage-Gate Innovation Summit, Miami, FL, November 2011.

17. Cooper (2014), endnote 1.

18. A. MacCormack, W. Crandall, P. Henderson, and P. Toft, "Do You Need a New-Product Development Strategy?" *Research-Technology Management* 55, no. 1 (January–February 2012): 34–43.

19. F. S. Wu and R. Haak, "Innovation Mechanisms and Knowledge Communities for Corporate Central R&D," *Creativity & Innovation Management* 22, no. 1 (March 2013): 37–52.

20. Wu and Haak (2013), endnote 19.

21. Section taken from: R. G. Cooper, "NexGen Stage-Gate®—What Leading Companies Are Doing to Re-Invent Their NPD Processes," *Visions* 32, no. 3 (September 2008): 6–10.

22. See Chapter 4, section on "Managing Risk."

23. Case source is Cooper (2014), endnote 1. See also Kirk (2013), endnote 12.

24. Source of the Innovation Project Canvas: P. Fürst, managing partner, Five I's Innovation Management, Austria.

25. L. Y. Cohen, P. W. Kamienski, and R. L. Espino, "Gate System Focuses Industrial Basic Research," *Research-Technology Management* (July–August 1998): 34–37.

26. See also R. G. Cooper, "Where Are All the Breakthrough New Products? Using Portfolio Management to Boost Innovation," *Research-Technology Management* 56, no. 5 (2013): 25–33.

27. See K. Beck, M. Beedle, A. van Bennekum, A. Cockburn, W. Cunningham, M. Fowler, J. Grenning, J. Highsmith, A. Hunt, R. Jeffries, J. Kern, B. Marick, R. C. Martin, S. Mellor, K. Schwaber, J. Sutherland, and D. Thomas, "Principles Behind the Agile Man-

ifesto," Manifesto for Agile Software Development (2001), http://www.agilemanifesto .org/principles.html

28. H. Takeuchi and I. Nonaka, "The New Product Development Game," *Harvard Business Review* 64, no. 1 (1986): 137–46.

29. See Cooper (2014), endnote 1; and N. Ovesen and A. F. Sommer, "Scrum in the Traditional Development Organization: Adapting to the Legacy," in *Modeling and Management of Engineering Processes, Proceedings of the 3rd International Conference 2013* (Berlin: Springer-Verlag, 2015), 87–99.

30. A. F. Sommer, C. Hedegaard, I. Dukovska-Popovska, and K. Steger-Jensen, "Improved Product Development Performance Through Agile/Stage-Gate Hybrids: The Next-Generation Stage-Gate Process?" *Research-Technology Management* 58, no. 1 (2015): 34–44.

31. The Chamberlain case first appeared in an article by the author: R. G. Cooper, "Agile-Stage-Gate Hybrids: The Next Stage for Product Development," *Research-Technology Management* 59, no. 1 (January 2016): 1–9.

32. Source of case: Cooper (2014), endnote 1.

33. Cooper (2016), endnote 31.

34. D. Karlstrom and P. Runeson, "Integrating Agile Software Development into Stage-Gate Managed Product Development," *Empirical Software Engineering* 11 (2006): 203–25. See also D. Karlstrom and P. Runeson, "Combining Agile Methods with Stage-Gate Project Management," *IEEE Software* (May–June 2005): 43-49.

35. B. Boehm and R. Turner, *Balancing Agility and Discipline* (New York: Addison Wesley 2004).

36. Cooper (2014), endnote 1.

37. J. Morgan, "Applying Lean Principles to Product Development," SAE International, Society of Automotive Engineers, http://www.sae.org/manufacturing/lean /colimn/leanfeb02.htm

38. G. Belair, "Beyond Gates: Building the Right NPD Organization," Proceedings, First International Stage-Gate Conference, St. Petersburg Beach, FL, 2007.

39. R. G. Cooper and M. Mills, "Succeeding at New Products the P&G Way: A Key Element Is Using the 'Innovation Diamond,'" *Visions* 29, no. 4 (2005): 9–13.

40. J. Spero, "Lean in R&D," IRI 2009 Six Sigma and DFSS in R&D Webinar Series, October 2009.

41. C. Fiore, *Accelerated Product Development* (New York: Productivity Production Press, 2005).

42. See Chapter 3, success driver #5; and Cooper (2013), endnote 26.

43. A number of excellent and accredited software solutions are available to support idea-to-launch systems. Contact the author for information: www.bobcooper.ca

CHAPTER 6: THE *AGILE-STAGE-GATE*® HYBRID MODEL

1. This chapter is based largely on three articles and a management report: R. G. Cooper, "Agile-Stage-Gate Hybrids: The Next Stage for Product Development," *Research-Technology Management* 59, no. 1 (Jan 2016): 1–9; R. G. Cooper and A. F. Sommer, "The Agile–Stage-Gate Hybrid Model: A Promising New Approach and a New Research Opportunity," *Journal of Product Innovation Management* 33, no. 5 (Sept 2016a): 513–26; R. G. Cooper and A. F. Sommer, "Agile-Stage-Gate: New Idea-to-Launch Method for Manufactured New Products Is Faster, More Responsive," *In-*

dustrial Marketing Management 59 (November 2016b): 167–80; and R. G. Cooper, "Next in New-Product Development: Agile-Stage-Gate Hybrids," *CIMS Innovation Management Report* (November–December 2016): 10-14. See also R. G. Cooper, "Best Practices and Success Drivers in New-Product Development," in *Handbook of Research on New Product Development*, ed. P. N. Golder and D. Mitra (Cheltenham, UK: Edward Elgar, 2017).

2. See K. Beck, M. Beedle, A. van Bennekum, A. Cockburn, W. Cunningham, M. Fowler, J. Grenning, J. Highsmith, A. Hunt, R. Jeffries, J. Kern, B. Marick, R. C. Martin, S. Mellor, K. Schwaber, J. Sutherland, and D. Thomas, "Principles Behind the Agile Manifesto," Manifesto for Agile Software Development (2001), http://www.agilemanifesto .org/principles.html

3. B. Reagan, "Going Agile: CA Technologies, Clarity PPM Division's Transformative Journey," *Digital Celerity*, San Francisco, CA, September 22, 2012, http://www .slideshare.net/DCsteve/going-agile-with-ca-clarity-ppm-agile-vision

4. Reagan (2012), endnote 3.

5. Beck et al. (2001), endnote 2.

6. B. Boehm and R. Turner, *Balancing Agility and Discipline* (New York: Addison Wesley, 2004).

7. J. B. Barlow, J. S. Giboney, M. J. Keith, D. W. Wilson, R. M. Schuetzler, P. B. Lowry, and A. Vance, "Overview and Guidance on Agile Development in Large Organizations," *Communications of the Association for Information Systems* 29, no. 1 (2011): 25–44.

8. B. Becker, "Re-thinking the Stage-Gate° Process—A Reply to the Critics," *Management Roundtable Report* (2006), www.roundtable.com; S. Lenfle and C. Loch, "Lost Roots: How Project Management Came to Emphasize Control over Flexibility and Novelty," *California Management Review* 53, no. 1 (2010): 32–55; and R. G. Cooper, "What's Next? After Stage-Gate," *Research-Technology Management* 57 (2014): 20–31.

9. Becker (2006), endnote 8.

10. Source: Agile–Stage-Gate expert P. Fürst, managing partner of consulting firm Five I's Innovation Management, Austria.

11. A. Begel and N. Nagappan, "Usage and Perceptions of Agile Software Development in an Industrial Context: An Exploratory Study," *ESEM '07: First International Symposium on Empirical Software Engineering and Measurement* (Washington, DC: IEEE, 2007), 255–64.

12. D. Karlstrom and P. Runeson, "Combining Agile Methods with Stage-Gate Project Management," *IEEE Software:* (May–June 2005): 43–49; and D. Karlstrom and P. Runeson, "Integrating Agile Software Development into Stage-Gate Managed Product Development," *Empirical Software Engineering* 11 (2006): 203–25.

13. Karlstrom and Runeson (2005): 49, endnote 12.

14. Karlstrom and Runeson (2005), endnote 12.

15. A. F. Sommer, C. Hedegaard, I. Dukovska-Popovska, and K. Steger-Jensen, "Improved Product Development Performance Through Agile/Stage-Gate Hybrids—The Next-Generation Stage-Gate Process?" *Research-Technology Management* 158, no. 1 (2015): 1–10. See also D. K. Rigby, J. Sutherland, and H. Takeuchi, "Embracing Agile," *Harvard Business Review* 94, issue 5 (May 2016): 40–50.

16. Cooper (2014), endnote 8; and N. Ovesen and A. F. Sommer, "Scrum in the Tra-

ditional Development Organization: Adapting to the Legacy," chap. 8 in *Modeling and Management of Engineering Processes, Proceedings of the 3rd International Conference 2013* (Berlin: Springer-Verlag, 2013), 87–99.

17. Barlow et al. (2011), endnote 7.

18. Sommer et al. (2015), endnote 15.

19. Source of bar-chart data: Sommer et al. (2015), endnote 15. Source of bar charts: Cooper and Sommer (2016a), endnote 1.

20. Sommer et al. (2015), endnote 15.

21. H. Takeuchi and I. Nonaka, "The New New Product Development Game," *Harvard Business Review* 64, no. 1 (1986): 137–46.

22. K. Schwaber and M. Beedle, *Agile Software Development with Scrum* (New York: Prentice Hall, 2013); and ScrumInc., "The Scrum Guide" (July 2013), http://www.scrumguides.org/scrum-guide.html

23. Construction-equipment company case is from Cooper (2016), endnote 1. Source: L. Cederblad, managing partner at Level 21 in Sweden.

24. The term "Power of Nine" was coined by Sommer. See Cooper and Sommer (2016b), endnote 1.

25. Section on heartbeat is from Cooper and Sommer (2016a), endnote 1. Adapted from D. Wells, "A Project Heartbeat," The Agile Process: http://www.agile-process.org/heartbeat.html

26. Wells (2009), endnote 25.

27. Section on within-team communication is from: Cooper and Sommer (2016a), endnote 1.

28. Source of sprint backlog chart: Fürst, endnote 10.

29. LEGO case and this section are from Cooper and Sommer (2016a), endnote 1.

30. Cooper (2014) in endnote 8; and Cooper (2016) in endnote 1.

31. Cooper (2014): 22, endnote 8.

32. Case is from Cooper and Sommer (2016b), endnote 1.

33. This section is taken from Cooper and Sommer (2016b), endnote 1.

34. Cooper (2014), endnote 8.

35. S. Kielgast and T. Vedsmand, "Integrating Agile with Stage-Gate®—How New Agile-Scrum Methods Lead to Faster and Better Innovation," *InnovationManagement .SE*, August 9, 2016, 1–15.

36. Source: Fürst, endnote 10.

37. Illustration is from Cooper and Sommer (2016b), endnote 1. See also Cooper (2016), endnote 1. Original source: L. Cederblad, managing partner at management consulting firm Level 21, Sweden.

38. This section is from Cooper and Sommer (2016b), endnote 1.

39. A. MacCormack, W. Crandall, P. Henderson, and P. Toft, "Do You Need a New-Product Development Strategy? *Research-Technology Management* 55, no. 1 (2012): 34–43.

40. E. Ries, *The Lean Startup: How Today's Entrepreneurs Use Continuous Innovation to Create Radically Successful Businesses* (New York: Crown Publishing Group, 2011).

41. P. Sandmeier, P. D. Morrison, and O. Gassmann, "Integrating Customers in Product Innovation: Lessons from Industrial Development Contractors and In-House Contractors in Rapidly Changing Customer Markets," *Creativity and Innovation Management* 19, no. 2 (2010): 89–106.

42. ScrumInc. (2013), endnote 22.

43. Quotation from Cooper (2016), endnote 1.

CHAPTER 7: DISCOVERY—THE QUEST FOR BREAKTHROUGH IDEAS

1. Arthur D. Little, "How Companies Use Innovation to Improve Profitability and Growth," Innovation Excellence Study, 2005, http://www.adl.com/reports .html?view=53

2. A guide to developing an innovation strategy is in R. G. Cooper, "Make the Right Strategic Choices in Product Innovation," Center for Innovation Management Studies Management Report, NC State University (January–February 2015), 1–7. See also R. G. Cooper and S. J. Edgett, "Developing a Product Innovation and Technology Strategy for Your Business," Research-Technology Management 53, no. 3 (May–June 2010): 33–40.

3. Source of figure: R. G. Cooper and A. Dreher, "Voice-of-Customer Methods Versus the Rest: What Is the Best Source of New-Product Ideas?" Marketing Management Magazine (Winter 2010), extended online version at http://www.marketingpower .com/ResourceLibrary/Publications/MarketingManagement/2010/4/38–48_Xtended version3.pdf

4. Sections taken from Cooper and Dreher (2010), endnote 3.

5. Example provided by Five I's Innovation Management Group, Austria.

6. See N. Franke, E. A. von Hippel, and M. Schreier, "Finding Commercially Attractive User Innovations: A Test of Lead-User Theory," Journal of Product Innovation Management 23, no. 4 (2006): 301–15. See also G. Lilien, P. D. Morrison, K. Searls, M. Sonnack, and E. A. von Hippel, "Performance Assessment of the Lead User Idea-Generation Process for New Product Development." Management Science 48, no. 8 (2002): 1042–59.

7. Adapted from: E. A. von Hippel, S. Thomke, and M. Sonnack, "Creating Breakthroughs at 3M," Harvard Business Review (September–October 1999): 47–57.

8. See for example:von Hippel et al. (1999), endnote 7.

9. E. A. von Hippel, S. Ogawa, and J. P. J. de Jong, "The Age of the Consumer-Innovator," MIT Sloan Management Review 53, no. 1 (2011): 27–35.

10. See LEGO Digital Designer, http://ldd.lego.com/en-us/

11. C. Hienerth, E. A. von Hippel, and M. B. Jensen. "Efficiency of Consumer (Household Sector) vs. Producer Innovation," SSRN eLibrary, https://evhippel.mit.edu /papers/section-1/

12. C. J. Beale, "On-Line Communities Shake Up NPD—an Introduction to the Value of This New Tool," Visions 32, no. 4 (December 2008): 14–18.

13. T. Brown, "Design Thinking," Harvard Business Review (June 2008): 85–92.

14. Superimposing Design Thinking model atop the first few stages in Stage-Gate is from Dr. A. Dreher, managing partner, Five I's Innovation, Austria.

15. "From Terrifying to Terrific: The Creative Journey of the Adventure Series," GE Healthcare—The Pulse on Health, Science & Technology, Sept. 26, 2012, http://newsroom.ge-healthcare.com/from-terrifying-to-terrific-creative-journey-of-the-adventure-series/

16. Different institutions have their own models for design thinking; most such models are much the same. The model seen in Figures 7.4 and 7.5 is based on one at the School of Design Thinking, Hasson-Platter-Institut, Potsdam University, Germany: http://hpi.de/en/school-of-design-thinking/design-thinking/mindset.html

17. O. Gadiesh and J. L. Gilbert, "How to Map Your Industry's Profit Pool," *Harvard Business Review* (May–June 1998): 3–11.

18. C. M. Christensen, *The Innovator's Dilemma* (New York: HarperCollins, 2000). See also R. N. Foster, *Innovation: The Attacker's Advantage* (New York: Summit Books, 1986).

19. G. Day and P. Shoemaker, "Scanning the Periphery," *Harvard Business Review* 84, no. 2 (November 2005): 135–48.

20. Day and Shoemaker (2005), endnote 19.

21. From D. Berger, "How Do You Get Those Big Growth Ideas," Proceedings, Beyond Stage-Gate: Bold Innovation for Real Business Growth, INNOVATE Consultancy, Jersey City, NJ, April 22–23, 2014.

22. Parts of this section on scenarios are taken from P. Schwartz, "The Official Future, Self-Delusion and Value of Scenarios," Mastering Risk, *Financial Times*, May 2, 2000.

23. K. Hardy, "Maximizing Return on Investment: Rust-Oleum's 'Focused' Idea Generation Program," Proceedings, Stage-Gate Summit 2010, Clearwater Beach, FL, 2010.

24. H. Chesbrough, "'Open Innovation' Myths, Realities, and Opportunities," *Visions* 30, no. 2 (April 2006): 13–15; and H. Chesbrough, *Open Innovation: The New Imperative for Creating and Profiting from Technology* (Cambridge, MA: Harvard Business School Press, 2003).

25. M. Docherty, "Primer on 'Open Innovation': Principles and Practice," *Visions* 30, no. 2 (April 2006).

26. "Open Innovation—A Fad or a Phenomenon? UC Berkeley and Fraunhofer Study How Large Companies Practice Innovation," Fraunhofer IAO, 2016, http://www.iao.fraunhofer.de/lang-en/about-us/business-areas/technology-innovation-management/1060-open-innovation-a-fad-or-a-phenomenon.html

27. Parts of this section are taken from "The Love-In: The Move Toward Open Innovation Is Beginning to Transform Entire Industries," *Economist* print edition, special section on innovation, October 11, 2007.

28. Source: *Economist* (2007), endnote 27.

29. H. Erler, "How Open Innovation Has Changed Since the Start of the Decade and Its Impact on Customer Value Creation," Proceedings, Stage-Gate Innovation Summit 2016, Cape Coral, FL, 2016.

30. These examples are from P. Boutin, "Crowdsourcing: Consumers as Creators," *Business Week*, July 13, 2006.

31. L. Huston and N. Sakkab, "Connect and Develop: Inside Procter & Gamble's New Model for Innovation," *Harvard Business Review* 84, no. 3 (March 2006).

32. J. Grölund, D. Rönneberg, and J. Frishammar, "Open Innovation and the Stage-Gate Process: A Revised Model for New Product Development," *California Management Review* 5, no. 3 (Spring 2010): 106–31.

33. M. Docherty (2006), endnote 25.

34. Adapted from Falco-Archer, "Patent Mining," 2005, www.falcoarcher.com

35. D. H. Pink, *Drive: The Surprising Truth About What Motivates Us* (New York: Riverhead Books/Penguin, 2009).

36. M. Maley, "Driving Global Innovation: Kellogg Company's Secret Ingredient—People!" Proceedings, Stage-Gate Summit 2010, Clearwater Beach, FL, 2010.

CHAPTER 8: INVESTING IN THE RIGHT PROJECTS—PORTFOLIO MANAGEMENT

1. This chapter draws on many sources, articles, and books by the author and co-workers: for example, R. G. Cooper, "Where Are All the Breakthrough New Products? Using Portfolio Management to Boost Innovation," *Research-Technology Management* 156, no. 5 (September–October 2013): 25–32; R. G. Cooper, "Portfolio Management for Product Innovation," chap. 7.2 in *Project Portfolio Management: A Practical Guide to Selecting Projects, Managing Portfolios, and Maximizing Benefits*, ed. H. Levine (San Francisco: Jossey-Bass Business & Management, John Wiley & Sons Imprint, 2005); and R. G. Cooper and S. J. Edgett, "Ten Ways to Make Better Portfolio and Project Selection Decisions," *Visions* 30, no. 3 (June 2006): 11–15. Portfolio management is described in greater detail in R. G. Cooper, S. J. Edgett, and E. J. Kleinschmidt, *Portfolio Management for New Products,* 2nd ed. (New York: Perseus Publishing, 2002).

2. Parts of this section are taken from an article by the author and coworker: R. G. Cooper and S. J. Edgett, "Overcoming the Crunch in Resources for New Product Development," *Research-Technology Management* 46, no. 3 (2003): 48–58.

3. See Figure 3.8 in Chapter 3. See also R. G. Cooper, "Best Practices and Success Drivers in New-Product Development," in *Handbook of Research on New Product Development*, ed. P. N. Golder and D. Mitra (Cheltenham, UK: Edward Elgar, 2017); and R. G. Cooper, "New Products—What Separates the Winners from the Losers and What Drives Success," chap. 1 in the *PDMA Handbook of New Product Development*, 3rd ed., ed. K. B. Kahn (Hoboken, NJ: John Wiley & Sons, Inc., 2013).

4. Portfolio management was originally defined in R. G. Cooper, S. J. Edgett, and E. J. Kleinschmidt, "Portfolio Management in New Product Development: Lessons from the Leaders—Part I," *Research-Technology Management* (September–October 1997): 16–28.

5. Parts of this section are taken from R. G. Cooper, "Maximizing the Value of Your New Product Portfolio: Methods, Metrics and Scorecard," (Stevens Institute of Technology: Stevens Alliance for Technology Management) *Current Issues in Technology Management* 7, issue 1 (Winter 2003): 1.

6. B. Nagji and G. Tuff, "Managing Your Innovation Portfolio," *Harvard Business Review* 9, no. 5 (May 2012): 66–74.

7. S. Bull, "Innovating for Success: How EXFO's NPDS Delivers Winning Products," Proceedings, First International Stage-Gate Conference, St. Petersburg Beach, FL, February 2007.

8. See, for example, "Net Present Value—NPV," Investopedia, http://www .investopedia.com/terms/n/npv.asp

9. T. Faulkner, "Applying 'Options Thinking' to R&D Valuation," *Research-Technology Management* (May–June 1995): 50–57.

10. D. Matheson, J. E. Matheson, and M. M. Menke, "Making Excellent R&D Decisions," *Research Technology Management* (November–December 1994): 21–24.

11. Cooper and Edgett (2006), endnote 1.

12. F. Black and M. Scholes, "The Pricing of Options and Corporate Liabilities," *The Journal of Political Economy* 81, no. 3 (May–June 1973): 637–54.

13. Source of ECV example: Cooper (2013), endnote 1.

14. S. J. Edgett, *Portfolio Management: Optimizing for Success* (Houston: APQC, American Productivity & Quality Center, 2007).

15. For a summary of research into success factors, see R. G. Cooper (2013), endnote 3.

16. Cooper and Edgett (2006), endnote 1.

CHAPTER 9: MAKING THE GATES WORK—GATES WITH TEETH

1. Sections in this chapter are from several sources: for example, R. G. Cooper and S. J. Edgett, "Best Practices in the Idea-to-Launch Process and Its Governance," *Research-Technology Management* 55, no. 2 (March–April 2012): 43–54; R. G. Cooper, "Effective Gating: Make Product Innovation More Productive by Using Gates with Teeth," *Marketing Management Magazine* (March–April 2009): 12–17; and R. G. Cooper, "How Companies Are Re-inventing Their Idea-to-Launch Methodologies," *Research-Technology Management* 52, no. 2 (March–April 2009): 47–57.

2. R. G. Cooper and E. J. Kleinschmidt, "Success Factors for New Product Development," in *Wiley International Encyclopedia of Marketing: Product Innovation & Management*, vol. 5, ed. B. L. Bayus (Chichester, West Sussex, UK: John Wiley & Sons, 2011).

3. Cooper and Edgett (2012), endnote 1.

4. The term "gates with teeth" comes from S. Jenner, "'Gates with Teeth': Implementing a Centre of Excellence for Investment Decisions," Proceedings, First International Stage-Gate Conference, St. Petersburg Beach, FL, February 2007. See also R. G. Cooper (2009), endnote 1.

5. S. Osborne, "Make More and Better Product Decisions for Greater Impact," Proceedings, PDMA Product and Service Conference "Compete to Win," Atlanta, GA, October 2006.

6. Cooper and Edgett (2012), endnote 1.

7. Section taken from Cooper and Edgett (2012), endnote 1.

8. R. G. Cooper and M. Mills, "Succeeding at New Products the P&G Way: A Key Element Is Using the 'Innovation Diamond,'" *PDMA Visions* 29, no. 4 (October 2005): 9–13.

9. Source of example: Five I's Innovation Management, Austria, a firm specializing in the design and installation of Stage-Gate in Europe.

10. Section taken from Cooper and Edgett (2012), endnote 1.

11. See S. J. Edgett, *Portfolio Management: Optimizing for Success* (Houston: APQC, American Productivity & Quality Center, 2007).

12. See S. Bull, "Innovating for Success: How EXFO's NPDS Delivers Winning Products," Proceedings, First International Stage-Gate Conference, St. Petersburg Beach, FL, February 2007.

13. Cooper and Edgett (2012), endnote 1.

14. Cooper and Edgett (2012), endnote 1.

15. Cooper and Edgett (2012), endnote 1.

CHAPTER 10: A PRODUCT-INNOVATION STRATEGY FOR YOUR BUSINESS

1. This chapter is largely based on R. G. Cooper, "Make the Right Strategic Choices in Product Innovation," *CIMS—Center for Innovation Management Studies Management Report*, NC State University, January–February 2015, 1–7. See also R. G. Cooper and S. J. Edgett, "Developing a Product Innovation and Technology Strategy for Your Business," *Research-Technology Management* 53, no. 3 (May–June 2010): 33–40; and R. G. Cooper and S. J. Edgett, *Product Innovation and Technology Strategy* (Ancaster ON: Product Development Institute, 2009), available on Amazon.com.

2. Section taken from Cooper and Edgett (2010), endnote 1.

3. B. Kirk, "Creating an Environment for Effective Innovation," Proceedings, Stage-Gate Innovation Summit, Clearwater Beach, FL, February 2009.

4. Benchmarking studies: see endnote 1 in Chapter 2.

5. Booz Allen Hamilton, *New Product Management for the 1980s* (New York: Booz Allen Hamilton, 1982).

6. D. J. Luck and A. E. Prell, *Market Strategy* (Englewood Cliffs, N.J.: Prentice Hall, 1968), 2.

7. I. H. Ansoff, *Corporate Strategy* (New York: McGraw-Hill, 1965).

8. R. E. Corey, "Key Options in Market Selection and Product Planning," *Harvard Business Review* (September–October 1978): 119–28.

9. Some sections in this chapter are taken from R. G. Cooper, S. J. Edgett, and E. J. Kleinschmidt, *Portfolio Management for New Products*, 2nd ed. (New York: Perseus, 2002).

10. Example taken from Joint Chiefs of Staff, "Joint Operations," Joint Publication 3–0, February 2008, http://dtic.mil/doctrine/docnet/courses/operations/jfcon/jp3_0 .pdf

11. Cooper (2015), endnote 1.

12. Cooper and Edgett (2010), endnote 1.

13. Cooper and Edgett (2010), endnote 1.

14. Cooper (2015), endnote 1.

15. R. G. Cooper, "Creating Bold Innovation in Mature Markets," *IESE Insight* 3, no. 14 (2012): 20–27; and R. G. Cooper, "Perspective: The Innovation Dilemma—How to Innovate When the Market Is Mature," *Journal of Product Innovation Management* 28, no. 7 (December 2011): 2–27.

16. From C. M. Christensen's disruptive innovation theory, as outlined in S. D. Anthony, M. Eyring, and L. Gibson, "Mapping Your Innovation Strategy," *Harvard Business Review OnPoint* (May 2006): 1–10.

17. G. S. Day and P. J. H. Schoemaker, "Scanning the Periphery," *Harvard Business Review* 83, no. 11 (November 2005): 135–48.

18. Adapted from Day and Shoemaker (2005), endnote 17.

19. C. M. Christensen, *The Innovator's Dilemma* (New York: Harper Collins, 2000).

20. See Christensen (2000), endnote 19.

21. Cooper and Edgett (2009), endnote 1.

22. Cooper and Edgett (2009), endnote 1.

23. See success driver #3 in Chapter 3.

24. G. Hamel and C. K. Prahalad, *Competing for the Future* (Cambridge, MA: Harvard Business School Press, April 1996).

25. Cooper (2015), endnote 1.

26. "Enduring Ideas: The GE-McKinsey Nine Box Matrix," *McKinsey Quarterly* (September 2008), http://www.mckinsey.com/business-functions/strategy-and-corporate -finance/our-insights/enduring-ideas-the-ge-and-mckinsey-nine-box-matrix

27. Cooper (2015), endnote 1.

28. R. E. Miles and C. C. Snow, *Organizational Strategy, Structure and Process* (New York: McGraw-Hill, 1978).

29. M. Adams and D. Boike, "PDMA Foundation CPAS Study Reveals New Trends,"

Visions 28 no. 3 (July 2004): 26–29; and M. Adams, The PDMA Foundation's 2004 Comparative Performance Assessment Study (CPAS), www.pdma.org.

30. M. E. Porter, *Competitive Advantage: Creating and Sustaining Superior Performance* (New York: Free Press, 1985).

31. P. J. Whalen, "Strategic and Technology Planning on a Roadmapping Foundation," *Research-Technology Management* 50, no. 3 (May–June 2007): 40–51.

32. For more on roadmapping, see R. E. Albright and B. Nelson, "Product and Technology Mapping Tools for Planning and Portfolio Decision Making," chap. 15 in *PDMA Toolbook 2 for New Product Development*, eds. P. Belliveau, A. Griffin, and S. Somermeyer (New York: John Wiley & Sons, 2004). See also R. E. Albright and T. A. Kappel, "Roadmapping in the Corporation," *Research-Technology Management* 46, no. 2 (March–April 2003): 31–40; M. H. Myer and A. P. Lehnerd, *The Power of Product Platforms* (New York, NY: Free Press, 1997); A. McMillan, "Roadmapping—Agent of Change," *Research-Technology Management* 42, no. 2 (March–April 2003): 40–47; P. Groenveld, "Roadmapping Integrates Business and Technology," *Research Technology Management* 50, no. 6 (November–December 2007): 49–58; and R. C. McCarthy, "Linking Technology Change to Business Needs," *Research Technology Management* 46, no. 2 (March–April 2003): 47–53.

33. The term "product roadmap" has come to have many meanings. Here the meaning is a *strategic roadmap*, which lays out the *major* initiatives and platforms the business will undertake well into the future, as opposed to a *tactical roadmap*, which lists each and every product release, extension, and version.

34. The term "technology roadmap" also has several different meanings. Here the term is used to denote a *plan for the business's expected technology developments* or acquisitions; by contrast, the term "technology roadmap" is sometimes used to describe an industry technological forecast, laying out what new technologies are anticipated in an industry.

INDEX

Mina, Oakville, ON, Canada

ROBERT G. COOPER is ISBM distinguished research fellow at Pennsylvania State University and professor emeritus at McMaster University in Canada. The author of several books, he is a fellow of the Product Development and Management Association since 1999.